PENGUIN BOOKS

MESOPOTAMIA

Gwendolyn Leick is an anthropologist and Assyriologist. She lectures in Anthropology at Richmond, the American International University in London and in Design Theory and History at Chelsea College of Art and Design. She also acts as a cultural tour guide in the Middle East, lecturing on history, archaeology and anthropology. She is the author of various publications on the Ancient Near East, including *A Dictionary of Near Eastern Mythology, Sex and Eroticism in Mesopotamian Literature* and *Who's Who in the Ancient Near East*.

Gwendolyn Leick

M E S O P

OTAMIA

THE INVENTION
OF THE CITY

PENGUIN BOOKS

PENGUIN BOOKS

Published by the Penguin Group
Penguin Books Ltd, 80 Strand, London WC2R ORL, England
Penguin Putnam Inc., 375 Hudson Street, New York, New York 10014, USA
Penguin Books Australia Ltd, 250 Camberwell Road, Camberwell, Victoria 3124, Australia
Penguin Books Canada Ltd, 10 Alcorn Avenue, Toronto, Ontario, Canada M4V 3B2
Penguin Books India (P) Ltd, 11, Community Centre, Panchsheel Park, New Delhi – 110 017, India
Penguin Books (NZ) Ltd, Cnr Rosedale and Airborne Roads, Albany, Auckland, New Zealand
Penguin Books (South Africa) (Pty) Ltd, 24 Sturdee Avenue, Rosebank 2196, South Africa

Penguin Books Ltd, Registered Offices: 80 Strand, London WC2R ORL, England

www.penguin.com

First published by Allen Lane The Penguin Press 2001
Published in Penguin Books 2002

031

Printed and bound in Great Britain by Clays Ltd, Elcograf S.p.A.

ISBN-13: 978-0-14-026574-3

www.greenpenguin.co.uk

Penguin Books is committed to a sustainable
future for our business, our readers and our planet.
This book is made from Forest Stewardship
Council™ certified paper.

Contents

List of Illustrations

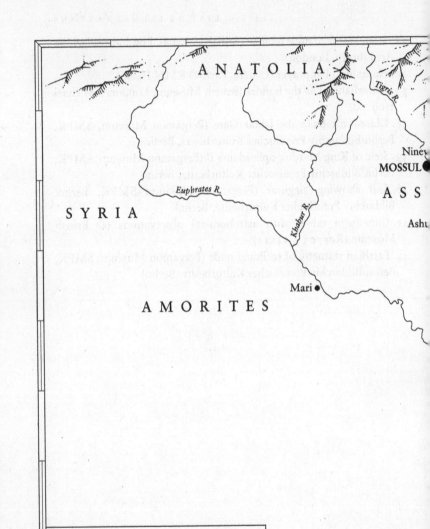

ANATOLIA

Tigris R.

Niney

MOSSUL●

Euphrates R.

ASS

SYRIA

Khabur R.

Ashu

AMORITES

Mari ●

Mesopotamia

Cities in caps are Moslem cities

| 0 | 100 | 200 km |

| 0 | 50 | 100 miles |

Preface

Mesopotamia is the name the ancient Greeks gave to a land corresponding approximately to present-day Iraq. It means literally 'between the rivers', referring to the Tigris and the Euphrates, which rise in the mountains of Anatolia to flow in more or less parallel courses down to the Persian Gulf. In contemporary usage, Mesopotamia has acquired a broader meaning, referring not just to the land between the two main rivers but also to their tributaries and valleys, so describing an area that includes not only Iraq but also eastern Syria and south-eastern Turkey. Its natural borders are formed by the mountain ridges of Anatolia to the north, the Zagros range to the east, the Arabian desert to the south-west and the Persian Gulf. Within this geographical context are two distinct zones, the first being the zone north of present-day Baghdad, where the Tigris and Euphrates come closest together. This is the area often called the Fertile Crescent, a stretch of land that runs from the Mediterranean coast to northern Iraq and benefits from the rainfall generated by the chain of mountains extending along the Syrian coast and southern Anatolia. To the south of this belt of hills and valleys stretches the Arabian desert. It was in the climatically favourable Fertile Crescent that the first human settlements and the beginnings of agriculture and animal husbandry originated some 10,000 years ago.

The second zone, between Baghdad and the Persian Gulf, is essentially a vast flood plain, the land having been formed by huge deposits of silt carried down by the rivers. This alluvial soil, with its high and varied mineral content, is potentially highly fertile, but the land is flat and there are no mountains to generate rain. Only after man had learnt to adapt to this environment, significantly through control of the waterways by means of canals and dykes, did it become possible to capitalize on the inherent economic potential of the southern plains. It was only then that the first large-scale communities began to develop, in which people began to profit from a system beyond subsistence to produce a surplus, diversify their cultural activities and live in increasingly large numbers in a new form of collective community, the city.

The invention of cities may well be the most enduring legacy of Mesopotamia. There was not just one but dozens of cities, each controlling its own rural and pastoral territory and its own system of irrigation. But since these communities were strung along the main waterways like so many pearls on a necklace, they had to arrive at forms of cooperation and mutual tolerance. Historians have tended to highlight the emergence of centralized states which exercised control over often extensive territories, but the most enduring and successful socio-political unit to emerge in Mesopotamia remained the city state.

This book seeks to tell the stories of ten Mesopotamian cities in a way that will do justice to this urban paradigm. The individual stories are heterogeneous, reflecting the often contradictory thoughts and conclusions of the archaeologists who have interpreted the physical evidence of sites, of the epigraphists and Assyriologists who have copied and translated the cuneiform tablets, of the historians, geologists and anthropologists who have considered the findings. Most importantly, each city tells its own story through its discovery and a gradual understanding of its historical development set beside how the Mesopotamians themselves wrote about it, what it was known for and which gods resided in its temples.

The collection of narratives concerning ten Mesopotamian cities that follows runs in a roughly chronological sequence from fifth-millennium Eridu through to Babylon, which lasted into the first few centuries AD. Each city has a place in a reality that has been reduced to an archaeological site in Iraq, more or less robbed of its secrets, more or less buried under sand-dunes. Each site has variously yielded its riches, from statues and potsherds to cylinder seals and jewellery, brick walls and tablets. Sheer accident of discovery has determined what has been found, whether it is palace archives or graves, temples or huts, a whole library from a period covering some thirty years or the architectural sequence for a temple spanning two millennia. What has been made of all these tangible bits and pieces is a further dimension, subjected to trends in intellectual fashion and the need to revise interpretations in the light of new findings and new ideas.

I have picked out some of these strands and ideas as one picks up sherds on a mound and used them as props to tell my narratives. The cities had their own interpreters, the scribes and savants of their time, so we will certainly hear their voices, however stilted they may sound in the awkward style of Assyriological 'translation'. Overall, a multitude of voices should emerge – of archaeologists and epigraphists, of ancient kings and their 'spin-doctors', of theologians ancient and not so ancient, of anthropologists and temple bureaucrats, of Babylonian businesswomen and divorcees. All these various strands of narrative have produced a different pattern for each city. But like some very old remnant of a beautiful fragment of textile, this reconstructed fabric of the past must be full of holes and badly worn parts that can never be restored or mended. Nevertheless the different fragments should allow us to build an impression of the richness and complexity of the original civilization that produced them.

Mesopotamia, like Egypt and classical Greece, is, though relatively little known, one of the great 'dead civilizations'. The quest for the roots of civilization formed part of the nineteenth-century obsession with origins and the great narrative of social evolution. Given that Victorian man was undeniably 'in advance' of most other manifestations of humanity, where, for him, did the decisive development from primitivism to civilization begin? For a long time the Greeks had been seen as marking the watershed between rude barbarity and rational, civilized life, though the Greeks themselves held the Egyptians in grudging admiration. The move towards apotheosizing the Egyptians as pre-classical representations of civilization owed much to Napoleon's ambition when he took scientists and 'savants' with him on his North African campaign. Champollion's subsequent decipherment of the Rosetta Stone marked the first step towards the appropriation of the past for the glory of European imperialism, a trend that Napoleon also pioneered, even to the extent of revitalizing the Roman practice of stealing obelisks. But quite apart from such politically motivated interests, the achievements of Egyptian civilization were plain for anyone to see who visited the grand new museums as they opened in all the major European and North American cities. The high quality of the ancient Egyptian artefacts, their superb draughtsmanship and artistry, clearly demonstrated a high level of cultural achievement.

Only gradually did public and scholarly interest turn to the other ancient peoples mentioned in the Bible, such as the Assyrians and Babylonians, who were equally 'oppressors of the Chosen People' and equally 'civilized', if only in terms of their literacy. Early excavations in the impoverished backwaters of the Ottoman Empire were initially driven by Franco-British rivalry for the spoils of antiquity. Intrepid explorers, such as Austen Layard and Émile Botta, attracted by the huge ruin heaps of upper Mesopotamia, were by the mid nineteenth century shipping home large quantities of Assyrian antiquities that caused a sensation when first exhibited at the Louvre or the British Museum. When the cuneiform tablets were deciphered by an Englishman, Colonel Rawlinson, the British public rejoiced. When more and more human-headed bulls arrived in Bloomsbury, they were thought to show some of the gravitas of the spade-bearded dignitaries of the Victorian age. As translations of the cuneiform texts became available, not only did the historicity of the Bible receive a much needed boost as a counter to Darwinism, but the sheer complexity and antiquity of Mesopotamian culture began to emerge. Pan-Babylonianism became all the rage – the cradle of civilization was, it was asserted, to be found between the rivers Tigris and Euphrates. So great was the popular appeal that the *Daily Telegraph* was able to send an expedition to Mesopotamia from money raised by public subscription.

During the twentieth century, as it progressed through the traumas of one world war, then another, and saw the break-up of the European empires, public interest in the ancient Near Eastern empires steadily waned. Not even the spectacular discoveries of Carter in Egypt or Woolley at Ur – both finding graves rather than palaces – could reverse a shift in the way human society and the human past were interpreted. Anthropology and prehistory came to be seen as more relevant avenues of study, and 'culture' rather than 'civilization' became the key concept. Only Egypt, which is for us almost entirely defined by its morbid obsession with life after death, has continued to fascinate the public.

Like that other much misunderstood ancient people, the Celts, pharaonic Egyptians have become part of New Age consciousness. The Mesopotamian peoples, the Sumerians, Assyrians and Babylonians, with their less spectacular art and crumbling mudbrick ruins, have no comparable place in public imagination.

None the less, despite dwindling budgets and a lack of public interest, generations of scholars have persisted with the task of dealing with all the excavated material, especially the thousands of tablets distributed in museum collections throughout the Western World, along with seals, pots, weights and sculptures. It could be said that these objects constitute a part of our present world and have been found at a time when skills were developed to make sense of them. Computer-aided technology now helps to store the complex information of economic texts and micro-technology allows for refinements of archaeological results. It is not just technology, however, but the questions being asked that have changed: cultural diversity, the relation of centre to periphery, social relations, power structures, economic systems, ecological change and gender issues are only some of the most recent concerns of historians and archaeologists. Such perspectives and goals inevitably reflect the thoughts and intellectual 'fashions' of our own time. The same texts, the same architecture, the same pots have been and will in the future be evaluated and understood in quite different ways that often say more about the society seeking such answers than about the ancient society itself. There are stories about the telling of stories, as any storyteller knows. I have tried to reflect such changing trends of interpretation in this book, since it is important to remember that history is a continuing process of asking questions and finding answers, not a rigid sequence of dates or events.

The most remarkable innovation in Mesopotamian civilization is urbanism. The idea of the city as a heterogeneous, complex, messy, constantly changing but ultimately viable concept for human society was a Mesopotamian invention. Certainly they invented a great many other things – bureaucracy, writing, mathematics and astrology – but these were sooner or later also invented elsewhere by other state societies, such as the Egyptians, the Chinese, the Incas or the Aztecs. We are only beginning to understand how the idea of urbanism developed uniquely in Mesopotamia and what could have triggered it. Environmental and geographical factors played a role, from the phenomenal potential productivity of the alluvial soils to the instability of a landscape in which cities occupied fixed points within an inherently unpredictable natural world. An absence of physical boundaries also mitigated against socio-cultural isolation; the scarcity of local resources necessitated long-distance exchange connections, and so on.

By the end of the third millennium, 90 per cent of the population in southern Mesopotamia was living in cities. By the mid first millennium Babylon was the world's largest and only metropolis, which Alexander the Great proposed to make the capital of his unprecedentedly vast empire. Alexander died too early to fulfil this dream; and under his successors the balance swung to the west so that Babylon became a backwater, an ivory tower of obsolescent scholasticism. By then, however, the idea of the city was as much part of contemporary life as writing, bureaucracy and hierarchical structures. The Hellenistic states and Rome exported these concepts, adapting them to suit the needs of colonial empires throughout the Mediterranean region and beyond.

The ancient Mesopotamian intellectuals were not above cynicism and irony, but they never doubted that their city was the only place for them to be. They knew that regimes came and went, that rivers changed their courses, that floods could obliterate individual cities, that overpopulation was not a good thing, but they were confident the City would never die. In our own age, when predictions are that a majority of the world's inhabitants will live in cities, this message may sound ominous. But we would also do well to heed the optimism of a plea to balance the benefit of human gregariousness and inventiveness with the dangerous glamour of the city as it was first epitomized by Babylon.

Note on the Text

Dates given in this volume are all BCE unless otherwise indicated.

Translations of original texts are reprinted as they appear in the publications indicated. Square brackets are used to show suggested restorations of the text; round brackets enclose words added to clarify context. Ellipses within round brackets, (. . .), mean that some lines have been omitted.

The text notes provide information about secondary sources used. The bibliographies list short summaries of available publications by chapter. A number of these are in foreign languages. Assyriology has a strong base in Germany, France and Italy, as well as in Britain and the United States. English translations of important scholarly texts are, however, relatively uncommon; I have quoted them if available.

The glossary provides a very short definition of archaeological, historical and some anthropological terms that recur throughout this book.

Chronology

PREHISTORIC PERIODS

Middle palaeolithic *c.*78,000–28,000 BC
Upper palaeolithic *c.*28,000–10,000 BC
Neolithic *c.*10,000–6000 BC
Chalcolithic *c.*6000–3000 BC
    Hassuna *c.*5500–5000 BC
    Halaf/Ubaid *c.*5000–4000 BC
    Uruk *c.*4000–3200 BC
    Jemdet Nasr *c.*3200–3000 BC

HISTORICAL PERIODS

1. Southern Mesopotamia
Early Dynastic I *c.*3000–2750 BC
Early Dynastic II *c.*2750–2600 BC
Early Dynastic III (Fara) *c.*2600–2350 BC
Dynasty of Akkad *c.*2350–2000 BC
Ur III *c.*2150–2000 BC
Old Babylonian *c.*2000–1600 BC
    Isin Larsa Dynasties *c.*2000–1600 BC
    First Dynasty of Babylon *c.*1800–1600 BC
Kassite Dynasty *c.*1600–1155 BC
Second Dynasty of Isin 1155–1027 BC
Second Dynasty of Sealand 1026–1006 BC
Dynasty of E 979–732 BC

Assyrian domination 732–626 BC
Neo-Babylonian Dynasty 626–539 BC

2. Northern Mesopotamia

Old Assyrian period c.1900–1400 BC
Middle Assyrian period c.1400–1050 BC
Neo-Assyrian period Empire 934–610 BC

POST-MESOPOTAMIAN HISTORY

Achaemenid Empire 539–331 BC
Hellenistic period 331–126 BC
  Seleucid Dynasty 311–126 BC
Parthian period 126 BC–AD 227
Sassanian period AD 224–642

ISLAMIC ERA: FROM AD 642

Abbasid Dynasty 750–1258
Ottoman period 1516–1914
British occupation 1914–21
Kingdom of Iraq 1921–58
Republic of Iraq 1958–present
  Saddam Hussein president since 1979

1 ERIDU

CREATING THE FIRST CITY

Eridu is the Mesopotamian Eden, the place of creation. This is the beginning of a story that relates how the Babylonian god Marduk created the world:

A holy house, a house of the gods in a holy place, had not been made, reed
    had not come forth, a tree had not been created,
A brick had not been laid, a brick mould had not been built,
A house had not been made, a city had not been built,
A city had not been made, a living creature had not been placed (therein).
(. . .)
All the lands were sea.
The spring in the sea was a water pipe.
Then Eridu was made, Esagila was built,
Esagila whose foundations Lugaldukuga laid within the Apsu.
(. . .)
The gods, the Annunnaki he created equal.
The holy city, the dwelling of their hearts' delight, they call it solemnly.
Marduk constructed a reed frame on the face of the waters.
He created dirt and poured it out by the reed frame.
In order to settle the gods in the dwelling of (their) hearts' delight,
He created mankind.[1]

This narrative is a myth of origin – how the world as Mesopotamian people knew it came into being, a charter for the notion of the city as a sacred place while, at the same time, the myth refers to a particular city, Eridu. The time before creation is described as an absence of all the characteristic features of civilized life as the Mesopotamians knew it. Amid the primeval sea, the first city, Eridu, and the great Marduk temple of Babylon, Esagila, are 'made' – or rather conceived through an act of divine thought that sparks off the process of actual creation. Just like the marsh dwellers of southern Iraq, who still build their huts on floating islands of reed, the god spreads mud upon a reed frame to fashion a platform. From this primordial, rather flimsy basis, the cities and their temples take their beginning. Henceforth the gods take up residence on earth and live in cities. And because the gods have the dwelling of 'their hearts' delight' in cities, Mesopotamian cities are always sacred.

Thus the Mesopotamian Eden is not a garden but a city, formed from a piece of dry land surrounded by the waters. The first building is a temple. Then mankind is created to render service to god and temple. This is how Mesopotamian tradition presented the evolution and function of cities, and Eridu provides the mythical paradigm. Contrary to the biblical Eden, from which man was banished for ever after the Fall, Eridu remained a real place, imbued with sacredness but always accessible. The strong local flavour of this mythical narrative, with its references to the particular conditions of the region, is striking and can only be understood if we consider the setting of Eridu.

Eridu is the ancient name of a site now known as Abu Shahrein. The etymology of the word *Eridu* is unknown and may well belong to a linguistic substratum of an early, pre-Sumerian culture. The Sumerians wrote it with the sign NUN, which looks like some kind of tree or even a reed. Eridu's geographical situation is unique. It is one of the most southerly sites, at the very edge of the alluvial river plain and close to the marshes: the transitional zone between sea and land, with its shifting watercourses, islands and deep reed thickets.[2] At the same time the western desert, stretching for many hundreds of miles and containing nothing but sand-dunes and rock-strewn wastes, is close enough to threaten the site and engulf it with sand. This placement meant that ancient Eridu had immediate access to the three widely different physical systems: the alluvium, the desert and the marshes, and hence to the different modes of subsistence: farming, nomadic pastoralism and fishing. Most importantly, however, the city commanded its own ecosystem, since it was built upon a hillock within a depression about twenty feet below the level of the surrounding land, which allowed the subterranean waters to collect together. This swampy place can still become a sizeable lake in the months of high water.[3] The earliest Mesopotamian texts, from the early third millennium, underline the importance of this lagoon. In Sumerian this was known as the **abzu** (in Akkadian *Apsû*). In the almost rainless southern regions, the most obvious and crucial manifestation of water was the **abzu**. At Eridu, so the texts say, it surrounded the religious centre and became synonymous with it. According to the Mesopotamian notion of the cosmos, the earth was a solid, disc-like expanse within a huge body of water. Below the earth was the **abzu**, above the earth the sky formed a more or less impermeable vault holding back the upper body of water, which at certain places and times fell as rain through the holes in the sky's ceiling. Eridu was the centre of the cult for the god or goddess of sweet water.

The text quoted at the beginning comes from a cuneiform tablet written in the Neo-Babylonian period, some time in the sixth century BCE. Hormuzd Rassam found it among the ruins of Sippar;[4] perhaps it belonged to the collection of a learned priest since it was written in both Sumerian and Babylonian. The creation story forms the introduction to a long incantation meant to be recited so as to purify the temple of Nabu at Borsippa.[5] Although this particular text version is of relatively late date (first millennium), the tradition that Eridu is the oldest city goes back to the very first written texts from the late fourth millennium; Eridu already heads a list of geographical names. The Sumerian King-list[6] begins with the following lines: 'After kingship had descended from heaven, Eridu became (the) seat) of kingship. Alulim reigned 28,800 years as king; Alalgar reigned 36,000 years. Eridu was abandoned, (and) its kingship carried off to Badtibira.'[7] The antiquity of Eridu was a matter of traditional knowledge, repeated again and again until it became a fact, or a cliché, so far as the scholars of the Western world were concerned who read these Mesopotamian texts before the site was discovered. The story of the archaeological exploration of Eridu shows how the received wisdom of ancient sources came to be both refuted and confirmed.

DIGGING UP ERIDU

The mount of Eridu, called Tell Abu Shahrein, which lies just some 24 kilometres south of Ur, had been targeted for excavation as early as the mid nineteenth century. It is a typical cone-shaped *tell*, or ruin-heap, half a kilometre in diameter, rising some 25 metres above the plain. Six smaller mounds were dotted around in the vicinity, indicating that the population centre moved throughout time, perhaps in accordance with the lagoon's shifting shoreline.

First attempts at excavation were made by J. H. Taylor on behalf of the British Museum, in 1854. The race was then on for all the newly created national museums of the Western world to be filled with artefacts from the most distant places and times for the greater glory of the imperial powers of the nineteenth century, symbolizing their command over time and space. In the mid nineteenth century highly crafted objects of great antiquity were particularly sought after – statues, reliefs and vessels made of precious metals – and any written documents in strange scripts were to be mastered and rendered intelligible through the advanced linguistic skills of Victorian scholars. The exploration of the great northern mounds in Assyria had already yielded carved stone reliefs, colossal bulls with bearded human faces and great quantities of cuneiform tablets.[8] All that Taylor found at Abu Shahrein was a mound of mud brick, heavily eroded and compacted. Since at the time methods to trace mudbrick walls had not yet been developed, his workmen tunnelled through the solid mass of earthwork in a generally futile search for 'antiquities'. Even the handsomely carved lion in black granite Taylor unearthed had to be left behind for lack of suitable transport.

The British Museum meanwhile continued to be filled with the popular Assyrian artefacts and Abu Shahrein was again left to the local foxes and jackals. In 1918 Campbell Thompson and in 1919 H. R. H. Hall explored the site for the museum yet again, but these attempts likewise produced few results. By the end of the Second World War in 1945 the colonial era of archaeology was over and the newly created Directorate General of Antiquities in Iraq chose the so far unpromising site as the target for the very first full-scale Iraqi excavation project.

The symbolic significance of this site played an important role as it was to bring new evidence 'for the strong thread of continuity which runs throughout the past of Iraq'.[9] The new Iraqi nation, the first Mesopotamian state to enjoy political self-determination after centuries of Ottoman and European rule, marked its new beginning with the recovery of the most ancient of cities so as to reaffirm the continuity of the local culture. It was also significant that the secular government chose a pre-Islamic site in an attempt to make its people proud of their ancient history and to help foster a sense of national, non-Muslim identity.

Work at the site began in 1946, with the Iraqi Fuad Safar as field director and the British archaeologist Seton Lloyd acting as technical adviser to the Department of Antiquities. The team spent three seasons until the end of February 1949.[10] From the beginning, the aims of the excavations were to produce a comprehensive and systematic exploration of the site, using the latest archaeological methods. The site was considered 'representative for the earliest epoch of human habitation in the drying Mesopotamia . . . as the setting for the evolution of Sumerian civilization . . .',[11] but the main political concern was to substantiate ancient claims for the site as a place of origin, not just for the Sumerian but also by implication for all of civilization, not least for that of the Middle East.

The Iraqi team began work on the 'acropolis', where the remains of a large stepped monument or ziggurat very similar to the one at nearby Ur[12] were clearly visible. This structure could be dated with the help of some inscribed bricks to the kings Ur-Nammu and Amar-Sin, rulers of the Third Dynasty of Ur (c. twenty-first century). Beneath one of the corners of the ziggurat workmen discovered walls of a much earlier edifice, which could on the basis of potsherds be dated to the late Ubaid period (c.3800). The term 'Ubaid period' derives from the Tell Ubaid site near Ur excavated by Sir Leonard Woolley in the 1920s. It refers to the Chalcolithic cultural levels of southern Mesopotamia, overlapping with the Halaf levels well known from northern Mesopotamian sites.

The Iraqi archaeologists decided to remove this late Ubaid layer to see if any earlier remains could be found underneath, and ended up with another sequence of eighteen occupational levels. At the lowest level, 'on a dune of clean sand', they discovered the very first building, 'a primitive chapel' no larger than 3 metres square. It contained a pedestal facing the entrance, and a recessed niche. The proposed date for this 'chapel' is 4900 or Ubaid level 1. The whole building, and all those of the subsequent layers, were made of sun-dried brick. This was an interesting feature in light of the fact that the typical Ubaid dwellings in the region, known from Woolley's excavations, were made from reeds, in a form of construction still used by the Marsh Arabs today: tightly wrapped, slim bundles of tall reeds serving as poles to form a framework covered with reed mats. Given that this was the traditional construction technique in the south, it was remarkable to find so much brick architecture at the earliest levels at Eridu, with all the important structures built in brick. The Ubaid culture is generally not well documented in southern Mesopotamia,[13] so the material recovered at Eridu helped to modify the impression, gained from Woolley's excavations, that the Ubaid in the south was a poorly developed primitive 'village culture'.[14]

The sequence of 'temples' showed they had been built on the same sites for hundreds of years. When the first 'chapel' of level XVII had fallen into disrepair, a new one was built directly on top of the ruins of the older walls. The new building was practically a reconstruction of the earlier one, with the addition of more sophisticated features, such as interior plastering. At the next level the plan was changed from an approximate square to a rectangle, nearly double in overall size. Then, at level XIV, the whole building had been levelled and all the earlier ruins filled in with sand and enclosed with a brick wall, to provide the basis for a new building elevated from the surrounding areas by 1 metre and accessed by a ramp. This showed features that had much in common with other monumental buildings of the time discovered in the north of Mesopotamia. A spacious central chamber (4.50 metres wide and at least 12.60 metres long) was surrounded by smaller rooms. Also characteristic was a rhythmical articulation of the walls by niches and buttresses, and a clear symmetrical layout.

The same layout was repeated when the building was reconstructed in the next two levels (X and IX). Then came a complete change in plan and general character. The walls became much thicker (70 centimetres) and the building covered much more ground. It had a central nave flanked by subsidiary side rooms. The walls, inside and out, were heavily corrugated, which made the high and dense walls more stable and produced a pleasing aesthetic effect as the play of light and shade created regular vertical patterns. Within the main chamber were several false doorways, one revealing a niche containing a spouted vessel full of fish bones. Buried beneath the pavement of the nave, directly below the 'altar', were a number of curious snake-like clay coils some 30 to 40 centimetres long. These may have had something to do with an underworld cult.[15]

At level VI the building became truly monumental. The walls of the previous building were once again levelled, to a height of 1.2 metres, and the space between them was packed with mudbricks. This formed another platform, extended considerably, to make room for the new structure. The denudation of the mound meant that not much of the plan could be recovered, but the main sanctuary was a very long room, measuring 14.40 by 3.70 metres. Twin doors were set into the shorter wall at each end. The podium was plastered, its surface burnt dark red. It was covered by a thick deposit of ashes, which also lay scattered all over the floor. Mixed with the ashes were large quantities of fish bones, as well as bones of smaller animals. Such remains extended over the whole of the north-eastern end of the chamber. The state of the bones indicated that the fish had been eaten, and curiously the remains had not been cleared out but were kept within the building. A small subsidiary room completely filled with ashes and debris to the consistency of clinker suggested that the fish remains and other offerings were burnt there.

After the collapse of temple VI preparations were apparently made for building yet another temple on top, at a higher level but more or less to the same plan. Only traces of subsequent buildings (temples V–I) remain because of extensive levelling at the end of the second millennium in preparation for the ziggurat. But since temple VI had been very dilapidated when the restoration attempts were made, it may well have been the last of the Ubaid 'temples' at Eridu.

From the time of the humble beginnings of the first 'chapel' to the huge and sophisticated temple VI more than a thousand years had passed. With hardly any interruption, one building had followed another on the very same spot, each succeeding one becoming larger than the one before, and as a consequence of carefully levelling the earlier remains the platforms grew higher and higher. A reconstruction by the Iraqi architects showed the last Ubaid 'temple' to be raised high above the ground, elevated by the successive layers of previous buildings. The interior furnishings, the platforms, niches and podia, also show a remarkable continuity of form and perhaps of purpose.

The archaeologists have routinely called these structures 'temples', a word signifying a place dedicated specifically to sacred ritual. It is not at all clear whether the Ubaid 'temples' were exclusively used for worship or seen as dwellings of the gods, as in later periods. What is certain is that they provided at least periodically a setting for particular activities. As has been pointed out, they were all filled with 'ordinary rubbish', small bones, unremarkable pottery and so forth. They were not apparently kept spotlessly clean or reserved for one specific purpose. Few objects of value were recovered: some clay figurines of naked male and female humans, small animal figures, a model snake decorated to look like one of the serpents still common around Abu Shahrein and the buried clay snake coils mentioned above. Otherwise there were only some beads of semi-precious stones, stone tools, obsidian blades, spindle whorls of clay and a copper axe.

It is clear that the buildings not only became progressively larger and better built with time, but that the interior arrangements – the pedestals, false doorways, symmetrically arranged niches – seem to have had symbolic as well as functional characteristics which point to ritual rather than mundane purposes. These late Ubaid temples may have anticipated the Mesopotamian temple architecture of the historical periods some 1,500 years later. Their plan, a central chamber flanked by side rooms with a free-standing podium in the middle, became a standard feature, as was the façade decorated with pilasters and niches. The custom of burying votive gifts and ritual implements was also never abandoned. Most significant perhaps was the idea of sealing the remains of earlier structures and their contents (to preserve their sanctity?) and then erecting the new building on top of the levelled ruins. Thus most Mesopotamian temples enshrined the substance of older temples and the very platform they stood on was made venerable by the accumulated sacred debris. As such they became a visible sign of continuity and antiquity.

It must be remembered that, especially in the southern plains, the features of the landscape were not as permanent as in other regions. The rivers would shift their beds, inundations destroyed cultivated areas, sand dunes encroached on deserted villages within weeks – all factors that threatened the desire for permanence and anchorage to a place. Only the cities, and especially the 'brickwork' of the temples, persisted throughout the ages and grew like living beings. This process can first be observed in Eridu. In the Babylonian narrative, the platform arising from the Apsu became the first seat of the gods; in the archaeological sequence, the simple hut-like structure on the sand was continually built over to become one of the most venerable sanctuaries in the country. Eridu's reputation in later times as the first shrine was amply justified by the archaeological sequence.[16]

THE SÈVRES OF THE CHALCOLITHIC

The archaeologists did not dig only on the main mound at Abu Shahrein, but also at several other, subsidiary sites. They discovered a small part of the residential quarters and an extensive cemetery. In all these areas, as well as in the 'temples' on the main mound, they found potsherds. Potsherds are always important in excavations, since they are invaluable for dating purposes. Other than that they are rarely particularly exciting. The pottery of the fifth millennium, however, is not only interesting for chronological reasons but is also very beautiful. Besides this it tells us something about the socio-cultural organization of the age. Both the northern Halaf and Samarra ware and the southern Ubaid and Hajji Muhammed ware – all named after their initial places of discovery – are instantly recognizable: they are thin-walled, mainly creamy in colour and decorated with a simple, striking elegance unparalleled in the whole of the prehistoric Near East. The patterns vary from freely applied dots and strokes to intricate geometrical hatching and zoomorph and human figures. The repertoire of shapes includes beakers, round and oval plates, bowls, spouted vessels, large and small jars, goblets, thin cups and coarser cooking ware.

Such high-quality pottery was made by skilled specialists at different centres of production; the pottery discovered at the early levels of Eridu (from the earliest in level XIX to level XIII) was locally manufactured. However, the distribution of the painted pottery went far beyond the areas of production. This pottery was no mundane, all-purpose household ware but an élite product; it needed special places for storage and display, was not easily transported and unsuitable for a nomadic way of life for which containers of unbreakable materials were preferred. But sedentarism and pottery go well together and it is conceivable that elaborately produced and decorated clay vessels may have contributed to popularize and proclaim the values of settled populations. Of course, they also have their practical functions since they were used for eating and drinking and serving food. Ethnographic accounts have demonstrated both the communicative purpose of decorated objects and the importance of collective feasting, sometimes called 'conspicuous commensuality' – a precursor to 'conspicuous consumption'. The term stresses the importance of the group bonding through shared meals, elaborately served and displayed. Such communal feasting strengthened the status of those who were able to procure the wherewithal, from the comestibles to the precious dinner service.

Anthropologists have argued that the emergence of prestige goods and precious tableware is connected to early forms of hierarchy – in which one group has secured access to territory and goods and is responsible for distribution.[17] The culture of the Chalcolithic (or Copper Age) in the Near East, of which the Ubaid is the southern manifestation, was characterized by increasing sedentarism, horticulture and exchange. Painted pottery from the latest phase (c.4000–3500) can be found all over Mesopotamia, Syria, western and southern Iran, Anatolia, and along the Persian Gulf. This points to a lively network of exchange throughout the region, which was to become even more intensified and organized during the subsequent age known as the Uruk period.[18] At Eridu the earliest settlement levels, built directly on the virgin sand, already have the Chalcolithic pottery typical of the southern Ubaid culture. Whoever decided to settle there was familiar with the technology and decorative repertoire.

As demand for such pottery increased, so the professional expertise developed; temperatures could be regulated more evenly and some form of tournette was used to produce even more regular shapes.

Locally produced pottery dominates in the earlier levels, enabling archaeologists to speak of 'Eridu ware'. Later all evidence for local manufacture ceases (after level XIII), for reasons unknown. The various floor levels of the 'temples' were strewn with Ubaid potsherds, though occasionally whole vessels and jars were recovered. This may suggest that the ceramics were used for actual meals, not just to bring offerings. If we remember the large quantities of ashes and of fish bones as well as the animal remains so common around the pedestals, it is tempting to see the consumption of food as an important part of the activities taking place. However, some types of pottery were only found in the 'temples' and may have served a more clearly defined ritual character. Little vessels, no more than 15 centimetres in diameter, with very thin walls and very elaborate decorative schemes, were sometimes found in clusters, one nestling inside the other (typical of levels X and XI). Also noteworthy are the so-called tortoise vessels, a speciality of Eridu. These had long spouts projecting diagonally from the shoulder and were also abnormally thin and fragile. One of them, filled with fish bones, survived in a niche behind the altar of temple VIII.

Particularly striking are the 'censers' common among the debris of the later 'temples'. The pierced triangular window openings could have allowed the smoke of incense to escape. The placement of the openings suggests doorways and the whole decorative scheme makes them look like miniature buildings – though ones more reminiscent of reed than of brick architecture.[19] Figurative terracottas were also found among the 'temple' debris, including fragmentary (female?) figurines, with the lower body covered with some sort of dress whose patterns are painted on with wavy stripes in black. It is unclear whether they represent any particular type of person or function or a deity. Other anthropomorph statues from the Ubaid cemetery levels are all nude.

BAD TEETH AND GOOD DOGS

The discovery of the Ubaid cemetery during the second season of excavation (1947–8) kept half the workmen busy for most of the season, and they produced remarkable evidence of the inhabitants of ancient Eridu. The cemetery was some distance from the main mound, on the outskirts of the late Ubaid settlement and contemporary with temple VI (c.3800). Some 800 to 1,000 people had been buried there, a modest number in comparison with the huge necropolis of Susa in southern Iran, where more than 2,000 interments from the same time have been found.[20] Only 193 of the Eridu graves were excavated. The bodies had been put in simple pits or brick boxes without a bottom. Each corpse was laid at full length on its back, with arms to the side or folded across the pelvis. Then the tomb was filled with earth to the level of the top of the walls and sealed with one or more courses of bricks. Sometimes the remains of previous burials were pushed aside to make room for another corpse, but there were never more than two adults in a grave, the third being invariably a child.

Funerary pottery was placed in a corner close to the right foot, generally a jar, a dish and cup. Occasionally there was evidence of food offerings. Meat bones were found in the earth filling or on top of the tomb. In one instance a male youth some fifteen years old had been buried with a dog, which was laid across the young man's lap with a bone placed in its mouth. Another grave also contained two fragmentary dog skeletons, perhaps of favourite pets. The human bodies wore beads and similar ornaments round neck or wrist, often made from obsidian. They seem to have been clothed, as bands of beads suggest a decorated fringe and belt.

Examination of the skeletons showed that the Eridu population was Mediterranean of the same type as that of present-day Iraq and neighbouring countries. Most of the variations occurred in the teeth and mandibles, with some individuals being 'notably prognathous and large toothed, their teeth being as large as those of Neanderthals'.[21] The large teeth were not necessarily an asset as many of the dead had badly worn teeth, sometimes ground right down to the gums, with resulting abscesses and caries. Whether this was due to a diet of grit-rich cereals or the result of disease is still unclear.[22]

The existence of a cemetery at any location shows that some people have claimed the right to bury their dead at that particular place. In this case, they were quite a large number of people, though what proportion of the Eridu population they represent at the time cannot be determined since only a small fraction of the residential area has been excavated. Cemeteries, especially in the Near East, never account for all deaths, since multiple practices of burial were maintained for undiscernible reasons. Some practices leave no archaeological trace, like that of exposing the corpse in the uninhabited desert where predators dispose of the remains. The practice of cremation is generally more common in fuel-rich areas, but secondary cremation after initial exposure also remains a possibility. Intramural burials, within courtyards or under the thick-walled buildings, were common in later periods, but the limited scope of the excavation of houses again prevents any conclusions as to whether some of the Ubaid population were buried in their homes. Finally the marshes and the lagoon itself could have served as final resting places.

In the later written tradition the Apsu is connected with the underworld. It is possible that the Eridu cemetery served the wider local community within a radius of some 25 kilometres as the preferred burial place.[23] Given that we do not know where and how the other people were buried, what does the cemetery of Eridu tell us about those who were interred there? Who were they? Family burials of a male and female adult together with a child[24] (and sometimes the family dog!) seem to indicate such social practices as monogamy and lineage prestige. Personal possessions, such as imported obsidian beads and ornaments, show that they had access to relatively precious articles (jewellery, clothes). Some of the objects, especially the obsidian and other stone beads, were of foreign origin and had been 'traded' or exchanged. Their presence in the graves indicates that the kin group had connections to distant places.

The pottery in the graves was also generally of high standard, and tall cups with ring bases were particularly common, perhaps used for libations. Several unique types of vessel, especially well made and beautifully decorated examples, were found only in the cemetery. Child burials were often furnished with miniature sets of bowls and jars. Other striking grave goods included a clay model of a sailing boat, complete with a little socket for the mast, and terracotta figurines. One example of a male figure survived intact. The figurines had slender proportions and curiously elongated heads with lizard-like faces. The upper parts of the chests are decorated with small round lumps which also run along the arms. The male figure holds a short stick in one hand. Whatever the significance of these representations, they were put into the tombs for a purpose, most likely in connection with funerary beliefs.

In summary, the whole procedure of burying the people in the Eridu cemetery involved considerable effort and planning. Tombs must have been marked on the surface to allow secondary interments of a spouse or child. The dead had to be furnished with suitable goods, with ornaments and decorated pottery. Furthermore, it appears that certain vessels were specially made for funerary ritual purposes, libations and so on. Cuts of meat and, in the case of children, whole small animals demonstrate that food offerings were also part of the obsequies. Some bodies were found covered in red ochre, though the excavators were unsure whether this had been done in antiquity, for symbolic purposes, or whether changes in the soil had produced the effect.

Altogether the Eridu graves indicated that the people buried there were in some way special. They uniformly had access to valuable artefacts; they could provide offerings and meat; they had the right to a 'proper' funeral complete with rituals and possibly subsequent care, while other people in the community clearly did not have this privilege. Why they should have such a differentiated status is not clear. It has been suggested that at this period some groups with extensive connections, forged and maintained by exchange (of goods, perhaps also of women), created a network of communication.[25] Such groups would extend the cultural horizons of the purely local communities and involve them in a much wider framework – a sort of Chalcolithic commonwealth of shared assumptions and ideas, archaeologically materialized in pottery and other prestige items. It linked the Mesopotamian north with the southern plains, with the plateaux and the river basin of Susiana in Iran. However, whether the Eridu skeletons belonged to an 'aboriginal' group or to 'newcomers', let alone whether they were the ancestors of the Sumerians, is a moot point. All that can be said is that the people buried in the cemetery of Eridu were 'different' because of their cultural habits and not for any inherent characteristic.

The same material culture items, with a few exceptions, were found in the graves and the 'temples'. But the same correlation could not be made between the dwelling houses and either the graves or the 'temples'. This could mean that the people who operated the activities in the monumental buildings were the same as those buried in the cemetery, that they may have had a particular ritual status through being connected to the Eridu ceremonial. At the same time, there were no marked differences in the quality and quantity of the funerary gifts, nothing to indicate that some individuals were distinguished from others, which speaks in favour of a collective identity, of a special group status. They may have been members of an élite, perhaps because they controlled interregional exchanges. The stamp seals found in the late 'temples' suggest that certain people had responsibility for transactions. They may have been tied to the agricultural exploitation of the Eridu region, with its cattle herding and barley fields, which could explain the sorry state of their teeth – having eaten too much sandy bread for too long. Unfortunately none of these suggestions can be substantiated because of the fragmentary nature of the evidence.

We know very little about the nature of society during the Ubaid period. For the Czech archaeologist Petr Charvát, it was the last of the true egalitarian societies with self-sufficient households, all equally engaged in subsistence activities.[26] Others find evidence of incipient hierarchies in at least some areas, where certain groups or households had greater access than others to some commodities. The crucial question is the role religion played in all this. If the large brick buildings were primarily for ritual purposes, did the people who organized their construction and maintenance derive any tangible 'profit' from their 'investment'? Did their connection with the 'sacred' serve to legitimize emerging differentiation among people, with one group having more command over the labour and produce of others?[27] The phrasing of such questions invariably betrays the writers' own ideological positions, with Marxian views focusing on class distinctions and control over the means of production as a main form of investigating societies. As such it is part of a modern narrative frame, the story of man's labour and who controls it. This can lead to some interesting results when there is enough material to consult. Unfortunately the Ubaid period remains inaccessible for more detailed investigations. The dead of the Eridu cemetery, with their joints of meat and pretty painted bowls and bad teeth, at once reveal and conceal the realities of their existence.

Ubaid Eridu

There is little doubt that in the Ubaid period a common culture developed which spread all over the Near East. However, old forms of life continued to exist alongside new ones, and this mixture of innovation and tradition is characteristic of Mesopotamia from the very beginning. Local communities were self-sufficient in terms of food production, skilfully exploiting the natural potential of a neighbourhood. In Eridu, the resources of the marshes and lagoon were prominent and the abundance of water made it suitable for the breeding of cattle and pigs.[28] The favourite food consumed in the 'temple' was fish, a preference perhaps induced by association with the Apsu.

As far as the spiritual achievement of this elusive, preliterate period is concerned, Charvát surmises that nothing less than 'the formation of the first universal religion' was at stake here, with Eridu playing a significant part, as perhaps the 'southern representative'[29] remembered by later tradition, where Eridu was seen as a source of all wisdom and the seat of the god of knowledge. While there is too little evidence to speculate on what form this 'universal religion' could have taken, an important component is the focus on ritual associated with built places. This does not suggest that these were the only forms of ritual, but that the architectural framing of ritual certainly became more important. Building at a 'sacred' site need not be the responsibility of any particular group alone, and even if it were the prerogative of some, the passing of time must mitigate against perpetual privilege. We have seen how the buildings could fall into disrepair and then be reconstructed, usually on similar lines but often bigger than before. Mudbrick needs constant maintenance and periodic rebuilding, and while the architectural body is inherently impermanent, it acquires solidity and mass through each act of reconstruction.

The participation in the ongoing process of maintenance and growth could have been as spontaneous as adding a stone to a cairn is in mountainous parts of world. It is tempting to envisage that the 'city' of Eridu as a ceremonial space belonged to everyone, to the marsh-dwellers and hunters, the cattle breeders and farmers, the settled and the nomadic. It perhaps became a focal point because of its remoteness from familiar social connections, a place good to be buried in, a place where you contributed to make a landmark, where the gods of the deep were nearer than in any other place, where you brought a dish of fish to cook in a dark chamber and then you went away. Only a relatively small population ever actually lived near by, and it is not clear in what relationship they stood to the main site. Eridu's example was not the only one. There were similar experiments going on in other places, such as Ubaid itself, and Tell Uqair, and also at Ur. But Eridu is not only exceptionally well documented for the Ubaid period, it also maintained the myth of its primacy to the subsequent ages of Mesopotamian history and right down to our age.

ERIDU IN THE HISTORICAL PERIODS

At the end of the Ubaid period there are signs of decline. The quality of the sherds deteriorates, the last 'temple' was allowed to persist in a state of dilapidation for a long time. The excavators suggested that at the beginning of the 'Uruk period', the archaeological level in the first third of the fourth millennium that follows the Ubaid, Eridu 'ceased to be a village supporting an agricultural community'. Only the central mound with its venerable succession of ruins was still in use. On the other hand, the public buildings were rebuilt on an even larger scale than before, in the monumental style characteristic of the 'Uruk culture'.[30] The whole of the mound was occupied with what the excavators describe as 'buildings of a religious character and dwellings for priests'.[31] Again the earlier ruins were buried beneath a large platform, this time with a limestone terrace.

Limestone and sandstone occur naturally at Eridu and it is one of the few cities in southern Mesopotamia where the city wall was built of gypsum.[32] The main 'temple' was also built with limestone and its walls were decorated with cone mosaics covered with thin copper plating. Other buildings of the same period (some with traces of wall paintings) were filled with sand during the Uruk period. Since layers of votive pottery were found embedded in the sand fill, it may have been a deliberate practice to preserve and at the same time terminate a building's use.[33] A retaining wall surrounded the whole of the mound, but it is possible that this was built later, during the Jemdet-Nasr period, around 3000. The seal of Eridu appears among the documents found at Uruk and Ur, as one of the old cities in the land.

For a few hundred years Eridu continued to exist primarily as a ceremonial (or religious) centre in the south, increasingly eclipsed by neighbouring Ur, which quickly grew in size. Then almost overnight it was completely abandoned, quickly buried under enormous drifts of sand that filled the deserted buildings, with only the main mound left standing. The temple itself was rebuilt twice in the protoliterate period, like an island in the desert, but the accumulation of loose sand seems to have made the areas surrounding the main mound uninhabitable. When, after some centuries, the area was once more inhabited, the population chose another spot, about a kilometre to the north, and few efforts were made to rebuild the shrine on the main mound.

The site only became important again in the Early Dynastic II period (c.2500). Either a ruler of the First Dynasty of Ur or a local governor built a large palace, composed of two identical buildings side by side. Why there were two buildings remains a mystery. They were built with so-called planoconvex bricks – rectangular with rounded tops – typical of the period.[34] The excavators suggested that whoever had resided in that palace also attended to the sanctuary on the main mound, but no traces of it remain as a result of the levelling of the site some five hundred years later, from the time when the kings of the Third Dynasty of Ur (Ur III) turned their attention to the old shrine of Eridu. The main architect of this project was king Amar-Sin (c.2046–2038). His father had built a colossal temple precinct with a massive ziggurat at Ur and the son followed that example. Inscribed bricks proclaim that Amar-Sin 'king of the four quarters' built 'for Enki, his beloved king, his beloved Apsu'.

There is no evidence that buildings other than a ziggurat were erected. Although the Ur king lavished resources and manpower on the ziggurat project, Eridu apparently did not become a functioning settlement at this time, let alone a city. It remained a sanctuary, made more prominent and important through the construction of the temple tower, but it was a symbolic site within the Ur empire – an ancient religious site revitalized by royal patronage. The Ur king appointed special priests and priestesses and some royal hymns suggest the coronation rites of the Ur III rulers were performed at Eridu.[35] It was also a destination for the cultic journeys of the gods, a popular form of spectacle and ritual in which the statues of various deities travelled by boat from one temple to another, up and down the country.[36]

In the following centuries the rulers of the Isin dynasties (2000–1800) at least repaired the massive brickwork. They also began an intensive search for buried temple treasure – many of their tunnels and shafts were found by the excavators. Then the shrine of Enki fell gradually into disrepair and for centuries Eridu became neglected and deserted. The cult of its main god, however, was not discontinued but moved to other cities. In fact it appears that the whole temple personnel of the shrine were moved to Ur during the time of Hammurabi (c.1792–1750) and the cult continued there in a chapel within the moon god's complex.[37] Only in the mid first millennium did the forsaken ruins once more receive royal attention when king Nebuchadrezzar II (605–562) attempted some restoration, according to a few inscribed bricks and administrative documents. Thereafter Eridu's temple fell into permanent ruin. Every temple in Mesopotamia, however, had its own artificial and miniature version of the Apsu – either a small pool, or simply a polished vessel filled with water. Thus the *numen* of Eridu could be represented symbolically at any place, and perhaps the fountains and pools which grace the courtyards in Middle Eastern buildings of much later centuries retain a faint memory of the old lagoon in the very south of Mesopotamia.

ERIDU STORIES

Of primordial mud, Enki's sex-life, drink and the Seven Sages[38]

Who were the gods of Eridu? From the texts dating from historical times we know the names of Enki (whom the Babylonians called Ea), the goddesses Nammu and Damgalnunna, and the divine couples Lahmt and Lahamu and Tiamat and Apsu; the names of their antecedents in the fifth and fourth millennia remain obscure. The single most important concept associated with Eridu is Apsu (Sumerian **abzu**).[39] It was conceived both as a natural phenomenon in abstract terms and as a personified entity. So, on the one hand, the Apsu designates the fertilizing aspect of groundwater and the creative potential of the muddy moisture. On the other, in mythological narratives,

Apsu can appear as a character. In the so-called Eridu Cosmogony, the primeval matter was composed of the mingled sweet and salty waters, personified as Apsu and Tiamat respectively.[40] This echoes the natural conditions of the marsh area where brackish and fresh waters come together. Apsu is conceived as the male, Tiamat as the female element; their offspring is called Mummu,[41] a sort of all female matrix who gives birth to Heaven and Earth, and it is this latter couple which begets the great gods. In later creation accounts, too, Apsu and Tiamat represent the original formless chaos which has to be subjected to a progressive series of differentiation. The original elements are powerful and dangerous, unpredictable.

There is a tension between these forces of nature and the subsequent stages of development which is often envisaged as a generational conflict. In the Babylonian epic of creation, the *Enuma eliš*, Apsu, 'begetter of the gods', is inert and sleepy but finds his peace disturbed by the noise of the younger gods so that he sets out to destroy them. His grandson Ea (Enki in Sumerian) is chosen to represent the younger gods and he puts a spell on Apsu, casting him into a deep sleep. The magic is meant to contain Apsu in the underground. From then on Apsu also becomes a mere place: the god Ea is said to have set up his home 'in the depth of the Apsu'. Henceforth Ea takes on the characteristics and functions of Apsu, which are enhanced by Ea's superior intellectual powers. The female counterpart of Apsu, Tiamat, is not so easily subdued, and unleashes hordes of monstrous beings to devour the younger generation of gods. Only Marduk, the son of Ea, and the champion of the younger gods, can overcome her, with the aid of the four winds and a magic net. He creates the known world from her body, cleaved in half like an oyster, and the Euphrates and Tigris flow from her eye sockets.

It is worth nothing that there is another, older tradition in which the primeval and creative matter was conceived of as female and personified as the Sumerian goddess called Nammu.[42] In divine genea-logies and some myths she is the mother of Enki and the mother-goddess who was said to have 'given birth to the great gods'. Nammu and the primeval waters are self-generative, bringing forth life by themselves, without a male partner. It is often thought that female deities are older than male ones in Mesopotamia and Nammu's cult; or rather, that the cult of the female principle as a watery creative force, with equally strong connections to the underworld, may well predate that of Ea-Enki.[43] With Enki in an interesting change of gender symbolism, the fertilizing agent is also water, Sumerian a, which also means 'semen'. In one evocative passage in a Sumerian hymn Enki stands at the empty river beds and fills them with his 'water'.[44] In other narratives (see below) he impregnates and irrigates at one and the same time.

The **abzu** also signifies the shrine (èš) of Eridu, the 'holy mountain', the architectural manifestation of the sacred place and form in the city. Water was the sacred substance *par excellence* – not least because of its fundamental importance for the economy of the desert climate. Water was essential, in magic, to purify and carry the spell, to assist in divination.

The ideas associated with the Apsu demonstrate how a particular geophysical setting inspired a religious and metaphysical concept. This was embodied in the buildings of the city of Eridu, which date back to the very beginning of settled life in southern Mesopotamia. The notion of water as the source of life in this world and beyond death evolved at a very early date and continued to inform Mesopotamian religious thought to the end.

During the first half of the third millennium, in the so-called Early Dynastic period, local deities became organized in a hierarchically structured pantheon of separate divine lineages. The Eridu system focused on Enki (Akkadian Ea),[45] presented as the son of the old Eridu goddess Nammu and the sky-god An, the chief of the Sumerian pantheon. Enki's wife was Damgalnunna and they both lived in the E-engur, the House of the Apsu, as the temple of Eridu was called. Their son was Asarluhhi, who was later identified with the Babylonian god Marduk. In addition there were many minor deities said to be related to the Eridu genealogy. Relationships between the various Mesopotamian gods and goddesses were a matter of political as well as theological importance. Lists of deities, arranged along kinship lines, were already established in the later fourth millennium, and the religious literature, hymns and cult songs further elaborate such interrelations.

Towards the end of the second millennium, Marduk assumed many of the functions of Ea/Enki without, however, fully replacing the older water deity. Enki was the 'master magician of the gods', a function later assumed by his son, Marduk. The Mesopotamians also made a connection between water and intelligence, or wisdom. When Enki (or Marduk) creates, he calls things into being through an utterance, a word, spoken to activate the inert primary matter. Enki's wisdom is of a practical as well as an esoteric nature, which fits in well with the creative aspect. He was the patron deity of various professional groups, such as leather-workers, washermen, reed-workers, barbers, weavers, builders, metalsmiths, potters, irrigation technicians, gardeners, goat-herds, as well as physicians, diviners, lamentation priests, musicians and scribes.[46] In mythological tales, Enki knows the solution to seemingly intractable situations.[47]

Eridu as the primary manifestation of the Apsu was also regarded as the place of knowledge, the fount of wisdom, and under Enki's control. Several narratives elaborate on this concept. Eridu as the storehouse of divine decrees is described in a Sumerian narrative called 'Enki and Inanna'. Enki, ensconced in the Apsu, is in possession of all the me, a Sumerian term which refers to all those institutions, forms of social behaviour, emotions, signs of office, which in their totality were seen as indispensable for the smooth operation of the world. These me belonged to Eridu and to Enki. However, Inanna, city goddess of Uruk,[48] desires to obtain the me for herself and take them to Uruk. For this purpose she sets sail to reach Eridu by boat, always the easiest way to get from one Mesopotamian city to another. Enki hears of her arrival and worries about her intentions. He instructs his vizier to receive her with all honours and to prepare a banquet at which both deities drink much beer. Enki falls fast asleep, leaving the way free for Inanna to load the precious me on to her boat, one by one, and sail away.

When Enki awakes from his drunken slumber and realizes what has happened, he tries to use his magic in an attempt to regain the me. Inanna manages to ward off the pursuing demons and arrives safely in Uruk. The ending of the story is unclear, since none of the existing text versions are well enough preserved, but it appears that a third deity brings about a reconciliation between Inanna and Enki. This is, of course, a typical Uruk story, concentrating on the local goddess and her superior power. Having liberated the me from the depth of the

Apsu, Inanna could not only enhance her own powers but also implement the decrees among mankind. The list of the **me** includes kingship, priestly offices, crafts and music, as well as intercourse, prostitution, old age, justice, peace, silence, slander, perjury, the scribal arts and intelligence, among many others.[49] The story also shows that, through Inanna's interference, they became immanent in the world. She liberated them from Enki's keeping at Eridu, where he presumably kept them locked away. Eridu is always connected with potential, with beginnings, though not necessarily with the realization of potential.[50]

The fertility of the Apsu and Enki's weakness for drink also feature in another Sumerian creation myth, 'Enki and Ninmah'. The myth begins with a kind of 'prologue in heaven'. The first generation of gods, collectively known as the Anunnaki, have been born, and through a series of marriages between gods further generations appear. They all have specific tasks assigned to them in order to keep the land well tended and irrigated. Some have to carry the baskets with earth, while the 'great gods' act as supervisors. The worker gods complain about their heavy labour and call upon Enki to think of a plan. Enki, apparently exempt from physical work, is fast asleep in the Apsu. Nammu, the mother-goddess, decides to wake him and tells him he ought to get up and create man.

Enki awakes but delegates the job to Nammu, instructing her that what she needs to do is take some of the Apsu clay and give it shape. Another goddess, Ninmah, assists her in this task, and assigns hard work to human kind. The gods celebrate the completion of man's creation with a banquet and Ninmah and Enki both become intoxicated. Ninmah proposes to make some more creatures and Enki is willing to decree their fate. She makes six humans, but they are less than perfect; all have some defect. Enki finally succeeds in finding a 'fate' or occupation for each of them. The one with failing eyesight is to become a singer, the barren woman is given a ritual function, the creature without sexual organs becomes a court official, and so on. Then it is Enki's turn to fashion new beings.

The text versions become corrupt at this point, but it appears that Enki makes two creatures. One is called Umul, who appears as completely unviable. He can't stand, sit, walk, talk or feed himself. Ninmah declares herself unable to do anything useful with him and curses Enki to remain for ever in the Apsu. Enki tells her that she must hold Umul on her lap – he appears to be the first baby. The story seemingly accounts rather humorously for physical and mental handicaps (resulting from the creator deities' tipsiness), the helplessness of human infants and the duties of mankind towards the gods, who have off-loaded the labour of sustaining the world on to human beings.

'Enki and Ninhursaga' is another Sumerian tale that makes much of Enki's impetuous sexuality. 'Young man Enki' is always lying in the marshes to spy on nubile goddesses. He manages to engender successive generations of female deities, until the last one, the spider and weaving goddess Uttu, extracts more from him than just his 'water' (a pun on the Sumerian word for 'semen'). He has to make a garden for her and plant it with cucumbers and fruit. Here the eating of the fruit, as in the Genesis story, leads to intercourse and the subsequent proliferation of plant life.[51]

The last of the Eridu stories is the Babylonian tale of Adapa, the priest of Ea. Copies of the text were discovered in the Egyptian city of Akhetaten (Tell el Amarna), the capital built by Eighteenth Dynasty pharaoh Akhenaton. In the fourteenth century heads of state throughout the Near East engaged in diplomatic exchanges of princesses, gold and other high-status items. The medium of their communication was Babylonian written in cuneiform signs. Tablets were transported from Egypt to Anatolia, from Palestine to Egypt, from Syria to Babylon, and vice versa. Mesopotamian learning thus reached distant courts.

Another copy of the story comes from the library of Nineveh, the most comprehensive collection of cuneiform literature. The Amarna version is somewhat different from the Assyrian, but the main plot is the same. Adapa is one of the Seven Sages created by Ea as exemplary human beings. He serves Ea as a priest in Eridu, where he is in charge of the food offerings to the god. He has to go fishing in the lagoon, which is generally so quiet that he needs neither rudder nor steering pole. One day, however, the south wind overturns his boat. The soaked Adapa shouts a curse at the wind that 'should break his wing'. His words have such power that the wind becomes immobilized and does not blow 'for seven days' (which means a long time). The failure of the wind (which brings cool air upland) is brought to the high god

Anu's attention and he demands that the culprit be sent to him for judgement. Ea, 'who knows heaven's way', decides to prepare Adapa for this important journey. He instructs his priest to put on mourning clothes and to tell the two gods Dumuzi and Ningishzida, whom he will meet guarding the gates of Anu's palace, that he is lamenting their disappearance from the earth. This show of contrition is meant to pacify the two vegetation gods who have suffered indirectly through Adapa's curse.

Adapa is conveyed to heaven, and there he follows Ea's advice to the letter. Dumuzi and Ningishzida duly promise to put in a good word for him and Anu's anger is appeased by their intercession. He asks Adapa where has his wisdom come from, and when he discovers that Ea was behind it, he offers Adapa oil, clothes and the 'water and food of life', which he says will cause him to 'become like the gods'. However, since Ea has also forewarned Adapa not to accept the 'water and food of death', Adapa rejects Anu's gift. At this apparent human folly, Anu breaks into 'divine laughter' and sends Adapa back to earth.

What was Anu's true intention? Did he mean to make Adapa, so accomplished in wisdom as to be almost divine, truly immortal? Or did he laugh at being outwitted by the wily Ea, who knows that what is 'water and food of life' for gods means the opposite for human beings? The purpose of the tale lies in this ambiguity, a reminder that man, even if he is like Adapa, one of the Seven Sages, cannot fathom the 'ways of heaven'.[52]

The Seven Sages were a manifestation of the ultimately unpredictable forces of the Apsu. They often appear in magic texts and incantations as the **abgal** (Akkadian *apkâllu*), fish-like creatures under the command of Enki/Ea. The masks worn by some priests represented on seals and a number of Assyrian reliefs are connected with the power of the Apkallu to ward off evil. They were also personified as traditionally seven 'culture heroes', sent by Ea to teach mankind the arts of civilization. In the late Babylonian composition known as the Erra epic, they are called 'the seven sages of the Apsu, the pure *parādu* fish, who, just as their lord Ea, have been endowed with sublime wisdom'.[53] They were the councillors of the antediluvian kings, also seven in number, and responsible for the invention and the building of cities. The city is therefore the product of divine intelligence.

For some reason the Apkallu also stand for hubris. A bilingual text from Nineveh records how each one managed to annoy an important god so that they were banished to the Apsu for ever. Just as in the other Eridu cosmogonies referred to earlier, the creative potential and the wisdom of the Apsu and its creatures are seen as dangerous and subversive. The tradition of their benevolent influence was one of the very last fragments of Mesopotamian lore to be transmitted to a new world. A Babylonian priest of Marduk, who lived during the reign of the Seleucid king Antiochus I (third century BCE), was the author of a volume called *Babyloniaca*. He wrote it in Greek, under the name Berossus. Only a few passages survive in the later Greek writings from his ambitious work, which was to summarize the history and literature of his ancient culture. One of the fragments concerns the fish-like monsters that Ea sent after the flood to teach mankind. One of them is called Oannes, the Greek form of Adapa's Sumerian name U-an.

THE HOUSE OF THE APSU

All these narratives about Enki and Eridu emphasize the connection between the locality, especially the Apsu, creation and fertility. Eridu is both primordial and immanent, the place where the world first became habitable, where brick and the city were invented. But as the Babylonian creation story emphasizes, the primary purpose of the 'first house' is worship.

The Sumerian collection of temple hymns begins with the hymn to Enki's temple in Eridu, called E-unir. These hymns are presented on tablets from the Old Babylonian period (*c.*1800), but according to the colophones they were originally edited much earlier, by a priestess of the moon-god at Ur, called Enheduanna, who lived in the twenty-third century.[54] Temple hymns offer a metaphorically rich evocation of the major Mesopotamian cult places, highlighting the particular aspects of the shrines:

E-unir, which has grown high, (uniting) heaven and earth,
Foundation of heaven and earth, Holy of Holies Eridu Abzu, shrine, erected
    for its prince

House, holy mound, where pure food is eaten
Watered by the Prince's pure canal,
Mountain, pure place, scoured with soap,
(. . .)
Your great . . . wall is kept in good repair
Into your . . . the place where the god dwells,
The great . . . the . . . beautiful place, light enters not.
Your firmly jointed house is clean, without equal,
Your prince, the great prince, a holy crown
He has placed for you upon your . . .
O Eridu with a crown on your head!
Growing . . . pure
Shrine Abzu, your place is a great place
In your place where they call upon Utu
Where the oven brings bread (good) to eat
On your Ziggurat, the lofty shrine, stretching towards the sky,
Where the oven rivals the Holy of Holies (or: Banqueting Hall)
Your Prince is the Prince of heaven and earth [whose] word was never altered,
. . . the creator, the wise one, the Lord Nudimmud has [E-engura] placed the
house upon you, has taken his place on your dais.[55]

The imagery of this text is not unique to the Eridu temple. Temples
are customarily likened to mountains and said to link heaven and earth.
The term 'prince' is a punning reference to the sign NUN, representing a
reed, which was used to write the toponym Eridu (NUN[ki])[56] and the
word **nun**, a title rendered here as 'prince'. The actual inner shrine,
'the holy of holies', is the room where the image of the god was kept
in darkness. Other important characteristics of the Eridu temple are
obviously the Apsu, here also used to refer to the 'sweet canal', and
the shrine itself. The ziggurat mentioned may be the one that the Early
Dynastic rulers could have built – of which there is no archaeological
evidence – or it may be the Ur III ziggurat and a later scribal addition.
The text also praises the food prepared in the sanctuary – another
custom with a long tradition, if we only remember the remains of
cooked food in the Ubaid period 'temples'. Finally the hymn reveals
the identity of the god: Enki, 'the creator, the wise one', who placed
the house on this spot and took his own place on the throne.

Fuad Safar had hoped that, in the excavation of the ruins of Eridu, 'being the most ancient and important shrine of Ea-Enki, as well as the seat of an important oracle, we should expect to find a Sumerian temple library, or at least, groups of tablets, connected with a centre of theological learning'.[57] No such library was discovered. Except for a few inscribed bricks, no written records were found. Eridu never was a 'centre of theological learning' in the historical period, since it never was a political centre or even a viable city in its own right. As early as the Uruk period (from the mid fourth millennium) Eridu was closely tied to Ur.[58] Some cities operated like twin cities, one as the symbolic and religious centre, the other as the administrative and residential quarters.[59] The revival of the sanctuary after the Jemdet-Nasr period could be linked to the rise of Ur in the Early Dynastic period, and the most ambitious architectural project, the building of the ziggurat, was undertaken by the Ur III king Amar-Sin.

The sanctuary was, during prosperous times, a major place of pilgrimage. Presumably the running of the temple would be covered by revenue generated through votive offerings and similar sources. For the costly maintenance of the buildings, however, Eridu had to rely on royal, that is to say state support. We saw that this dependency on official, supraregional investment was only feasible when the central government had the economic means and when it was deemed ideologically advantageous. During the Ur III empire, the revitalization of ancient cult centres became a priority to further the legitimacy of the Ur rulership, which was proclaimed as having very close relations with the great gods of Sumer. Enki's shrine was not only local, it was also one of the most ancient and prestigious. The vast expenditure on the ziggurat of Enki was justified as a means of re-establishing the proper functioning of the shrine – for the benefit of the whole country, courtesy of the king of Ur. At Ur there was an important scribal centre and most of the texts concerning the god Enki were preserved and perhaps composed at Ur. A separate intellectual centre away from Ur and the censure of court officials would not have been in keeping with the firm ideological control of the Ur government. Their efforts to invest in Eridu's symbolic value certainly helped to keep alive the memory of the shrine's antiquity and its association with the god Enki. Even when the Babylonian deity Marduk – in terms of divine genealogy the 'son of Enki/Ea' – assumed most of the functions and powers of the old god, Ea remained a 'great god' – primarily as a master of magic.

Throughout the ages, Mesopotamian tradition identified Eridu as the most ancient of cities, as a holy place, the very site of creation. Mesopotamian notions of the city have little to do with size, population density or political status. Except for the two legendary kings mentioned in the Sumerian King-list, there were no kings in Eridu. It was not a centre of political power during any of the historical periods. Nor was it very important economically or strategically. Eridu's importance was mainly symbolic. It stood for Mesopotamia's link with the beginning of the world, proof of the astounding longevity of its civilization. It was also very holy. At Eridu the features of the landscape – especially the large body of sweet water, a sort of lagoon at the edge of the desert – were seen as manifestations of divinity. Once the special nature of the place became marked out and built over, over and over again, in a continuous effort for a thousand years, it had accumulated enough credibility to retain the status of a very important place despite its small size and despite long periods of actual physical decay and neglect. Eridu became part of the cultural landscape, sometimes more as a concept, sometimes magnificently reconstructed.

Just as the Apsu, the most potent symbol of Eridu's sanctity, could be present in any temple of the land, in analogy to the ever-present though hidden underground water-table, so Eridu was ever present and immortal, even when its ruins were covered by sand. Eridu and Mesopotamian culture have the same origin, with their fish-like creatures emerging from the primeval slime. They mark the beginning of a process that continues to this day.

2 URUK

WARKA AND THE 'MOTHER OF CITIES'

In 1856 members of the Royal Asiatic Society were told that a ruin
site had been found in the remote desert region of southern Mesopotamia, huge in size and impressive in its height of accumulated debris.
Sir Henry Rawlinson, well known for his success in deciphering the
cuneiform script, went on to surmise that this place, which the Arabs
called Warka, might be none other than the biblical Erech, mentioned
in Genesis 10 as one of the four cities in 'the land of Shinar' founded
by Nimrud, son of Cush. Although Rawlinson admitted he was unable
to read the cuneiform name with precision, he noted that it was
described as 'the city' *par excellence*. He was also convinced of Warka's
very high antiquity, and regarded it as the mother-city from which all
other cities sprang.[1]

Almost 150 years later, we know that Warka was indeed the site of
a city called Uruk by the Sumerians – the name having survived for
five millennia – and the question as to what extent it should or could
be regarded as the 'mother of cities', as the matrix of urban development, continues to be hotly debated by archaeologists, historians and
anthropologists.[2]

It all began in 1849. Sir William Loftus, a member of the Perso-
Turkish boundary commission, spurred by Austen Layard's spectacular discoveries of Assyrian palaces a few years previously, had gone to
investigate the south Mesopotamian plain. In his *Travels and
Researches in Chaldea and the Susiana* (1857), he records his first
impression of Warka: 'Three massive piles rose prominent before our
view from an extensive and confused series of mounds, at once shewing

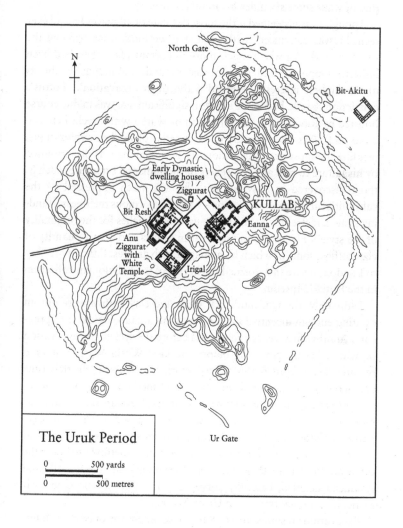

North Gate

Bit-Akitu

N

Early Dynastic
dwelling houses

Ziggurat

KULLAB

Bit Resh

Eanna

Anu
Ziggurat
with
White
Temple

Irigal

The Uruk Period

Ur Gate

0   500 yards

0   500 metres

the importance of the ruins which we – their first European visitors – now rapidly approached.' The site was huge, with a still discernible ring of walls some six miles in circumference.

Though Loftus deemed it the most desolate of all places he had ever seen, he was convinced 'with each step we took, after crossing the walls, that Warka was a much more important place than had been hitherto supposed, and that its vast mound, abounding in objects of the highest interest, deserved a thorough excavation'.[3] Loftus's conviction that he had come across a significant site was in due course boosted by Rawlinson's identification of Warka with Erech. Between 1850 and 1854 he had undertaken a series of modest explorations, tackling the most prominent mounds. Although he was disappointed by his failure to find any bas-reliefs or monumental sculptures such as those discovered at Assyrian sites, he was much impressed by the substantial architectural remains – walls of enormous thickness, standing some 2 metres high ('their very ugliness vouches for the originality of the style'). He also found cuneiform tablets and a vast quantity of clay coffins, some of which he managed with greatest difficulty to ship to London, where they formed the kernel of the Babylonian collection in the British Museum.

Ultimately, though, mudbrick walls and clay coffins were not an exciting enough incentive for the Victorian archaeological entrepreneurs. Another fifty years had to pass before the systematic excavation of Warka began. Not long before the First World War, a German research team from Berlin started work in 1912–14. By that time archaeology had acquired the status and methodology of a science rather than of a treasure-hunt for antiquities. German archaeology, as pioneered by Robert Koldewey, who had worked in Babylon, gave particular attention to architecture, and most campaign leaders at Warka were trained architects. They perfected methods to trace the often no more than faint outlines of crumbled mudbrick walls and produced detailed, carefully surveyed plans and elevations in their meticulous annual reports on Uruk–Warka.

Excavations resumed in 1928 to 1939 (when war once more interrupted) and again from 1953 to 1990. Although epigraphy, the study of texts, became another important focus after the discovery of archaic tablets in the 1930s, the archaeologists at Warka still concentrated on architecture. Considering that Uruk had the earliest, grandest and most numerous monumental buildings in Mesopotamia, it was well served by the enthusiasm and technical expertise of the German excavators. On the other hand, present-day archaeologists lament the fact that their pronounced preference for architectural ensembles was responsible for the neglect of stratigraphic recording. The attitude summarized as 'pottery is rubbish' meant that millions of potsherds, vitally important in establishing habitation sequences, were thrown aside into spoil heaps. Furthermore, the original find-spots of even the most conspicuous objects were only vaguely indicated in the records. During the 1980s previous results were re-examined and new soundings made, and detailed surface surveys provided more reliable information about settlement size and patterns of habitation.[4] The rural hinterland was also explored to determine the infrastructure of the fourth millennium occupation period.[5] However, excavations at Uruk are suspended for the time being as a result of the imposition of UN sanctions on Iraq, which makes all access to archaeological sites very difficult.[6]

Whenever the archaeologists do return to Warka, they will have plenty more work awaiting them. After all, the ruins cover an area of 550 hectares, and 18 to 28 metres of settlement layers can be counted.[7] After thirty-seven archaeological campaigns, starting in 1912, large surfaces of the site, at least 100 hectares in area, remain untouched. Most of the excavation works have hitherto concentrated on the largest mounds, the most prominent of which, known in antiquity as Eanna, occupies the centre of the ruin. It has a dense sequence of nineteen building levels for the early fifth millennium and fourth millennium, with some later remains from the second millennium. Kullab, the western and highest mound, was only occupied during the fourth millennium. In addition, there are large ruins from the first millennium, such as the huge Anu temple and other ceremonial buildings, on smaller mounds at the periphery as well as nearer the centre.

Most of the archaeological information about Uruk therefore concerns either the early 'Uruk' period of the fourth millennium, or the later phase, especially the Neo-Babylonian and Seleucid epoch (the latter half of the first millennium). Unfortunately there is little evidence from the third millennium, when, as we know from contemporary inscriptions, Uruk was an important political and ceremonial centre. Virtually nothing has been excavated from the Akkadian period (2350–2150), except for some surface pottery. The most recent survey has shown that Warka was still an important site as late as the seventh century AD, when it guarded a part of the Sassanian western border. It was then conquered by 4,000 Arab horsemen in AD 654. The Sassanians fled and Warka remained a deserted waste until the arrival of European explorers in the nineteenth century.

The discussion of Uruk which follows will concentrate first on the archaeological evidence and interpretation of the fourth millennium remains, and then proceed to review how Uruk was portrayed in Mesopotamian literature, paying particular attention to its tutelary goddess, Inanna-Ishtar.

THE URUK PERIOD

It is generally a matter of chance for archaeologists to work on a site which reveals artefacts and buildings which are, at the time of discovery, unlike any other comparable examples. When such finds occupy a hitherto undocumented slot in the chronology of a region, the excavators often choose to name the 'culture' after the site. Leonard Woolley's deep-sounding at Tell Ubaid therefore inspired the term 'Ubaid' to be used for the southern Mesopotamian phase of the Chalcolithic period, though it subsequently became clear that Tell Ubaid was a much more marginal and minor settlement in comparison with other sites excavated after Woolley's work was over.

At Warka, the most striking and significant levels of excavations date from a period after the Ubaid layers. It became clear that here was evidence of a very different culture, of which Uruk was a major centre. Levels X to III represent a certain homogeneity and continuous development and are as such representative of a separate cultural phase in Mesopotamia, named, after the initial and most prominent find-spot, the Uruk culture or Uruk period, which lasted from c.3800 to 3200. Unlike the Ubaid culture, however, the Uruk phenomenon is not restricted to southern Mesopotamia. It is becoming increasingly clear, from archaeological work carried out in such areas beyond the present Iraqi borders as Syria, southern Turkey and western Iran, that the Uruk culture is present in a very wide geographical area beyond the Mesopotamian heartland, from south-west Iran to northern Syria and southern Anatolia. Uruk period artefacts and buildings are immediately recognizable: the pottery has a clearly defined stylistic range, the architecture is characterized by multi-functional and monumental buildings, and most important are the cylinder seals and tablets written in an early form of cuneiform script. The Uruk period represents perhaps the most intriguing puzzle in Mesopotamian history because of the many questions raised by the unprecedented spread of one material culture over so wide an area and the development of urbanism for which Warka is the most striking and the grandest, but by no means the only, example.

THE ARCHAEOLOGICAL SEQUENCE AT WARKA

Eanna

The deep-soundings of the Eanna mound showed this area to be the oldest, continuously inhabited part of Warka. The earliest levels (XVIII–XVI)[8] belong to the Ubaid culture, represented by the typical Ubaid painted pottery and clay sickles. Layers XVI–X show a gradual fading out of Ubaid material culture (the last Ubaid pottery being found in level XII). The designation and archaeological nomenclature of phases XVI to IX are still being negotiated; summarily one can say that there are indications of a change in the material culture. The Eanna soundings are not particularly useful for these early phases, and excavations in other sites have provided a clearer picture of this emergent new culture.[9] Of particular interest are clay tokens with simple designs thought to specify commodities of exchange; they first appear in layer XVII. New architectural techniques, such as the use of clay cones for mosaic wall decorations, were gradually introduced. The first metal tools, and imported stone, limestone and obsidian, came in at level XI.

What is now seen as fully fledged Uruk culture sets in after level X (c.3800 BCE). While the Ubaid potsherds show delicate patterns and thin profiles, the most conspicuous Uruk pot, found in huge numbers at any Uruk site, is a misshapen and lumpish clay bowl, a throw-away mass-produced container known as the so-called bevelled-rim bowl (abbreviated BRB). Archaic signs associate this bowl with food and it has been argued that grain rations, or perhaps some cooked food, were handed out to workers.

The other highly typical Uruk object is the cylinder seal, an oblong piece of stone engraved with patterns or pictorial scenes which appeared in slight relief when rolled over a damp clay surface; they were invented in Uruk VII (c.3600). Monumental architecture at Uruk dates from the Middle Uruk phase (c.3400), considerably later than at Eridu. Mud-brick seems to have been out of favour here for centuries and the buildings were constructed in a variety of new techniques. The so-called Stone Cone Temple, for example, was built on a platform of rammed earth made waterproof by a layer of bitumen. The foundations of the building were made of limestone set in lime mortar and the walls above consisted of a kind of cast 'concrete', made of gypsum and pulverized baked bricks. The interior walls, preserved to some 3.5 metres high, were built of limestone and cast concrete. The whole building was of an impressive size (28 by 19 metres). The central chamber and two corridors were surrounded by three massive walls. The central cellar-like room had a podium based on reed mats, and there were also water tanks and shallow drains. These subterranean chambers were then buried under huge loads of stones laid so as to alternate with layers of clay. It is a strange edifice, with its hermetically sealed underground rooms, the purpose of which remains quite obscure.

In the next layers, the buildings became even more monumental. As at Eridu, the excavators chose to call these huge structures 'temples', but while at Eridu there was a formal continuity of layout and plan which made such terminology plausible if not conclusive, the Uruk buildings showed much diversity of plan and circulation patterns. The so-called Limestone Temple of Eanna V was 62 metres long and 11.30 metres wide. A central narrow oblong space (9 by 58 metres), either open to the sky or roofed over, was surrounded on four sides by subsidiary rooms, all of which were accessible from the outside. The walls consisted of limestone blocks and were deeply corrugated into niches and buttresses, a technique more suitable for brick architecture. A staircase gave access to the roof.

The classical period of Uruk culture was reached in levels ivb–a. It is remarkable that there was a rapid succession of buildings: new structures were continuously put up, pulled down and built again. However, the experimental phase of construction came to an end and all the public monuments were now built in mudbrick, with the wall surfaces often disguised by clay-cone mosaics with geometrical patterns of reminiscent of textiles. The buildings were set at various angles around large terraces. Most impressive was the northern front of the terrace with its 30-metre-wide colonnade, formed by massive engaged pillars, also decorated with mosaic patterns. 'Temple D' (45 by 80 metres) had a T-shaped main space, with subsidiary chambers and deep funnel-like entrances that pierced the thick mudbrick walls, which were elaborately recessed. 'Temple E' looked quite different. It consisted of a square central courtyard (20 by 20 metres) surrounded on each side by hall-like oblong chambers (15 by 5 metres) and adjacent smaller rooms. The building had multiple and symmetrically disposed entrances which led through the chambers into the courtyard.

The overall impression of the Uruk monuments is of well-planned public spaces, undefined in terms of purpose but designed for maximum accessibility, with great care being taken to ensure easy circulation. In addition to these open spaces and permeable buildings there were quite different, unprecedented structures, sometimes of vast dimensions. A sealed construction, similar to the Stone Cone building of level vi, is the 'Riemchen Building', so-called after the characteristically thin and elongated bricks (called *Riemchen* in German). It was built on a pavement in stones bound with bitumen. Above it was a chamber surrounded on all sides by corridors, and all spaces were filled with storage jars, animal bones, textiles, metal vessels, sculptures, weapons and architectural ornaments that seem to have been taken from the Stone Cone Temple.

In level iii an entirely new complex of buildings was erected over the carefully levelled remains of the Uruk ivb structures. The reason why the entire architectural ensemble was destroyed is far from clear. The building types of iva remained much the same as before, T-shaped halls, possibly with vaulted roofs, flanked by subsidiary rooms and giving on to wide open courtyards, terraces and gardens. The remains of a bath, comprising a series of rooms waterproofed with bitumen, has also been recovered.

Kullab

The western mound of Kullab seems to have had a longer and different history of use. While the Eanna district, with its large, permeable buildings, was on flat ground, Kullab was raised on a substantial terrace with higher structures on top that must have been visible for miles around. Even in the earliest phase the building stood on a platform accessible by a ramp. Successively enlarged (some ten building phases have been identified), the platform accommodated various buildings with symmetrical layouts and copper decorations. Each time the area was rebuilt, the remains of the earlier structures were included in the subsequent terraces, which contributed to the elevation of the platform from its surrounding area, the same procedure as in Eridu. The most famous building, known as the White Temple, was built on the south-west part of the terrace and had a coating of white gypsum plaster on the walls and floors that was still preserved at the time of excavation. There were staircases presumably leading to the roof. At some point the temple was sealed, the doors blocked off, and the whole area covered and filled with bricks and debris.

The end of the early history of Kullab marks the beginning of the last archaic phase of Uruk, level III. While the high terrace was immured and deserted, the Eanna district continued to be in use, though here all the existing architectural structures erected in phase IVa were also destroyed and obliterated. The central terrace was enlarged to an L-shaped plan, with several subsidiary courtyards, many of which have narrow sunken pits with traces of fire. Inventory and furnishings from previous buildings were deposited in special structures that were sealed, as had been the practice in earlier phases. The famous city walls of Uruk were probably also built during phase III, at the beginning of the third millennium.

This brief description of the architectural phases of the Uruk period at Warka demonstrates the intensity and scale of building activities within the relatively short period of some four hundred to five hundred years. The most remarkable fact is the periodic levelling and reconstruction of the whole architectural ensemble, at least in the Eanna district. In other periods, occupational strata arise because of natural decay from the extensive use of mudbrick, or because of warfare. In the Uruk period there is little evidence of erosion and natural damage, nor of military action or other forms of violence. It appears that the destruction of the existing buildings was the result of a deliberate decision. Walls were systematically reduced in height, the openings blocked and interior spaces filled up. The equipment and accumulated debris were enclosed in structures specifically designed for this purpose. Then the whole area was sealed under a new terrace and new buildings erected on top.

In later historical periods, Mesopotamian temples were often reconstructed over the remains of earlier structures, sometimes replicating the same ground-plan by building new mudbrick walls over the stumps of the old walls. In the Uruk period there is no such continuity. The orientation, size, layout and decorative schemes were all subject to alteration. Architecture, or at least a particular form of public architecture, became experimental. Substantial buildings with representative and perhaps ceremonial functions had already been built in the Ubaid period, as we saw at Eridu. In fact the tripartite plan with symmetrically placed entrances and subsidiary rooms remained substantially the same. The articulation of walls by recesses and flat buttresses had also been developed before. So there was no lack of traditional architectural forms available, especially in regard to brick-built structures. Yet the Uruk builders were prepared to invest in untried methods of construction, making use of a range of materials other than the ubiquitous clay. For load-bearing walls, they used locally quarried limestone, mould-cast concrete, stone alternating with trampled clay and bottle-shaped clay cones embedded in concrete. The outer surfaces could be treated in such a way as to conceal these materials completely. The walls could be whitewashed with a lime-and-clay mortar, or finished with gypsum plaster and simply painted. But the preferred Uruk form of decoration was the cone mosaics, composed of cone-shaped clay or stone pegs of different colours (mainly white, black and red).

Another structural element typical of the Uruk period architecture, and afterwards practically disappearing from the Mesopotamian repertoire of building techniques, is the semicircular engaged pillars. These were tied into the retaining wall and faced with the same cone-mosaic decoration. Since no walls were preserved for more than some 2 metres at the most, it is impossible to decide whether they had any specific load-bearing function.

The monumental architecture of the Uruk period is curiously distinct from the vernacular architectural traditions informing the Ubaid culture, rooted in a familiarity with local materials and well-suited to the climatic conditions and subsistence pattern of the region. The Ubaid builders constructed magnificent and occasionally truly monumental mudbrick structures, but for some centuries the architects at Uruk tried out new methods, new materials, new forms of decoration. This inventive intensity does not appear to have been driven by economic considerations that aimed to save labour or expenditure.[10] Limestone had to be quarried some distance away, cut and transported to provide the stone slabs in some of the buildings, or subjected to burning and chemical processes to produce concrete, which then needed wooden or reed shuttering. The millions of individual clay or stone cones used in the decorative mosaics were equally labour-intensive to make and hardly cheap to produce. There was a conscious effort to break with building tradition regardless of cost, in terms of man-hours and the logistical problems of procuring stone and figuring out how to use it. The implications of such a prodigal investment of energy will be discussed below.

The stunning architecture of Uruk received the main focus of attention from the excavators, but equally interesting were the artefacts discovered within the buildings. Some of the buildings appear to have been constructed specifically for the secure disposal of the contents of previous buildings, which makes the dating of such objects difficult. All that can safely be said is that they cannot be earlier than the building layers within which they were found. The lack of stratigraphic data, however, affects the dating of the other great Uruk invention, writing, which is thought to have occurred in the Middle Uruk period.

BUREAUCRACY AND WRITING

This discussion of the Uruk culture began with an examination of the architectural evidence and the first development of an urban design strategy. The other important innovation of the Uruk period was the invention of bureaucracy and, as a consequence, the invention of time-resistant accounting. The overall success of Uruk as the main centre of distribution was dependent on the efficient handling of the administrative coordination of the economic exchange system. Two strategies were crucial for this success, and both developed already existing ideas into much more versatile tools. These were sealing and writing.

Stamp seals had been in extensive use throughout the Ubaid time. When goods were transferred from one place to another, they could be transported in bulk, their integrity guaranteed by the sealed wrapping. Similarly, collective storage facilities could be supervised by controlling the doorways with seals. In the Uruk period these practices continued but on a much larger scale, and a great many more people were involved in the administration. To be able to identify individual officials and the institutions they represented, the seals had to be identifiable. Since the relatively small surface of a stamp seal does not allow for much variation of pattern and design, the Urukians invented the cylinder seal. This object as such is not much bigger than a stamp seal, but when its surface is rolled over a moist clay surface, the design space becomes much larger and can accommodate quite complex pictorial images.

For some scholars[11] the use of seals during the Uruk period emphasizes the reciprocal nature of exchanges, the sender's seal being as important as the recipient's. The iconography of seal designs certainly appears to bear some relation to types of institution and perhaps to the nature of the commodities being treated. But even in cases when one can establish a connection between a motif and an administrative category, the reason for the connection remains obscure. To some extent they were like heraldic devices, with the semiotics of the design being secondary to the purpose of identifying the bearer and destination. The repertoire of designs consists of animal and human figures, usually separate but in some instances interacting. The animals are recognizable beasts of the steppe (lions, gazelles, birds) or domesticated: cattle, sheep, but rarely pigs. Composite, fantastic creatures also occur, such as the well-known dinosaur-like monsters that intertwine their necks into a corkscrew pattern.

People on seals perform a variety of occupations: some are engaged in repetitive tasks (pigtailed women weaving); some engage in the transport of commodities, on foot or by boat; some are seen to receive them, others appear to frolic, dance, perform some ceremony and have sexual intercourse. There are also men armed with spears, bows and arrows, or maces, guarding bound prisoners. The seal designs fill out our scant knowledge of how life was lived by referring to a multiplicity of tasks, some tedious, some pleasant, some routine. Yet even here there is little evidence for hierarchical social structures, of personalized power, a theme that will dominate the glyptic repertoire of later periods.

The other important bureaucratic tool of the period was the storage of information on clay tablets, which made it possible to keep track of the flow of certain commodities. The archaic tablets are currently being analysed and transcribed in Berlin, where modern data-processing systems are being used to unlock the messages encoded.[12] As mentioned before, it is possible to make sense of the Uruk tablets, even if not all the signs can be reliably identified. It becomes clear, for instance, that different systems of numerical codes were used, depending on the type of commodity. There were separate number symbols for types of grain, types of beer, textiles, metals and so on. Institutions and officials also had their symbolic signs. Generally the information could be distributed in random fashion on the tablet surface. There was no general direction in which to decode the signs. In the archival tablets, receipts and tallies were often written on the reverse of the tablet. Some of the signs have clear representational value, an ear of corn standing for barley, a wavy line for water; some signs depict containers and vessels. Other signs appear more abstract, or at least the reference is unclear. The fact that the writing surface was damp clay militated against detailed representational graphemes, such as the Egyptian hieroglyphs, compared with which they look awkward and much clumsier. This is not to say that the Uruk period lacked style and the ability to draw, as the seal designs clearly show. But writing on damp clay does not encourage detail and makes curved forms especially difficult to execute. Thus the signs became increasingly simplified and began to look less and less like the objects they originally depicted.

The messages that could be encoded are administrative: receipts, tallies, allocations of goods and rations, allocations of responsibility to offices, projections of yields and expenditure of labour, distances of travel and so forth. The contents of the tablets were easily understood within the administrative context. They served to store such information on non-perishable material as long as it was necessary to keep it. After that they were discarded. The fact that the early tablets do not encode speech, that they use a system of notation rather than 'writing' in the sense with which we are familiar, has been interpreted as a sign of primitiveness, or at least of this being an early experimental stage in a development towards 'full writing'. But it is quite possible that the information was encoded in a linguistically non-specific form so as to make it more flexible and useful for an ethnically and linguistically diverse region.

INTERPRETING THE URUK PHENOMENON

The Uruk period, especially the middle and mature phases, from about 3500 to 3200 BC, is a particularly tantalizing example of how limited our understanding of the past actually is. We have all the tangible evidence of a fully fledged urban 'civilization', with all the classical hallmarks, monumental architecture, art, several thousands of cuneiform tablets and cylinder seals. This has prompted pronouncements that we have here the first pristine state organization, with social stratification, a state religion, even colonial outposts, all based on an intensive irrigation-based agriculture. In fact most of these conclusions are hypothetical. Very little is known about how Uruk society was organized, why people chose to live in such large numbers in one place and why they should have expended so much labour on public works.

The archaic cuneiform tablets reveal certain complexities in the organizational structure which may have some bearing on the configuration of Uruk society as a whole.[13] Social categories appear undifferentiated, there are 'men', 'women' (presumably married, able-bodied), 'over-seers' and the various administrative and productive centres, represented by just two signs that seem to refer to buildings in which respective activities were carried out. The highest office on the bureaucratic level at least was accorded to the EN and NIN, the former a male and the latter a female title. The texts suggest that the EN was an apex of a chain of commands, but it is impossible to determine to what extent this was a ceremonial or truly executive function. The parity between the sexes is also a noteworthy characteristic of Uruk society. But the different levels of competence and responsibility the archaic tablets reveal need not be taken as referring to social categories or 'classes' across the whole of Uruk society. It is possible that they were primarily administrative categories to begin with, with symbolic or status differences only eventually coming to be associated with privilege and greater power.

Generally the texts withhold more than they reveal. As a result, the hard facts, the plans and debris and tablets, need even more imaginative interpretation than is customary in a discipline that has always formed a somewhat uneasy alliance between scientific method and a speculative, experimental evaluation of 'evidence'. The following survey presents some of the most influential theories about the Uruk culture.

Hans Nissen from the Free University in Berlin has been actively involved in the archaeological exploration of Uruk for many years. In his accounts he stresses the environmental importance for culture formation.[14] According to his theory, all Babylonia was under water during much of the Chalcolithic period. As a result of climatic changes around the middle of the fourth millennium, the southern plains of Mesopotamia became habitable as the waters receded. But there was still enough surplus water to allow the land to be intensively worked with the farming techniques that had evolved in the northern parts of Mesopotamia and Syria. The virgin alluvial soil could support arable farming, the raising of livestock, especially cattle and pigs, and horticulture. In addition, the marshlands and steppe had plenty of game, fish and other wildlife resources. This huge potential for food procurement made southern Mesopotamia an extremely attractive proposition for settlements. Proportionally small areas of land could feed a much greater number of people than in those areas which relied on rainfall.

Nissen sees Babylonia in the mid fourth millennium as a hugely exploitable ecosystem with no existing land claims by any particular indigenous groups of any size. This accounts for the decrease of settlements in the north and the great concentration of population in the south. The concomitant higher population density and the possibility for conflict stimulated the need to 'establish rules enabling people or communities to live together' which 'is far more important in encouraging the higher development of civilization than the need to create purely administrative structures'. He sees in southern Mesopotamia, as exemplified by Uruk, the maximizing of potential by techniques developed and refined elsewhere, which applies not only to food-producing techniques but also to organizational structures.

The result was a rapid rise in the size of Uruk which continued to grow into the third millennium until it covered some 550 hectares. He locates the hub of the city in the district known as Eanna in later periods, which at the height of the Uruk period functioned as a large-scale economic unit that controlled agricultural production and animal husbandry, as well as crafts, directed public building activity, and was responsible for festivals and sacrifices. Nissen's theory that the alluvium, at least around Uruk, quite suddenly became available with a huge resource potential that could be maximized without too much initial effort in terms of labour expenditure, proved an important counterpoint to earlier theorists who had emphasized that artificial irrigation and its supervision produced a bureaucratic élite who were the motors of social change into 'oriental despotism'.[15]

Nissen's model does not account for another phenomenon of the Uruk period, the existence of smaller and sometimes very large contemporary settlements in other parts of the Near East, within quite different cultural settings, that produced typical Uruk-period artefacts: seals and seal impressions, 'bevel-rimmed bowls', clay tablets with the pictographic script of the period, and, where accessible, monumental buildings and planned 'urban' layouts.[16] Most of these sites are located near important waterways, linking them to southern Mesopotamia.[17] The discovery of these 'Uruk' sites in such distant places raises the question of who lived there, who built and managed them, what their function was, how they related to their own hinterland, what was their relationship with the perceived centre of the Uruk culture in southern Mesopotamia, and why they seem to appear suddenly and then become deserted at the end of the fourth millennium.

The Californian anthropologist Guillermo Algaze has suggested that colonialism by the Uruk centre was the mechanism that triggered a cultural expansion.[18] He postulates that the south had the organizational and military means to exert a direct influence on the hinterland so as to have access to all those commodities that the agriculturally productive alluvial plain so notoriously lacked: hardwood timber, minerals and metals. The Uruk government established enclaves and outposts which ensured and enforced the regular transfer of metals (especially copper, lead, gold and silver), minerals (semi-precious stone and obsidian) and timber from the periphery to the centre. Exports from the centre were surplus grain, leather products, dried fish, dates and textiles. Algaze sees few advantages for the people of the periphery, a standpoint reflecting the ideological basis of the anthropological critique of colonialism. For him the Uruk culture represents the first imperial expansion in the Near East that pulled highlands and lowlands, the eastern plains and the mountains of Anatolia, into one interrelated network dominated and managed by the Uruk élite. His theories have spurred archaeologists to pay more heed to local developments in the area traditionally perceived as the 'periphery', but his general assumption that Uruk had the military means to generate and sustain a colonial 'empire' has found little support.

The question of how Uruk society was organized is one of the most difficult and controversial issues. Most scholars agree that Uruk society, at least at the central sites, was hierarchically organized under the leadership of a professional élite (perhaps represented by an individual 'ruler'), who exerted power over the population through the control of the administration and religious life.[19]

One of the most imaginative interpretations of early Mesopotamian society comes from the Czech Assyriologist Petr Charvát.[20] He argues that Uruk society was essentially egalitarian, even a sort of primeval 'welfare state' characterized by 'corporate undertaking and corporate consumption'. This means that a body of responsible persons made decisions on behalf of the wider community and saw to the distribution of material goods and foodstuffs within the Uruk 'corporation'. While Charvát also recognizes that there was an imbalance in the resources available to different regions, he does not believe that the Uruk centre exploited the periphery. Instead he postulates that there was a wholesale redistribution of surplus, an equal circulation of goods throughout the whole region within the Uruk world to benefit all contributors equally.

Charvát concedes that the solution of the considerable managerial complexities of such corporate distribution must have been organized professionally, a situation which can lead to the assumption of public power by the executive group. He is convinced that no such takeover occurred in the Uruk system, since the archaeological records show none of the expected indicators of social differentiation, no separate residential facilities for élite families, no signs of privately owned wealth. In his most recent study, based on an examination of the archaic tablets,[21] he describes Uruk society as 'loosely ranked'. The texts distinguish between individual people (personnel), who work in the workshops, warehouses and offices, and the institutions they relate to professionally. The institutions are both relatively small and local, as well as larger and regional. The highest level of administrative responsibility is the office of EN and his female counterpart NIN, whom he believes fulfilled important ritual functions. The EN had executive powers and possibly a high status. Charvát believes that the Uruk community was held together by an intricate distribution system which would make the efforts of individual persons and communities worth their while in return for an equal compensation. Furthermore, the ideology of 'democracy', or at least of equal access to resources, would have been reinforced by public rituals and other practices that communicated the message that everybody was equal.[22]

Collective effort and collective values underpin all sectors of public life in this vision of Uruk culture. It explains the invention of cylinder seals as emblems of collective entities, of writing and other technological advances as the result of experiments designed to ensure greater efficiency in administration and production to maximize the equal distribution of goods and services. It was, in this theory, the harnessing of collective will that made it possible to generate and maintain such high levels of productivity over such a large territory.

Other scholars have advocated the centrist state model. Uruk was 'a hierarchically organized political system in which state institutions controlled large-scale economic activities'.[23] Susan Pollock, in her most recent publication,[24] characterizes fourth millennium society as consisting of generally self-sufficient households, side by side with organizations that 'controlled large, hierarchically ordered and specialized work-forces producing luxury and mundane goods'. She doubts that 'temples' were such centres of production at that time, suggesting that the ceremonial buildings procured their wealth through a 'tribute system and ritual offerings' instead. She finds little evidence that production of 'most mundane goods was carried out under direct administrative control', but that distribution was subject 'to some degree of administrative regulation'. The most common form of extracting goods and labour was through a tribute system which significantly increased the workload of some sectors of population, most notably of women, who were the principal producers of woollen cloth.

These theories provide some insight into the possible background of the Uruk culture but leave the position of Uruk the city unexamined. Only two small sectors of the late Uruk city have been investigated, and both Eanna and Kullab were representative only of the ceremonial centres of the city. There is no evidence of private residential areas and, significantly, no graves. We also lack barracks and workshops, which are well documented in other Uruk towns.[25] We therefore know very little about the actual conditions of life in the city. On the other hand the available evidence makes it clear that Uruk was a very special place in the Near East in its day. For one thing, it was the only really large urban centre in the fourth millennium. The site covered an impressive 5·5 square kilometres. Athens in the fifth century BC reached only between 2 and 5 square kilometres and imperial Rome in AD 100 was only twice the size of fourth millennium Uruk.[26] The reasons for this growth still elude us. If Uruk was the hub of the complex production and distribution system scholars now envisage, it must have attracted a varied population from many parts of the Near East. Furthermore, Uruk did not have just one but two major ceremonial and religious centres, Eanna and Kullab respectively.

The city may have grown out of two originally distinct localities. Throughout the fourth millennium the western mound, Kullab, and Eanna in the centre of the present ruins, exhibit idiosyncrasies in architecture which may point to ideological (or theological) differences. In later periods, Kullab was sacred to the sky-god An and Eanna was the precinct of the city goddess Inanna.[27] The favourable geographical position has already been alluded to. Uruk also had the most spectacular public architecture, unprecedented and unrivalled at the time. In the following discussion I would like to take a closer look at the monumental buildings at Uruk and what we can learn from them.

THE MEANING OF THE URUK 'TEMPLES'

The excavators summarily designated most of the monumental structures as temples and assigned them a primarily religious character. On
the other hand, administrative tablets were also found at both Kullab
and Eanna. Of course, the intentional scattering of objects and tablets
throughout Eanna obscures any knowledge of whether the tablets
were also written and stored there. The example of Eridu has shown
that, even when there is a continuity in the design and interior equipment, it does not necessarily follow that previous buildings also had
an exclusively cultic purpose. The Uruk buildings, especially in the
Eanna district, are much less 'typical' in their variety of plan, orientation, patterns of circulation, building techniques among other factors.
They seem to have been built for any number of purposes, for functions
and banquets, for the storage of valuable items, for receptions and
rituals, for processions and perhaps decision-making purposes. The
western mound, usually designated as the 'Ziggurat of Anu', exhibits
a number of features similar to Eridu VI and later Sumerian temples
and could have served as a 'sacred precinct' with greater plausibility
than the Eanna area with its variety of typologies.

Architectural structures, even if their exact purpose is unknown,
can to some extent be analysed as to how their spatiality is expressed.
It is noticeable at first glance how transparent the plans of many of the
large buildings are at Uruk. The multiple openings of the structures
suggest that the separation between outside and inside was constantly
negotiable, allowing a free flow of entering and leaving. This accessibility may suggest a communal and egalitarian orientation in
Uruk society, as does the similar transparency of early Greek civic
architecture.

The treatment of the wall surfaces with mosaic patterns on both
inner and outer walls minimized the difference between interior and
exterior. The geometric patterns, closely imitating woven and pleated
fabrics, suggest textile wall hangings and lend an intimate aspect to
what are large open spaces as well as to inner rooms. This textile skin
also incidentally contradicts the monumentality of the architecture.[28]
Charvát has also pointed out that the use of mosaic patterning may

49

signal both social complexity and an 'emphasis on communal, corporate behaviour patterns'[29] in which single elements are typically enmeshed within a larger unity.[30]

The third factor, not discussed before perhaps because of Western habits of considering architecture in terms of self-contained buildings, is the spaces between, inside and around the built edifices. These terraces, platforms and courtyards were just as important. The famous colonnade of the Pillar Hall, 30 metres wide, abutted on to a long rectangular courtyard, also surrounded by half-columns. It is by no means certain that this elaborate ensemble was only the outer face of a building behind.[31] It may have served as a backdrop to a public square. There is also the possibility that some of the spaces, supplied with cisterns and conduits, could have been planted and might have served as gardens.[32] More than the size of the buildings or their particular layouts, the open spaces and the free circulation of the main buildings themselves are indicative of an attitude that stresses openness and visibility. There is no trace of the temenos and enclosures that would become so typical of later periods. Instead this very early manifestation of urban design emphasizes common access and perhaps a common purpose.

Such a stance is difficult to reconcile with a divided, class-based society ruled by an oligarchic élite who devised elaborate and time-consuming building works to keep the masses usefully employed to stop them from becoming disruptive for sheer idleness.[33] Large monuments are highly visible proofs of collective enterprise, but it may be too cynical to argue that such complex and labour-intensive building operations were invariably put up under duress. The later Uruk period has a very experimental feel to it, an almost restless energy, as the frequent demolition and changes in technology make clear. Any direct connection with an overt claim to perpetuate traditional rights or political power is unlikely under such circumstances, again in contrast to later historical periods. The Uruk public monuments, not just in Warka but in many other sites, all share these characteristics of open spaces, large and well-built edifices, of transparency and easy access.

If one were to summarize the attitude behind the Uruk design strategies, it would be multi-functional, civic and egalitarian, allowing for a wide range of activities to be carried out openly. They could be

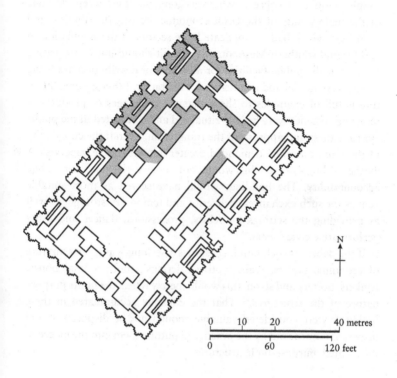

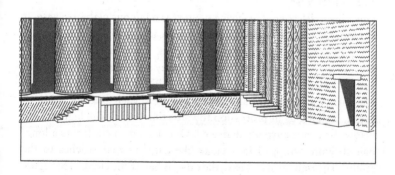

of ritual, religious, economic or administrative nature, and also allow simple onlookers to observe what was going on. If we accept that one of the main remits of the Uruk economic life was distribution and exchange, which had to implicate large sectors of the population in and beyond southern Mesopotamia, then it should not be surprising to see that the public facilities for all stages of distribution are being given a ceremonial and a bureaucratic character. Ethnographic literature is full of examples to show that the exchanges of products in pre-state societies were heavily ritualized and conducted in the public eye to witness and approve of the transaction. Even if the complexity of the Uruk economy demanded greater administrative supervision, as the sealings prove, this would not remove the need for public accountability. The buildings would have served as most suitable venues for such exchanges, deliveries and temporary storage, as well as providing the settings for feasts, processions, dances and other performative civic events.[34]

If the debris of such buildings shows a seemingly puzzling mixture of economic tablets, seals, 'votive offerings', tools, animal bones, trinkets, pottery and so on, this would merely reflect the multi-purpose nature of the structures.[35] That the contents accumulated in these buildings were considered valuable enough not be disposed of and dispersed is borne out by the practice of putting them into the inaccessible, sealed, purpose-built structures.[36]

The Warka Vase

One object discovered in such a context is a famous alabaster vase. It has four horizontal bands of shallow relief carvings. The lowest register contains a regular wavy line, symbolizing water. The next band of relief is divided into two parts: ears of barley and date palms are below, and in the upper part are rams and ewes. The middle register depicts upright, clean-shaven, bald and naked men, each bearing a jug or vessel, walking as in procession towards their right. The highest field below the rim is partially damaged. One nude man confronts a long-haired figure wrapped in a cloak-like garment that reaches to the ankles. The right arm is raised, the other is below the cloak. This figure is usually identified as female. Next to this person are reed posts, symbols of the deity whose name was read as Inanna in Sumerian. She faces a figure who is partially obliterated, only a foot and part of a long skirt being visible.[37] Behind the female figure is a large ram on whose back stand two human figures. Both wear a long skirt and their hair hangs loose down their backs. The first holds an object that looks like the symbol for EN. Then there are various objects, large vessels, two vases, a ram and a sheep, a bull's head, two platters with perhaps more food.

The procession of ritually naked men bearing vessels filled with produce suggests a formal occasion. They are stripped of all accoutrements that might suggest distinction or rank. Shorn and denuded, they walk together in a single purpose, towards a single goal. At the uppermost band of images the goods are neatly arranged, two of each kind, and the reed bundles serve to mark out a particular place for them. Whether this should be taken as the realm of the sacred (Inanna's) or as a more general demarcation of purpose remains unclear. The different clothes and hair fashions introduce difference, at least of function if not of status. The cloaked figure acknowledges the person bringing the heaped basket, raising one hand in a gesture that may be a blessing or greeting. If this does refer to a religious rite, it does so by implicating the divine in man's efforts to live off the bounty of the land. The produce is the yield of the land and one is also reminded that water is the basis of the economy. There is a simplicity and single-minded purposefulness in the scene, stately and timeless, dignified and measured.

The vessels and baskets that feature on these reliefs are the same ones that occur on the administrative tablets, and have the same shape as those whose sherds fill the strata of Uruk. They embody the reality of the Uruk culture, the economic source of its enormous wealth and its meticulous distribution. It presents a well-ordered and well-managed world, sustainable and stable, confident of meeting the challenges of collective life, perhaps the vision of the urban élite who celebrated the ritual aspects of distribution.[38]

INTERPRETING THE ARCHITECTURE

The architectural framework at Uruk may have served to facilitate ritual behaviour as depicted on the alabaster vase, but it also helped to anchor a tradition or a custom to a place which could in turn foster common bonds. It would have served to demonstrate and facilitate the economically vital exchange process and perhaps at the same time instil egalitarian and 'urban' values of intergroup cooperation and consensus.

The Uruk culture's investment in monumental architecture thus had various outcomes. It helped to consolidate the cultural identity of people by shared labour and responsibility; it provided landmarks that proclaimed in stunning visibility the wealth, expertise and common effort of the community; it provided focal points for special activities (display, exchange, ritual) and furthermore helped to spread the ideology of the culture far and wide. Whether one interprets the distant cities in northern Syria or Iran as colonial outposts or as manifestations of a global enterprise culture, the architectural amenities helped to communicate and perhaps replicate the alchemy of Uruk social self-understanding.[39]

The periodic destruction of the Warka Eanna and Kullab monuments is equally noteworthy. It is tempting to see the dismantling of edifices as expressing a reluctance to accept the validity of permanence of an institution or of practices associated with it. That this was also carefully orchestrated and not a wanton form of revolutionary upheaval is suggested by the deliberate preservation of all the accumulated articles of use. If construction unites the people by participating in the creation of the future, then ritual destruction makes it possible to project disappointment for failure on to the past. Then the past and the memory are sealed and a new foundation laid quite literally upon the levelled remains. The new terraces would provide a *tabula rasa* for new beginnings and the assertion of civic values of equality. If that process was indeed ritualized, it would also prove that the 'Uruk élite' was particularly subtle at orchestrating public support and at diffusing discontent, since the rebuilding does not signify social change.

The next phase of monumental buildings adjusts and reorients, changes methods of construction, but on the whole things remain the same: large monuments within which tablets, seals, objects of value and mundane use accumulate. The architecture of Uruk demonstrates the inherent ambiguity of this culture: between frenzied innovation and tradition, egalitarian values and attempts at centralized administration, the acquisition and destruction of wealth, challenge to authority and civic self-understanding. Such fluctuations and contradictory currents were to remain characteristics of urban life.

THE END OF THE URUK CULTURE AND LATER PHASES

As the city grew larger and more populous, attracting more and more people eager to escape the drudgery of subsistence farming, and perhaps also the narrow horizons of traditional communities, the demands on the remaining rural population increased. Tension and unrest seem to have been met with violent repression; pictorial scenes on seals and other objects show groups of prisoners, their hands bound behind their backs, forced to their knees by guards with spears and clubs. The many mace-heads discovered in the Eanna depositories and the large quantities of sling-shot balls and arrowheads also point to the use of military force. It seems that, by the end of the fourth millennium, the urban experiment was taking on a new momentum. If, as Nissen believes, the climate changed so that much less water was carried by the rivers, it may have prompted even more people to seek their survival in the city, which would have made life in the city more precarious. Perhaps the levelling of the Uruk IV Eanna and the final demise of Kullab were a reaction to such unrest, promising a new beginning and a more just compensation.

The destruction of Eanna and Kullab may mark the end of one of the most innovative periods in prehistory, but it did not signal the end of Uruk or the end of urbanism. This time is badly represented archaeologically at Warka, but it is clear that the city continued to grow in the Jemdet-Nasr and subsequent Early Dynastic periods (first half of the third millennium). In fact it reached its greatest extent and largest population in the early part of the third millennium. The most significant architectural project of this period was the construction of the walls of Uruk. Later tradition was to credit Gilgamesh, king of Uruk, with this monumental task. This is how he invites a visitor to admire his work:

See if its wall is not (as straight) as the (architect's) string, inspect its . . . wall, the likes of which no one can equal.
(. . .)
Go up on the wall and walk around, examine its foundation, inspect its brickwork thoroughly. Is not its foundation of baked brick, did not the Seven Sages themselves lay out its plan?[40]

Some 9 kilometres of ramparts encircled the city, enclosing not just an inner centre but also including suburbs and wasteland (for brick manufacture), gardens and probably some grazing ground. The wall did indeed have burnt-brick foundations. It was more than 7 metres tall and the gates were protected by projecting towers.[41] Gilgamesh, despite his fairy-tale adventures, famously failed in his quest for eternal life. Mesopotamian tradition insisted on heroes being culture heroes. He became immortal by making a significant contribution to the greatness of his city by availing himself of the city's ultimate cultural invention: writing.

Look for the copper tablet box, undo its bronze lock, open the door to its secret, lift out the lapis lazuli tablet and read it, the story of that man, Gilgamesh, who went through all kinds of sufferings.[42]

Uruk's greatest story, as told some thousand years after Gilgamesh's reign, thus summarizes the two major inventions that we still associate with this city: monumental urban architecture and writing. Uruk continued to exist, through prosperous and inauspicious times, for a very long while yet. The shrines of Uruk, of Inanna (Ishtar) and Anu, became some of the great sanctuaries of the country, endowed with royal patronage and popular dedications. In the first millennium it became an important centre of commerce again, as well as a place of learning; astronomy especially flourished at Uruk, well into the Seleucid period. One could write a history of Mesopotamia based on the lifetime of this city alone, even if the archaeological evidence is still very patchy at present. Uruk is mentioned in many Sumerian,

Babylonian and Assyrian texts. There are many stories about Uruk. The one just related responds to the current revival of interest in 'origins' of institutions and cultural forms that belongs to an age uncertain about the viability of its own civilization.

INANNA'S URUK

The preceding sections have dealt with prehistoric Uruk and the challenges this material presents to present understanding. Perhaps all the concerns about central control and the emergence of state organization so much debated at the present time could also be seen as a reflection of the Uruk sacred to the sky-god An, whose ziggurat watched over the city. An represents patriarchal authority. He was called the 'father of all the gods' and invariably he heads the lists of deities that the ancient Mesopotamian scholars were forever compiling and copying. But as we have seen, Uruk An is not the only deity. He shares the patronage of the city with a goddess – a goddess whose scintillating personage is vividly described in numerous hymns and songs, narratives and myths.

The name of Inanna, or, as the Babylonians were to call her, Ishtar, was written with a sign representing an upright bundle of reeds with a looped top. This symbol occurs on the alabaster vase described above (pages 52–3) and on numerous other pictorial scenes. Nothing is known about her origins or character in the Uruk period, and in the texts before and in the third millennium she appears as a heroic 'lady of the battle' who helps her favourite human subjects to achieve supreme office as kings. No doubt different religious notions developed by different peoples and ethnicities merged to inform the character of the goddess as she appears in the later texts. By the time of the Third Dynasty of Ur (2150–2100) she is clearly associated with sexual desire and libidinous energy. In some love-songs she is Bride, who rapturously rejoices over her body and welcomes her Bridegroom to revel in sensual delight.

The Ur king Shulgi (2094–2047) is praised for his skilful lovemaking as Inanna's mythical consort and other narratives describe the relationship between the goddess and the ruler.[43] She is also celebrated as the Queen of Heaven, the mistress of the sky, and her emblem is the planet Venus in its double manifestation of morning and evening star. Her restless ambition for greater power is the theme of several narratives, as in the myth already summarized in which she tricks Enki into giving away the divine me.[44] The story of her visit to the underworld, which is preserved in both Sumerian and Akkadian, is also framed as a bid to extend her influence into the realm of the dead, which is ruled by her pale *alter ego*, her sister Ereshikigal. The Sumerian story relates that Inanna is fully aware of the dangers awaiting her on her journey and that she prepares by leaving instructions with her female vizier as to what should happen if she fails to return. Upon her admittance to the underworld, she is made to pass through the Seven Gates, where she has to divest herself of all her insignia of power until she is shown naked and vulnerable to her sister's presence. In the ensuing struggle, she is rendered completely lifeless.

Inanna's absence from the world above is vividly described in the Babylonian version:

> No bull mounted a cow, no donkey impregnated a jenny,
> no young man impregnated a girl in the street
> the young man slept in his private room
> the girl slept in the company of her friends.[45]

This sudden loss of libido threatens the continuity of life and the wise god Enki (Ea) has to find a solution which will bring Inanna back. He creates beings that transcend the established gender categories and these manage to penetrate the underworld and persuade or trick Ereshikigal into handing over the corpse of Inanna, which they sprinkle with the Water of Life, provided by Enki. The revived Inanna is then allowed to leave, but she has to obey the laws of the underworld by providing a substitute to take her place among the dead. She ascends to earth, picking up her garments and jewels at each successive gate, and when she sees her lover Dumuzi patently not mourning her demise but occupying her own throne, she hands him over to the demons of the underworld.

A number of texts refer to Inanna's cult and festivals, and the different phases of the moon and the heliacal appearance and disappearance of the planet Venus called for special celebrations. Her ritual personnel also incorporated a contingent of transsexuals and perhaps homosexuals, as well as numerous women who escaped the narrow bonds of patriarchal marriage in the service of the love goddess. The late Babylonian poem of Erra contains a passage which describes a totally unacceptable state of affairs in each of the major cities of Mesopotamia. This is what it has to say about Uruk:

> Even Uruk, the dwelling of Anu and Ishtar,
> city of prostitutes, courtesans, and call-girls
> whom Ishtar deprived of husbands and kept in their power,
> Sutean men and women hurl abuse;
> they rouse Eanna, the party-boys and festival people who changed
>   masculinity to femininity to make the people of Ishtar revere her.
> The dagger bearer, bearers of razors, pruning-knives and flint-blades,
> who frequently do abominable acts to please the heart of Ishtar:
> you set over them an insolent governor who will not treat them kindly,
> who persecuted them and violated the rites.[46]

It is the oppression and persecution of Inanna's people which calls for censure, not their 'abominable acts', which belong to the goddess's remit of protecting all manifestations of desire and libido, regardless of civic norms.

Inanna stands for the erotic potential of city life, which is set apart from the strict social control of the tribal community or the village. She frequents the taverns and alehouses, where men could meet single women, and she is said to prowl the streets of Kullab in search of sexual adventure. Copulation in the streets was apparently a normal and joyful event, and the young people sleeping in their own chambers is singled out as a most worrying state of affairs in the lines quoted above. There has been much debate about 'sacred prostitution' and the incidence of normal prostitution in Mesopotamia.[47] The discussion of such matters reveals and reflects both traditional views filtered through Judaeo-Christian ethics and feminist perspectives. We still know very little about the realities of urban life in Mesopotamia, but it is worth noting that there existed a positive paradigm of 'free love' that was associated with Inanna-Ishtar. In the Hebrew Bible, Babylon is portrayed as the city of licentiousness, but the Mesopotamian poets present Uruk as a city of festivals, its streets full of singing and dancing, and they refer to 'its population of beautiful and voluptuous women, women with luxuriantly curly hair and available women in general'.[48] Uruk, 'mother of cities' in so many respects, was perhaps the capital of a trading empire as early as the fourth millennium. It may have invented bureaucracy and central control, but it may also have been the first to develop mentalities and facilities to challenge conventional sexuality – a vital if not uncontroversial function of the city down to our own days.

3 SHURUPPAK

When Sir William Loftus undertook his survey of promising mounds in the 1850s, a local emir tried to interest him in a site called Fara, where small antiquities, such as cylinder seals and carved figurines, were supposed to 'flow like water from the mound'. But Loftus was not impressed with what he saw and another fifty years passed before Hermann Hilprecht began a cursory excavation and recommended it as a worthwhile project to Robert Koldewey from the German Oriental Society. Koldewey was already committed to Babylon, but for two seasons he allocated some time to Fara. The Germans set about digging trenches and regular pits some 2 metres deep. They found a large quantity of seals and seal impressions, 840 tablets, several large houses and a number of graves. The city had been burnt, a dreadful fate for the inhabitants but a good thing for archaeologists since many artefacts were still *in situ* and the mudbrick walls as well as the tablets had been baked hard in the conflagration and thus survived for millennia.

The written documents allowed the site to be identified as the ancient Sumerian city of Shuruppak, well known from the Gilgamesh epic as the home of the flood-hero Utnapishtim. But despite such promising finds, Koldewey abandoned the excavations in 1903. In 1931 the University of Pennsylvania was set to continue, mainly because of the city's legendary past. However, H. Schmidt, the director of the excavations, found the circumstances too trying. He was put off by bad weather, problems with water supplies, and the fact that the whole site was scarred by the German excavators' old trenches and their spoil dumps covered much ground. He did find more seals, tablets, some graves, as well as large pits lined with baked bricks, but there were no spectacular new discoveries and no monumental architecture. After the one season, funding had dried up and Schmidt became more interested in Iran. Since that time, Fara has been left undisturbed, except for a brief survey carried out in 1973 by Harriet Martin from Birmingham. She published a synthesis of the previous excavations' results, together with her survey and a brief description of epigraphic research carried out in the meantime.[1] Despite the relatively scant effort spent on the excavation of this site, it has proved to be of great interest, primarily because of the written records.

Shuruppak is no Uruk. To begin with, it is much smaller, only a quarter the size of Uruk, extending to only 100 hectares in its most prosperous period. Nor was it inhabited for millennia as Uruk was. Shuruppak lasted for only about a thousand years, roughly the whole of the third millennium BC. It lay in the middle of southern Mesopotamia, half-way between Uruk and Nippur, on the Euphrates near the head of four watercourses. During the Uruk period there had been some villages and a small town in the area, and the city of Shuruppak emerged in the Early Dynastic period I (ED I 3000–2750), growing fairly rapidly until the end of Early Dynastic III (ED III 2600–2350), when it covered some 100 hectares. This was the phase terminated by the great fire and the one that was most productive from an archaeological point of view. Later levels are badly eroded, but it seems it was an important city in the Ur III period (up to 2000) – the city walls date from this time – but fell into terminal decline after the disintegration of the Ur empire.[2]

The architectural remains from the most prosperous period can hardly be called monumental, and the excavators failed to locate a temple – it may not have had a major sanctuary. It is not mentioned in later Mesopotamian tradition as the seat of any important dynasty and does not feature in any extant royal inscriptions as being involved in wars and conquests. Nevertheless an important period of Mesopotamian history has been named the Fara age.

THE FARA AGE

This refers to the time-span known to archaeologists as Early Dynastic IIIa. The accidents of destruction by fire and the erosion of subsequent layers of habitation preserved the layout of some of the buildings and objects of daily use, but also, most important for our understanding of the city, the thousand clay tablets and seals. The term Fara is mainly used in connection with the written remains of Shuruppak since, from this period on, textual evidence becomes the primary source of information for Mesopotamian urban society, supplementing the archaeological data of pottery and architectural remains. The dating system from then on reflects the written records about political hegemonies mainly based on native 'historiographical' works such as King-lists.

Before we take a closer look at what constitutes the Fara phenomenon, we need to consider what happened in the time between the end of the Uruk period and the last phase of the Early Dynastic period that we associate with Fara.

FROM THE URUK PERIOD TO FARA: THE SHRINKING PARADIGM

The Uruk period marked the first stage of urbanization, with one major centre (Uruk) as the focus of a dense network of corporate rural settlements. The Uruk culture came to an end around 3100, as can clearly be seen from the more or less sudden disappearance of Uruk culture artefacts in the Syrian, southern Anatolian and Iranian sites. The institutions of bureaucratic control were abandoned and replaced by distinctly local forms of social and economic life. In Mesopotamia, the change can be seen in settlement patterns: rural communities and small villages become progressively rare. Environmental factors may have played a role. Nissen advanced the theory of a progressive drying up of secondary watercourses; intensive cultivation may also have hastened the decline of agricultural productivity.[3]

During the Uruk period, the city of Uruk, with its substantial rural hinterland, had been the only really big urban area. Now we see the abandonment of the previous small-scale farming settlements and the foundation, alongside already existing urban centres (such as Ur), which grew in size, of new city centres with access to virgin soils in the alluvial plain. Each of these cities controlled its own rural territory and was responsible for the supply and maintenance of water. Cities were located at strategic points in terms of access to waterways, and thus the wellbeing of any city was directly linked to successful claims to water rights. Furthermore, since the rivers in the alluvial plain have a tendency to shift from one branch to another, the fate of all southern cities depended on the behaviour of the rivers. Shuruppak, a rural town during the Uruk period, grew rapidly in the Jemdet-Nasr period (3100–2900). As Martin has observed, 'undoubtedly its position on the Euphrates near the heads of four watercourses flowing down the eastern Euphrates was at least responsible for this boom'.[4] Similarly she sees the decline of Shuruppak in the later periods as a result of a weakened economy caused by the shifting of the Euphrates to its western branch.

The most important difference between the Uruk period and the subsequent phases of Mesopotamian history (the transitional Jemdet Nasr and the Early Dynastic periods) was the emergence of regional and isolated centres and the loosening of the close ties between northern and southern Mesopotamia. In comparison with the wider horizon of the Uruk age, this was a more parochial world. The southern alluvium became a culturally separate domain which was politically and economically divided into several (eventually about twelve) independent units or 'city-states'. Such self-sufficient smaller units were relatively simple to maintain and sustain. Shuruppak is a well-documented example of one such new centre.

NEW WAYS OF WRITING

Very few written documents have been found from the period following the decline of the Uruk period to the last phase of the Early Dynastic period which we know as the Fara age. This may be because of the limited number of excavated sites from the period, or the element of sheer chance in discovering or not discovering tablets. It is also possible that there was less demand for writing after the dissolution of the Uruk administration. Certainly in many of the more distant Uruk cities writing was given up altogether. This was not, however, the case in southern Mesopotamia, despite the scarcity of texts from the intermediate Jemdet Nasr time. On the contrary, the value of writing seems to have been so firmly associated with the concept of an urban culture that it continued to be transmitted. However, a comparison between the Fara texts and the Uruk period (IV) texts demonstrates that a very important change had occurred.

The difference is not one of content or context. Writing was still used primarily to record administrative data. But while the Uruk scribes had invented a system that recorded facts and data in a pictographic form which can be understood but not read, we can read the Fara texts because they are written in a particular language, which happens to be Sumerian. Conventionally the Uruk period writing is regarded as an 'archaic' form of communication, a primitive early development that failed to achieve the target of 'true' writing. But the 'archaic' system fulfilled its primary task of encoding complex numerical data and administrative responsibility more than adequately.[5] Moreover, given that the system also had to operate in the multilingual and multicultural context of the Uruk world, this form of writing was better than one tied to a specific language. The disadvantages of the 'archaic' writing, its limitation to content (lists and book-keeping), and the proliferation of signs, were balanced by the relative ease with which such 'literacy' could be acquired and by its broad communication base.

With the disintegration of the Uruk economic network and the relative political and economic isolation of southern Mesopotamia, such considerations ceased to be relevant. The more homogeneous cultural horizon of the alluvial plain finds expression in the development of writing in a particular idiom. Why Sumerian came to be the language represented by writing is still uncertain. Mesopotamia was never linguistically or ethnically homogeneous and the personal names in the early texts clearly show that languages other than Sumerian were spoken at the time. Much has been written about the apparently 'sudden' appearance of the Sumerians in Mesopotamia and their possible origins.[6] They were thought to have come from the mountains because of their predilection for ziggurats, and were seen to have been engaged in rivalry and conflict with the people who spoke Semitic languages. None of that can be substantiated. Linguistically, Sumerian is not related to any of the known groups of languages and attempts to link it to Ural–Altaic languages, because of a shared characteristic of adding syntactic elements to the main word – agglutinating them – have proved fruitless.

The question of the origin of the Sumerians remains intractable and all we can state is that, at the beginning of the Early Dynastic period, this language was chosen to be rendered in writing. Perhaps the Sumerians did become politically dominant and exercised control over the scribal centres in the early cities. It is also possible that it was even then a prestige language reserved for written communication irrespective of whether or not the 'Sumerians' were politically powerful. Some of the earliest royal inscriptions, for instance, were commissioned by kings who bore Semitic names. Whatever the motivations were originally, once it was adopted Sumerian remained the foundation of Mesopotamian writing, even when, in time, other languages were rendered in the same system. Knowledge of Sumerian was still considered a sign of true learning and wisdom nearly three thousand years later.[7] Like Sanskrit or Latin, it acquired a cultural value as the link to an old and still vital tradition. Even among modern Assyriologists, those mastering Sumerian have an unofficially higher status than those dealing with 'easier' languages.[8]

The process of adapting the writing system occurred towards the end of the Uruk period and is conventionally designated as Archaic Level III.[9] Let us consider how the 'archaic' system of word signs was converted to writing Sumerian. The principle by which a form of writing based on symbols without phonetic characteristics may be converted into a system of writing that can also reflect parts of sounds (phonemes) is quite simple. It is based on the fact that, in every language, there are words with different meanings that sound the same, such as 'bee' and 'be' or 'dear' and 'deer' in English. In Sumerian, many words were apparently monosyllabic, and quite a few consisted of just one vowel sound. The word for 'water' was a.[10] In a grammatical context, the syllable 'a' could stand for a whole range of syntactical functions, depending on whether it was put before, between or after a chain of semantic elements. The archaic sign for water consisted of two parallel wavy lines. If one works within an existing repertoire of signs that refer to objects that can be represented in a standard form (a type of drawing), such as the wavy lines, then there will already exist quite a number of such signs for a large variety of concrete things (types of vessels, animals, buildings and so on). When these signs are taken to represent a word in a particular language, as, for instance, when the stripy insect is recognized by an English speaker, he will read 'bee'. In English the sound 'be' can also be an infinitive verbal form, or a syllable within other words, as in 'be-lieve'. By drawing a 'bee' in all cases where a 'be' sound is wanted, the functional possibilities of the sign multiply since it can refer to the primary, pictorial referent, the 'bee', or stand for the sound in a variety of contexts.

In Sumerian, any time the sound 'a' needed to appear in writing, two wavy lines were used, and context would make it clear whether it was meant to be read as 'water', a grammatical component or a syllable in a compound word. This principle, known as homophony, was the main structural device in the adaptation of the archaic cuneiform system for specific languages.[11] The disadvantage was that the script became a hybrid of pictographic and phonetic signs that had a much greater potential for confusion than the purely pictographic one. Writing became more complicated, special markers had to be introduced to signal that a group of signs referred to a specific category of words, such as personal names, or stars, or animals, or whatever. In practice, scribes developed professional expertise tailored to suit the type of work they were engaged in: bureaucratic, legal (recording of court cases or drawing up of contracts) and communication (missives or public inscriptions). All these types of written tasks had their own special features and scribes relied on a limited repertoire of signs. Only the advanced scholar would have complete command over all the possibilities and intricacies of the script and vocabulary.

In keeping with the conceptual dissociation from the primary pictorial image, the signs themselves changed their appearance. They were no longer drawn with a pointed stylus, which had always been cumbersome on the damp clay surface of the tablet. Rounded forms assumed a linear form, and the lines could be executed much faster by pressing a stylus with a triangular profile into the smooth clay, which resulted in the characteristic wedge shape of the strokes (Latin for 'wedge' is *cuneus*). When the direction of reading the tablets also changed, the original image was even less recognizable because the signs appeared to be turned by 90 degrees so that what was originally drawn horizontally, such as the two wavy lines for 'water', was now vertical.[12] This change contributed to the increasing abstraction of the signs and the reduced number of 'strokes' performed with the stylus, which made writing much faster.

These fundamental changes to the writing system were introduced in all southern cities which became independent regional centres in the early third millennium, including Shuruppak, Ur and Abu Salabikh, as well as, much further afield, the Syrian city of Ebla. There is a remarkable uniformity in the repertoire and the formal characteristics of the individual signs. The administrative élite of these cities must have recognized the necessity to regularize the writing system within the southern Mesopotamian region so as to facilitate economic exchange and cooperation. It also points to a close network of contacts within the scribal communities; a passage in a text from Ebla mentions the expected arrival of a 'mathematics professor from Kish'.[13]

The Fara tablets

Nearly a thousand tablets were recovered from the Early Dynastic III phase of ancient Shuruppak, among which the majority record transactions and receipts and belong to the main administrative centre of the city. However, there were among those economic texts also reference works in the form of lexical lists, and tablets referred to as 'school texts' in earlier publications. It is now clear that the 'school tablets' of Fara, like those from the slightly later archives found at Abu Salabikh and Ebla, preserve the first literary texts in Mesopotamian history. Some scholars believe they represent 'the first great flowering of Sumerian literature and the culmination of the archaic Sumerian tradition of scholarship'.[14] But while it is now possible to classify some of these tablets as 'literary', they are not easy to understand, let alone translate. Although writing had developed considerably towards the codification of spoken language, it cannot be said to transmit a complete message. The greatest problem for the modern scholar is the fact that the signs were not arranged in the order in which they were meant to be read, but distributed at random within a given space marked out by lines on the tablet. Furthermore, grammatical elements are only rarely indicated. As such the 'texts' are really 'no more than mnemonic aids'[15] to retrieve information. In connection with oral commentary and aural learning, they made perfect sense.

The 'Instructions of Shuruppak' and the writing of oral tradition

It is clear that the earliest literary texts are located squarely in an oral tradition. They were proverbs, riddles and aphorisms, as well as some incantations or magic spells. One collection of proverbial sayings and admonitions is known as the 'Instructions of Shuruppak', attributed to the legendary antediluvian king of the city bearing the same name. Early versions of the texts were discovered at Abu Salabikh.

It is sometimes argued that the impetus for the creation of written versions of orally transmitted knowledge comes from a fear of losing it. Since writing already had a long history in Mesopotamia, it is unlikely in this case that the proverbs were committed to writing as a rescue operation. A more plausible explanation is their suitability for scribal training. With the shift from symbolic notation to the rendering of speech, the scribe had to extend his ability to express actual sayings, and since a proficiency in proverbs was already a sign of wisdom, they became an important part of scribal education, providing the vital link between orality and literacy. The Fara tablets reflect the transition from primarily logographic writing (where a single sign expresses a whole word) to one which reflects phonetic and grammatical values, and as we have seen, the process of deciphering a message written in this manner relied on oral commentary. Slightly different, more expanded versions of proverbs from later texts also confirm the view that there was a tradition of maintaining an oral exegesis. Modern collections of Mesopotamian proverbs, both in Sumerian and Akkadian, as well as the bilingual versions, are based on school exercise tablets containing one or several proverbs, sometimes copying the teacher's example from one side of the tablet on its reverse.

Part of a school's teaching apparatus was its proverb collections, comprising hundreds of sayings in a thematically arranged system. This grouped together proverbs under a common catchword, as, for instance, 'poverty', 'scribes', 'fox', 'donkey', 'dog', 'marriage', 'city'. Since the proverbs reflect the general milieu of a stratified, urban and agrarian society and the particular Mesopotamian setting, the marshes, canals, city streets and quaysides, one gets glimpses of the reality of ordinary people's lives. At the same time, they are undoubtedly the product of a particular social group, the literate professionals, as the number of proverbs concerning scribes and the process of training clearly shows. The 'Instructions of Shuruppak' differs from other collections in so far as it has a more coherent literary structure, the advice being given by the father, Shuruppak, to his son. This is how the oldest version, preserved on tablets from Abu Salabikh and Fara, begins:

> The intelligent one, who knew the (proper) words and was living in
>   Sumer –
> Shuruppak, the . . .
> gave instructions to his son:
> My son, let me give you instructions,
>   may you pay attention to them!
> Do not neglect my instructions!
> Do not place a field on a road, it is disastrous.
> Do not buy an ass (etc.) . . .
> Do not build a house in a . . . it is . . .
> Do not buy a prostitute, it is horrible (?).
> Do not make a well in a field, the water will do you damage.
> Do not give evidence against a man, the city will . . .
> Do not guarantee (for someone), that man will have a hold on you.
> (. . .)
> Go far away from quarrel,
> stay far away from taunt.[16]

The extant text takes up some sixty lines, divided into sections that are always introduced by the refrain 'Shuruppak gave instructions to his son' followed by the exhortation to pay attention. The later, classical version was much expanded to 282 lines. It combines practical advice ('Do not buy a steppe ass', 'Do not scatter your sheep into untested grazing ground'), moral precepts ('Do not steal', 'Do not break into a house', 'Do not commit murder'), cautioning to observe social etiquette ('Do not beat a farmer's son, he will break your irrigation canal', 'Do not have sex with your slave girl, she will call you: Traitor (?)', 'When you are drunk, don't judge', 'Do not speak with a girl when you are married, the slander is strong') and proverbial sayings ('Love maintains a family, hatred destroys a family', 'When drinking beer all the harvest is drowned'). The 'wisdom' of these texts is conservative in tone, and assumes an unalterable social structure where the 'wise' person is aware of his respective social standing and acts appropriately ('Authority and possession, strength and aristocracy. You should submit to strength', 'You should bow down to the mighty man'). The focus of interest is that of the household owner, responsible for his kin and retainers and mindful of thrift and good husbandry. There is much emphasis on doing the right thing at the right time, on foresight and planning and sobriety. They also reflect the ideology of the late Early Dynastic period, with differences in wealth and social status.

Proverbs, on the other hand, have a timeless quality and have parallels in most cultures since they react to common human failings in face of the demands for selflessness, reliability and respect demanded by all social intercourse. Anthropologists regard proverbial sayings as a social control mechanism, part of the armature of an ongoing critique of other people's behaviour, being, like gossip, a way of ensuring the social norms are upheld. In non-literate societies such strategies serve to uphold the correct attitude and condemn selfishness, greed and jealousy. However, since proverbs are aphoristic, typically short and complete in themselves, their truth value is limited. They can be applied to a variety of situations and many proverbs contradict each other. A person with a good repertoire of proverbs would always be able to find one either to condemn or praise. This is also reflected in the larger proverb collections from Mesopotamia, where proverbs with contradictory messages are grouped together within a common associative field.

Another category of texts from Fara is magical spells and incantations, again some of the earliest examples so far known. The formulaic expressions are also closely linked to an oral tradition and sometimes echo proverbial sayings. Again the translation is very difficult and remains tentative. Here are some examples of Shuruppak spells:[17]

> The south wind is tied up,
> the north wind is tied up,
> the Tigris is tied up in a hose,
> illness is tied up in the body of the person.

This suggests that, since winds and the river floods are uncontainable, disease should likewise not be retained in the body of the patient.

> If the child is female, may she (the Great Midwife?) let spindle and . . . emerge.
> If it is male, may she let the curved stick and club emerge.
> May Ningirima let the spell (emerge?).

Perhaps this was meant to determine the sex of an unborn child.

> Tamarisk, tree of An.
> From all its branches it is pure.
> Tamarisk, from your roots Enlil and . . . emerge.

The indigenous tamarisk was primarily used for magic purposes; from its wood all kinds of ritual implements were fashioned and even its charcoal had purifying properties.

> May he scream like a monkey tied to a rope,
> may his illness come out like a . . . spell (?),
> like a broken vessel (?) may Ningirima loosen the spell.

Magic spells often use metaphorical references, here the demon who caused the disease is forced to leave like an uttered scream. Ningirima is a goddess much invoked in Sumerian magic.

It has already been mentioned how the modification of the script from a bureaucratic recording device to speech-based system made the acquisition of literacy more difficult. However, as far as the scribes were concerned, the possibilities of wielding greater influence increased, especially as they penetrated the management structures of temples and other large estates, where they were indispensable not only for the administration but also for their ability to engage with the dissemination of ideological propositions to influence public opinion. Although we do not know how scribes were recruited or who organized their education, it appears that the profession reproduced itself by acquiring students either from their own families or by a process of adoption. The sealings from Shuruppak show that a great number of scribes (at least eighty are known) were active at the same time.[18] In House IX at Shuruppak, the contents of all the tablets were either literary (mainly proverbs) or lexical, suggesting that this building accommodated a scribal education centre. Such concentrations of reference material and exercises were also found at the contemporary site of Abu Salabikh.[19]

Encyclopedic and other lists

Ancient wisdom entailed the knowledge of names and words; Solomon in the Bible knew the 'names of birds and fishes', and as we have seen, Shuruppak 'the intelligent one, knew the words'. The main vehicles for the written codification of this knowledge were the lexical lists.

Those discovered at Shuruppak and the other late Early Dynastic cities demonstrate that there was a continuity from the later Uruk period, bridging some five hundred years. Many new forms of lists were also created, on the other hand, and it is fair to say that the lexical tradition of the Fara period scribes was one of the most remarkable intellectual achievements of the third millennium.

A comparison between the archaic lists and the Fara lists reveals that, although the general graphic order was maintained as the lists followed the old sequence of lexemes or main entry signs, they were not exact copies of the older versions. The Uruk period lists recorded the names of birds, fish, cattle, pigs, trees and wooden objects, cities and regions, as well as professions and titles. The salient feature which determined the given context was a graphic marker, also called determinative, which preceded each entry. One glance at a given list therefore established the category of items it dealt with. While the lists of animals and objects proceeded by representing a characteristic feature, such as the shape of a vessel or a plant, with the script referring to a tangible reality, the lists of place-names and professional titles consisted of abstract symbols which either had to be invented for the purpose or else drew on already established pictorial symbols such as those used on sealings. It is clear that the lists dealing with abstract signs were comparatively more important for the scribal training and it is not surprising to find many examples and excerpts from such lists. The lists also dealt with sub-categories and associative fields. So, for instance, in the main entry 'date-palm' in the series that collects tree and wood terminology, we find not only all the parts of the date-palm, from crown to roots and bark, the stages of growth and decay, but also the uses to which all these parts could be put. In the canonical version of this particular list, from the mid second millennium, the main lexeme 'date-palm' has hundreds of such sub-entries.[20]

The professions list also reflects a hierarchical social order. The first group of entries all refer to a 'head' of a department ('Head of Barley', 'Head of the Plough', for example) which suggests a supervisory capacity. Professional titles in all stratified societies show, on the one hand, a tendency towards conservatism while, on the other, their meaning shifts to quite different functions. The very archaism of a title denotes privilege and legitimation by a long tradition, even as many titles at the contemporary British senior administrative level exemplify. At the same time, new posts appear and some older offices become obsolete. The Fara professions list makes such innovations, introducing the category of tax-collector.[21] The Early Dynastic lists are the first attempts to modernize the list tradition, but they seem still to retain the archaic symbolic association. It is likely that an oral commentary was necessary to make sense of quite a number of signs and it appears that the oral and written tradition used Sumerian as the language of scholarly discourse.

Not long afterwards, when cuneiform writing became adapted to other languages, as the example of Ebla shows, the standard reference lists also provided the mainstay of scribal training, but the list of symbolic signs was augmented by a parallel column which translated the meaning into the local Semitic language. When Sumerian ceased to be a dominant scribal idiom sometime at the beginning of the second millennium, the Mesopotamian scholars also created pronunciation columns and translations of the main signs. The lexical lists became the bedrock of all subsequent cuneiform learning. When, some thousand years later, the rulers of Levantine principalities wanted to exchange diplomatic missives in Babylonian, the scribes who set up schools there brought their lists and added another column for the local language. The same procedure can be observed in Anatolia and Elam.

By the late Early Dynastic period, the lexical reference works show a singular uniformity across a huge geographical area, from southernmost Ur to Kish in the north, to Ebla in Syria, to Susa in Elam, regardless of political and ethnic divisions. At Shuruppak the following types of lists were found: thematic or encyclopaedic lists which group together the names of bovines, fish, birds, plants, containers, textiles, metal objects, all arranged in a fixed order. Then there was a singular list of professions, known only from Fara, which begins with **sanga** (a high position in the temple administration), and proceeds to craftsmen and members of the cult personnel. There were also parts of a list of mathematical and economic terminology (of obvious importance to scribes engaged in administration), and lists of the names of deities. The Shuruppak version is particularly interesting since it enumerates primarily divine names composed with **nin** (a title traditionally held by a woman),[22] although not all these names need refer to goddesses. At a later time, numerous male gods had names composed with **nin** (such as Ningirsu and Ninurta, who were rather 'macho' warrior gods), but it is still significant that the female element played such an important role.

The lexical works were not just systematic series of graphemes for the purpose of scribal training, they were also a conceptual tool for the intellectual understanding of reality through the process of finding the right name for everything and to gain some sort of magic power through the evocation of the named. In the myths, the gods need only utter the names of things for them to come into being; similarly, what is not named has no existence and is unfathomable. Human beings construct a meaningful relationship to their environment by giving names to things that matter and ordering these names into classificatory systems which define man's place in the world.[23] The Mesopotamian thematic lists are no doubt based on such traditional taxonomies – as we have seen, the categorical sign acts as a conceptual framing device in the list. However, the act of committing orally constructed taxonomies to writing meant that the loosely categorized data – the 'names of things' – had to be organized into a graphic system. The solution was to adopt the linear list format, which simultaneously arranged the entries in order of importance or relative rank. Hence the god lists and professions lists reflect the relative status and precedence of divine beings and human occupations.

In the thematic lists, the names of plants, animals, man-made things and natural phenomena are listed according to their symbolic and/or practical importance to Mesopotamian culture. The tree list begins with the tamarisk, which had the greatest magical properties, the animal list with the sheep. The lists therefore also reflect a value system as well as a conceptual repertoire, so that the thematic lists became highly complex systems of recording and classifying Mesopotamian culture. The lists provided a link not only to the beginning of cuneiform tradition but also to creation itself. This explains the inherent conservatism of these works, which retained many obsolete signs, words and categories.

On the other hand, the involvement of scribes in the maintenance and management of public life meant that to some extent the lists needed to be kept up to date, or that commentaries should elucidate obscure meanings. The alphabetic forms of writing that allowed for a direct representation of sounds, without any primary pictorial referent, could be learned easily without buying into the whole cumbersome cultural apparatus of a mixed system such as cuneiform. With the exception of technical glossaries, lexical works are unknown in the classical world. The conceptual ordering of the world was thus freed from the constraints of naming and the confines of the specific written sign. Perhaps this helps to explain the difference between the Greek capacity for abstract and rational thought and the apparent lack of it in Mesopotamian thinking.

THE ADMINISTRATION OF SHURUPPAK AND THE 'HEXAPOLIS OF SUMER'

When Shuruppak was destroyed at the height of its prosperity and growth, the city covered some 100 hectares and had a population of between 15,000 and 30,000. The Fara tablets – unlike the archaic tablets from Uruk, which were generally found amid the infill of demolished structures within the Eanna district, with individual tablets turning up quite out of context – occurred *in situ*, in the buildings in which they had been stored as archives.[24] Recent studies of the available documents have shown that all of the 430 administrative texts were written within a very short period lasting no more than six months.[25] This means that we have a brusquely interrupted slice of bureaucracy covering only a part of a single administrative period. It appears that documents of allocations with a fixed expiry date and other written transactions were routinely destroyed or recycled at the end of such a period, or at least removed from the current archive context.

The most important find-spot was building xv, dubbed Tablet House by the German excavators; some 322 tablets were found there. Other archives were situated in different buildings, but it has become clear that they all belonged to the same administrative centre responsible for all the workforce of the city. This centre employed no less than 2,000 people and had at its disposal large tracts of state-owned land planted with cereals (mainly barley) to be used as ration payments for the workers. Other important agricultural activities were the raising of livestock, especially of sheep, whose wool was a major economic resource when worked into textiles. Unfortunately the main archive dealing with wool and textiles is not preserved. One of the smaller tablet collections deals primarily with donkeys; it contains the names of some 1,200 workers and reflects the importance of these animals for traction, transport and warfare.

The administrative tablets give us a good idea of the meticulous organization of the centre, with its clear boundaries of competence and bureaucratic responsibility. There were numerous managerial units, composed of between 20 and 100 employees, supervised by officials called **ugula** and **nimgir**. These were in turn subject to control by a head of department. At the apex of the system was the person who occupied the highest political office, called the **ensi**.

Of particular interest is an archive discovered at the northern tip of the mound which refers to men and officials coming from other Sumerian cities, as well as a particular group of people called **guruš**, who came to Shuruppak for certain services. The large numbers of these people, ranging from 1,300 to 160,000, are remarkable. The **guruš** seem to have been counted in units composed of 680 men and could be assigned to different officials. While some of the tasks they performed seem to have been agricultural, a number of texts specifically mention that they were military, in which case they constituted an enormous concentration of soldiers dispatched from all parts of southern Mesopotamia. There are no other texts to shed light on the political events of the time, since none of the 'historical' inscriptions from contemporary cities refer to any particular conflict under the leadership of Shuruppak. The very fact, however, that contingents of able-bodied young men were moved from one part of the country to another, to perform a variety of duties, some peaceful corvée work, some defensive or offensive, suggests that there must have been a degree of cooperation between cities.

The central administration was clearly responsible for local affairs as well as for wider political association.[26] The texts repeatedly mention the names of five other Sumerian cities that clearly had regular contact with Shuruppak. These were Adab, Lagash, Nippur, Umma and Uruk. Kish seems to have been important, too, and may have been recognized as a separate though friendly power. The six cities seem to have maintained a very high degree of cooperation and exchange. This entailed contributing manpower to communal projects, as the **guruš** exemplify, and provisioning them from special funds, agreement on free travel within each other's territory, and perhaps a common policy towards other political entities within and without the country. The texts often mention that a central place called KI.EN.GI plays a pivotal role in this alliance of six cities. The location of this centre is still unknown. In later periods Kengi was used as the name for 'Sumer' in distinction to 'Akkad', but there is no evidence that this was the case in the period covered by the Fara archives. Perhaps the meeting place for an inter-city organization gave its name to a region rather than vice versa, as Jacobsen has suggested.[27]

Shuruppak seems to have played an important role in the alliance, not least because of its central location. The efforts of the six cities to pool their resources and coordinate their defence did not work for ever, as the sudden destruction of Shuruppak demonstrates. The question remains as to who was responsible for this act. A likely candidate is the city of Ur, which clearly had no diplomatic or economic relationship with any of the allied cities. Furthermore, the rise of Ur as an important political centre immediately after the end of the Early Dynastic III period may be the result of a military success. The Ur kings Mesannepada and Meskalamdug both bore the title 'King of Kish', which suggests at least a temporary hegemony over the northern city. In this case, some of the wealth found in the Ur cemeteries may well have been looted from Shuruppak.[28]

SOCIETY

The Fara texts allow us a glimpse of the workings of the central administration and the relationship with allied cities. The internal social structure of the city is more difficult to determine since much rests on the interpretation of the tablets' context. Are the buildings in which they were found public or private? Excavated remains of large residential units with one or several courtyards, surrounded by rectangular rooms and enclosed by a perimeter wall, show they were able to accommodate a nuclear family and dependants, as well as provide storage and some form of accounting. In older excavation reports, these structures were habitually designated as 'temples', since early theories focused on the primacy of the 'temple economy' as the main production unit. Some scholars, following the terminology of Max Weber, suggest that the main economic unit of the Early Dynastic period was the *oikos*, a kin-based household owning land and productive facilities which generated wealth.[29] They interpret the sealing legends that closed storage spaces and the administrative tablets as belonging to the control of the household, a statement much disputed by others, who see them as belonging to a central organization.[30] The practice of inscribing the names of individuals on seals could either signify the emergence of private ownership and the formation of an élite or merely indicate administrative responsibility. The written material is from such a short period it by no means presents a comprehensive picture of all the economic activity of the city during this time.

Is there any other proof for an emergent class system? One such indication is the practice of providing some individuals with valuable grave goods. The graves of Shuruppak could have provided useful material, but only a fraction of the ninety-odd excavated graves were recorded. The dead were often buried within their former domestic space, either simply wrapped in matting or enclosed in a pottery coffin. The grave goods indicate certain differences in status, as some individuals were given simply pottery vessels while others had more valuable metal and stone dishes, tools and jewellery.[31]

The extent of private enterprise is another matter of debate. One individual was called Anzud Sud, according to his distinctive cylinder seal, which bore his name. The imprint of his seal has been found in a variety of contexts. For Charvát this proves that he 'had a right to approve of disposal of community property'[32] and operated in some form of official capacity for the community, but he goes further to make him the head of a private concern, growing his own crops and raising his own livestock and even controlling some manufacturing. Other authorities (such as Nissen) have denied that such opportunities existed.[33] A recent compromise in the controversy is to characterize the economic and social structure of the Early Dynastic period as a mixture of collective and private systems, represented by the 'temple' (or 'palace') and the Weberian household (*oikos*).[34] It has also been recognized that kinship groupings became important. Land was held collectively by the patrilinear family, who had to consent to any transfer of landed property by collectively sealing the documents. The family's common origin was emphasized by reference to shared ancestors, as the genealogical passages in contracts show. People without family attachments were often the poorest members of society and employed by the large organizations, such as temples and palaces. Prisoners of war formed a sizeable contingent of such persons.[35]

The gender relations of the Early Dynastic period show a strong differentiation of sexual roles. This can be seen in the graves of Shuruppak and other sites, where women lie on the left-hand side while men lie on the right. The female dead were given spindle whorls – a reminder that women and children made important contributions to the lucrative textile production. There are also references to female offices in the administrative texts. According to Charvát, there was a marked decrease in feminine status in comparison with the Uruk period, but the evidence for the social status of women is almost entirely circumstantial.[36]

WARFARE AND COMPETITION

The fate of Shuruppak shows the fragility of peace in the Early Dynastic period. City walls had been built since the early centuries of the third millennium, no doubt to offer security to the population within and to safeguard the stores and other wealth. Inter-city aggression, as well as raids by peoples from outside Mesopotamia or by non-sedentary groups near by, posed a constant threat of violent incursions, from damage to crops and agricultural installations to full-scale fighting within cities. A Sumerian literary text, 'Gilgamesh and the Agga of Kish', preserved on Old Babylonian copies, is set within this period.[37] It describes a conflict between the cities of Uruk and Kish, when Kish demands Uruk's submission. Uruk is led by its king Gilgamesh, who easily persuades the assembly of young men to support a military confrontation with Kish, much against the advice of the assembly of elders.

In this account a strong leader, backed by the ranks of local male youth (the **guruš**), engages another city in fighting. Gilgamesh wins the encounter through a ruse. The scenario fits the period where conflicts between individual cities were common, usually over access to and control of water. Since cities were strung vertically along the main riverways, the further upstream a location the greater the possibilities of controlling the water-supply. The city of Kish, the adversary of Gilgamesh's Uruk in the narrative, had a particularly favoured position on the upper Euphrates after the major shifting of the river to its western branch[38] at around 3000. We have seen how alliances and cooperative measures provided some safeguard against common enemies and helped to prevent disruptive rivalry between neighbouring cities. But as has been pointed out, after the fall of Shuruppak and the break-up of the Sumerian alliance a flare-up of inter-city conflict occurred.[39] The best-known conflict was the long-drawn-out struggle between Umma and Lagash over a disputed territory, of which the rulers of both sides left long and detailed inscriptions. Despite efforts to mediate a permanent solution and safeguard peace, the two cities engaged in repeated and bloody warfare, destroying each other's temples, slaughtering the inhabitants and despoiling the arable land.

Furthermore, as warfare became more professional and a source of revenue as much as a matter of defence against an outside enemy, political control over other cities could be decided by force of arms. In the later tradition, as exemplified in the Sumerian King-list, only one city at a time could legitimately exercise 'kingship' over the land. The changeover from one city to the next was expressed with the formula: city x was smitten with the weapon by Y; kingship was carried off to

Y. Although such works as the King-list should not be taken as 'history', they nevertheless express the indigenous attitude to changes in political power. The fall of Shuruppak marked the end of a period of intercity collaboration and triggered the intensification of internal conflict. Two hundred years later, one city was to emerge victorious and its ruler, Lugalzagesi, imposed his sovereignty 'over the land'.[40] From then on, the political struggle was not only one between individual cities, but between hegemonic state systems and individual cities. Particularism, with each city looking after its own interests, and imposed centralization by one dominant political centre, became the new polarities.

SHURUPPAK IN LATER TRADITION: THE FLOOD STORIES

In later memory Shuruppak was not, like Uruk, for instance, remembered for its victorious or heroic kings, its wealth or a particular deity. Instead Shuruppak was famed as the home of a wise man who survived the flood by building an ark, a sage who transmitted wisdom to future generations. The flood-hero was known under various names. He was called either 'Who Found Life' (rendered as Utnapishtim in the Gilgamesh epic and as Ziusudra in the earlier Sumerian version of the flood story) or 'Exceedingly Wise' (Atra-hasis in the Babylonian flood myth). All accounts see the deluge as a punishment sent by the gods, most notably by Enlil, who has an unpredictable temperament.

According to the Babylonian myth of Atra-hasis, the longest and most comprehensive of Mesopotamian flood stories, the reasons for Enlil's displeasure were the intolerable noise made by the multitude of human beings, their ceaseless clamour which disturbed the peace of the gods. He tries to decimate their number by various means, such as disease and famine, before he decides to send a great flood as a final means of eradicating mankind. His plans are foiled by the god Enki (Babylonian Ea), who realizes that the gods need man to perform the vital task of offering sacrifices. He therefore instructs his protégé, the wise man of Shuruppak, in what manner he could counteract Enlil's plans. Enki has to resort to this subterfuge of using a human being because Enlil has bound the other immortals by oath not to thwart his scheme. All that Atra-hasis has to do is follow Enki's advice to the letter. So when the heavenly sluice gates are opened, he is ready to embark on his vessel, together with his wife and the seeds of all living things. While all else perishes, they are saved, and when after a long time the waters subside, they disembark and bring a sacrifice which attracts the starved gods 'like flies'.

Enki remonstrates with Enlil about his desire to destroy mankind and orders the mother goddess to create new human beings to populate the world anew. Atra-hasis and his wife are given eternal life and made to live in a remote place at the edge of the world as a reminder to the gods not to annihilate mankind ever again. As a further compromise, to safeguard the peace of the gods from the human noise, Enki institutes measures to limit human reproduction by decreeing that classes of women be unable or forbidden to have children, as well as infant mortality in the guise of a child-snatching demon. Atra-hasis represents the link between the old world and new postdiluvian world and the continuity between them. In his unique immortality – together with his wife he is the sole exception to the divine decree that only the gods should have eternal life – he is a permanent witness to human ingenuity.

That flood stories should be popular in the alluvial plains of Mesopotamia is not surprising. Rivers are liable to sudden shifts of course since there are no natural obstacles to stop them meandering. Archaeologists have found deposits of silt in several places, including one at Shuruppak, where Schmidt identified an 'inundation level' composed solely of alluvial silt between the Jemdet-Nasr and the Early Dynastic I level. The city was rebuilt a little bit further away and life reasserted itself. It appears that floods were local phenomena rather than the whole-scale destructions of the myths since none of the archaeologically documented layers of silt are from the same period. Nevertheless, for the affected region the effects of a sudden flooding would have been devastating enough to leave a lasting impression. The flood level also speaks for the authenticity of the association with Shuruppak as the last antediluvian kingdom, since it is likely that the transition from the Jemdet-Nasr to the Early Dynastic period also marked the relative leading importance of Shuruppak at this time in Mesopotamian history.[41]

The wise man of Shuruppak, his knowledge of 'words' and his

devotion to his god, epitomize the specific values much admired in Mesopotamian culture. The message of the flood-heroes and the eponymous sage Shuruppak is that the most lasting achievements of urban civilization are not buildings and walls, since they can be swept away and turned to ruins and fields; and not power, since the gods control all destiny, but knowledge and humility.

4 AKKAD

Akkad[1] was one of the most famous of Mesopotamian cities, whose wealth, splendour and glorious rulers were to be remembered for millennia; it has yet to be identified and excavated. We have so far no archaeological record of the city's existence, no foundation deposits, no archives, no graves, no stratified sequence of debris, no architectural remains, no inscribed bricks to identify the site. All the same, the reality of Akkad as the new capital of a state founded by Sargon of Akkad has never been doubted because the name of the city appears in written documents from the second half of the third millennium from other Mesopotamian sites, quite apart from frequent references to Akkad in the cuneiform literature, omens and royal titles. Akkad was known as the centre of the most successful empire ever, which reached to the corners of the world.[2] So prestigious was its name that Babylonian kings called themselves 'king of Akkad' right down to the Persian period.

The most prominent kings of Akkad were figures of legendary renown who assumed a paradigmatic importance as either singularly successful or calamitous. The cuneiform literature about Akkad and its kings is a remarkable example of historical and political reflexivity. In the words of the American scholar Piotr Michalowski, 'Akkad became the vehicle of textual meditations on history, kingship, and power.'[3] It is therefore important to take a close look at this highly important genre of cuneiform literature and discuss in some detail the historical background that informs the development of a central state and the institution of kingship. In the last section I will introduce one of the reflective pieces of writing about a famous Akkadian king, the so-called 'Curse of Agade'.

AKKADIAN ROYAL INSCRIPTIONS: THE FIRST HISTORICAL RECORDS?

The majority of sources about the history of the Akkadian empire are preserved on tablets written some five hundred years after the events, during the Old Babylonian period (c.1800–1600). They are copies of original royal inscriptions of early Akkadian rulers, such as Lugalzagesi of Uruk, Sargon, Rimush, Manishtusu and Naram-Sin, covering a time-span from c.2370 to 2223. These copies were collected in the form of anthologies, two of which are preserved. The original inscriptions were written on statues and stelae that once stood in the courtyard of the Ekur temple at Nippur[4] and were written in Sumerian or Akkadian, and in bilingual versions.[5] The Old Babylonian scribes not only copied the old versions faithfully, they also noted in the colophons the sort of monuments they had been copied from.[6] They were much admired at this time as the first and most venerable examples of the genre, and students copied and memorized extracts from these Akkadian royal inscriptions. Thus they influenced the style and format of later tradition. However, in addition to the Old Babylonian anthologies, some original inscribed statues have been found, such as those which the Elamite king Shutrukh-Nahhunte I (1185–1155), who was an avid collector of historical monuments, had taken to Susa in southwest Iran where French archaeologists found them.

Royal inscriptions are interesting not only because of their historical information, their accounts of battle and conquest, but also for their political relevance as instruments of royal propaganda. The very first royal inscriptions developed from the custom of dedicating objects of value to a god. This was an old tradition, as the rich inventory of the prehistorical temples at Eridu showed. However, a donor could make a permanent record of his gift in the form of an inscribed message. The earliest one so far found, from c.2600, written on an alabaster vase, simply records the name, title and city of the person who made the donation: 'Mebaragesi, **lugal** (king) of Kish.' Another reads: 'To (the god) Zababa, Uhub, prince of Kish, son of Puzuzu, conqueror of Hamazi, has dedicated (this vase).'[7]

The first royal 'inscription' consists of just three words. Nevertheless it is symptomatic of a new practice: to perpetuate the memory of the individual and his high status – the alabaster vase becomes the recipient of memory. Furthermore, the inscriptions often link military conquest to the act of offering, since at least some of the spoils of victory were given to the gods as their share of booty and, at the same time, transferred into the safekeeping of the temple. That this was a privilege is emphasized by the use of title, which implies political power ('king'). It seems that only people who had assumed supreme office perpetuated their memory through an inscription on an object of symbolic value. Of course, in the context of bureaucracy, many names were recorded routinely, as the more than eighty names of literate officials from Shuruppak have demonstrated, but such records were not regarded as a record of individual existence, and as we have seen, archives were regularly cleared out and the tablets discarded.

Other than military success, the royal inscriptions also commemor-ate building projects sponsored by the king: 'For Ninhursaga, when A-anepada, king of Ur, son of Meskalamdug, built the temple of Ninhursaga, he carried the holy chariot, for the life of A-anepada, he dedicated this bowl to her.'[8] The kings often document themselves as the builders of public monuments or the restorers of the architectural fabric of temples. The donation of valuable objects or the inauguration of a restored or newly built temple were no doubt ritualized as a performance, as a form of victory parade, for instance, perhaps culmin-ating with the entry of the successful leader of troops into the sanctuary to deposit some of the spoils of war to the city gods; or as a seasonal festival where the ruler participates by making his own more spectacu-lar votive prestations. On such occasions the texts inscribed on the objects may have been read out aloud, and at least some of the inscribed monuments may have been intended for public display. This would have entailed public knowledge of the text, not because everyone could actually read it but because the oral version of the text would be available in some form.

At the same time, the practice continued of dedicating smaller artefacts, such as vessels, weapons, small statues, or tablets made of precious material, to the gods with the idea that they were meant primarily for the attention of the gods; they were often hidden or deposited within the brickwork of the building to partake of the avowed eternal lifespan of the temple. Often the inscriptions address a future king who might come across them in the course of renovating a temple, and they exhort him to treat the object with respect and not to remove it from its original emplacement.

By the end of the Early Dynastic period, the 'public' royal inscriptions had become several hundred lines long. They served not only to commemorate the name, title and deeds of a powerful local ruler, but were also meant to influence the public opinion of the present and future generations. There has been a tendency to treat the 'historical' information of royal inscriptions as factual and reliable, but in recent years the propagandistic aspects of royal inscriptions have received much attention, a reaction against an often over-literal interpretation of such sources as primary historical data.[9] Royal inscriptions were produced whenever a ruler commanded access to literate personnel trained to produce such texts, which was not an automatic by-product of kingship. Indeed, the collaboration with trained scribes was an indication of political stability. As time went on and a great number of old royal inscriptions from previous ages became available for study – as in the Old Babylonian period – they informed the popular image of royalty, which could then be manipulated by the educated élite to exercise a measure of control over possible excesses of central power. In the Akkad period, the scribes in the service of rulers exercised the function of 'spin-doctors'; their task was to develop ideological arguments to counter opposition from other centres resisting the forces of central control; they had to justify a new form of government which concentrated power in the hands of an individual king.

At the very end of the Early Dynastic period (c.2370), the inscriptions of Lugalzagesi, who called himself king of Umma, summarize the old attitude and at the same time prepare the way for a new age. His first text on a silver vase affirms the boundaries of Shara, the tutelary goddess of his city Umma; that the gods of his city, together with the other great gods of Sumer, had chosen him to be leader, had in fact created and nurtured him to fulfil his destiny, to conquer Kish and to restore the boundaries of his city. He also heaps maledictions against anyone who in future times would profane these stelae.

His second inscription, preserved on numerous fragments of calcite vases, presents an idyllic and pastoral vision of the peace and well-being that the whole country enjoys under his reign: the roads are safe 'from the Lower Sea to the Upper Sea', terror is eliminated, 'the people irrigate the fields joyfully'; Uruk passes its days in gladness, 'Ur lifts its head to the sky like a bull, Umma lifts an arm heavenward'. The final prayer asks the great gods to prolong his life, 'to make people sprout up like grass', to make the heavenly stalls prosperous and that he shall remain for ever the 'first shepherd and irrigator of the country'.[10] This gentle scene, however, could only come about through the unchallenged supremacy of Lugalzagesi, 'king of the whole country', whom the great gods chose to be the 'supreme manager of the gods'. It is he who intercedes with the gods, sacrifices and libates at Enlil's shrine in Nippur. The responsibility for the whole country is thus in the hands of one powerful king. Legitimized by the great gods, he rules supreme and the land is at peace.[11]

To appreciate the differences in the interpretation of rulership and government, we need to examine the terminology of élite titles and especially the implications of the term **lugal**.

LUGAL AND THE RISE OF KINGSHIP

The discussion of titles and nomenclature of offices is notoriously difficult, especially since there may over time have been regional differences as well as changes in meaning. In the Uruk period the highest office seems to have been occupied by one person who alone had the right to the title **en**. According to Charvát's analysis, even the highest office of the Uruk hierarchy was part of the 'civil service', though the names of people holding the **en** post were not recorded, nor were there any signs of ostentatious display or accumulation of wealth. During the Fara period, the **en** office appears to have shifted to the religious sphere; an analysis of the economic texts suggests that the main duties of the **en** at this time were connected with the cult, especially in fertility rituals.[12] In the later literary traditions of the Old Babylonian period, a person became **en** by 'marrying' the goddess Inanna. This concept of legitimizing control through divine consent became an important factor in the ideology of Mesopotamian rulership.[13] It seems to have been widespread during the Early Dynastic period. At the same time the

lugal (the sign means something like 'head-man', 'boss') became more important. During the Uruk age it denoted some overseer of personnel, clearly subordinate to the **en**. At the end of the Uruk period, especially at Ur, he seems to have assumed greater responsibilities and become a spiritual and secular leader.[14]

The rise of individual patriarchal households,[15] the accumulation of capital in the form of productive land and specialized craft production and the increasing secularization of political power facilitated the rise of individual leaders. The rivalry between city states and their vulnerability to attack from outside raiders made investment in armaments and military training imperative. The **lugal** benefited from conflict and the possibilities of pillage by enlarging his following. He also commanded institutions, and people owed special allegiance to him, as some personal names show. The primary institution associated with the **lugal** was the *é* – usually translated as 'palace' – the 'household' under the authority of the **lugal**. The Early Dynastic evidence shows that this office, perhaps first becoming synonymous with direct leadership of the city, arose in archaic Ur, and became an increasingly common form of governing city states. In contrast to the **en** office, which needed the recognition of the temple and was bestowed on a suitable candidate, the **lugal** position could be inherited and followed a dynastic succession.[16] He also had the prerogative of controlling systems of measurements and the right to leave written records of his deeds.[17]

In other cities we also see some evidence for a two-tiered hierarchy. At Shuruppak, for instance, the title held by the local ruler was **ensi**, who could acknowledge the superior authority of a **lugal**, who seems to have held sway over a larger territory.[18] Rivalries between cities and military engagement, either for defensive or aggressive reasons, could well have contributed to an over-arching system of control under the authority of an individual ruler. The greater the territory acknowledging the sovereignty of this ruler, the greater was his power. The Sumerian phrase **lugal.kalam.ma**, 'King of all the Land', is thought to denote sovereignty over all of Sumer; it was first used by the kings of Uruk.

Lugalzagesi, who started off as **ensi** of Umma, having conquered most of the Sumerian city states and taken possession of Uruk, called himself 'king of all the lands, king of Uruk, king of the country'. He refers to the 'land' several times in his text, as we have seen before. For the first time, here is a ruler who regards his office as a mandate for a centralized form of government that includes all the city states of Sumer. This vision of a state that comprised the totality of the country as a political unit was new. We have seen in the previous chapter how cities, though jealously guarding their spheres of influence and forever watchful for any infringement of their boundaries, would collaborate and recognize a common culture which was urban, literate and bureaucratically organized. The secularization of power and administration, and the concentration of wealth by families and households, prepared for the individualization of power. The **lugal** was often a charismatic individual, with personal characteristics and ambitions, rather than a bureaucrat or 'priest'. This does not imply that there was an inherent conflict between 'secular' and 'religious' leadership. More pertinent was the tension between local (city state) independence and integration into some larger unit (kingdom).

While we can to some extent trace an internal Sumerian development of kingship, it is also possible that this form of aristocratic rule originated in a different environment from the Sumerian city state. Such a region was the area north of the alluvial plain, where the Tigris and Euphrates come close together. It had a rather different ecological and geographical situation from the southern plains.[19] The slightly sloping terrain prevented the rivers from shifting their courses too much. Michael Mann[20] has suggested that this zone, just north of Kish, was of particular importance for all of Mesopotamia because not only could it support a mixed economy, combining irrigation-based agriculture and herding, but it also commanded a strategic position astride the trade routes to all cardinal directions. He characterizes the region as a 'transitional march',[21] dominated by competing warlords, usually able fighters who tried to extend their power by raiding and raising tribute for protection. In such circumstances, leadership is tied to successful military exploits, with the chief's popularity depending on his ability to secure respect and income. This heterogeneous border culture, with its social flexibility, so argues Mann, bred courageous adventurer-kings, quick to seize opportunities for plunder and tribute.

Another view suggests that the region was united into 'a single territorial state, whose gravity point usually remained at Kish',[22] as early as the Early Dynastic period II. The title 'king of Kish' suggests a claim to the rulership over this whole region; it appears first in writing with Mesilim (c.2400). However, when this title was borne by southern rulers it may have had a different implication. According to Hans Nissen's theory, the area around Kish was crucial for the ecological stability of the alluvial plain since it was at this point that the flow of the rivers, relatively close together, could to some degree be manipulated. He proposed that 'from the consolidation of the irrigation system on, it was of decisive importance for the south of the country to be kept under control at this danger point ... The title "king of Kish" would have been the well-earned distinction of the southern Babylonian ruler who carried out this function.'[23] Perhaps such a scenario seems to put too much faith in the effectiveness of south Mesopotamian diplomacy; Enshakushanna of Ur, for instance, simply reports that he destroyed Kish, but it is clear that attempts to unite the north and all the independent city states of the south originate in the Kish area.

THE AKKAD STATE

Many claims have been made about the radical change brought about by the Akkad state. It was considered the first supra-regional political entity in the ancient Near East, the first government to streamline administration throughout Mesopotamia, the first regime to introduce charismatic kingship, the first to manipulate public opinion by 'propaganda', the first to introduce international trade, and so forth. On the whole, there is simply not enough information to substantiate any of these assumptions, which are often based on a perceived fundamental difference between the 'old' world of the 'Sumerian city states' and the new world order of the dynamic and expansionist 'Semitic' and centralist Akkad state. Furthermore, our perception of what was new or traditional is often filtered through later local traditions which draw attention to certain features that had a relevance at a particular time when the comments were made.

Legend and fact, contemporary and later perspective, intermingle in this period more than in any other. Fact and fiction, history and historiography, have become so intertwined that some scholars prefer to concentrate entirely on the relatively scant economic and legal documents of the period and discount the possibility of using any of the later material for an understanding of the Akkad period.[24] The following account tries to deal with both aspects, the factual data available and the later echo in the Mesopotamian literary tradition.

Sargon

The Akkad period begins officially with the reign of Sargon (2340–2284).[25] Akkad became the capital of a state which incorporated eventually all the Sumerian city states and extended its power further afield, if not, as the old texts claim, to the 'four corners of the world'. To date the beginning of this period to Sargon begs the question as to whether Lugalzagesi, who had established his sovereignty over some fifty governors in the south and thus commanded a small empire, should not be counted as part of the new age. After all, he claimed on his royal inscription that he had made all the foreign lands subservient to him, 'from the Lower Sea along the Tigris and Euphrates rivers to the Upper Sea'. The Old Babylonian scribes who edited the collections of royal inscriptions obviously thought so and included Lugalzagesi in their anthology. He certainly brought an end to the independence of the Sumerian city states. The Sumerian King-list,[26] on the other hand, with its structural neatness and preference for dynastic continuity, assigns Lugalzagesi a separate chapter, as having exercised kingship over Uruk for a period of twenty-five years. It goes on to say:

Uruk was defeated (and) its kingship was carried off to Agade. In Agade, Sargon, whose father was a gardener, the cup-bearer of Ur-Zababa, the king of Agade who built Agade, (he) reigned 56 years as king.[27]

This schematic arrangement is still followed by the customary division of the third millennium into a 'Sargonic' or Akkadian period. Archaeologically speaking, the material culture of this period is much more elusive and there is little evidence for a fundamental change during the second half of the third millennium.[28]

The name of Sargon has been regarded as an official name, usually taken to mean 'true, rightful king' (Akkadian: *sarru kenu*), but recently it has been suggested that Sharrukan may in fact have been his birth-name.[29] His origin and background are obscure; in his own inscriptions he does not give any reference to his paternal ancestors. Since he achieved such extraordinary fame, he was given a fictionalized background, derived from popular tales, which emphasize his rise from obscurity to 'king of the world'. One such tradition is referred to in a passage from the Sumerian King-list. A Sumerian text gives a fuller version: Sargon's (unnamed) father, a 'gardener', enters the service of Ur-Zababa and is promoted to the high office of cup-bearer. The gods decree that the reign of Ur-Zababa should come to an end and Sargon becomes king.[30] Another variant is preserved on Babylonian tablets. Here Sargon's maternal ancestry gets elaborated.

> Sargon, the mighty king, king of Akkade, am I.
> My mother was an en-priestess(?), my father I never knew.
> My father's brother inhabits the highlands.
> My city is Azupiranu, which lies on the bank of the Euphrates.
> She conceived me, my en-priestess mother, in concealment she gave me birth,
> Set me in a wicker basket, with bitumen she made my opening watertight.
> She cast me down into the river from which I could not ascend.
> The river bore me, to Aqqi the water drawer it brought me.
> Aqqi the water drawer, when lowering his bucket, did lift me up.
> Aqqi the water drawer did raise me as his adopted son.
> Aqqi the water drawer did set me to his gardening.
> While I was still a gardener, Ishtar did grow fond of me,
> And so for . . . years I did reign as king,
> The black headed people, I did rule and govern.[31]

Here the mother's high status (en priestesses were often of royal blood) is emphasized, as well as the paternal origin as an outsider 'from the mountains'. The city Azupiranu is not a real city, but refers to the highlands where aromatic *azupiranu* herbs grow.[32] This legend also stresses the miraculous circumstances of the hero's birth and survival, in a tradition that has numerous parallels, not least that of Moses. The truth value of such stories is negligible.

However, the statement that Sargon built Akkad is very likely factual. Though the city has not been identified archaeologically, we know it was in the region north of Kish, Mann's 'transitional march'.

Recent suggestions located the city near the confluence of the Tigris and its eastern tributary, the Diyala river.[33] As a new foundation, it would have to have been nearer the north-eastern fringe of the Babylonian plain to escape attention and interference from the south. The lack of agricultural potential could be offset by the profits from trade connections. The Tigris, with its deeply cut river-bed, was comparatively useless for irrigation purposes but good for riverine transport along the north–south axis. The Diyala connected the area with the Hamrin region, from which the Iranian plateau could be reached. Several sites could fit the bill. Tell Muhammed, on the outskirts of Baghdad, has been proposed as the most likely location, but excavations by the State Antiquities Organization have not progressed beyond late second millennium levels.

In any event, Sargon built himself a power base in the area north of or around Kish and developed a well-trained and well-equipped military contingent. It is unclear what happened at Kish: whether it was Sargon or Lugalzagesi who dethroned the incumbent ruler, Ur-Zababa. Sargon may have had to move his base to Akkad because of a failed *coup* at Kish,[34] but the next logical step was to attack the person who commanded most power in the south: Lugalzagesi, who may have been enjoying the pastoral peace of the lands too much to prepare for a challenge. Sargon struck at Uruk, broke down the city walls, won the battle and took Lugalzagesi prisoner. Then, betraying a characteristic sense of performance and civic drama, he paraded the 'king of all the lands' 'in a neck-iron to the gate of Enlil at Nippur'.

The victory over Uruk was followed up by a series of battles against other Sumerian cities, Ur, Lagash and Umma. Only then did the 'god Enlil not let him have a rival, gave him the Lower and the Upper Sea and the citizens of Akkad held (posts of) government'. It is clear from Sargon's own inscriptions that his success was based on military superiority; he claims to have fought thirty-four battles, destroyed many city walls and had '5,400 men eat daily before him'. Not content with his sovereignty over Mesopotamia, he led successful campaigns against principalities in the east, and made successive raids along the Euphrates and to the west of it, to Mari and Ebla. He reports that he gained control over the sea-coast traffic ('boats from Magan and Meluhha moored at Akkad') and asserted his command over the

Middle Euphrates region and Syria right up to the 'Cedar Mountains'.
Not much else is known about him and his reign, and the actual extent
of his realm is still unclear. However, the fact that he had managed to
unite the whole of Mesopotamia, appointed his own men as governors,
and was known and perhaps feared in areas much further afield, as
well as the fact that he ruled for an unusually long time (the Sumerian
King-list gives him fifty-six years), left a lasting impression on the
succeeding generations. In the later tradition, he was seen as the most
successful king ever. He was thought to have ruled over no less than
the 'totality of the lands under heaven', 'from sunrise to sunset, the
sum total of all the lands' as one text explains.[35]

Sargon's inscriptions were assiduously collected and copied, and
tales of his birth and conquests circulated in oral as well as literary
form. Many of these tales were invented to suit particular political
circumstances. The story of Sargon's peaceful intervention in a dispute
between Anatolian merchants, filled with references to the difficulties
of crossing mountains and rivers, is known as 'The King of the Battle'.[36]
The historical context of this story is most likely the time of the Amorite
king Shamshi-Addu,[37] who was keen to revitalize the interrupted trade
connections between Upper Mesopotamia and the copper-producing
principalities in central Anatolia.[38]

By the Old Babylonian period, Sargon had become a model hero.
When the Babylonians compiled a collection of historical omens,
Sargon featured prominently as a 'Good and Successful King'. The
'omen of Sargon' therefore augured well, promising world domination.
Like Charlemagne in Europe, or King Arthur in Britain, he became an
archetypal king who ruled long and well.

The evaluation of Sargon's achievements in real terms is more
problematic. His scale of operations went further than any of his
predecessors, but much of what is generally ascribed to Sargon may
have taken place gradually under his successors. The foundation of
Akkad, however, is very likely his own work. Akkad is the first city in
Mesopotamia to operate as a real capital. The international trade,
much emphasized in the contemporary texts, must have contributed
to the comparatively cosmopolitan atmosphere of the city, which in
turn became legendary. As long as the remains of Akkad's buildings
stay buried, however, we cannot substantiate such claims. The city

remained conceptually linked with Sargon as its founder and some of his glory reflected on it. The name may have been that of the village or small town which he took as his base;[39] it was subsequently applied not just to the city but to the country around it (*māt akkadim*; in Sumerian **ki.uri**) and used in distinction from the southern 'Sumer' (rendered as **ki.engi**). Furthermore, it was applied to the written language, a more syllabic form of cuneiform writing more suitable for the rendering of the Semitic language. The main impetus for this development seem to have originated in the Syrian town of Ebla: it has been suggested that the scribal culture of the Fara period already owed much to the collaborative impact of the Syrian experiments.[40]

Sargon did much to propagate this version of cuneiform, and the basis for the inscriptions written in this 'Akkadian' system.[41] His use of the old title 'king of Kish' is typical of the possibilities opened up by syllabic writing, since in the Akkadian version it can stand for *šar kiššati*, usually translated as 'king of the universe'.[42] Sargon established some equality between the traditional 'Sumerian' system and the new 'Akkadian' language. Some of his royal inscriptions were written in either language, and bilingual versions were also put up. Under his successors, written Akkadian became more widely used for administrative purposes, which points to the change of personnel from the native clerks to 'men of Akkad'. He also followed the southern custom of setting up inscribed statues and stelae in public places; the forecourt of Nippur was perhaps the most prestigious site,[43] but other cities have also yielded public monuments.[44]

The purpose of such public art was to establish a visual presence of the king throughout his realm, to propagate the military and peaceful achievements of his government and to create some form of common iconography which would build a bond between the different peoples ruled more or less directly by the Akkad kings. This awareness of the political potential of art was again nothing new, as the Uruk culture artefacts have shown. During the Akkad period, we see a complete change less in terms of imagery and iconography than in style. Akkadian art is characterized by grandeur and a difference in scale which leaves space around the main figure of the royal protagonist to make him appear as set apart from other human figures, as well as proportionally taller.[45] There is also a sense of dramatic tension, with scenes being depicted just after a climactic point. The best-known example of this trend is the stele of Naram-Sin, which depicts his victory over the mountain-dwelling Lullubi people.[46] Here the king, wearing a horned crown which marks him as super-human, stands near the summit of a mountain, receiving the submission of the enemy leader, while slaughtered soldiers tumble head-first down the slopes.

Much has been made in the past of the alleged differences between Sumerians and Semitic Akkadians, contrasting the free-spirited if cruel Semites with the bureaucratic and parochial Sumerians, the former producing leaders that were typical empire builders like Sargon while the stereotypical Sumerian ruler was a bald and 'spiritual' priest-king. The ancient written sources never mention ethnic affiliations. The population is simply the people of the land, called the 'black-headed ones', and neither language nor origin seem to matter.

A life-size head of copper discovered among the Akkadian period levels of Nineveh has customarily been described as a portrait of Sargon, or at least of one of his descendants. It is a remarkable work of sculpture and almost intact, save for a gash in one cheek. Since statues of kings were by no means uncommon at the time, it could well represent one of the Akkadian kings, and it reflects an ideal of male beauty that even to modern eyes epitomizes the image of a noble Arab sheikh – sporting a luxuriant full beard and long locks. The busts of Early Dynastic rulers and potentates have, by contrast, clean-shaven faces and heads and well-rounded cheeks. The difference in hair fashion may point to cultural differences between the northern regions and the south, unless the shaved head denoted a class of higher officials; as the statues of dignitaries from Mari seem to show, where long and carefully trimmed beards are worn with a bald pate. Another possibility is that the long hair, with artfully pleated strands and crimped locks, that we see on the head of Sargon was really a wig, much like the luxury version made of sheet gold found by Sir Leonard Woolley in the tomb of a king of Ur.[47]

Sargon's successors

After Sargon's long reign, his sons succeeded him, first Rimush, then the elder brother Manishtusu. It is not clear for how long they ruled; probably between nine and fifteen years each. The death of the old king signalled a chance for the independent city-states of the south to regain their freedom. Rimush had to put down a revolt by Ur, Adab, Lagash, Umma and Zabala, and Elam also had to be resubdued by campaigns. The Sargonic state relied substantially on a well-trained military force. It is not quite clear how the soldiers were recruited and provisioned, but it seems that the allocation of land was one possible way of rewarding at least senior officers for their services.[48]

The most important contemporary monument is the black diorite 'obelisk of Manishtusu', which records the acquisition of large areas of land in the northern part of the country. These land rights had been collectively owned by a patriarchal kinship group, who had to agree to the alienation of property in exchange for silver. To what extent they were forced into the sale by the king is not clear. Another stele, found at Girsu, could possibly be dated to Rimush. It also 'records the distribution of arable land by the king to people of his household, which he may have acquired after his defeat of Lagash'.[49] The visual decoration on the monument shows the defeat and execution of (hostile) soldiers. According to administrative records from southern cities such as Girsu, the Akkadian royal household expanded at the expense of local institutions.[50] Such a policy no doubt strengthened the economic basis of the state, but it also caused resentment and fostered opposition.

The accession of Manishtusu's son Naram-Sin (2260–2223) may also have triggered a crisis: no less than 'all the four corners of the world rebelled against me', as he records. Again the Sumerian city states, led by Kish, Uruk and Nippur, took the initiative and the more far-flung outposts of the empire followed suit. How widespread and general this revolt really was is unclear. Some inscriptions that were deemed to be contemporary and historical sources for the rebellion have subsequently been identified as pseudo-historical compositions from the Old Babylonian period, especially those concerning the conflict with Kish.[51] The battles of Naram-Sin and his lion-like fury are the subject of later literary compositions in which he fights alongside the plague-god Erra; there is also one in which the 'mighty king' is shown to be but an instrument in the hands of the god Enlil. While certain themes may have subsequently been added or exaggerated, there is no fundamental reason to doubt that a challenge to Naram-Sin's authority did flare up into a violent conflict. It is also possible that Naram-Sin himself exaggerated the amount of resistance and emphasized the successful repression of a major rebellion movement so as to strengthen his position as supreme ruler of a centralized state. But whatever the extent of actual opposition, he certainly took another highly important step to legitimize his dominion and by so doing reformulated the notion and function of kingship. Shortly after the 'rebellion', his name in the texts appears as written with the sign denoting divine beings. He refers to the circumstances of his divinization in the following inscription on a statue:

Naram-Sin, the mighty king of Agade: when the four corners of the world opposed him with hostility, he remained victorious in nine battles because of the love of Ishtar and even took the kings who had campaigned against him prisoner. Because he succeeded when heavily pressed in maintaining his city in strength, his city [i.e. its inhabitants] implored Ishtar of Eanna, Enlil of Nippur, Dagan of Tuttul, Ninhursaga of Kish, Enki of Eridu, Sin of Ur, Shamash of Sippar, Nergal of Kutha to have him as the god of their city Agade and they built him a temple in the midst of Agade.[52]

In other texts, too, Naram-Sin is called the 'god of Akkad'. The king had moved officially into a higher category of being – that of a deity – and declared himself the main channel of communication between the great gods of the country and his subjects, 'the black-headed people'. Statues of the king received the sort of attention hitherto reserved for those of gods, and Akkad, a new city which, unlike Uruk or Eridu, could make no claims to be an ancient sacred site, became sacred because it was the seat of the divine king. The process of deification has close parallels to that of the Roman emperors and must be understood as a propagandistic attempt to justify far-reaching administrative and economic reforms and changes in the political system. Scribes close to the royal household made a point of using the divine determinative when writing the king's name, but it was by no means a universal practice.

Naram-Sin became the protagonist in quite a few literary compositions which originated in the Old Babylonian period and became popular classics of the scribal curriculum; they reflect both the historical circumstances and the intellectual currents of their time.[53] It is noticeable that, while Sargon is overwhelmingly described in positive terms – his humble birth and usurpation of power were presented as divinely decreed – Naram-Sin's position is more ambiguous. In one very popular work, 'The Curse of Agade' (see below), he is shown to have caused the fall of the capital through his disregard for the gods.

The state Naram-Sin held together by an iron will and brute force began to fall apart in the succeeding generations. Naram-Sin's son, Shar-kali-sharri, ruled for another twenty-five years (c.2223–2198) and, according to his inscriptions, he carried on much like his predecessors, though his main military engagements were with peoples from the eastern and western fringe of his empire, the Gutians and the Amorites respectively. He also faced persistent opposition within Mesopotamia. It appears that after his death most of the southern city-states shook off the central control of Akkad and asserted their independence. The last few descendants of Sargon ruled over only a small rump state around the former capital. The state broke apart as central control collapsed. The Sumerian King-list reflects this by the phrase, 'Who was king, who was not king?' and then lists a few more names as kings of Akkad, summarizing that eleven kings had ruled for 197 years. Later tradition ascribes the demise of the Akkad state to the Gutians, people from the Zagros hills, described as 'hordes' in the Sumerian King-list. The proximity of Akkad to the eastern hills obviously presented an element of risk, since any wealthy city at the fringe of cultivation is a potential target for non-urban tribal peoples and any weakening of control and defence would attract raiding parties. Eventually the Gutians were said to have assumed overall political power, at least in the northern plains. The southern cities, however, prospered,[54] especially Lagash, perhaps finally profiting from the redistribution of landholdings which the Akkadian kings had forced on to the city states.

Despite the glamorous image of the Akkad 'empire', which owes much to subsequent generations of Mesopotamian scribes, we know little about the actual extent of the realm or how it was organized.[55] The royal inscriptions from Sargon onwards claim that the empire stretched from the Lower Sea (the Persian Gulf) to the Upper Sea (the Mediterranean), but there is little to substantiate Mesopotamian control over regions beyond the Euphrates in the west. There are some rock reliefs that record successful raids by Naram-Sin into more distant regions, such as Pir Huseyn in eastern Turkey or Darband-i-Gaur in the Zagros mountains. But altogether the archaeological data from peripheral regions thought to have been under Akkadian control are fragmentary and often contradictory. Naram-Sin's boast that he destroyed Ebla has been linked with the destruction of its Early Dynastic palace, but since the chronology of Ebla and the Akkadian period is by no means established, this remains entirely unproved. One is on surer ground at the north Syrian site of Tell Brak, where bricks and other items inscribed with the names of Naram-Sin and his predecessor Rimush have been found, as well as monumental architecture. The excavators suggest the city was the site of a substantial Akkadian garrison that may have controlled a wider area in the Habur region in north-east Syria, where some Akkadian tablets have been found at Tell Leilan. It is likely that this constituted the northernmost extent of Akkadian direct influence, and a fire in the intermediate levels suggests that the occupation was not consistently effective throughout the Akkadian period. Control over Elam and Anshan in the Iranian west is, however, documented by texts found at Susa.

The situation with regards to the Persian Gulf trade connections is also problematic.[56] Mesopotamian pottery and other artefacts from the Early Dynastic period have been found along the coast at Oman and the United Emirates, as well as in Qal'a I at Bahrein, which suggests that trade connections at least existed.[57] Although there is no proof for the existence of direct political control over peripheral regions suggested by the royal propaganda, an internally united Mesopotamia with strong connections to such commercially important regions as the upper Habur valley, the Persian Gulf and Susiana, must have stimulated the economy and long-distance trade. Raids and razzias may have helped to generate booty and tribute payments from marginal areas. The reorganization of land tenure, at least in some parts of the country (certainly around the Kish region and at Lagash), may have helped to raise agricultural productivity on state-held land. In different cities, the Akkadian kings appointed members of the royal family to fulfil important functions, such as governors and senior temple officials, which helped to consolidate central control and taxation.

All of this lasted about a century, until centrifugal tendencies in the south mitigated against central control and the 'empire' began to lose credibility further afield, until the territory of Akkad was reduced to its original extent around the city of Akkad.

'THE CURSE OF AGADE' [58]

This text, like so many of the other literary compositions about the Akkadian kings, could have been written at any time between the actual fall of the city (c.2150) and 2000, but it most probably belongs to the Third Dynasty of Ur, the period of the next unified state in Mesopotamia. Numerous copies, mainly from the Old Babylonian scribal centres, have survived. It was a popular text, some 281 lines long, transmitted in Sumerian. The extent to which it reflects real historical events, and whether it can be taken as evidence for ethnic conflict between Sumerians and Semitic Akkadians, has given cause to much speculation among scholars. What has become clear is that the story serves to suit the political agenda of the Ur III kings, who glorified their own achievements and, as in this text, presented the ruler of an earlier 'empire' as hubristic in comparison.[59] The theological framework also matches the ideological system of the Ur III period.

The text begins with a reference to Enlil's frown. Enlil was the god of Nippur – in the Sumerian myths he is leader of the Sumerian gods[60] – who resided in a temple called Ekur. The frown of Enlil is a literary topos that always spells disaster for the frowned-upon city. In this composition Enlil's frown triggers the fall of Kish and 'slaughters the house of Uruk'. Sargon's name appears only once. He is clearly just an instrument of divine will, to whom the god gives sovereignty and kingship. The goddess Inanna is now introduced, who seeks to establish her cult in Akkad, 'like a youngster building a house for the first time, like a girl establishing a woman's domain'. Her presence assures the well-being of the city:

> So that the warehouses are provisioned,
> that dwellings would be founded in the city,
> that its people would eat splendid food,
> that its people drink splendid beverages,
> that those bathed (for holidays) would rejoice in the courtyards,

that the people would throng the places of celebration,
that acquaintances would dine together,
that foreigners would cruise about like unusual birds in the sky,
that even Mahashi would be re-entered on the tribute rolls,
that monkeys, mighty elephants, water buffalo(?), exotic animals,
would jostle each other in the public square –
thoroughbred dogs, lions, mountain ibexes, alu – sheep with long wool –
(so that all this might happen) Holy Inanna did not sleep.
At that time, she filled Agade's . . . with gold,
she filled its shining . . . with silver,
delivered copper, tin, and blocks of lapis lazuli to its granaries,
sealed them away in its silos.
She endowed its old women with advice, she endowed its old
men with counsel, she endowed its young women with dances,
she endowed its young men with martial might.
She endowed its little ones with joy.
The viceroy's children, (still) cradled by nursemaids,
played *algarsur* instruments.
Inside the city was the *tigi* drum, outside it, the flute and the *zamzam*.
Its harbour, where ships docked, was full of excitement,
all foreign lands rested contentedly,
their people experienced happiness.
Its king, the shepherd Naram-Sin,
rose like the sun on the holy throne of Agade.
Its city-wall touched heaven, like a mountain,
Holy Inanna opened wide
the portals of the city-gate, as for the Tigris going to sea,
ships brought the goods of Sumer itself upstream (to Agade),
the highland Amorites, people ignorant of agriculture,
came before her there with spirited bulls and spirited bucks,
Meluhhans, people of the black mountains,
brought exotic wares down to her,
Elam and Subiru carried goods to her like pack asses.
All the governors, temple administrators, and land registrars of the
    Gu'edena,
Regularly supplied monthly and New Year offerings there.
This in Agade's city-gate . . . ![61]

This lengthy introduction is interesting because it describes a particular ideal of a capital city which owes its prosperity to international trade and tribute rather than to agricultural output. The outward signals are the presence of foreigners, exotic animals and the produce of distant countries, which is 'sealed away in silos'. The wealth generated provided the wherewithal for regular temple offerings and public festivals, when people would dress up and eat and drink well. The presence of the king, 'like the sun on the holy throne', signals that this type of city is associated with larger political units, with 'empires' that connect together normally independent entities and stimulate long-distance exchange as well as tribute.

The description fits Ur at the end of the third millennium as much as Akkad a couple of centuries earlier, as it does the Assyrian royal cities, as well as Babylon in the first millennium. This 'capital city' lacks the sustainability of the classic Mesopotamian city with its self-sufficient agricultural economy. The capital prospers as long as the political fortunes of the regime prosper, but it is vulnerable to change and its wealth becomes a liability since it makes it a target for covetous rivals or opportunistic raiders. No doubt the Mesopotamian kings were well aware of the inherent dangers, but the official discourse needless to say presents the rise and fall of capitals in a theological language, implying a tenuous relationship between gods and, equally important, between kings and gods.

The Sumerian text next describes the crisis at Akkad as the consequence of Enlil's disapproval, which forces Inanna to withdraw from the city and abandon her sanctuary. Within a short time, the other gods follow suit. They also take away the royal insignia, including the crown and throne, and their own prerogatives which they bestow on a city: Enki its wisdom, Utu its counsel. The reasons for Enlil's ominous 'silence' are never made clear. Cooper suggests that Inanna wanted to build a new temple, which would have entailed official permission from Enlil. His 'silence' was a sign that he had decided to withdraw sovereignty from Akkad, which meant that the other gods, including Inanna, had to vacate their sanctuaries and thus leave the doomed city without divine support.

The text now turns to the king. Naram-Sin sees in a dream vision that Akkad would no longer exist, that it would 'plunder its own riches, that its temples and stores would be scattered'. The knowledge of impending doom paralyses the king. He falls into a seven-year-long depression, having abandoned his regalia and 'covered his chariot with reed-mats'. After waiting all this time, Naram-Sin again tries to obtain a favourable omen from Ekur. But the omens remain negative. The situation has reached stalemate. Without Inanna's presence and the blessing of the other gods, the city is unviable.

Naram-Sin now takes an entirely unprecedented step. He decides to force Enlil to deliver a pronouncement, to alter his divine will. He musters his troops and bears down on Enlil's temple of Ekur, to demolish it as if it were a huge ship. Naram-Sin 'sets his spades against its roots, his axes against the foundations until the temple, like a dead soldier, falls prostrate'. Then he sets to to despoil its storerooms, he penetrates into the 'holy bed-chamber, casts the holy vessels into the fire'. Large ships dock at the temple to remove goods from the city. 'As the goods are removed from the city, so is the good sense of Akkad removed.' This triggers Enlil's revenge: 'Enlil, because his beloved Ekur was destroyed, what should he destroy for it?' He decides to wreak his vengeance through a barbarian invasion, through Gutium, 'a people who know no inhibition, with human instincts but canine intelligence and with monkey features'. Like a firebrand or a flood they sweep over the land and leave it wasted for generations. 'No one escapes their arms, messengers no longer travel the highways, boats no longer travel the rivers.' They drive the penned animals into the open and assert nomadic habits. Inside the cities, not on the open countryside, they plant gardens. 'For the first time since cities were built and founded, the vast fields did not produce grain, the inundation ponds produced no fish, the irrigated orchard yielded neither syrup nor wine.'

There is widespread famine, the dead are left unburied, and 'the great sanctuaries were remodelled to tiny reed chapels'; only lamentations and dirges can be heard. Enlil himself mourns. He withdraws to his holy bed-chamber and lies down fasting. The other gods are alarmed by Enlil's withdrawal. In order to 'cool his angry heart', they curse Akkad: 'May the city that destroyed your city, be done to as your city.' Then follows a long litany of imprecations, invoking death, destitution, social disintegration and finally oblivion. The divine curse is fulfilled and the poem ends abruptly with, 'Akkad is destroyed – hail to Inanna.'

This poem dwells on the ruin of the 'empire' and the anger of Enlil so as to make a contrast with the contemporary revival of Mesopotamia's fortunes under the next imperial government, the Third Dynasty of Ur. The kings of Ur made a great show of their patronage of the great temples of Sumer, especially the Ekur at Nippur. There is no evidence that Naram-Sin sacked the temple of Enlil. On the contrary, his statues were worshipped at Ekur long afterwards, and the invasion of the Guti happened much later. But 'The Curse of Agade' exposes an ideological concern for the right relationship between the gods and the absolute ruler.

Traditionally, as we have seen at Eridu, the gods dwelt within their cities; their temples were their houses and estates, where they lived with their spouses and children and servants. The whole notion of Sumerian urbanism was intimately connected with this in-dwelling of the divine. Mesopotamian religion never fully envisaged the transcendental infinite presence of gods; it needed them to be tied to a place. Their holy bed-chamber occupied the inner recesses of the temple estate. Heaven was no further than the temple roof. By providing the gods with lodgings and sustenance, the city partook of the essence of divinity.

The fundamental principle was one of mutual exchange, comparable to that which defined the city's relationship with the surrounding country. Just as the fertility of this rainless land could only be harnessed effectively with the well-organized teams of labour, equipment and storage that the city provided, so the survival and happiness of the gods depended on human effort. This is explained in numerous myths depicting the miserable fate of the gods before they were able to shift the burden of subsistence, the 'digging of canals', to people who were created specially for this task. Through feeding the gods, the city became viable, but it depended on the willingness of deities to take up and retain residence. Inanna did her utmost to furnish Akkad with wealth and happiness, but she lacked a basis of operation, a large temple. The building of temples was seen as an essential requirement for the city's existence.

Such an undertaking was a momentous task. Not only was it necessary to ensure the purity of the ground, and to observe innumerable complex rituals to guarantee the successful completion of the building, a process described in great detail by Gudea, the ruler of Lagash.[62] It also needed the approval of the great gods, signalled by the process of delivering oracular verdicts from the great temples. In practice this could give the major temples, especially the Ekur, a measure of political influence. Certain decisions which might alter the balance of power or have other major consequences, such as a foreign campaign, might at least be delayed through an inconclusive oracle, while others could be approved swiftly and unanimously. Kings could try to minimize the danger of opposition by appointing members of their household to senior temple offices, but the professional training of the diviners, which took many years, ensured that their loyalties would be more firmly associated with the temple than the palace.

Naram-Sin's aggression against the Ekur could also be seen as a typical palace fantasy, the description of an act of vengeance on the obstreperous temple machinery by projecting it on to a famously single-minded and much-admired former king. In comparison with such blatant aggression, the fiscal restructuring of temple revenues initiated by the Ur III kings was harmless. 'The Curse of Agade' was equally popular in the Old Babylonian period, and we know that Hammurabi too had to tread a careful path between reform and tradition.[63] But while the poem may have served to stress the piety of the Ur III and Old Babylonian rulers, it also involved a fundamental idea that royal hubris constitutes a threat, a critique of the excess of political power.

Akkad survived the occupation of the Gutians; the city was mentioned in economic texts intermittently until the first millennium. But it never regained its status as a Mesopotamian capital. The memory of Akkad remained associated with the Sargonic dynasty, which later tradition made into the prototype for all imperial aspirations. If Akkad was indeed occupying the same site as Baghdad, there is a striking parallel between the city of Sargon and the city of al-Mansur and the Abbasid caliphs, a city as filled with exotic foreigners, merchant caravans and stories to provide entertainment for a thousand and one nights.

5 UR

Ur, like Uruk and Eridu, had its origins in the Ubaid period, the very beginning of permanent settlements in southern Mesopotamia. It was also a major ceremonial and religious centre, and certainly during the historically documented periods it housed the shrine of the moon-god, called Nannar in Sumerian and Sîn in Akkadian. Favourable communications also assured economic prosperity, and the city, especially during the third millennium, enjoyed considerable political power, first as an independent city, then as the capital of a centralized state during the Third Dynasty of Ur. As the seat of government it benefited from massive building programmes, from substantial city walls to vast religious precincts. The prestige of the well-endowed temples of Ur outlived the political influence of the city and many later rulers saw it as advisable to maintain and endow the sanctuaries with grants, donations and architectural projects. Even when it lost its economic importance as a result of shifts in the transport links, Ur never, as Eridu did, fell into desolation throughout the millennia of Mesopotamian civilization. Like other ancient southern cities, it was splendidly restored by Nebuchadrezzar II (605–562). The city only died when the ceremonial function no longer suited a changed political climate, as happened when Mesopotamia became incorporated into the Achaemenid empire (550–330). Even before that time, however, the cult of the moon-god had shifted much further west, to Syrian Harran.[1]

In this chapter I would like to demonstrate how the archaeological and epigraphical sources from the third millennium and early second millennium highlight the connection between the religious prestige of the city and the political aspirations of its rulers.

EXCAVATING UR

The ruins of the ancient city of Ur lie fifteen miles south-west of Nasiriyah, half-way between Baghdad and the Persian Gulf, and are known locally as Tell al-Muqayyar ('the Mound of Pitch'). Like so many Mesopotamian sites, it is now surrounded by sandy desert, while the Euphrates runs some ten miles further east than it did in antiquity. The city was once close to a side-arm of the river, which flowed into the lagoon situated before the Persian Gulf. This geographical position meant that Ur had access to the sea, as well as to the other major waterways that drained into the lagoon. In historical times the sea traffic was of particular significance for importing and exporting commodities.

The conspicuous ruin hill that rises more than forty feet above the ground was first investigated by J. H. Taylor, British consul at Basra, as early as 1854. The British Museum had commissioned a survey of the southern ruins and he chose Tell al-Muqayyar as his headquarters. The ancient identity of the city was soon revealed by the numerous inscribed tablets, and though this proved to be the 'Ur of the Chaldees', well known from the Bible as the home of Abraham, no substantial excavations were undertaken at the time. The foreign interest in antiquities, however, prompted local people to search the previously shunned *tells* for saleable items. The south Mesopotamian sites produced hardly any sculptures, but they were overflowing with cuneiform tablets that fetched a good price in the bazaars at Baghdad. Thousands of tablets ended up in numerous private and public collections, torn from their contexts and often badly handled. Eventually the market became so swamped with them that the tablets plummeted in value. This clandestine plundering of scientifically valuable material – or so it appears to the Western scholar – could be stopped only by properly organized excavations.

The British Museum was particularly interested in profiting from a political situation which gave Britain a free hand in southern Mesopotamia. The first opportunity came during the First World War. Campbell Thompson, a former assistant at the British Museum, happened to be on the Intelligence staff of the army in Mesopotamia and managed to do some digging at Eridu and Ur. This led to a campaign, directed by H. R. H. Hall (1918–19), who also worked at nearby Eridu and al-Ubaid. Financial difficulties dogged the British Museum campaigns until they were resolved when the wealthy University Museum of Pennsylvania proposed to undertake a joint expedition. There was considerable American interest in the site, not least because of the biblical connection. Leonard Woolley, the experienced British archaeologist, then directed the excavations from 1920 to 1934.[2] The most spectacular findings, especially the contents of the 'Royal Graves', ended up in London, though the 'spoils' were otherwise equally shared between the Pennsylvania and British museums. In the late 1970s, the Iraqi government, under Saddam Hussein, ordered the partial restoration of the most substantial monument, the ziggurat of Ur-Nammu, which became something of a tourist attraction for visitors and foreign business people in the Basra area. During the Iran–Iraq war it was rumoured to have accommodated anti-aircraft guns. It is still one of the most impressive ancient monuments in southern Iraq.

The long continuous habitation from at least 5000 to 500 BC resulted in a deep and rich deposit of remains at Ur. The excavators faced a roughly oval site, with the longest dimension measuring over half a mile, the old bed of the Euphrates being to the north and west. The remains of the sanctuary were near the surface in the north-eastern corner, topped by a hillock of the ziggurat, with the latest Neo-Babylonian building phase giving shape to the ruins. Only a comparatively small portion of the city was excavated, and the very earliest Ubaid layers hardly at all. It seemed that during the fourth millennium Ur must have been a centre of pottery production, since there was a vast deposit of broken pottery (known as the 'Great Sherd Dump'), beginning in Ubaid times, continuing into the Uruk period and terminating in the Jemdet-Nasr period (around 3000). There was a lot of hard-baked clay debris with evidence of pottery kilns and even a terracotta component of a potter's wheel. The 'dump' also contained a cylinder seal and the small steatite statuette of a bear.

A lot more information was gleaned from the third millennium layers. Leonard Woolley was particularly struck by a thick layer of pure clay deposit some eight feet thick, which separated the Ubaid layers from what he considered the 'Sumerian' strata. Here, he concluded, was evidence for the 'flood of Sumerian history and legend, the flood on which is based the story of Noah'. Although he pointed out that this was a local phenomenon, he still considered that it might have wiped out the original inhabitants of the country, leaving a remnant 'impoverished and disheartened ... Then into this almost empty land there came people of a new race and settled down by the towns and villages side by side with the survivors of the old stock ... The union of the two stocks gave birth to the Sumerian civilization.'[3] The flood deposit in his reconstruction of historical development neatly divided the antediluvian aboriginal culture from the postdiluvian Sumerian high culture, though he allows for some racial and cultural mixing![4]

The Ur cemeteries and the 'Royal Graves'

Woolley's most famous and spectacular discoveries were made in the cemetery area, which lay outside the walls of the old town. The first cemetery belonged to the Jemdet-Nasr and the earlier Early Dynastic period (first third of the third millennium), in which the dead were deposited in pits, usually on their sides in strongly flexed positions. The grave goods give important clues to the cultural horizons of the epoch.[5] There was polychrome pottery, but metal was obviously important and well worked. It was used for silver earrings, copper and bronze mirrors, spoons and pins, and for various implements and vessels, such as copper bowls, lead tumblers and bowls. At a later date, perhaps because of increased sea transport, stone bowls and vessels made from steatite or chlorite from the Persian Gulf replaced metal grave goods. Long-distance connections to the East are implied by beads and ornaments made of carnelian and lapis lazuli. Although no architectural remains of this period were excavated, the grave goods suggested that at least certain sections of the population of Ur had access to luxury items brought from far afield, while the standards of working metal and stone suggest familiarity with the material and a highly developed aesthetic sense.

Another of Woolley's extramural soundings revealed eight continuous layers of organic refuse, interspersed with seal impressions. They belonged to the Early Dynastic I period. An unusual number of door sealings were found, occurring here for the first time in Mesopotamian history. In the next level, the area began to be used as a cemetery and retained that function until post-Akkadian times. It contained more than 2,500 graves and seemed contemporary with the seal-bearing strata.[6] Most of the bodies were wrapped in reed matting and put in simple pits, as in the Jemdet Nasr cemetery, and were given some grave goods, though quite a number were buried without. It was among these modest burials that Woolley made his most famous discovery, the sixteen élite tombs he identified as the 'Royal Graves'. They were proper chambers of mudbrick and even stone, elaborately vaulted with an apsidal end, and situated in a deep pit approached by a ramp. After the main burial had taken place in the chamber, the pit was used for offerings and subsequently filled with earth.

A unique feature of these graves was that they contained what appeared to be the principal body as well as the bodies of men and women interpreted by Woolley as 'servants' and perhaps sacrificial victims. The wealth and quality of the objects buried with the deceased was and still is astonishing. Nothing like it had been found in Mesopotamia before. There was a lot of gold and all the precious materials available at the time: ivory, semi-precious stones, bronze (both tin and arsenic), and some vessels shaped from a very hard igneous rock that must have taken a great many days to fashion. Males were given hand axes, daggers, knives, whetstones, as well as gold head-dresses made of metal bands set with stones. Females wore golden hair ribbons, leaf-shaped hair ornaments, combs, earrings and choker-type necklaces. Some individuals had both male and female artefacts (one was male, one female).[7]

The best-preserved tomb belonged to a woman identified by her lapis lazuli cylinder seal as Pu-abi,[8] the first sign of it being an antechamber in which lay the bodies of five men with copper daggers at their waists. Underneath a layer of matting were the skeletons of ten women, arranged in two rows, elaborately bedecked with golden head-dresses and necklaces. Near by were the remains of a beautifully decorated harp, its body topped with the head of a golden bull with a beard of lapis lazuli. Further down Woolley came to a sumptuously ornamented sledge chariot, and the crushed skeletons of two oxen and a heap of the most gorgeous funerary goods, including a lapis lazuli and ivory gaming board, golden tools and weapons, bowls of soapstone, copper dishes, vessels, jugs and cups of silver and gold, all piled up together.

An inlaid wooden chest that had perhaps once contained clothes concealed a hole in the floor which gave on to another tomb chamber, with its own shaft and antechamber. This contained six male and nineteen female bodies, draught animals, the same kind of luxurious offerings, a lyre and the model of a boat in silver. The grave itself had been disturbed and partially looted; the male body was identified by his seal as that of A-kalam-dug, king of Ur. The lady Pu-abi's tomb lay behind this grave and, though the vaulted brick roof had caved in, it was otherwise intact. The body of the queen lay on a wooden bier, a golden cup near her hand and her chest completely hidden by a mass of beads of silver, gold and precious stones, remains of bejewelled cloaks and ornaments. The golden head-dress she had worn over a huge padded wig still encircled the crushed skull, ribbons and circlets hung with leaf-shaped pendants and a comb-like ornament ending in five pointed stars. Mrs Woolley spent some time modelling the face above the cast of one of the better preserved female heads and this became the basis for a museum exhibit, which was to show the head of the ancient queen adorned with the reconstructed original jewellery she was buried in.[9] A second diadem lay beside her, originally a strip of leather sewn with thousands of lapis lazuli beads inset with miniature golden animals and rosettes. Two other female bodies lay in crouched positions next to the bier and the whole chamber was filled with costly offerings, including cosmetic colouring in seashells. Woolley surmised that the male burial was the earlier one and that Pu-abi's tomb was placed above it.

Another tomb belonged to a certain Meskalamdug, said to have been a king (**lugal**). He wore a golden helmet shaped like a wig, now in the Iraq museum. A shaft grave whose owner could not be identified contained seventy-four bodies, sixty-eight of them women, all elaborately dressed, and all the females had lyres next to them. As Woolley described the scene:

They were disposed in regular rows across the floor, every one lying on her side with legs slightly bent and hands brought up close near the face, so close together that the heads of those in one row rested on the legs of those in the row above. Here was to be observed even more clearly . . . the neatness with which the bodies were laid out, the entire absence of any signs of violence or terror.[10]

The famous Standard of Ur was found here, with its separate sides showing scenes of war and peace, as well as two figures of he-goats, an image dubbed by Woolley as the 'ram caught in a thicket'. The question as to how the bodies of the people in the antechambers met their deaths has been much discussed. Woolley thought it 'most probable that the victims walked to their places, took some kind of drug – opium or hashish would serve – and lay down in order; after the drug had worked, whether it produced sleep or death, the last touches were given to their bodies and the pit was filled in'.[11] Fragments of cloth showed that the women had been wearing garments of bright red wool with long sleeves, and this led Woolley to imagine that

it must have been a very gaily dressed crowd that assembled in the open mat-lined pit for the royal obsequies, a blaze of colour with the crimson coats, the silver, and the gold; clearly these people were not wretched slaves killed as oxen might be killed, but persons held in honour, wearing their robes of office, and coming, one hopes, voluntarily to a rite which would in their belief be but a passing from one world to another, from the service of god on earth to that of the same god in another sphere.[12]

This is a good example of the power of narrative strands in archaeological assessment. Woolley was careful to base his theory of the sacrificial victims on circumstantial observations, to assemble clues. He pointed out that bodies could not have been moved after death without disturbing the delicate ornaments and to the fact that a large copper cauldron was placed near by, apparently connected to the goblets given to each of the deceased – presumably to facilitate death by poisoning. On closer inspection, none of these 'proofs' hold up: the handling of bodies after interment is a well-known practice in many cultures, especially in the Mediterranean area, and Woolley's inability to even conceive of such customs owes as much to Victorian sensibilities about death as to his lack of ethnographic knowledge. Another fanciful theory to explain why people should have been put to death was proposed by Cyril Gadd, who suggested that the bodies belonged to male and female priests who had assumed the roles of gods and goddesses for the celebration of a sacred marriage rite.

We simply do not know for certain what happened in the 'death pits',[13] but alternative interpretations have been proposed, partly on the basis of recent examinations of the skeletal remains, the original excavation notes and anthropological parallels. First of all, cauldrons and goblets were common in other Early Dynastic grave sites. They were probably used for libation rituals and not necessarily connected to a poison draught. Furthermore, the severe decomposition of the skeletons made any statements as to just how individuals met their deaths nothing more than speculation. It has also become clear that the male and female burials are not from the same time, though all burials fall within a relatively brief period. According to recent suggestions by Petr Charvát (1993), one also needs to consider the sociological context, especially since the rich grave goods and the elaborate architecture of the major tombs make it clear that they must have belonged to persons who had a high standing within the community. He sees 'no obstacles to a proposition that the main burial might have been surrounded by corpses "stored up for the occasion" and belonging to people who fervently wished to be laid to rest in the proximity of persons whose charismatic significance is likely to have been acknowledged by the whole community'.[14] He thus interprets Woolley's voluntary human sacrifices as secondary burials and explains the presence of the dead 'attendants' as motivated by a wish to demonstrate allegiance beyond life. Closer inspection has revealed that some of the bodies had been manipulated and possibly excarnated before their second interment.

Another interesting issue that has recently come to the fore is the question of female status as reflected in the Ur graves.[15] Although the skeletons unearthed by Woolley had not been examined by specialists and some of the ascribed gender identifications are doubtful, it is clear that more women than men were buried in the Early Dynastic IIIa cemetery. A study of the grave goods and the personal items of the deceased showed that they expressed gender differences. Certain items made a body culturally male or female. There is no doubt that femininity had powerful connotations and that some women occupied high positions in public life; the title **nin**, as worn, for instance, by Pu-abi, signified a very important female office which may have implied a close connection to the religious sphere.[16] Other items of female apparel have also been interpreted as 'badges of office'. Furthermore, it has to be remembered that both males and females had the right to be buried with secondary interments ('retainers'). It appears that, at least in ceremonial contexts, certain women were regarded as especially powerful and seem to have derived their elevated rank from professional status rather than from kinship affinities as daughters or wives of powerful men. This is of considerable importance and it appears that, at least at Ur, it was possible for some female officiants to achieve considerable political and religious influence, a point to be referred to further on.

THE EARLY DYNASTIC KINGDOM OF UR

The late phase of the Early Dynastic age (twenty-fourth century) shows signs of a fully hierarchical society. This is supported by the iconography of the seals and the Standard of Ur, as well as the signs of office that suggest professional specialization by different institutions, from administration to the military, with graded distinctions of rank. The sixteen 'Royal Graves' may well be 'the encoding of social structure in visible signs',[17] but any reconstruction of the social fabric must remain tentative. What can be said is that the Ur élite commanded considerable resources and took care to justify its status through participation in public rituals which may have provided a form of supernatural sanction for social position. The iconography of the seals, especially those featuring banqueting scenes, which were mainly worn by women, may suggest that ritualized feasting was an important culture theme and possible practice.

Elaborate burial rites for the most significant individuals stress the importance of the dead for the community. Such ancestral cults are well attested from later Mesopotamian periods, when the spirits of dead kings and other high-status persons were thought to continue their benevolent intercession on behalf of the community as long as funerary rituals and mortuary offerings were kept up.[18] It also appears that high status had more to do with the cult of the moon-god Nannar, the city god of Ur, than with any secular authority.[19] The graves also give an insight into the material culture of Ur in the mid third millennium. The standard of craftsmanship shows familiarity of working with metals and precious stones and a high technical competence. Materials from faraway places (lapis lazuli from Budakhshan, for instance) prove that Ur commanded resources sufficient to participate in long-distance trade and exchange.

As we have seen, the architectural remains of Early Dynastic Ur were removed or superseded by the structures built during the time of the Third Dynasty, some five hundred years later. Only some of the city walls may go back to this period. We have also seen how at this time cities began to be surrounded by massive walls. These could be built quickly as the result of the innovation of a new type of brick which allowed a new form of construction. This so-called planoconvex brick was flat-bottomed with a bun-like top. The bricks were mould-made in standard sizes (usually 21 by 16 centimetres), but apparently without skimming off the surplus. They could be laid flat, with mortar filling the gaps, or, similar to drystone walling, sideways with the long sides outwards. When the direction of the inclination was changed after each course, it resulted in a herringbone pattern. Parts of the walls, especially in structurally vulnerable parts next to openings, such as doorways, were laid in straight courses to produce a counterweight to the angled courses. A major advantage of this method was that laying the bricks at an angle was easier and could be done by unskilled workers. It was also very suitable for building curved walls and rounded corners, a typical feature of Early Dynastic enclosures – again a labour-saving device, since right-angled corners in massive brick structures need particular strengthening.[20]

Rubble-filled casemate types of wall were a similar application of relatively unskilled and time-saving building techniques.[21] Technical innovation is usually a response to a need; it is likely that the increasingly militant competition between cities made defence a matter of urgency. The availability of labour gangs[22] and regular troops indicates the conscription of people for public work projects. Another view on the proliferation of large-scale building projects is that they would have been a deliberate effort to create work, to absorb surplus labour by engaging in long-term projects to employ a variety of craftsmen as well as unskilled workers, and to teach an urban workforce discipline.[23] The collective benefit from such projects, especially temples and fortifications, justified the expenditure of effort and materials. To what extent the finished buildings also contributed to enforce social boundaries[24] is less clear, especially since there is very little evidence of residential areas of the time.[25]

The most important sanctuary of the city was the temple of the moon-god Nannar. It had a ziggurat which was first built around 3000. Parts of the huge temple enclosure wall, built with planoconvex bricks, remain; it was 9 metres thick. The ceremonial complex was surrounded by subsidiary parallel chambers for storage. Among the few Early Dynastic tablets discovered were some revealing that pigs were given out as part of the regular offerings to the gods and subsequently consumed in the palace.[26]

Very little is known of the history of Ur at the time. Some of the rulers of Lagash wrote that they had conquered Ur, but omitted to mention the names of the defeated rulers. The Sumerian King-list has nothing to say about Lagash. Instead it records that 'kingship' passed from Uruk to Ur and lists Mesannepada as the first king of the first Ur dynasty, which comprises a total of five kings. Revised dating of the 'Royal Graves' suggests that some of the later burials may be contemporary with the Mesannepada dynasty, and that some of the dead may have been members of his family.[27] Woolley discovered a foundation tablet in the ruins of the Early Dynastic temple at nearby al-Ubaid, which was written by A-anepada, who calls himself the 'son of Mesannepada king of Ur'. Mesannepada's own seal, discovered in the Ur cemetery, bears the title 'king of Kish'.

As we have seen, some scholars trace a possible connection between the destruction of the Kish palace, the fire that finished off Shuruppak and the use of this title by the southern ruler. The son of A-anepada, called Meskiaga-nuna, became king after his grandfather. His wife dedicated a calcite bowl for 'the life of her husband', as its short inscription says. (It is, incidentally, the oldest inscription written in Akkadian so far discovered.)[28] The last two kings of the first Ur dynasty had Akkadian names, a clear indication of the linguistic and ethnic contacts between Sumerians and Semites even in this southern region. The last phase of the Early Dynastic period was characterized by rival claims to hegemony over the whole country; the King-list records a number of dynasties which, in accordance to the linear list format, appear to have succeeded one another. In reality, many of these ruling houses were contemporaries.

Nothing is known about the Second Dynasty of Ur, and even the names in the King-list are too damaged to be legible. However, it is certain that the centre of power shifted from the south to the north, where first Lugalzagesi of Kish, then the kings of Akkad, held sway over the land of 'Sumer and Akkad'. Ur was defeated by Sargon, who destroyed the city walls and incorporated it into the Akkadian state. Ur's position during this time is told in a poetic work which has only recently been recognized for its historical importance.[29]

A WOMAN'S VIEW OF HISTORY: THE STORY OF ENHEDUANNA

This story concerns a formidable woman known as Enheduanna, the first female author in history. We have already mentioned her name as the reputed editor of the Sumerian temple hymns in connection with Enki's temple at Eridu.[30] She made an enormous impression on generations of scribes after her lifetime; her works were copied and read centuries after her death. Recent scholarship has revoked earlier doubts about the authenticity of her literary creation and puts it firmly in the context of the Akkadian period under the rule of Sargon's grandson Naram-Sin. We even have a likeness of Enheduanna on a calcite disc bearing her name and the line 'en-priestess, wife of the god Nannar'. A relief shows a woman with a turban-like head-dress standing before the seated god.[31] Enheduanna did not only edit temple hymns, she was also the author of a long and very difficult Sumerian literary composition known as *Nin-me-šara*.[32] My discussion of this challenging text is based on the most recent edition and translation by the German Sumerologist Annette Zgoll.[33]

The poem, preserved on some ninety different tablets from Nippur, Ur, Uruk and other cities, begins with a praise of the goddess Inanna, of her peaceful as well as her destructive powers. Then the author switches to a first-person account of the miseries she is suffering because of an individual called Lugal-ane, who has forced her to abandon her sanctuary and barred her from the performance of her sacred duties. Having lost her connection to the moon-god Nannar, she appeals directly to Inanna and challenges the decision of Lugal-ane. To solve the dilemma, she also seeks a judgement from the great god An, who decides to favour her plea and restore the priestess to her former post at the moon-god's temple at Ur.

The *Nin-me-šara* seems to refer to the political difficulties of Enheduanna's situation. According to her seal, she was appointed an en-priestess by Sargon. This amounted to an act of considerable interference in the religious affairs of Ur, even if the term 'daughter of Sargon' was metaphorical rather than reflecting a real blood affili- ation.[34] On the other hand, once appointed as 'wife' of the moon-god Nannar, chief deity of Ur, she also had to act in a manner that reflected her close connection to the god and his city. During the reign of Naram-Sin the southern cities, including Ur, rebelled against the Akkadian government.[35] We also know that this revolt was headed by a certain Lugal-ane, whom Naram-Sin names as the rebel leader of Ur. According to the poem, Lugal-ane challenged Enheduanna's legitimacy for the en-ship and forced her out of Ur. The author expresses this very real and surely terrifying situation not as a struggle between human protagonists, but as something happening on a higher level between the respective deities. Inanna represents Akkad, Nannar rep- resents Ur, and the ultimate arbiter is the sky-god An of Uruk. Annette Zgoll has convincingly shown that the text is structured like a legal case, ending with a final judgement uttered by An. The crucial point is the identification of the Akkadian dynastic goddess Eštar (or Ishtar) with Inanna of Uruk and her incorporation within the Mesopotamian pantheon.

It is possible that the solution, proposed by Enheduanna, was to declare that Inanna was Nannar's daughter; this would have justified the goddess's power over Ur and southern Sumer. Not surprisingly, Lugal-ane rejected any claim to usurp Nannar's undisputed rulership. The deadlock was only broken when Enheduanna, from her exile, obtained a divine omen from An, instructing her to return to the Gipar, the traditional residence and cult place of the **en** at Ur. This was no doubt a courageous if not a foolhardy decision. Lugal-ane issued dire threats and, apparently by force, prevented her from gaining entry. Once more she was forced to leave, but this did not stop the intrepid priestess from using her influence to achieve her goal. It is not clear what role the priesthood and leadership of Uruk played in the whole affair, but she managed to obtain the final judgement of An, who wholeheartedly accepted Inanna's new position of power.

The *Nin-me-šara* abounds in imagery that exults the material prowess and terrible energy of the goddess. At the same time, this exultation elevates her above Nannar. The triumph of Inanna may also reflect the triumph of Enheduanna, whose skilful manipulation of the ideological system helped to secure the imperial claims of the Akkad dynasty and secure her own position. She was no doubt an extraordinary woman, brave and ready to defend herself, an able negotiator, a scholar and poet.

Enheduanna's 'victory' at Ur had far-reaching consequences for the future of that city. Although it lost its political independence during the Akkadian period, it continued to flourish despite Sargon's diversion of maritime traffic to his new capital Akkad. The graves of the 'royal cemetery' continued in use, albeit without the extremely ostentatious funerary apparel of the Early Dynasty III tombs. There is no sign of a break in tradition or any lack of prestige objects. Even the practice of secondary burials for certain types of persons was maintained.[36]

Excavations yielded hardly any material from the Akkad period or the time of Gutian hegemony that came afterwards, mainly because those levels were obliterated by the major reconstruction programme of the Third Dynasty kings. It appears that the southern cities remained relatively independent from domination by the Gutians, as the rise of the city of Lagash under Gudea demonstrates. Ur at that time seems to have been governed indirectly from Lagash, at least intermittently. The last of the much resented Gutian rulers, Tirigan, 'the serpent, the scorpion from the mountains, who violated the gods and took away the kingship of Sumer',[37] was finally defeated and driven out by Utu-hegal, the ruler of Uruk, who put his vanquished foe and his family in a yoke before him. Seven years after this victory, Utu-hegal died and domination over Sumer passed to Ur-Nammu (c.2113–2096), maybe his brother,[38] who had perhaps been a governor at Ur during Utu-hegal's reign. At any rate, Ur-Nammu chose Ur to be the seat of a new state and he founded the most successful of all the dynasties of this city, the Third Dynasty of Ur, or Ur III for short.

UR IN THE UR III PERIOD (*C.*2113–2029)

Unlike the first two dynasties of Ur, the third was not simply one among several Mesopotamian polities whose influence was largely confined to the area surrounding the city itself.[39] On the contrary, the kings of Ur III created another centralized state which had, as its heartland, all of Sumer and Akkad, from the Persian Gulf to the southern Jezirah, and large parts of the western Iranian hilly flanks and plains, including Susiana and the Tigris valley with its eastern tributaries up to Nineveh, as peripheral regions dominated by the Ur government. This heterogeneous empire was held together by an army of civil servants, since bureaucratic control was regarded as a more reliable instrument of sustained influence than military might. This was probably a legacy of the previous centralized state, the Akkadian empire, whose kings had also attempted to standardize administrative procedures throughout their territories. After the collapse of Akkad, the practice of training and employing large numbers of scribes was maintained in the various Mesopotamian urban centres, though it lapsed in peripheral regions.

The Ur III tablets

During the hundred years of Ur III, an enormous amount of written documentation was produced, with even the most mundane trans-actions, such as the purchase of a single sheep, being recorded. As a result there are more tablets from this period than of any other. Hundreds of thousands of tablets were discovered in various Mesopot-amian sites, a large number of them being unearthed by unauthorized diggers who sold vast quantities to dealers, especially during the last decade of the nineteenth century when 'Assyrian' antiquities were hugely popular. Originally coherent archives thus became scattered throughout the world and a significant number simply disappeared from lack of expert care or interest.

Most of the tablets came from smaller mounds, and their discovery sometimes prompted archaeological campaigns like the one by de Sarzec in 1984 at Telloh, though the 3,000 tablets he found were but the meagre remains of plundered archives that had previously contained some 35,000 tablets.[40] Though the administrative texts were originally despised as mere 'laundry lists', their value as a source of information about many aspects of Mesopotamian culture soon came to be recognized. While some 25,000 have so far been published, the task is far from finished and the economic, anthropological and political analysis of the Ur tablets alone provides plenty of material for future generations of cuneiformists. The largest archive collections come not from the city of Ur itself but from smaller centres as well as from Telloh, Drehem (ancient Puzrish Dagan, a livestock centre) and Jokha (ancient Umma).

The Ur III bureaucrats worked within a hierarchically structured system that allowed competent officials to rise through the ranks. We can follow the careers of quite a few such people, thanks to the practice of recording the names of the scribes in charge. The tablets were also dated according to the system of year names (see page 125). The tablets record incoming and outgoing produce and livestock, details of contract labour, of work done and rations paid, projections of future agricultural yields as well as the actual harvest gain, allocations of seed grain and, of course, computations and receipts for taxes. The personal names of thousands of people employed by, or enslaved to, the large institutions, are preserved, and at least occasionally the tablets contain information about family size and residential customs.

A centralized economy and administration

It is clear that the state had monopolies over the production of certain items, especially textiles. Linen and woollen cloth were made into garments and the quality, cut and design were strictly controlled. Dress was a highly visible means of signalling status and some types of garments were worn exclusively by certain professions and people. As in the early days of the Industrial Revolution in Europe, women and female children were the primary producers of textiles and their status and working conditions similarly came below most other occupations.[41]

To maximize productivity, the state administration introduced various standard measures.[42] These largely replaced the earlier custom of individual cities controlling their own systems of weights and measures. Silver became the main unit of accounting and was in circulation in the shape of rods, from which the appropriate amount in weight was snipped off. Most importantly, the agricultural management seems to have been improved and investments were made by the central authority to implement superior irrigation techniques. Livestock raising, especially of cattle, seems to have been concentrated in the northern valleys that were climatically more suitable for the purpose. Fishing, fowling, horticulture and the growing of date-palms all became integrated within the economy, as the administrative texts show. This does not, however, mean that all economic activities were strictly regulated. We only have the official records of large institutions, such as temple or crown-owned estates. Smaller and private landholdings were evidently not obliged to keep accounts.

A new calendar was introduced, valid for the whole country, with years named after a significant event: for instance, 'Year the king's daughter married the ensi of Anshan' or 'Year the temple XY was inaugurated'. This custom had been in use since the Akkadian period.

Politically the country was divided into provinces, each with its own capital, and governed by an ensi (provincial governor) appointed by the king. The ensi was responsible for the maintenance of stability and the collection of taxes and answerable to the king. Individual cities were thus firmly integrated into a centralized state, and even temple holdings were controlled by government authority.

Ur as capital city

The fact that the first two kings of the Ur III dynasty had long periods in office – Ur-Nammu reigned for eighteen years, his son Shulgi for forty-seven – contributed to the successful implementation of reforms and administrative changes. The city of Ur became the capital of this wealthy empire and was, as the seat of the ruling dynasty, the primary focus of their building activities. In fact, the present appearance of the ruins, cleared by Woolley and restored by the Iraqi Antiquities Department, could be said to reflect the glory of the Third Dynasty.

The huge ziggurat, the best-preserved example of this typical Meso-potamian building type, is the one that was built by Ur-Nammu and completed by his son and successor, Shulgi (2094–2047). It stood within its own enclosure and was orientated to the points of the compass. It was built in three stages, rather like a huge sandcastle, with one layer on top of another, each a bit smaller than the one below. The core was of mudbrick, probably encompassing the ruins of an earlier structure, and this core was faced with a 2.4-metre-thick skin of baked brick set in bitumen to protect it from erosion. The lowest stage measures 61 by 45.7 metres at ground level, but somewhat less at its top, since the walls were, rather than vertical, inclined for added stability. It is 15 metres high.

Only a few metres of the second stage are preserved. Access to it was by three ramps, the middle one of which rose from the ground at right angles to the outer face, with a lateral ramp on each side, parallel to the body of the ziggurat. It is not certain how the stairs continued and how many stages there were originally. Nor do we know whether or not there was a high temple on the ultimate platform. The whole massive structure was very carefully built with ample drainage pipes to the core. Woolley also discovered that the brickwork was reinforced and insulated with thick layers of reed matting, which are thought to have spread the weight of the brickwork more evenly and absorbed moisture from the core.

The ziggurat, elevated on its own platform and surrounded by double walls, must have been an impressive landmark as it towered above the city walls. Its Sumerian name was **é-temen-ní-gùr-ru**, 'House whose foundation platform is clad in terror'. Woolley believed that the terraces were not paved but planted with trees, like 'hanging gardens', with the niches in the burnt-brick cladding serving for drain-age and to secure watering hoists. Such a 'pine-topped crag-like' struc-ture suggested to him that the original conception of the ziggurat was to be a Mountain of God[43] – a support for the notion that the 'Sumerian homeland' was a 'wooded and high-lying country' and that, upon their arrival in the flat south Mesopotamian landscape, they had to build 'the high place which nature had failed to provide – using brick instead of stone and slime (bitumen) for mortar'.[44] There is little archaeological support for the existence of plantations on ziggurats, and it would have demanded considerable ingenuity and labour to maintain any vegetation in such an exposed place. There is also nothing in the Mesopotamian literature that would substantiate any such practice. Nor is it likely that the ziggurat was meant to imitate or evoke a natural mountain. On the contrary, the strict orientation to the points of the compass, the architectural features, such as the regular, rhythmical articulation of the buttresses and recesses in the façade and the elaborate stairways, all emphasize the artificiality of the construction. The ziggurat is also a further development of the old practice of layering one platform above another, of encasing and elevating foundations on to ever higher levels. It has been pointed out that in areas prone to flooding this was also a practical device and the towering sanctuaries must have been reassuring sights as high and therefore safe places, not necessarily to keep the people safe, but to protect their gods, upon whose benevolence all life depended. It also allowed the chosen representatives of humankind to approach the heavenly sphere more closely.

To what extent they also served as observatories for astronomical experiments, another cherished theory, is unknown. The ziggurats in the context of the southern city were as urban in their connotation as the downtown high-rise skyline is in our age. In our capitalist world, skyscrapers accommodate corporate business and symbolize dynamic enterprise, with the straight sides and almost invisible taper emphasizing essentially democratic values. In Mesopotamia, the ziggurats suggest eternal values and a hierarchical social order. Their broad foundations rest firmly on the ground and ascent is slow and processional, hundreds of steps on broad ramps leading to the higher platform. Skyscrapers only became possible after the invention of electric lifts! The ziggurat was functional, too. Though solid and inaccessible inside, and not hollow, it incorporated accumulated sanctity from previous building, again firmly enclosed and protected. As an architectural structure its purpose was entirely ceremonial, the purest expression of urban monumental architecture in Mesopotamia.

For Woolley, steeped in biblical imagery, the ziggurat brought to mind a vision 'which showed to Jacob ladders set up in heaven and the angels ascending and descending on them' as he imagined 'priests in robes of state bearing the statue and emblem of Nannar up and down the triple staircase against the background of coloured brick'.[45] He was not far off the mark with this spectacular evocation, since some texts do indeed describe, though summarily, the celebration of rites on the ziggurat, and on the flat temple roofs alongside. Bearing in mind my contention that the mass spectacle and publicly performed rituals were of the utmost importance for the collective experience of the city, and, at that time, for the whole of the country, it seems no wonder that the founders of the first coherent, centralized state built ziggurats, and not just at Ur, though naturally the largest and most important was erected in the capital. Nearby Eridu was revived, and Amar-Sin, grandson of Ur-Nammu, built the ziggurat there. In terms of social semiotics, these structures also fitted the age, since the tiered ziggurat could be understood as a vast, three-dimensional symbol of hierarchical society whose uppermost level touched the realm of divinity.[46]

The ziggurat, though the most visible feature from afar, was only a part of the religious ceremonial precinct of Ur. As has been mentioned earlier, the whole area stood on an artificial platform retained by a heavy brick wall (up to 22 metres thick and 8 metres high) with a strongly inclined outer face (45 degrees). The flat buttresses repeated the rhythmical articulation of the ziggurat, which underlined the conceptual unity of the Ur sacred precinct. The north-west side was dedicated to the moon-god Nannar. It comprised the courtyard, enclosed by a double wall with an elaborately buttressed façade and one massive gate tower. Next to it was a large square building called the Enunmah, the purpose of which is not clear. Perhaps it served as a treasury.

The Gipar and Ur in later history

The south-east side, sacred to Nannar's spouse Ningal, was occupied by a huge and complex building known as the Gipar. It is one of the most interesting monuments of Ur, mainly because of its importance for the religious life of the city.[47] This Ur III structure was probably built above an earlier building that may have gone back to the Early Dynastic period: remains of walls with the characteristic planoconvex bricks have been found. Since we know that the Gipar was in use during the Akkadian period when Enheduanna, succeeded by Naram-Sin's daughter Enme-Nannar, was in residence, and thereafter when Ur-Bau of Lagash installed his en-priestess, the building had been in continuous use up to the beginning of the Ur III period, at which time it was much enlarged and completely reorganized.

According to traditional procedure, the builders began by erecting a terrace over the razed earlier structures. On top of that, occupying the whole surface, they built another sub-structure, tracing the complete plan of the eventual building in thick short mudbrick walls. This space was then filled in and levelled, and above it rose the real walls. Inscribed door sockets name Ur-Nammu as the builder. His grandson Amar-Sin contributed with furnishings such as doors.[48] Enclosed by the same kind of heavily buttressed wall as all the other buildings of the enclosure, it was internally divided in half by a corridor running across the whole width of the building. The internal arrangements comprised courtyards, surrounded by rooms of varying sizes. These have all the characteristics of domestic architecture, as well as of service areas, including ample storage, kitchen facilities and similar secular amenities. The building not only served as the main residence of the en-priestess and her numerous entourage and servants; it was also the residence of the goddess Ningal, who had her own 'apartments' almost parallel to those of the en. The central courtyard was surrounded by multi-functional rooms, just as in a private house; there were storage jars and an archive detailing the running of the estate, and the *cella*, or cult room, with its anteroom exactly corresponding to the reception room. Here the statue of the goddess was placed on a raised dais.

In addition to this divine establishment, there were further ritual installations close to the priestess's living quarters, and as we know from texts, she was expected to devote time 'to pray for the life of the king'. The excavations have shown clearly that this building continued in intermittent use a long time after Ur III. In the period following the demise of the dynasty, the role of the en (Akkadian: *entu*) had become so important that there was even a cult for the dead priestesses whose tombs were within the Gipar; some still received regular and special offerings sixty years or so after their deaths.[49] Interestingly, the comprehensive restoration work at the time was undertaken by an en-priestess, Enannatum, daughter of Ishme-Dagan of Isin (c.1953–1935 BC), according to inscribed bricks.

The Gipar then experienced periods of successive decay and restoration until the office finally fell into oblivion. Only during the last phase of Mesopotamian independence was the institution revived one last time. This happened in the course of initiatives by the last Babylonian king, Nabonidus (555–539), to revitalize obsolescent temples and offices. We know about this only from the king's lengthy inscriptions describing this enterprise. As he records, no one alive at the time knew about such priestesses and he only found out about them from an old inscription left by Nebuchadrezzar I (1126–1105), which depicted a priestess and listed her accoutrements.[50] In his search for authenticity, he copied the dress and the regalia for his daughter Ennigaldinanna, the last *entu*-priestess. She had a collection of antiquities in the Gipar consisting of old inscribed bricks and votive offerings. This Babylonian princess, self-consciously reviving or rather reinventing an ancient office, represents the last in a long line of women, from Enheduanna in the twenty-third century onwards, who mediated between the political aspirations of their fathers and the timeless exigencies of the gods.

Ur III kingship: the royal hymns

Although the old Akkadian royal inscriptions, still visible on the statues displayed at Nippur, were studied and transmitted in scribal circles, they were not the blueprint for the Ur III royal inscriptions. Perhaps the disintegration of the Akkadian empire, the long years of foreign domination and the struggle to overcome the separatist tendency of the old cities militated against the official glorification of political and military power. It must also be remembered that the new 'empire' was operating from two traditional southern cities, Uruk, the home of the dynasty, and Ur, the new capital. The long tradition of local forms of rulership in each of these cities influenced the outward form and the language of royalty in this age. It is therefore also not surprising that the Ur III kings emphasized their religious and ceremonial role and reinterpreted high priestly offices in order to strengthen their own sacerdotal functions.[51]

Although the strength and success of the Ur government depended to no small extent on conquest and the use of force, victories and battles were, with rare exceptions, proclaimed through year names rather than literary compositions. The royal hymns which became the main literary genre of the Ur III state are thus very different from the Akkadian royal inscriptions. They generally choose not to dwell on worldly achievement, the Ur III kings being anxious to show their respect for tradition and religious customs. At the same time, they succeeded in achieving quite unprecedented control over religious institutions and temple estates, and they gave themselves the supreme right to assume the most important ceremonial and ritual roles. The idea of the king as supreme mediator between the gods and the people had by then become an old tradition and the Akkadian cult of kingship was revived. This created the distance between the king and his subjects necessary to implement radical political and economic changes.

The royal hymns were an important medium for the formulation and propagation of these ideas. They survive mainly in the form of Old Babylonian school copies. The genre flourished particularly during the reign of Shulgi, son and successor of Ur-Nammu, who ruled for forty-seven years from 2094 to 2047. There are several different types of royal hymns, some addressed to the king in an elaboration of the formulae that invoke divine blessings 'for his life', others much more complex and providing for utterance by the king himself. It is very likely that they were performed and sung at ceremonial occasions at the court.[52] The language of all these hymns was Sumerian, even as it was the language of all official written documents, and it has been suggested that this was another attempt to widen the gulf between the ruling élite and the common people, who at that time (if they ever had done) no longer spoke Sumerian.[53] The efforts of the courtly poets to produce finely honed Sumerian literature, replete with all the artifices of the craft, demonstrate the continuing vitality of the language in intellectual circles.[54] The most important remit of these hymns was to reiterate the special status of the king as 'chosen by the gods',

> Shepherd Shulgi, when your seed was placed in the holy womb,
> your mother, Ninsun, gave birth to you, your personal god, pure
> Lugalbanda, fashioned you, mother Nintu nurtured you, An gave
> you a good name, Enlil raised your head, Ninlil loved you.[55]

and to immortalize his name:

> For the king to make his name
> pre-eminent for future times,
> so that Shulgi, king of Ur,
> make the song of his strength, the song of his might,
> the eternal message of his all surpassing wisdom,
> to transmit (it) to posterity for future times
> I laid it before the strong one, the son of Ninurta,
> before his eyes for future times.
> He praises his strength in song,
> wisdom, the precious gift, which is his, he praises.[56]

All aspects of the king's personality were subject to praise: his looks and stature – 'My king, who is as strong as you? Who can rival you?' (Shulgi D refrain) – his intelligence, his athletic prowess, his skill in the ancient royal arts of hunting (he fights the lions face to face rather than set a trap) and his learning: 'No one can write a tablet like me (. . .) adding, subtracting, counting and accounting, (I) completed all (the courses)' (Shulgi B, C).[57] He excels at music, his voice is exceedingly sweet and he plays even the most difficult of instruments. He is also skilled in the reading of omens; no one can interpret the livers as expertly as he.[58] These hymns naturally flatter and exaggerate, but they also reveal which qualities and accomplishments were deemed praiseworthy at the court. Certainly music and poetry played an important role, and it appears that even some of the royal ladies also attempted to compose (or at least commission some minstrel) lyrical pieces, often alluding to sexual intimacy with the king.[59]

It is tempting to dismiss these paeans to the perfect ruler as typical products of sycophantic court poets that have limited relevance to the world beyond the royal palace. It is hard to imagine that these highly crafted songs in a none too current language would have been 'popular'. They are interesting, though, for the concept of kingship proposed. On the one hand, the king is undeniably human, albeit a particularly accomplished specimen, who fulfils his royal duties with zeal and wisdom. On the other, he is distinguished by a close affinity with the gods, not just as a representative of mankind but in some way as related to them. The most interesting relationship is that between the king and the goddess Inanna, a subject we have already touched upon in other contexts.[60]

The king as the consort of Inanna

In Ur III times, especially during Shulgi's reign, the king is regularly called the 'husband/consort of Inanna', not just 'beloved', like the Akkadian kings, or 'chosen in the heart of Inanna'. In fact, several royal hymns specifically allude to the sexual nature of the bond. In the following extract from one of the Shulgi hymns, the goddess speaks about the king as the shepherd Dumuzi, who was traditionally the lover and bridegroom of Inanna. There were numerous songs celebrating their courtship.[61]

> Since by his fair hands, my loins were pressed,
> Since the lord, the one lying down by Holy Inanna,
> The shepherd Dumuzi
> In (his) lap smoothed me with milk
> Since in my . . . pure arms . . . he relaxed,
> Since like choice . . . (and) choice beer . . . he touched
> [since] the hair of my lap he [ruffled] for me,
> Since with the hair (of) my . . . he played,
> Since on my pure vulva he laid his hands,
> Since in . . . of my sweet womb he laid down,
> Since like 'his black boat' he . . .
> Since like 'his black barge' he . . .
> Since on the bed he spoke pleasant (words),
> I (also) will speak pleasant (words) to my lord,
> A good fate I will decree for him.[62]

The goddess is so pleased with his love-making that she blesses him in the customary expression by 'decreeing a good fate'.

In many of the Ur III texts concerning Inanna, her libidinous power is her main asset. She is the goddess of a primal drive strongly resembling the Freudian *id*. Inanna is described as ambitious to the point of aggressiveness, as one 'who loves battle' and is endowed with a huge sexual appetite. In contrast to the fertilizing and impregnating powers of the male gods, such as Enki, her special gift is desire, associated in the texts with the vulva, whose orgasmic potential is seen as boundless.[63]

Enheduanna in Akkad times had emphasized the destructive potential of Inanna's vitality, the terrible *me* of the goddess. Now, in the Ur

III period, we have another case of adjusting theological thinking for political reasons. The king as Inanna's consort is a complex notion, belonging at one level to the metaphorical kinship with the major deities that expresses the ruler's close links with the gods of the land. The king is called the 'child' of Ninsun, the 'brother' of (the divine) Gilgamesh, the 'son' of Lugalbanda and the 'husband' of Inanna. As the husband of Inanna, he is also Dumuzi the Shepherd. There are many stories about the Shepherd. He acts like a real shepherd; he is out in his sheepfold, surrounded by copulating animals. Inanna impatiently longs for the consummation of their union. But he is also doomed; most famously in the myth 'Inanna's Descent into the Netherworld'.[64] A number of songs and poems dwell on his restless and ultimately futile flight from the demons of the underworld.

The royal hymns that portray the king as Dumuzi do not refer to the unhappy fate of Dumuzi. Instead in these he fulfils the role of bridegroom of the goddess, in the same way as Enheduanna had been called the 'bride of Nannar'. Perhaps this may be seen as a reinterpretation of the old en-office, traditionally held in Ur by a female and by a male in Uruk. This may also explain the popularity of stories about the kings of the First Dynasty of Uruk, who ruled nearly a thousand years before the Ur III kings. Current in these narratives is the notion that the intimate relationship with Inanna was of fundamental importance to the ruler. The stories all concern the rivalry between Uruk and the land of Aratta, which is described as being somewhere in the eastern mountains.

The outcome of the cities' rivalry is presented as hinging on the question as to which en, that of Uruk or that of Aratta, will please Inanna more. Enmerkar at some point even taunts the en of Aratta with the assertion that he can only see the goddess in a dream, while he, Enmerkar, actually lies down with her, 'in sweet slumber', and that he accompanies Inanna 'for fifteen double hours on the adorned bed'.[65] These stories may well incorporate older narrative themes, and should not be seen as completely new fabrications of the Ur III court poets. However, the stress on the male en-ship as a typical Uruk institution and the source of secular power remains significant. Shulgi, having assumed the title of 'en of Inanna', could use the Uruk narratives to make a point about his own conquests and reforms that were presumably sanctioned by Inanna's 'love'. His fictional kinship with the gods, and especially his 'marital' relations with Inanna, were perhaps meant to deflect criticism for his more controversial reforms, such as his interference in temple administration. From his twenty-first regnal year onward, he put many of the hitherto independent old Sumerian temples under state control and exacted taxes from them.[66] Only a few, such as the Inanna temple at Nippur, enjoyed relative self-determination.[67]

Another of Shulgi's hymns describes the king's tour of all the major shrines of his realm.[68] Such public displays were important since they allowed the ruler to put on a terrific show with lavish offerings and ostentatious display. Again we see the importance of public ritual against the backdrop of the Mesopotamian cities, and the intimate connection between the religious, ceremonial sphere and *realpolitik*. A strong centralized government with far-reaching mechanisms of control still needed to make certain that the old institutions, especially the main temples in the cities, were not too much in opposition. The king could achieve a measure of direct control over the chief official position in the temple hierarchies and declare certain sectors, especially the economically productive ones of agriculture and textile manufacturing, dependent on state supervision, but all this needed to have divine approval. Appointments, for instance, were made upon oracular decision (which could be repeated until the ritually correct and politically acceptable verdict was reached); major reforms could be justified as being based on the counsel of the gods.

The king's impeccable credentials to display his close collaboration with all the major deities were equally vital. The various cults of the city gods were brought into a dynamic system whereby the divine statues went on long 'journeys' along the main waterways, 'visiting one city after the other' as if they were relatives; which of course they had all in some way become as a result of the rearranged official pantheon organized along patrilinear kinship structures that echoed those of the contemporary society.

The end of Ur III

The success of the Ur III government in exercising such unprecedented control was also a contributory factor in the dynasty's downfall. The complex mechanism of bureaucracy impeded quick decision making. The over-production of cereals led to increased strain on the soil and a fall of productivity. The tax exaction system, which continued to be efficient, became more and more burdensome to larger sections of the population. New waves of immigration, coming from the western desert fringes and beyond into the Akkadian heartland, destabilized the political balance in the dependent territories.

The Amorites, or Martu, as the newcomers were collectively called, were tribally organized groups, but not necessarily the wild and lawless nomads the Mesopotamian texts portray. As in subsequent periods of mass immigration, the newcomers could count on some existing networks, either through clan connections or reciprocal exchange, which allowed them to establish a foothold among the populations already in place. In Babylonia and the middle Euphrates regions especially, Amorite chiefs carved out new domains of influence, and a fierce rivalry for grazing grounds, arable land and political influence ensued. The Ur government lost control over the eastern and north-eastern provinces, and then, in a desperate attempt to stop the spread of revolt and immigration, king Shu-Sin (successor of Amar-Sin, c.2037–2027) ordered a wall 170 miles long to be built. The last Ur III king, Ibbi-Sin (c.2026–2004), faced not only continuing expansion by the pastoralist tribes but also rebellion within the Sumerian heartland. Through a mixture of diplomacy and military action, he managed to maintain a precarious peace, until finally his policy of securing support through short-term alliances with increasingly powerful provincial rulers failed. The situation may be gleaned from a series of letters the king exchanged with a certain Ishbi-Erra, a former governor of Mari, a vassal and official of Ur, who had gained much influence in Middle Babylonia. When the capital experienced an acute shortage of food, Ishbi-Erra was able to hold the city to ransom over shipments of grain. He formed alliances with Nippur and Isin, playing one off against the other, teaming up with other enemies of Ur and eventually taking control over the remnants of the Ur III empire and founding a new dynasty at Isin.

The city of Ur was devastated and destroyed, not by the Amorites or Ishbi-Erra's troops, however, but by the long-oppressed inhabitants of Elam and Shimashki, provinces in western Iran that had been annexed by Ur. The destruction was thorough and devastating. The sacred precinct was sacked and burnt, the temple treasuries plundered, the residential districts razed, and those survivors not taken into captivity faced slow death from starvation or disease as the surrounding fields were torched and the waterways became contaminated. This at least is the scenario depicted in a long Sumerian poem of some 520 lines.[69]

'The Lamentation over the Destruction of Ur'

The poem evokes the suffering of the city, its gods and people, as well as the effects of the capital's destruction on the country as a whole. This is generally expressed in negative sentences, as a discontinuity of the normal state of affairs:

> That on the banks of the Tigris and Euphrates 'bad weeds' grow,
> That no one sets out for the road, that no one seeks out the highway,
> That the city and its settled surroundings be razed to ruins,
> (. . .)
> That the hoe not attack the fertile fields, that the seed not be planted in
>   the ground,
> That the sound of the song of the one tending the oxen not resound on
>   the plain,
> (. . .)
> That the song of churning not resound in the cattle pen.

The gods abandon their shrines and the temples become defiled, the en-priests are abducted, the cattle and sheep of the temple estates slaughtered, the treasuries looted. Then the situation at Ur itself is described, a state of famine depriving even the king of food and drink, all storehouses being empty. Even 'the dogs of Ur no longer sniff at the base of the city wall', for there are no longer any scraps to be found. The gods then decide that the long-suffering country be restored again, that the evil should befall the enemy nations instead. The poem ends with a series of positive decrees or blessings and, in a reversal of the initial curses, heralds the return to a state of prosperity:

That the Tigris and the Euphrates (again) carry water – may An not
 change it,
(. . .)
That there be watercourses with water and fields with grain – may An not
 change it,
That the marshes support reeds and new shoots in the canebrake – may
 An not change it,
(. . .)
That the land be populated from north to south – may An not change it,
(. . .)
That cities be rebuilt, that people be numerous – may An not change it,
(. . .)
May a good abundant reign be long lasting in Ur.
Let its people lie down in safe pastures, let them copulate!
(. . .)
O Nannar – oh your city! Oh, your temple! Oh, your people!

As the translator of this poem points out, the text was written to
show the continuity between the Ur state and the succeeding dynasty
of Isin created by the ex-Ur governor Ishbi-Erra, although the Isin
government is never explicitly mentioned. The composition was mod-
elled on the 'Curse of Agade', but here the hapless last king of Ur,
Ibbi-Sin, is not accused of any sacrilegious act but presented as the
victim of a fate decreed by the gods.[70] The great gods, especially Enlil,
can bestow political might and prosperity on a city of their choice, and
they can equally withdraw this support without apparent reason. Now,
so the poem implies, it is the turn of Isin, and its very triumph over Ur
is a sign that the gods approve of the change.

Ishbi-Erra and his followers were quick to present themselves as
legitimate heirs of the Ur state and took over most of the ideological
trappings of the former 'empire', though neither Isin nor Larsa – both
cities vied for hegemony – managed to maintain their hold over Sumer
and Akkad. But apart from the political message of the Ur lamentation,
it gives an insight into the ideal vision of Mesopotamian life. It evokes
the rivers as the basis of all life, of the natural resources of marshes
and the well-managed farmland resounding to the songs of ploughmen
and dairy maids. Urban life is characterized by joyful activities, the

'bellowing of the temples' – a reference to the sounds of drums and other instruments – the abundance of food offerings, the smell of roasting meat; with an ordered social life, a functioning judiciary and elaborate rites performed by specialists.

Lamentations over destroyed cities became a genre of Sumerian literature in which a worst-case scenario was contrasted with the normal functioning of city and countryside. They were recited on the occasion of potentially dangerous activities which the gods could interpret as aggressive – especially the demolition of temple buildings for restoration purposes. The underlying theme, however, is that cities, dynasties and states are part of an ongoing ebb and flow of destruction and rebirth. The sack of one city, even the most devastating attack, does not mean an end for all cities, the demise of a royal line is not the end of kingship, a change of government does not imply a radical change of life for most citizens. Mesopotamians, perhaps because of their experience of an inherently unstable ecology, took a long-term view of the fundamental resilience and viability of their culture. The lamentations over destroyed cities were historical records lamenting actual destructions as an affirmation of faith that 'cities be rebuilt again', that life will continue.

As for the city of Ur, the fall of the Ur III dynasty meant that it lost its importance as the capital of an imperial power. But the city itself revived and continued to thrive for many more centuries. As a centre of learning it was very important in the Old Babylonian period and retained this prestige far longer than its political fame. It continued to be one of the great cult centres as the seat of the moon-god Nannar and his consort Ningal, with their strong links to the fertility of livestock, until the very end of the Mesopotamian era.

We have seen how the Kassite rulers rebuilt the sanctuaries and how the Babylonian kings contributed to the restoration and maintenance of Ur's temples. The old tradition of commerce was also maintained, as economic tablets show.[71] Ur is one of the best examples showing the tenacity of the Mesopotamian urban idea and how the accumulated sanctity of the religious precinct, combined with an urban infrastructure of considerable complexity, provided a matrix which could withstand political and economic failure and, even more important, success. Akkad and Nineveh, even Mari, never recovered from their glory of having been the epicentre of political power. Ur survived not only the destruction of the Elamites but the most centralized state system that the Near East had ever seen.

6 NIPPUR

The ancient place-name Nippur has survived for millennia, the modern village being called Niffer. It lies near the modern city Diwaniyah along the old Shatt el-Nil river bed, in the middle of the Babylonian plain. The Nippur region was marshland and in the 1880s accessible only by boat.[1] In Mesopotamian times the city lay on the Euphrates,[2] linked by this waterway with Sippar in the north, Kish, Abu Salabikh downstream, and Shuruppak and Uruk further south. Nippur's position in the geographical centre of Babylonia was an important factor in its development.

EXCAVATIONS AT NIPPUR

Nippur's ruins cover more than a square mile of land, with the highest point reaching 25 metres above ground. The site is bisected by a deeply cut watercourse, known by the local inhabitants as the Shatt el-Nil. There are thus several mounds on each side of the gully formed by the old river bed.

This large *tell* attracted the attention of explorers at an early date. The English adventurer and archaeologist Austen Layard arrived in 1851. He started to open up trenches at different points of the mound, an undertaking he was forced to abandon after a fortnight by the adverse climate of the region. He never returned.[3]

By the 1880s the Americans were beginning to take a keen interest in Near Eastern archaeology and joined in the race to discover more and better evidence for substantiating the truth of the Bible and to find antiquities.[4] When the University of Pennsylvania decided to send an expedition to Mesopotamia it chose the as yet unclaimed site of Nippur.[5] With no experience in the field, and no knowledge of local custom, J. P. Peters led the first season in 1887, a venture that ended with the siege and capture of the American camp, following the death of a tribesman who had been shot for stealing. Undeterred by this initial failure, Peters returned the following year and began, with his characteristic zeal, to explore the mound using a system of his own devising, digging trenches, tunnels and shafts at different points and dumping the spoil anywhere, the heaps of which soon reached alarming proportions.[6] Pressure to deliver results in order to secure funding apparently made such 'irrational' digging almost inevitable.[7] And the results were impressive: some 17,000 tablets were sent to Philadelphia.

In 1890 the highly ambitious German Assyriologist H. V. Hilprecht took over, assisted by the English architect H. Valentine Gere, who had worked with Flinders Petrie in Egypt. Hilprecht was keen to put the excavations on a more scientific footing and tried to copy the methodology of the German archaeologist Robert Koldewey, who was working in Babylon at the time.[8] Having spent one season on the site Hilprecht declared that the major work was done. Eager to put his site on the map and to score points for his adopted country, he widely circulated the idea that he had discovered the Temple Library of Nippur and publicized an account in his popular book *Exploration in Bible Lands* (1903). Its publication caused major controversy among scholars, his enemies pointing out that most of the tablets had in fact been shipped to America during the previous digs and that in any case 'Mesopotamia had no libraries'.[9] Hilprecht fought back by publishing several scholarly volumes on the tablets from the Temple Library.[10] There was also much controversy and unpleasantness over Hilprecht's position at Pennsylvania's new museum (founded in 1898), and squabbles over the ownership of tablets. The outbreak of the First World War put a stop to any further plans of excavation for the time being.

In 1948, the Chicago Oriental Institute, in temporary collaboration with Pennsylvania,[11] resumed work and began with systematic excavations which lasted for nineteen seasons, from 1948 to 1990.[12] This sustained effort produced important results: the temple of Inanna was found to have had a very long history, from the Early Dynastic period in the early third millennium until the Parthian occupation in the third century BC. Of particular interest were the excavations of the residential quarters of the city, where the Old Babylonian levels especially clearly showed the fluctuations of wealth and population density.[13] In one area, which became known as the 'scribal quarter',[14] large numbers of tablets were found in private houses which belonged to the local intellectual élite of the time.

The American team also made environmental-archaeological surveys which helped to establish the changing ecological situation of the city.[15] At Nippur one can see clearly the extent to which a Mesopotamian town depended on the fluctuations of the river course. Furthermore, Nippur's role within the early system of the southern city states and within the centralized kingdoms is unusual in so far as the city was never a seat of government but derived its prestige from a position of neutrality and its potential for legitimizing hegemony over the whole country. Finally, Nippur was a town of academics, a Mesopotamian Oxford or Cambridge, which gained it a reputation as much for intellectual snobbery as for erudition in obscure disciplines. The chapter will end with one of the few surviving stories from the oral tradition, which features an ordinary citizen who triumphs over an adversary through his wit and ingenuity.

HISTORY OF OCCUPATION

The earliest levels of occupation are only known from deep soundings and from discarded potsherds that became embedded in subsequent layers, but they prove that the site had been inhabited since the Ubaid period (5000 BC). The extent of the Ubaid settlement is unclear. It appears that the area later occupied by the Ekur, as the main temple of Nippur was called, was already a ceremonial or religious centre at that time. Towards the end of the fourth millennium, the western mound seems to have been occupied as well, as Uruk pottery and Jemdet-Nasr material have shown.[16] The city continued to expand along both sides of the river during the Early Dynastic and Akkadian periods (c.2600–2150).[17] The temple precinct of the Ekur was much enlarged at this time and a new temple, dedicated to Inanna, was built.

As with all major Mesopotamian cities in the mid third millennium, a massive wall protected the city.

As a recent survey of the settlement patterns of southern Mesopotamia has shown, the number of settlements in the Nippur–Adab region remained stable throughout the fourth millennium and then increased sharply from the Early Dynastic period onward.[18] Nippur reached its greatest size during the Ur III period, expanding to approximately 135 hectares.[19] The sanctuaries were rebuilt on an even grander scale, the domestic quarters expanded southwards, and the city wall was strengthened by Ibbi-Sin (c.2026–2004), who records this project as having occurred in the sixth year of his reign.[20]

In the Isin-Larsa and Old Babylonian periods (from c.2000 to c.1700) the city shrank in size and the entire southern mound became deserted. Neither were the walls serviceable, but some parts, especially the eastern half of the city, continued to be inhabited. A major catastrophe seems to have befallen Nippur in the eighteenth century, perhaps because of a shift of the Euphrates, which left the city cut off from its water supply. It was totally abandoned by 1720 BC.[21] Sand covered the city and perhaps only a skeleton staff remained within the Ekur temple to maintain minimal services.[22]

The recovery of Nippur took place in the fourteenth and thirteenth centuries, during the Kassite period. The Euphrates had returned; this time it ran west of the city, as indicated on an ancient map. The old river bed became known as 'Canal in the Middle of the City'.[23] The Kassite kings rebuilt the temples of Enlil and Inanna and constructed administrative buildings on the western mound. The city began to flourish again, although the old map shows that it did not reach the same size as before. Then fortunes changed again during the period known as the Dark Age of Babylonia, from the end of the Kassite period (1155) to c.800. Probably only a small village-size settlement remained on the old temple mound. Babylonian records report that the statue of Enlil had been stolen by Sutean and Aramaean tribes.

The city revived in the eighth century and grew rapidly in the seventh century, during the reigns of Shamash-shumu-ukin and his brother, Ashurbanipal.[24] The principal shrines were reconstructed, including the ziggurat, and residential quarters sprang up again in the southern districts. It is not clear where the Euphrates ran at this time – perhaps once more through the middle of the city.[25] In the sixth century Nippur's population included not only Babylonians and Aramaeans, but also large groups of exiled peoples who had been deported from their homelands. This practice had been initiated by the Assyrians to quell insurrections in colonial territories and provide labour and skill for agricultural and architectural projects in Assyria.[26] In and around Nippur, Lydians and Phrygians from western Anatolia were in one such community, Urartians and Melidans from central and eastern Anatolia in another.[27] There were also Greeks, Tyrians and Philistines from Gaza; as well as possibly Judaeans. Altogether more than eighty-nine settlements along sixty known canals are known in the Nippur region.[28] Some of these foreign groups were still living there two hundred years later.

The city was in decline during Neo-Babylonian times, but it became important again during the Achaemenid period (550–330), when the Persians built a new temple and several palace-like constructions. The economic prosperity of certain sectors of the population at least can be gleaned from the archives belonging to the wealthy Murashu family.[29] The city continued to grow in the Seleucid and Parthian periods (c.331 BC–AD 224). The large number of Seleucid coins shows it to have been an important site, and in the Parthian period (especially during the first century AD) Nippur became one of the largest cities in southern Mesopotamia. The Court of Columns (made of specially shaped burnt bricks) is the best-known monumental structure of this time. The city continued as an urban centre throughout the Sassanian and Early Islamic periods (AD 242–750) and had another peak of occupation during the Early Abbasid Dynasty, when Baghdad was the seat of the sultanate (AD 800). Thereafter it was abandoned again until the fourteenth and fifteenth centuries. This was the last urban phase in the city's long existence. During the Ottoman period, Nippur declined into the scattering of villages that exists on the site today.

This brief survey shows very clearly how closely the fate of Nippur depended on the behaviour of its main water source, the Euphrates. This is not unique to Nippur. Other cities along the river's course were similarly affected. The level plains of southern Mesopotamia provide no natural impediment to the movement of rivers, and especially not to a powerful waterway like the Euphrates, which carved itself a new bed every once in a while, only to revert to a former course at whim. In modern times, dams have slowed the current of the river, which makes it more controllable.

Gibson's account also demonstrates the relative fixity of the 'city'. While the populations expand or shrink, or even dwindle to almost nothing, the city with its shored-up, solid bulwark of building layers persists without losing either the status of city or its sanctity. This is the result of a belief that the *genius loci*, the city god, may choose to absent himself (or herself) for a while, but is nevertheless fundamentally tied to the place. The god's return may be signalled by a change in climate, by the waters' return or by renewed political stability. The sands are then swept out of the dilapidated temple precinct and a new beginning is marked by the restoration of the sanctuaries.[30] The prestige of Nippur as the seat of major Mesopotamian deities also made it politically expedient for hegemonic rulers to invest in the city, either by contributing valuables to the temple treasuries or by engaging in building activities. That they were anxious to commemorate their devotion to Nippur's gods in writing is shown by a number of inscribed objects or foundation documents that have been discovered, dating from the Early Dynastic period right through to Neo-Babylonian times.

NIPPUR AND ROYAL IDEOLOGY

All Mesopotamian cities were thought to depend entirely on the benevolence and active protection of the city gods. Since mankind was specifically 'invented' by the gods to provide services for them, the care of the local deities was, as a number of cosmogonic texts explain, the main duty of the citizens.[31] But the relationship between a city and its gods was not a straightforward contractual arrangement. As we have seen, Eridu was a sacred place because it was a manifestation of the Apsu. It was only secondarily associated with such divine personalities as Nammu, Enki and Damgalnunna. Eridu was thus in historical times the 'seat of Enki-Ea',[32] but once the Apsu could be represented in abstracted form as a shiny vessel or a pool that any temple could acquire, the site itself became less important. The Uruk tales of Enmerkar and Lugalbanda underline the idea that the goddess Inanna had to be seduced and wooed by the Urukian kings to concentrate her support on Uruk.[33]

In 'The Curse of Agade', the goddess decides on a whim to choose Sargon's new city for her home, but just as abruptly she deserts it again.[34] As soon as the gods leave, even temporarily, the city suffers and declines, only to revive upon the gods' change of heart. The question as to what might prompt deities to desert or return was answered in different ways, but first and foremost by the fatalistic acknowledgement that it cannot be answered because the ways of gods are different from mankind's. Gods are simply unpredictable. This attitude is perhaps a deep-seated response to the inherent ecological instability of Mesopotamia.[35] Why some cities should have a long-term successful relationship with their gods and others apparently not, or less so, is another question that interests the modern scholar as much as the ancient thinker. Uruk's triumph over 'Aratta', the mystical competitor 'in the distant mountains', is explained in various narratives that show how kings, through their intelligence, ingenuity or the support of powerful magicians, win the goddess's favour in contest.

The belief system that linked the survival and prosperity of the cities with the favourable disposition of gods also provided a basis for political manipulation. Military aggression against another city could be justified as acting on behalf of the city god;[36] the assumption of power by an individual could be ascribed to his special selection by the deity. All these themes were well developed during the Early Dynastic period, but there is no indication that any one city deity was fundamentally more important than another. With the emergence, some time towards the end of the Early Dynastic period, of a centralized political system in which a particular city claimed supremacy over as many other cities as possible, the ideological interpretation changed. This involved a restructuring of the individual city deities' relationship with one another and the promotion of one god as the ultimate arbiter of imperial control. The deity to emerge as the supreme instance of legitimization was Enlil, the god of Nippur.[37]

The reasons for this choice are still enigmatic. The most widespread theory, repeated in practically all standard works on early Mesopotamia, was proposed by Thorkild Jacobsen in 1957.[38] Nippur and Enlil, he argued, 'were recognized as the undisputed source of rule over

Sumer as whole', not because of a supremacy based on conquest but because Nippur was 'an original all-Sumerian place of assembly for the purpose of electing a common ruler'.[39] He envisaged the Early Dynastic political system as a form of alliance much like the classical Greek *amphictiony*, in which the local rulers of each city assembled to decide on important, supraregional matters, as all belonging to the Sumerian Federacy, or 'Kengi-League'.[40] In the course of time, as the concept of kingship developed, the assembly conferred or approved the assumption of power at Nippur, often following a military victory. Jacobsen based his analysis primarily on literary texts of a much later period, in which the gods were described as coming together at Nippur under the stewardship of Enlil.

It has since become clear that these ideas belonged to the Ur III period. A very important component of the Ur III ideology was the notion that there could only ever be one king to exercise legitimate control and that only the god Enlil had the authority to give validity. He alone could bestow 'kingship' on one city after another. Any ruler aspiring to the title 'king of the land', which implied control over all of Sumer and Akkad, had to be officially recognized and crowned by Nippur.[41] The Ur III scribes, who were well acquainted with the third millennium royal inscriptions, compiled a list of dynasties in which only one of the many contemporary city states is said to have exercised kingship. The result is known as the Sumerian King-list, which to some extent still informs the terminology of modern historians.[42]

Another pseudo-historical document relating to Nippur is the so-called 'Tummal Inscription',[43] which records the history of the Ekur, Enlil's main temple at Nippur, and that of the Tummal, shrine of Enlil's consort Ninlil. The first king listed as the builder of Ekur is Mebaragesi of Kish (Early Dynastic period II). His son Agga is accredited with the construction of the Tummal, followed by some other Early Dynastic kings, Gilgamesh of Uruk, Mesannepada of Ur, and then straight on to the founder of the Ur III state, Ur-Nammu, and his successors. The text thus emphasizes that the Ur III kings observed the ancient custom of royal construction work at the Nippur temples in response to their election to kingship.

The Ur III 'tradition' of Nippur's role as king-maker proved remarkably tenacious. It was wholeheartedly adopted by the successors of the

Ur dynasty, the comparatively petty kings of Isin and Larsa, as well as by the Old Babylonian kings such as Hammurabi. Only towards the end of the second millennium did Marduk, city god of Babylon, usurp Enlil's function as bestower of kingship (Akkadian *ellilutu*, 'Enlilship'). The city of Nippur profited from this tradition in a variety of ways: the temples received many donations and costly gifts; kings anxious to seem traditionally pious contributed to the never-ending building maintenance or embarked on wholesale reconstructions;[44] the town was often granted exemption from labour or military services and taxes.[45]

While we can see how the Ur III scribes adjusted theological and historiographical notions to suit a centralized state system, they were not inventing the whole story but building on existing beliefs and institutions. Although Jacobsen's theory that representatives of all Sumerian cities met in assemblies has not been substantiated by Early Dynastic sources, some cities did form alliances.[46] There is no evidence in the Fara texts, however, that Nippur had a special status or that Enlil was a particularly important deity at that time. On the contrary, according to epigraphic and archaeological sources, Inanna, Enki and Ningirsu were the main gods, with cults and shrines not just in their original 'homes' (Uruk, Eridu and Lagash) but in many places throughout the land.[47] It seems that the elevation of Enlil was initiated or at least propagated on behalf of the city of Lagash, one of the most powerful cities in the period after the fall of Shuruppak (*c.*2350). This can be seen clearly in the main propaganda texts, the royal inscriptions. Enlil of Nippur becomes the father of Ningirsu and heads the list of the gods to whom his son swears the treaty oath.[48] This may have been due to a political alliance between Lagash and Nippur. Other rulers allied to Lagash adopted a similar phraseology.[49]

A result of the active promotion of Enlil was the reorganization of the pantheon, or rather the attempt to create a pan-Sumerian coherent kinship system for all the diverse city gods and goddesses of the land. Ningirsu, city god of Lagash, became the son of Enlil; previously he had been called the son of Enki and Ninhursaga.[50] Enannatum's successor Entemena further consolidated the influence of Lagash and continued to derive his legitimacy from Enlil in Nippur. The priesthood of Nippur was actively engaged in this process and at least one

Nippurite temple official appears in the Lagash texts.[51] Naturally the promotion of their deity could only benefit the city. It also gave the Nippur élite considerable political influence since it provided support for the claims to sovereignty of any suitable candidate, not necessarily a Lagash ruler. This happened during the reign of Uru-inim-gina (c.2378–2371), who through a series of reforms also managed to alienate the support of other Sumerian cities.[52] Although the king sent gifts to Nippur, it did not stop the priests of Enlil extending their support to Lugalzagesi of Umma, who defeated Uru-inim-gina. His long inscription on stone bowls that he dedicated to Enlil makes the Nippurian god responsible for his triumph:

When Enlil, king of all the lands, gave to Lugalzagesi the kingship of the nation, directed all the eyes towards him, put all the lands at his feet, and from east to west made them subject to him . . . Enlil permitted no rival, under him the lands rested contentedly, the people made merry and the suzerains of Sumer and the rulers of other lands conceded sovereignty to him at Uruk.[53]

As we have seen in the case of Akkad (Chapter 4), Lugalzagesi subsequently established the first united monarchy in Sumer and in turn strengthened the position of Nippur.[54] When Sargon of Akkad took away the kingship from Lugalzagesi after a series of battles, he displayed his new power in a brutally convincing way by leading the king of Uruk in a neck-stock to the Gate of Enlil at Nippur.[55] In the course of the Akkadian period, the importance of Enlil became solidified into a standard component of the ruling ideology and was revived by the Ur III government. At the same time, Nippur began to build on its status as a place for assemblies to arbitrate in all manner of decisions, especially legal cases, which were heard in the courtyard (kisallu) of the Ekur.[56]

The city's prestige as a politically neutral though influential city was responsible for its special status, which the local élite was careful to foster. This situation was most precariously maintained in turbulent periods, when rival dynasties fought for supremacy. In the aftermath of the collapse of the Ur III state, Isin and Larsa were engaged in just such a struggle and Nippur veered in its support from one to another, as can be seen from year names used in the city.[57] Such a situation was no doubt difficult for the senior temple officials and the inhabitants of the city. Although the use of force against Nippur seems to have been a rare occurrence, it remained a possibility and the population sought refuge elsewhere at least once during this time. It is not clear what real political weight the conferral of recognition by Enlil had at this point, but the consequences for making the right choice must have been contested and debated among the Nippur leadership, since the city relied to some extent on royal support. The kings of the First Dynasty of Babylon continued to acknowledge Enlil's rights to legitimize kingship.

Hammurabi declares in the prologue to his famous 'law code' that he was given 'Enlil-ship' by the great gods (Akkadian *ellilutu*). This abstract term isolates the supreme decision-making powers of the god, which would eventually be separated from Enlil and given to Marduk when the theological system was reorganized during the Second Dynasty of Isin, and Enlil lost his superior position in favour of the Babylonian Marduk.[58] But while Enlil's authority may have been contested by the Marduk priesthood, it did not fundamentally diminish the prestige of Enlil or his city.

Having surveyed the political development of the ideological basis of Enlil's temple at Nippur, what do we know about this god?

ENLIL

In most popular reference works about Mesopotamian deities, his name is taken to be Sumerian, composed of the title en and the component lil, 'wind, ghost', and hence translated as 'Lord Air'. He was thought to represent the third component of atmospheric deities, together with An (heaven, above) and Enki (earth, below) occupying the place between heaven and earth. This assumption is based on later Babylonian theology, as represented by the Creation epic (known by its Babylonian title as the *Enuma eliš*). Here Marduk assigns the main gods different spheres of influence: Ea reigns over the Apsu, Anu in heaven, and Enlil in between the Anu's celestial abode and Marduk's temple at Babylon. This does not specifically connect him to the element 'air', which was not a cosmic notion in Mesopotamia. In recent years the etymology of Enlil has been re-examined and it is now thought that the name is the Sumerian rendering of an originally

Semitic word, the very word for 'god', *'il*, the root form of such well-known Semitic divine appellatives as El and, of course, Allah.[59]

Semitic-speaking people had been present in southern Mesopotamia well before the Fara period, and they brought with them their own gods, such as the various manifestations of weather gods generally associated with the Fertile Crescent and mountainous regions. Some divine personalities, well known from literary sources of the late third millennium, were the result of hybridization, or an amalgam of originally separate deities. This appears to be the case with Inanna, the goddess of Uruk, who merged with the Semitic Eshtar into a novel deity combining martial prowess with the powers of procreation and libido. Enlil is listed in the Fara god-lists, but he came relatively late to Nippur, where he may have replaced Enki.[60]

We have seen that the archaeologists discovered remains of monumental installations below the Early Dynastic shrine and that there were several temples at Nippur during this period. It seems that Nippur attracted the cult of several deities, a fact that may have something to do with its geographical position in the centre of the alluvial plains, between Jezirah and the deep south. It is possible that in this quite densely populated area, Nippur functioned as a neutral place for diverse groups of people who not only spoke different languages but represented different modes of living (farmers, herders, gatherers). By bringing their gods here, they may have been able to secure a representation of their interests. This might explain both the proliferation of deities at Nippur and the longevity of its reputation for political neutrality and a place where adjudications could be made. Enlil was the most famous and the most institutionalized arbiter of divine decision.

Enlil not only has an apparently Semitic name, he was also always associated with the word **kur**, which signifies both the physical realm 'mountain' and the cultural term 'foreign'. Furthermore, Enlil has all the characteristics of a weather god. Weather gods are typically unpredictable and often have irascible tempers; their favourite home is invariably a mountain.[61] Enlil's epithets are **kur.gal**, 'great mountain', and **lugal.a.ma.ru**, 'king of the storm'. His temple, it will be remembered, was called the **é.kur**, 'the house (is a) mountain'. All the extant versions of the flood story credit Enlil with control over 'the sluice gates of heaven' that drown the earth. The element of violence and sudden fury is as much in keeping with storm gods as is their benevolent rationality. In the Mesopotamian context, where agricultural production was independent of rainfall, the positive and fertilizing powers of weather gods were not so strongly stressed as in their traditional homelands, such as Syria and Anatolia. Accordingly, Enlil was feared and respected rather than loved, since his force was felt primarily in sudden floods, raging storms and, even more threateningly, the shifting of river courses.

In the later mythological tradition, Enlil's relationship with mankind is always problematic: he is easily roused to anger and impulsively gives in to his urge towards destruction. The flood myths describe how, when the noise generated by the masses of humans drives him to distraction, he immediately decides to wipe them off the face of the earth.[62] In contrast, Enki/Ea realizes in his wisdom that the gods depend on mankind and finds ways to foil Enlil's plans for annihilation. The customary connection of weather gods with fertility was also modified in the Mesopotamian myths. The major water symbol was, as we have seen, the subterranean Apsu, and Enki therefore represented the fertilizing powers of water. Various literary texts praise Enki's phallus as the male source of life-giving 'water' and his luxuriating in the marshes stands for the powerful connotations of moisture, dampness and fertility that inform the metaphors in Sumerian writing about joyful eroticism.[63]

Enlil's role in this context is interesting. Enlil's shift from northern weather god to pan-Mesopotamian 'father of the gods' is told in several narratives. In one story, 'Enlil and Ninlil',[64] he impregnates the nubile Ninlil in the marshes, despite her warnings that she is 'too young for kissing' and he will get punished. Indeed, Enlil's case is debated in the courtyard of the Ekur (as we have mentioned, the traditional place for problematic legal decisions!) and he is expelled from the city. Ninlil follows him, and they trick each other into mating three more times, begetting three underworld gods. A related story, 'Enlil and Sud',[65] also deals with his premarital adventures, except that this time he behaves in the culturally condoned manner. When he sees the young goddess, he politely inquires about her parents and then goes through the motions of formal proposal, the delivery of bridal gifts and finally the wedding. They marry in the traditional Mesopotamian manner and proclaim the victory of culture. The final lines of the hymns praise Nisaba, Ninlil's mother – who, as goddess of grain and writing, combined nature and culture.[66]

The story of 'Enlil and Ninlil', with its riverside location and emphasis on impregnations, works within the paradigm usually associated with Enki: phallic eroticism and potency. But the point is emphasized that this unlawful intercourse does not happen in some licentious swamp region, but in Nippur, a city that, perhaps more than any other in Mesopotamia, prided itself on learning, justice and moral standards. If Enlil is to be accepted as a Nippurian deity, he has to conform to the rules of civilized life. Ninlil's actions save him from his banishment and she is rightly praised in the concluding lines of the poem. In 'Enlil and Sud', the god follows the other traditional way of becoming acculturated, by marriage to a local 'girl'. The theme of a non-urban male marrying a city girl was very popular in Sumerian literature. Best known are the songs that celebrate the wooing of Inanna by the shepherd Dumuzi, who delights Inanna with his rugged outdoor manners.[67] 'The Marriage of Martu' describes how the unnamed daughter of Numushda accepts the proposal of the deeply uncivilized Martu, described with outright urban prejudice as belonging to people 'who eat raw meat, have no house and will have no decent burial'.[68]

The manner of Enlil's acceptance into the circle of Nippur gods, and his ambiguous role in the flood stories, point to a certain ambivalence about this god, which may betray a veiled criticism of Enlil's close connection with kingship, which was also a double-edged sword for his priesthood to handle.

NINURTA

The other important and equally ambiguous Nippurian god was Ninurta. His temple, the Eshumesha, was one of the largest temples in the city. He was known as the 'first-born' of Enlil, though, according to 'Enlil and Ninlil', the moon-god Nanna had been their first child. Ninurta was both an agrarian and a rain god, very contradictory roles for a Mesopotamian deity. A text dealing with the various tasks connected to the growing of barley was entitled 'Instructions of Ninurta'. A Sumerian hymn calls him 'the farmer of Enlil', whose 'life-giving semen' fills the canals and lets the barley grow.[69] However, there are other texts which stress the characteristics of a storm god.

One particularly revealing composition, known as 'The Return of Ninurta',[70] was written in the Old Babylonian period and copied many times thereafter. The long text is mainly taken up with an extensive hymn-like passage of self-praise uttered by Ninurta, the narrative framework concerning his return from having done battle in the **kur**, a summary term for the troublesome mountain regions to the north and east of the Mesopotamian plains. Ninurta is victorious over the hosts of the **kur** and drives his chariot, laden with war trophies, back to Nippur. In full battle regalia, surrounded by his captains, he is set to enter the Ekur, his father's temple: 'Ninurta, storm of the rebellious lands, swept like a flood, destroying the fortresses of the rebellious lands', comes with such force that his progress frightens the gods. Even Enlil is 'frightened in his residence'. At the same time, the envoy of the gods assures Ninurta that, because he has been so successful against the enemy, 'Enlil need send out no other god beside you.' When he hears this message, Ninurta

put the whip and goad away in the rope box, leaned his mace, the arm of battle, against the rope box and entered the temple of Enlil. He drove his captive wild bulls into the temple (. . .) and laid out the (booty of) his plundered city.

The gods are duly impressed, particularly his mother Ninlil, and 'even great mountain Enlil humbled himself'. Ninurta then begins his self-praise. Starting with an enumeration of his trophies, he sings about his awe-inspiring weapons and his irresistible and terrifying strength, concluding that he is simply 'the most able among the gods'. As Ninurta proceeds to leave the Ekur, he is humbly asked to 'be pacified toward your beloved city' and invited to return to his own temple, the Eshumesha, to 'tell your young wife, lady Ninnibru, what's in your heart, and to make favourable pronouncements for the king'. The concluding lines are:

Strong one, Deluge of Enlil, Ninurta, magnificent scion of Ekur, Pride of the father who engendered him, your praise is sweet.

In this myth, Ninurta shows that he is of the same stock as his father: he is a veritable 'deluge', and his youthful vigour is as yet unchecked. As in many myths, the younger god exaggerates the parental force and threatens to take over the father's power. The gods are worried about his excessive strength and only flattery seems to placate the overblown self-esteem of the young warrior. In fact, nothing happens, he shows off his trophies, is duly admired by the assembled gods and returns to his own temple and the company of his consort. The equilibrium and status quo are maintained. The text also vividly alludes to the potential danger of a victorious king as he approaches the city in triumph. It expresses the ambiguous reaction the city inhabitants and local government must have felt when a fully armed triumphant army made its way towards Nippur. As Cooper points out, the myth also affirms that the success of any real king in his battles ultimately depends on the will and support of Enlil and his son Ninurta.

The tension between Enki and Enlil (it is widely thought that Enlil's cult expanded at the expense of Enki's, which may account for a literary revenge by the priesthood loyal to Enki) is also passed on to Ninurta. In fact, it allows the tension to be articulated, since Ninurta is like a caricature of Enlil in terms of the exaggerated impetuosity. In the composition known as 'King, (the) Splendour of his Storm is Overwhelming' (**lugal-e ud me-lam-bi nir-gal**),[71] Ninurta journeys to Eridu to seek Enki's blessings, and behaves in a demanding and belligerent way. Enki's response is lost, but Ninurta returns satisfied. Another text sees his arrogance punished. Ninurta discovers that the young of the Anzu-Bird to whom he has apparently entrusted them, have dropped the Tablets of Destiny, and they have fallen into the Apsu. Ninurta now has to ask Enki's permission to retrieve them and Enki refuses. When Ninurta insists and even attacks Enki's vizier, Enki creates a giant turtle out of the Apsu-clay, which bites Ninurta's toes. Enki then digs out a pit into which both the young god and his tormentor fall. Only the supplications of Ninurta's mother persuade Enki to set him free and he reminds Ninlil that she now owes him a favour.

INANNA

Inanna's temple at Nippur was at least as old as the Ekur of Ninurta, according to the excavated structures. During the second half of the third millennium, Enlil, and to some extent Ninurta, were the deities most often invoked in written texts, and Inanna's temple seems to have received much less royal patronage, but this changed in the Ur III period when Shulgi ordered her temple to be comprehensively rebuilt and enlarged. Like other major deities, she had an original home base, Uruk, as well as temples in other cities.

It appears that, from the Ur III period onwards, the Nippur priests serving Inanna tried to define the particular manifestation of the deity she was thought to display there. One Sumerian hymn written during the Old Babylonian period, perhaps reworking earlier versions composed for the occasion of her taking up residence in the newly reconstructed temple, defines the range of her influence. She is the evening and morning star, the protectress of the flocks, who out in the rough sheepfold drinks from the trough with the animals. She seats the children of the afflicted on her lap, takes part in the sacrifice to the dead at New Year and joins An and Enki in the pronouncement of justice.

Her womanly side is also shown in all its complexity: like a homeless woman roaming the streets, she picks up strangers for company; as a harlot she goes to the tavern to find a man; or as the wife of Dumuzi she spends the night in her chamber, rejoicing in his arms.[72] Her relationship with Enlil was apparently neutral enough to merit no mythological elaboration. One hymn[73] states that she received special prerogatives from Enlil, 'who put the sky as a cap on my head, the earth as sandals on my feet'.

We can see that Nippur had several well-functioning sanctuaries apart from Enlil's Ekur, and each temple also had chapels for other major gods. In addition, Nippur was a major destination for 'journeys of gods'. This was a tradition, particularly during the Ur III period, of transporting the statues of deities from their home temples to other gods' temples, on a visit. One long Sumerian poem describes how the moon-god Nanna-Suen travelled to Nippur to seek Enlil's blessing.[74]

Nippur's investment in temples and its policy of political neutrality assured the city's special status for most historical periods. When Shulgi's reforms affected most sanctuaries, making them production places under central government control, the Inanna temple at Nippur enjoyed relative independence and self-determination, as the recently published archives show.[75]

TEMPLES, SCHOOLS AND ARCHIVES

Nippur was full of temples. A tablet discovered in a terracotta jar full of inscribed objects lists the total surface areas covered by temples in the city. During its time of composition, in the Kassite period, there were twenty-two shrines in the city, not counting the large ones of Enlil and Ninlil, Ninurta and Ninnibru.[76]

The concentration of temples and the absence of a secular governing body characterized the social, economic and political structure of the city. Rivalries between the different temples must have occurred, especially when royal largesse was directed at one temple to the exclusion of others. The 'Curse of Agade' seems to suggest, for example, that the Akkadian Naram-Sin, though certainly falling short of vandalizing Ekur as the text insists, at least diverted offerings from Enlil to Inanna.[77] The response of the injured priesthood was, as usual, a literary diatribe, cursing the memory of sacrilegious ruler, albeit not during his lifetime![78] When Naram-Sin confronted the rebellion of the southern cities, the priesthood of Ninurta backed a rival pretender to power, going so far as declaring him a legitimate king. The rebellion was suppressed and the Akkadian king asserted his authority. However, his successor, Shar-kali-sharri, was eager to ensure the support of Nippur and the priesthood of Enlil. These are just some examples of the interaction between politics and religion so characteristic for Nippur.

Temple organization
The establishment of several major temples, even if they were not equally prosperous or influential at all times, also accounts for the large number of personnel attached to each and the unusually high

concentration of literate persons. A significant percentage was attached to the sanctuaries and fulfilled one or several posts. The agricultural holdings of the temples were vast, and outlying positions supplied further commodities. During the Ur III period, most of the livestock for the temples came from Puzrish-Dagan (modern Drehem), as the archives discovered there demonstrate. Hundreds of thousands of people were involved in the activities connected to the temple economy. The temples also supervised the production of leather goods, woollen textiles and other craft articles. Hired labourers and dependants worked the fields, tended the gardens and kept the irrigation works in good order. Their livelihood came from the produce of their labour in the form of rations, mainly barley, oil and beer, the latter being a rich source of vitamin B and, since it was made with pure water, a healthy beverage albeit with a low alcohol content. The temple personnel also comprised singers and musicians, exorcists and diviners, and numerous other cultic specialists.[79]

It is still very problematic to discern particular functions and status from the titles borne by temple officials. There were variations of meaning depending on the deity, and changes throughout history are not reflected in the conservative nomenclature of titles. There was also considerable overlap between cultic duties and more secular positions. At Nippur especially, religious titles were linked to the political state of Nippur, which seems at least during the Ur III period to have been governed by a heterogeneous collective, the assembly of Nippur citizens, the governor (**ensi**) of the city, and the highest priests of the Enlil and the Ninurta temples.

Temple offices were enumerated according to status, either by usufruct of temple lands, which could then be leased, or rations, some of them large enough to be further distributed, some to cover subsistence needs. Some temple offices could be inherited, others were bestowed by the king, the temple authorities or, at least since the early second millennium, acquired through adoption. This was not infant adoption, but the incorporation of a non-related adult individual into the family in exchange for economic support. The adoptee was given otherwise inalienable agricultural property or temple offices in return. The archive of a certain Mannum-meshu-lissur illustrates a good example of this custom.[80] He was a typical *nouveau riche* businessman who became absorbed in a propertied but increasingly impoverished high-status family, then used his position to acquire large amounts of land and real estate which were tied to lucrative positions within the temple hierarchy.

Despite the number of large religious institutions, only one relatively small temple archive has as yet been discovered at Nippur. It dates from the Isin-Larsa and early Old Babylonian periods (specifically from year 1 of Lipit-Enlil of Isin to year 28 of Rim-Sin of Larsa – a time-span from c.1934 to 1794).[81] It is of great interest because the tablets employ a form of bookkeeping which lists incoming and out-going offerings and rations expenditures. One side includes the nota-tion sá-du and listings of various deities, sanctuaries and cult objects that were to receive the sá-du (Akkadian *sattuku*) offerings, the reverse side has the heading 'expenditure' and lists specific amounts of food-stuffs for individuals who are listed by their name or profession, usually in a consistent sequence. This shows that in practice the deities were presented with food and other items, which were then redistributed according to a predetermined ratio among the temple personnel. The degree of complexity involved in such calculations shows that some central authority was responsible, but it is not yet clear which organ-ization was in charge.

The scribes at Nippur

Further excavations may yet unearth the archives of the other great temples. The vast estates, with their thousands of dependants, could only have been administered by a large and well-trained bureaucratic staff. Furthermore, the demand for 'decisions' stimulated the provision of professional expertise, in either the study of oracles or legal matters. Finally, the liturgy of the gods involved the recitation of cultic songs, hymns and incantations, and there was also a demand for specially commissioned literary works, to commemorate the dedications of statues or the restorations of buildings by potentates. All these serv-ices depended on a large number of literate clerks, scribes and professionals.

It is therefore unsurprising that the tablets found at Nippur repres-ent an unusually complex collection of written material. Nearly 30,000 have so far been discovered, a large number of them dating from the third millennium. Most are written in Sumerian, and they include 2,100 literary tablets, the major proportion of all so far known. Almost all major Sumerian compositions come from Nippur, together with lexical texts and related reference works, as well as later Babylonian 'scientific' texts in the Mesopotamian sense – divination, omen collections, medical texts, astronomy.

The emphasis on a scholarly transmission of Sumerian, which had by the time of the Ur III period ceased to be a spoken language, seems to have been one of Nippur's special missions. Most of the literary tablets were found in houses in the 'scribal quarter' of Nippur, and date from the Old Babylonian period. Other urban areas (defined as TA and TB in the archaeological record) are well documented for a time-span of two hundred years (*c.*1923 to 1739), covering the turbulent times from the end of Ur III to the beginning of the Old Babylonian period, ending with the eighteenth-century catastrophe that led to the complete abandonment of the city in around 1720.[82]

During Ur III times, the 'scribal quarter' was primarily an administrative district, with senior officials living in large architect-built houses. The plans of the houses reflect the pattern still common in the Middle East nowadays: a single doorway leads into a large courtyard surrounded by various rooms and storage facilities; private rooms are arranged behind or at either side of a reception room. In larger houses it was possible to separate public and private spaces by one or more additional courtyards, and they also had facilities such as bathrooms, kitchens and stairways. The subdivision of large units into several smaller ones illustrate the difficult times when the city passed between the control of Isin or its rival Larsa. When the kings of Isin secured Larsa's domination over Nippur, this ushered in a two-hundred-year period of relative peace and prosperity. The residential areas TA and TB were reorganized, although TB continued to be inhabited by administrators and TA remained largely residential. The changes reflected in the plans of the buildings related to changes in the population and an increase of wealth.

One of the manifestations of prosperity was the greater importance of literacy. Several houses had facilities for scribal training, such as courtyards for teaching, with benches and containers for clay and water. Numerous tablets were found in these courtyards – exercise tablets, lexical lists and literary excerpts. It seems that most of the residents educated their children there, since school tablets were found in nearly all the houses. These schools, known as é-dub-ba ('tablet houses'), flourished until the reign of Samsu-iluna, Hammurabi's successor, when an economic crisis, probably caused by ecological problems, severely disrupted the life of the city. Scribes, as economically unproductive elements of society, were among the first to leave the city.[83]

Scribal schools, which are particularly well documented during the Old Babylonian period, are also known from other cities,[84] because of literary compositions which were set in the milieu of the é-dub-ba. The particular conditions of the early second millennium were what allowed for a greater diversity of scribal training. Methods of teaching and the curriculum were nevertheless surprisingly uniform in different cities and the main reference works were used for many centuries, copied again and again.

Sumerian, very much like Latin in the Middle Ages, was seen as the foundation of literacy. It acquired the status as a learned, professional form of communication. 'A scribe who does not know Sumerian, what (kind of) scribe is he?' asks one proverb.[85] The whole scribal training after the end of the third millennium was therefore based on a bilingual competency, as some passages in the often humorous 'Edubba texts' show, as where a student denigrates the abilities of one of his colleagues: 'He is a deaf fool when it comes to the scribal art, a silent idiot when it comes to Sumerian.'[86]

The training of scribes proceeded in stages. In the beginning the student learnt the basic skills of shaping and handling tablet and stylus.[87] Then he studied the syllabaries,[88] which taught the equivalent of the ABC, the standard sequence of sign values and their pronunciation. 'A fellow who cannot produce a–a, how will he attain fluent speech?' From there he progressed to lexical lists, usually beginning with god-lists: 'I have written (a tablet) from the different names of Inanna up to (the names) of animals living in the steppe (and the names of different) artisans!'[89] says one of the eager pupils in a dialogue. These lists, originally drawn up in Sumerian and arranged in groups according to the first sign denoting a category (such as 'animals of the steppe'), were useful vocabularies, since they gave the translation of the Sumerian entry in Babylonian.[90] Numerous school tablets, easily recognizable from their round shape designed to fit easily into the palm of a hand, contain excerpts from the standard lexical texts.

From such general linguistic training, teaching progressed to more specialized professional subjects. One such composition that may have originated in Nippur was called *Ana ittišu* after its first entry, a compendium of law and legal phraseology, again a bilingual text.[91] Letter writing in Babylonian was practised by following collected examples and students needed to be proficient in taking dictation and reading the contents aloud.[92] Scribes were also taught how to compose a public inscription for a stele, and royal inscriptions from previous dynasties were copied assiduously. Even more important was a thorough grounding in mathematics: 'Do you know multiplication, reciprocals, coefficients, balancing of accounts, administrative accounting, how to make all kinds of pay allotments, divide property, and delimit shares of fields?' asks the teacher in the so-called 'Examination Text A'.[93]

It is likely that not every student became adept in all the subjects taught and that individuals would select the 'courses' most suitable for their chosen profession. Those who aspired to the greatest learning would spend many years in acquiring the status of a senior scholar who could then pass on his learning. Familiarity with literary works was much encouraged during the Old Babylonian period, as the thousands of tablets with excerpts from well-known texts show. It has been suggested that some literary compositions, such as the school dialogues and perhaps some of the royal hymns, were composed in the Edubba. There were, as has been mentioned, quite a number of such scribal training establishments in Mesopotamia, and we sometimes know the names of the persons who ran them.[94] But as one appreciative student put it in a letter, 'in Nippur the Edubba is unique'.[95]

The reputation of Nippur's great learning is lampooned in another Edubba text, however. The main protagonist here is a doctor from Isin, a city famous for healing. The good doctor has cured a citizen from Nippur who has suffered from the effects of a dog bite, and the grateful patient promises the physician that, should he ever come to Nippur, he will feast him on fine food and give him high-quality beer to drink. When the doctor asks for directions as to how he might find his host, he is told to

enter by the Grand Gate and leave a street, a boulevard, a square, Tillazida Street and the ways of Nusku and Ninimena to your left. You should ask Nin-lugal-absu, daughter of Ki-agga-Enbilulu, daughter-in-law of Nishu-an-Ea-takla, a gardening woman of the garden Henun-Enlil, sitting on the ground of Tillazida selling produce, and she will show you.

The doctor manages to follow these complicated instructions and finds the woman, but when he asks her in Babylonian where to find his man, she answers all his questions in Sumerian. He suspects she must be cursing him and so she has to translate her responses for him. The little tale concludes: 'What a fool he is! The students ought to get together and chase him out of Great Gate with their practice tablets!'[96] In Nippur, so the tale would have us believe, even vegetable sellers spoke Sumerian.

The outstanding cunning and wit of the ordinary citizens of Nippur is the theme of another story, again associated with the literate city, which is one of the few folk tales to be known from Mesopotamia. The tale is now known as 'The Poor Man of Nippur',[97] its protagonist being Gimil-Ninurta, a wretched individual who 'lived in his city Nippur in abject misery'. He regularly goes to bed hungry and has no change of clothes to wear. He has just enough money left to buy a goat in the market and debates with himself what he should do with the animal. If he were to bring it home, his family would be angry, and furthermore there would be no beer to go with it. So he decides to take the goat to the mayor's house in the hope of being invited to a meal and given a decent drink in return for his gift. Off he goes to the mayor's with his goat, and presents himself to the doorkeeper. He is duly admitted to the mayor and recounts the reasons for bringing him the goat. Unfortunately the mayor does not respond as he has hoped, but gives Gimil-Ninurta only 'some bone and gristle and third-rate beer' before having him thrown out. Gimil-Ninurta manages to shout to the doorkeeper that, for the disgrace he has suffered, he will repay him threefold.

To carry out his revenge, Gimil-Ninurta first goes to the king and asks him for the loan of a new chariot for a day, as well as clothes fit for a nobleman. He also catches two doves and stuffs them inside a box, which he seals with a seal. Thus equipped, he drives right up to the house of the mayor, who, not recognizing him in his finery, receives him with all honours. Gimil-Ninurta informs him that he has come to bring gold for Ekur, the temple of Enlil. The mayor thereupon slaughters a fine sheep for a generous meal and, although the mayor is sleepy, Gimil-Ninurta keeps him up very late. When his host finally succumbs to sleep, Gimil-Ninurta slips out into the night, opens the box and releases the two birds, which fly away. 'Wake up mayor, the gold has been taken and the box has been opened!' he calls out, ripping his new clothes in anguish, and then sets about the hapless mayor, giving him a thorough thrashing until he cries for mercy. He also compensates his guest with a substantial amount of gold and gives him new clothes. As he leaves the house, Gimil-Ninurta calls out to the doorkeeper that, 'This was number one.'

His next ruse is to don another disguise to make him look like a doctor. He then presents himself again to the mayor, who shows him his bruises. Gimil-Ninurta informs him that he always carries out his healing in private, but once they are alone together in a private room, he ties the mayor up securely and gives him another beating from head to toe. 'I have requited two, one remains,' he shouts to the doorkeeper as he leaves.

For his last trick he pays a man with a goat and tells him to go to the mayor's house, shouting so everyone would hear him: 'I am knocking on the mayor's gate, I'm the man with the goat!' While the man does as bidden, Gimil-Ninurta hides under a bridge, 'like a dog', and watches the mayor emerge from his house, bringing with him the people of his household, male and female, who rush off in pursuit of the man. When all but the mayor have gone, he comes out from under the bridge and seizes the mayor, beating him a third time. Thus did the resourceful poor man of Nippur avenge an insult suffered at the hands of a powerful official.

Although a majority of the Nippur tablets date from the Isin-Larsa and the early old Babylonian periods, significant numbers date from later times, when Nippur again experienced prosperity and peace. The city never lost its association with learning and literacy, and one very interesting archive, comprising some fifty tablets, dates from the fourth century BC, long after Babylon had been defeated by the Persians, during the reigns of Darius II and Artaxerxes II.[98] The tablets belonged to the prominent family of Belshunu, an exorcist priest and his sons. Belshunu was a descendant of an ancestral scribe called Ab-sum-mu, 'the Sumerian', and the sons were also literate temple officials. They thus constituted one of the old scribal families whose ties to the Ekur went back for generations. The economic tablets shed light on the material aspects of their lives, such as the care of the estates that came with their offices and details of their supervisory duties. The professional tablet collection comprised excerpts from lexical lists, a copy of an Old Babylonian royal inscription, a hymn to Nergal, a list of deities, as well as a list of stones with magical properties, various rituals and incantations, lists of other products needed for magic rituals and a commentary on medical diagnostics and prognostics. It also included an astronomical text and the oldest known horoscope, cast on the occasion of the birth of one of Belshunu's sons.[99]

The archive thus documents how, towards the end of the Achaemenid period, the religious life in Nippur was still functioning and the ancient scribal tradition still being upheld by some of the city's old literate families, who looked after the administration, liturgical services and their professional specialisms. As Joannès points out, the sons of Belshunu were contemporaries of Plato, and the archive not only represents Nippur's long association with learning but also testifies to an interest in new developments, such as astronomy and astrology.

7 SIPPAR

A TALE OF TWO CITIES

Sippar lies some 20 kilometres south of Baghdad, where the courses of the Euphrates and Tigris come closest together. Like so many other Mesopotamian cities, its fate depended on the often erratic behaviour of these rivers, and the close proximity and interaction of the two flows resulted in particular hydraulic effects. According to geo-archaeological surveys the rivers were actually connected when the site was first inhabited during the Uruk period.[1] Deposits of silt left by the Euphrates formed levees to make a habitable elevation above the flood plains. The city itself was situated along the Euphrates. The high content of sediment carried by this river had the gradual effect of burying the older Tigris channels, pushing that river further to the east. At the same time, the raising of the river bed caused a shift of the Euphrates further westwards, which resulted in a steady separation of the twin rivers, leaving an area of land which could be cultivated.

Sippar's location not only ensured a relatively stable supply of water but also had important implications in terms of infrastructure. The main form of communication was along the rivers by boat. Sippar had access to both major streams and their side-arms, though, during the historical periods, the Euphrates was far more important than the Tigris as a navigable waterway. Sippar also occupied a central position in the wider Mesopotamian context, being within easy reach of the Assyrian plateau, the Jezirah and the middle Euphrates region that controlled access to the Syrian valleys. It is therefore not surprising that Sippar should always have been an important trading place. Because of its mercantile role, it was also rather more cosmopolitan than most other Mesopotamian cities.

Sippar was also an important religious centre. Two main deities were worshipped here in separate large temples: the sun-god Shamash and Annunitu, an Ishtar-like goddess. Since the sun-god was seen as an arbiter of justice in Mesopotamia, Sippar gained prestige as a city of fair dealing.

The site produced two layers of evidence, comprising, on the one hand, documents from the Old Babylonian period, spanning a period from about 1800 to 1600, and on the other, records from the middle of the first millennium, the last phase of Sippar's prosperity. The archaeology was complicated by the fact that its ruins were spread over two distinct sites, one being a mound now known as Abu Habbah, the other called ed-Der.

THE SITE AND ITS EXCAVATORS

In 1880, Hormuzd Rassam, a native of Mossul, who had worked with Austen Layard and gained possession of a comprehensive excavation licence from the Ottoman sultan, was entrusted with a mission to secure antiquities for the British Museum. When he came across the mound of Abu Habbah, conveniently elevated above the cultivated fields, the local sheikh readily granted him permission to explore the ruins. With a luck that came to be proverbial, Rassam had straight away hit on a most remarkable location. He had thought it best to begin digging at the highest point, which looked very much like the remains of a ziggurat, and sure enough, when the workmen had cleared away the surface debris, they uncovered a chamber with a bitumen-covered floor.

I lost no time in having the asphalt pavement broken into and examined, and to the surprise of the workmen and to my not a little delight, an inscribed earthenware basket, with a lid, was discovered in the southwest corner of the chamber, about 3 feet below the surface. Inside we found a stone tablet, 11½ inches long by 7 inches wide, inscribed minutely on both sides with a small bas relief at the top.[2]

It was a foundation document written by the Babylonian king Nabu-apla-iddina (c. 870) and carrying a neat inscription on the relief to say that it depicted the sun-god Shamash in his shrine called Ebabbar in Sippar. At one stroke it was possible to identify both the site and the part of the building in which the box had been found. Rassam instantly connected the name Sippar with the Sepharvaim mentioned in the Bible (2 Kings 17:24, 31), a passage recording that the king of Assyria settled people from this site in Samaria to replace the deported local inhabitants.[3] Much encouraged, Rassam continued his explorations for three months. He made a preliminary plan of the Ebabbar and estimated that it contained some 300 rooms and courtyards, of which he cleared around 170. His efforts were amply rewarded, for not only did he hit on what must have been the treasure chambers of the temple, filled with precious votive objects, he also found thousands of cuneiform tablets.

Unlike those he had previously unearthed in the Assyrian palaces, these tablets had not been baked in antiquity and 'the clay had become so friable that as soon as they were exposed to the air they crumbled to pieces'.[4] His solution was to bake them *in situ*, with the result that they clumped together. Nevertheless he estimated that he had been able to ship a consignment of some 50,000 tablets to London before he had to leave Sippar abruptly when his permit from the sultan was withdrawn. The contents of the many crates he sent to the British Museum not only contributed some of the most interesting objects to the museum's collection, quite apart from the rich epigraphic material, but also provided an insight into the history of Sippar, for which detailed archaeological evidence was lacking.

The oldest object was a stone vase from the Jemdet-Nasr period (*c*.3000). There were numerous other objects and vases from the Early Dynastic period, among them a statue dedicated by a king of Mari called Iku-shumugan, which provided the earliest historical record from Sippar so far known (*c*.2500). The Akkadian kings Manishtusu, Rimush and Shar-kali-sharri contributed inscribed mace heads and other stone objects, venerable artefacts that were preserved in the temple along with other donations from kings, a stele from Hammurabi (1792–1750), boundary stones from Kassite rulers and the sun-god tablet of Nabu-apla-iddina (*c*.870). The most recent datable object was an argonate vase with an Egyptian cartouche, given to the temple during the Achaemenid period. That the site was still occupied during Parthian and Sassanian times was shown by pottery and glass that must have come from private houses or graves.[5]

Rassam's knack of finding the richest seams at archaeological sites thus contributed in a large measure to our present knowledge of Sippar. His success and hasty departure, however, also had an adverse outcome for archaeology in that it encouraged the local Arabs to do their own digging, especially for tablets. Substantial quantities of tablets undoubtedly disappeared through inexpert handling, but, despite their poor state of preservation, large numbers of them reached the antiquities markets and ended up in the collections of the Louvre and the museums of Berlin and Philadelphia among various other institutions. Wallis Budge from the British Museum was also able to purchase in Baghdad a number of tablets secretly dug from the ed-Der mound.[6]

In 1894 the French sent a team headed by Vincent Scheil to continue the excavations. Scheil was also unable to spend more than a few months at Sippar. His records are now supplemented by more recent reports by Iraqi archaeologists. He also published some seventy tablets.[7] In the 1930s the German excavators of Assur spent some time at Sippar, doing 'quick triangulations' to establish the architectural evidence of the Neo-Babylonian temple precinct.[8] After the Second World War, the Iraqi Directorate of Antiquities made a brief survey at ed-Der.[9] It remains a puzzle, however, why such a prominent site was never systematically excavated. Most of the scholarly literature about Sippar is based on written sources discovered by Rassam, or by 'illicit' diggers without archaeological back-up. More information began to come to light in the 1970s, when a Belgian expedition, well provided with funds and technical equipment, was sent to ed-Der to make extensive surveys and engage in geophysical research focusing on environmental factors. This team also undertook more conventional excavations in the area of the Eulmash and the city's residential quarters and made soundings at Abu Habbah.[10]

The mound of Abu Habbah had been identified as ancient Sippar at the outset, on the basis of the sun-god foundation tablet, but the situation at ed-Der had proved more complex. Some scholars even thought it was Akkad, the capital of Sargon in the third millennium. Only when the tablets acquired by Budge for the British Museum were examined had it become clear that it was the Sippar of Annunitu.

The picture was also complicated by the fact that the city had been known by a number of different names in antiquity. This gave rise to

(*Above left*) Halaf-style terracotta jar, fashioned
and painted by hand. *c.*4500 BC. (Louvre, Paris)

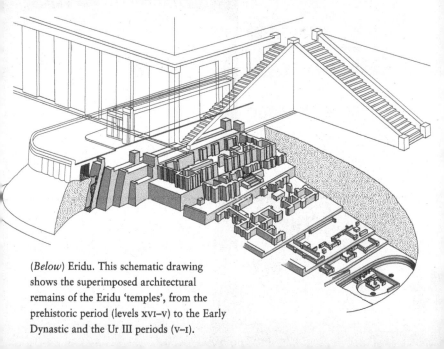

(*Below*) Eridu. This schematic drawing
shows the superimposed architectural
remains of the Eridu 'temples', from the
prehistoric period (levels XVI–V) to the Early
Dynastic and the Ur III periods (V–I).

Alabaster vase from Uruk, found at level III within the Eanna precinct. 92 cm. (Iraq Museum, Baghdad)

(*Below*) Detail from the top register (of the vase) showing a female figure receiving a basket with offerings. Behind her are the upright reed bundles which in historical times were associated with the goddess Inanna (Iraq Museum, Baghdad)

(*Left*) Limestone cylinder with engraved hunting and pastoral scene.
(*Right*) Administrative text on a clay tablet which shows the numerals as round or crescent-shaped impressions formed by the writing implement and the pictographic signs for various commodities, such as fish and some liquid substance, as represented by a jar (left-hand corner). Both from Uruk. (Pergamon Museum, Berlin)

Clay-cone mosaic covering the engaged round pillars on the façade of a public building in the Eanna district at Uruk. The patterns are suggestive of reed matting or textile hanging. (Pergamon Museum, Berlin)

Accounts text on a clay tablet from Shuruppak which concerns the sale of a field and a house. A good example of the neat and compact writing which characterizes the Fara tablets. 8.5 cm × 2 cm. (Louvre, Paris)

Another sale contract from Shuruppak. The writing style of this tablet is markedly more archaic than that of the tablet above. 10.8 cm × 10.4 cm. (Louvre, Paris)

Copper head of an Akkadian king who wears a ceremonial wig held together with a diadem and has a carefully dressed beard. It was found at Nineveh. 30 cm. (Iraq Museum, Baghdad)

Akkadian cylinder-seal impression which, according to the inscribed panel on the left-hand side, belonged to 'Adda, the scribe', no doubt a wealthy individual who could afford such an exquisitely carved artefact. It shows a number of Mesopotamian deities, such as the sun-god Shamash rising between two mountains in the centre. On his right stands the water-god Ea, with fish flowing from his shoulders, while opposite him is a winged and armed goddess, perhaps representing Inanna/Ishtar. Next to her stands a bearded warrior god with a mighty bow. The scene is completed on the right by a double-faced deity and a lion. (British Museum, London)

The ziggurat of Ur-Nammu at Ur. Before restoration.

Foundation deposits which commemorate the building activities of Ur-Nammu. The carved figure shows the king carrying the basket for the ritual shaping of the first brick. Foundation deposits typically included tablets fashioned from precious metals, as well as various beads, pearls and less permanent offerings. From Ur. (Oriental Institute, Chicago)

(*Opposite*) This inscribed sandstone stele commemorates the victory of the Akkadian king Naram-Sin over the Lullubi. The king, wearing horned crown, a sign of divinity, receives the surrender of the enemy. In a masterly condensed fashion, the artist represents the relentless ascent of the Akkadian soldiers to the mountainous terrain inhabited by their foes, who are tumbling down the precipice or are simply trampled underfoot. The king stands in super human grandeur and isolation, protected by the celestial gods whose symbols mark the apex of the stele. Discovered at Susa. 200 cm × 105 cm. (Louvre, Paris)

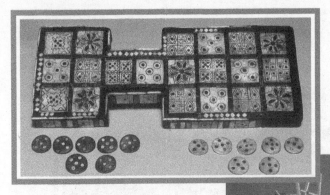

(*Above*) Sumerian gaming board discovered in the 'Royal Graves' at Ur. The body was made of wood, with mother-of-pearl and lapis lazuli insets. (British Museum, London)

(*Right*) Reconstructed lyre with a golden bull's head and inlaid pictorial scenes. From the 'Royal Graves' at Ur. (British Museum, London)

(*Left*) Golden head-dress and jewellery discovered in the grave of Queen Pu-abi as originally reconstructed by Mrs L. Woolley, having used a female skull found in the tombs. (British Museum, London)

Detail from the so-called Standard of Ur, actually the soundbox of a stringed instrument, which shows a royal banquet above and the receipt of animal tribute below. From the 'Royal Graves' at Ur. Inlay with shell and lapis lazuli. (British Museum, London)

Gypsum statuette of an affectionate couple found within the temple of Inanna at Nippur. (Iraq Museum, Baghdad)

(*Left*) Terracotta face of demon as constituted by divination entrails. Old Babylonian. From Sippar. (British Museum, London)

(*Right*) Neo-Babylonian (Seventh-century) tablet with a map indicating Babylon in the middle, situated on the Euphrates, Assyria and its mountainous borders to the north and the marshes of southern Baylonia. From Sippar. (British Museum, London)

(*Below right*) Barrel-shaped clay tablet recording the restoration of the temple of the Sun-god in Sippar by Nebuchadrezzar II (605–562). (Oriental Museum, Durham University)

(*Above*) Alabaster cult socle from the Ishtar temple in Ashur. It shows the Assyrian king Tukulti-Ninurta I, first standing, then kneeling before the divine emblem. 60 cm × 57 cm. *c.*1220 BC. (Pergamon Museum, Berlin)

bove) Early Dynastic alabaster statue of vorshipper, found in the lower levels of Ishtar temple at Ashur. 46 cm. *c.*2400 (Pergamon Museum, Berlin)

(*Right*) Octagonal baked-clay prism with a votive inscription by Tiglath-Pileser I of Assyria (*c.*1109 BC). This format allowed for very lengthy inscriptions to be transcribed on to a single object. 56 cm high, 17.5 cm wide. From Ashur. (Pergamon Museum, Berlin)

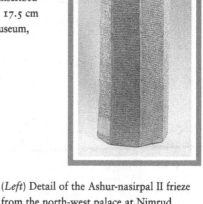

(*Left*) Detail of the Ashur-nasirpal II frieze from the north-west palace at Nimrud. Above a stylized tree of life appears a winged bearded deity in a disc which is widely believed to represent the god Ashur. 883–859 BC. (British Museum, London)

(*Above*) Relief from the north palace at Nineveh, showing King Ashurbanipal hunting lions from his chariot. *c.*640 BC. (British Museum, London)

(*Below*) Relief from the palace of Sennacherib at Nineveh. A harpist a▪ a female musician process through tʰ gardens, famous for their exotic tree A telling touch is the decapitated heː suspended from the branches of the tree in the middle. Seventh century. (British Museum, London)

Relief from the south-west palace at Nineveh. This detail shows two scribe The beardless one in front, probably ː eunuch, holds a clay tablet, while his colleague prepares to take notes on a scroll, presumably to write in Aramai which was widely in use at this perioᵈ *c.*640 BC. (British Museum, London)

33. (*Right*) Relief from the palace of Sennacherib at Nineveh depicting the siege of the Jewish town of Lachish. It shows an Assyrian battering ram in full action, the collapsing walls of the fortress, and the inhabitants of the town being led into captivity or exile. *c.*701 BC. (British Museum, London)

34. (*Below left*) Clay tablet from the library of Ashurbanipal at Nineveh. It forms part of the Gilgamesh epic and contains the episode of the flood. Seventh century. (British Museum, London)

(*Left*) Bronze and gold statue showing the Babylonian king Hammurabi at prayer. *c.*1750 BC. (Louvre, Paris)

(*Below*) Glazed-tile relief from the Ishtar Gate at Babylon. It shows the *mušhuššu*, a dragon-like animal sacred to the god Marduk. The creature has the head of a viper, the body of a reptile, the front legs of a lion and the back legs of an eagle. (Pergamon Museum, Berlin)

(*Right*) Tablet showing the Assyrian king Ashurbani-pal carrying a basket of earth to symbolize his efforts in restoring the temple of Marduk at Babylon, which had suffered from the devastation wrought on the city by his father Sennacherib. *c*.660 BC. (British Museum, London)

Impression of a Babylonian cylinder-seal showing a ziggurat with its five superimposed terraces. *c*.1000 BC. (Pergamon Museum, Berlin)

Babylonian cuneiform tablet with astronomical observations. The initial line reads, 'Night of the 18th, last part of the night, the moon was behind Beta Geminorum.' The date can be deduced from such astronomical information as 61 BC, when Babylon was under Parthian rule. (British Museum, London)

Statuette of a reclining nude from the Parthian period. The figure shows an interesting combination of Greek and Mesopotamian stylistic sensibilities. The fluid and sensual curves of the body contrast with rigid pose of the arm and the summary treatment of the head. Between first century BC and second century AD. (Pergamon Museum, Berlin)

the assumption that Sippar was surrounded by satellite towns, all with names compounded with 'Sippar', such as Great Sippar, Walled Sippar, Yahrurum Sippar or Amnamum Sippar (both tribal names), Steppe Sippar or Annunitu Sippar.[11] But since there are no additional tells in the area, and since a careful analysis of the context in which the names were used made it clear that the scribes were using different terms in accordance with local usage,[12] it was finally recognized that Sippar must be a twin city. Abu Habbah was the place with the Ebabbar, the temple of the sun-god, while ed-Der had the Eulmash, the temple of Annunitu, these being respectively known as Great Sippar and Sippar Amnamum. While the two sanctuaries determined the identity of the two parts, they were considered to have been a single political unit from the mid third millennium onwards.

SIPPAR'S HISTORY

The soundings and surface surveys of the more recent expeditions have finally made it possible for Sippar's history of occupation to be pieced together. From surface finds it appears that Abu Habbah was the older settlement, established sometime in the Uruk period, while the most recent soundings have reached Early Dynastic levels.[13] As the votive objects from Rassam's temple collection showed, the sanctuary of the sun-god was important enough in the third millennium to receive highly valuable gifts from kings as well as local rulers. The site was, with its temple, in almost continuous occupation through to the Neo-Babylonian period, and even later into the Sassanian period. Occupation of the second tell, ed-Der, may reach back to the Akkadian period; Ur III levels are clearly attested. From then on it continued to be inhabited for as long as the other Sippar existed.

The majority of the written sources from Sippar that date from the early Old Babylonian period shine a spotlight on the life of the city. Many of these documents were found in private houses and the so-called *gagum*,[14] usually translated as 'cloister'. One other sizeable corpus of texts dates mainly from the sixth century and derives primarily from the temple archives. Other historical epochs are poorly represented by written documents, and so, for a reconstruction of the broad outlines of Sippar's history, we need to rely on sources from other Mesopotamian cities.

Sippar's status as one of the three privileged cities, together with Nippur and Babylon, means it is often mentioned in royal inscriptions and annals. Its geographical position repeatedly made it a key site in the political struggles for supremacy in Babylonia, and in the conflicts between Assyria and Babylon, as well as between Mesopotamia and its eastern neighbours, such as Elam and later Persia.

In the Sumerian King-list, Sippar was said to have been the seat of an antediluvian dynasty even before Shuruppak, with one king, Enmeduranna, reigning for 21,000 years. In some cosmogonic texts, Sippar, like Eridu, is mentioned as one of the oldest cities in the land. In fact, as we have seen, little is known about Sippar from the period before the second millennium. The cult of Shamash seems to have been important enough for the temple to have received costly gifts from Akkadian kings and other local rulers. During the Ur III and the subsequent Isin-Larsa periods (c.2150–1800), the southern sun sanctuary at Larsa eclipsed the Sippar temple.

Things began to change in Sippar's favour with a shift of power from south to north following the growing influence of the people known as the Amorites, who had begun to move into Mesopotamia from the western deserts at the end of the third millennium. Efforts by the rulers of Isin and Larsa to stem their migration into southern Mesopotamia proved futile. Sippar, as the northernmost city of the plains, then became particularly important to the new Amorite rulers, who wanted to extend their area of influence southwards. The earliest kings of the dynasty that ruled the country from the city of Babylon, apparently a recent foundation, tried to exercise control over Sippar with intermittent success. The takeover finally came about in the twenty-ninth year of Sumu-la-ila in 1838 BC. There is a year-name to record the rebuilding of the Sippar city wall, which may have been destroyed in fighting.[15]

The kings of Babylon did much to promote Sippar and made it a premier religious centre in parallel with Nippur in the south. The city thrived under their patronage and the temple and the cloister in particular became prosperous. The peak of growth for Sippar was attained during the reign of Hammurabi (1792–1750), and most of the Old Babylonian Sippar tablets date from his time. Hammurabi's long period in office allowed him to implement several important administrative reforms. He was particularly concerned with the welfare of Sippar and called himself the 'renewer of Ebabbar for Shamash',[16] a reference to his restoration work at the sun-god's temple. He also repaired and reinforced the city walls, a necessary precaution against the restless tribes threatening his kingdom. His benevolent policies were maintained by his dynastic successors, but gradually the political situation worsened and the authority of the Babylonian kings weakened as they lost control of the southern cities and became embroiled in conflicts with neighbouring petty kingdoms.

In 1595, the Hittite king, Murshili I, came down the Euphrates in a lightning attack and sacked Babylon. How Sippar fared at the time is not known, but an urgent missive from the city governor to the Babylonian king warns him of imminent danger and that the enemy stands prepared to attack. It seems some disaster befell the city as there are no more documents till centuries later. It is likely that the city revived under the Kassite dynasty (c.1600–1155), which ruled over Mesopotamia from nearby Dur-Kurigalzu. The Kassites were a people from the Caucasus who had begun to settle in the East Tigris region at the beginning of the second millennium. These foreign kings were thoroughly acculturated in the Babylonian tradition and were particularly keen to patronize the old religious centres and hence invested heavily in temple restorations. Although there is no documentary proof for their building activities at Sippar, the Shamash temple was fully functioning by the time when the Second Dynasty of Isin had taken control of Babylonia. Nebuchadrezzar I (1126–1105) restored temples throughout the land and his work at Sippar is documented by an inscribed boundary stone (*kudurru* in Babylonian).

Difficult times were nevertheless ahead. A text dating from the reign of Adad-apla-iddina (1069–1048) reports that Aramaean and Sutean tribes ravaged the countryside and destroyed Sippar so thoroughly that the cult there ceased for a period of about a hundred years.[17] The city's recovery, or that of the religious precinct at least, occurred in the tenth century. Peace returned as Babylonia grew strong again, and a peace treaty with Assyria secured a political stability that lasted for 150 years. Rassam's sun-god tablet in the earthenware box dates from this time, when the king Nabu-apla-iddina (c.870) created new endowments for the Ebabbar.

When relations between Assyria and Babylonia took another turn for the worse, Sippar, lying on the border between the two states, came very much in the line of conflict. During the wars of Sennacherib against his arch-enemy, the southern tribal leader Marduk-apla-iddina (c.700–690), the king installed the Assyrian crown prince as regent in Babylon. He was also at war with Elam (a then powerful state in western Iran), and the Elamites, making use of Sennacherib's engagement in the southern provinces, captured Sippar (c.694). In the meantime, an anti-Assyrian faction in Babylon seized the Assyrian crown prince and delivered him into the hands of the Elamite king, who was based, by now, at Sippar, where it seems the prince died as a hostage. This turn of events deepened Sennacherib's resentment against Babylon, on which he vented his fury in a savage attack. Neither did Sippar escape his anger. The Assyrian king destroyed the temple of Annunitu and took away the cult statue of Shamash, along with other Babylonian deities.

Kidnapping of divine statues was common practice, for the loss of a city god was seen as a great calamity. As if to prove the point that misfortune follows the absence of its god from a city, Sippar suffered a devastating attack and a wholesale massacre at the hands of the Elamites when Sennacherib's successor renewed the war against Elam. But Esarhaddon (680–669) was conscious of the sacrilege his father was seen to have committed against the holy cities of Babylonia, and was keen to make amends. He began a programme of rebuilding the destroyed sanctuaries, a policy continued by his son Ashurbanipal, who in 669 restored the exiled gods to Sippar and other cities.

The city began to revive and it enjoyed another golden age during the sixth century, after the fall of Assyria. Nebuchadrezzar II and his successors endowed the temples lavishly and rebuilt the severely damaged fortifications. Nabonidus, the last of the Babylonian kings (555–539), reported that he had restored the Ebabbar temple and noted the discovery of the old foundation documents deposited by his ancient royal predecessors, among them Hammurabi. Nabonidus' reconstruction of the Ebabbar constituted the last building activity at the temple precinct, the ruins of which were still in a relatively good state of preservation when Rassam and the other excavators investigated the site in the 1890s.[18]

The last large collection of texts comes from the Ebabbar during the time of Nabonidus,[19] but the downfall of Babylon was at hand and the Persian king Cyrus II defeated the Babylonian army at Opis. Having accepted the surrender of Sippar in 539, he entered the city to await the capitulation of Nabonidus, who was taken into Persian exile. The change of government seems to have made little difference to the city and texts show that the temple continued to function under Achaemenid rule. The city continued to be inhabited, probably on a much reduced scale, during the Seleucid and the ensuing Sassanian Persian dynasties, until, sometime towards the end of the pre-Christian era, it was abandoned for good.

OLD BABYLONIAN SIPPAR

The major published source about Old Babylonian Sippar, simply called *Ancient Sippar*, was written by the American scholar Rivkah Harris,[20] who made use of the abundant administrative and legal documents and was particularly interested in how the city functioned economically, and how the workers were organized, from farm hands to bureaucrats and temple personnel. Unfortunately the great majority of these tablets came from one particular institution, the 'cloister' or 'enclosure' (*gagum*), which gave a rather skewed perspective on the city as a whole.[21] Even so, because the *gagum* was so closely involved in a whole array of economic activities, it was possible to make general assumptions about the working of the city.[22] Some additional material has come to light, such as letters and legal contracts, but we do not have the archives of the temple itself, nor of the central administration. Neither do we have the records of Sippar's apparently well-established merchant community. Harris's conclusions about the social context of the *gagum* texts are therefore highly speculative. Furthermore, basic questions, such as what the population of the city may have been, estimated by Scheil as a modest 5,000, remain unanswered.

The texts do illustrate, however, how Sippar came increasingly under direct control by the central Babylonian government. Hammurabi installed a garrison in the city and the main institutions came under royal authority, while government representatives kept the king informed through correspondence. On the other hand, the city benefited from royal investments, particularly in defences and the upkeep of its waterways, as well as in temple building. The city had formerly been governed by a council of 'elders' headed by a lord mayor, but by the time of Hammurabi's successor, Samsu-iluna (1749–1712), the government body of Sippar was composed of representatives of the Harbour, as the merchants' quarter was called, and a royally appointed official. During the early periods covered by the archives, these bodies were responsible to the citizens, but in later years they came to be answerable to central government. This tightened supervision was put into effect by personnel directly in the service of the crown. The military presence established by Hammurabi was always under the king's direct command and the officer in charge was never a native of Sippar. Legal affairs were decided by local judges, though litigants could ask for a royal verdict if they were unsatisfied with an outcome.

As was often the case during periods of strong centralization, the government attempted to gain control over the temples. In Sippar this could be seen to have occurred in the middle of Hammurabi's reign. From then onwards temple officials refer to themselves as 'servant of the king' rather than 'servant of the Ebabbar' (or the god). Through appointments to leading positions in these administrative institutions, the king could thus consolidate his influence over the city. The main issue was the collection of taxes, of which there were all kinds. Professionals, such as scribes, physicians, tavern keepers or judges, often paid their tax in silver, but more commonly the agricultural field tax was submitted in kind, primarily in barley but also animals.

Large numbers of officials were responsible for the calculation and collection of these taxes, though it is not clear how efficient the system actually was. The produce was stored in royal granaries and used for the provision of workers, soldiers and animals employed in connection with royal projects. Grain could also be given out on loan, as documented by the accounting office of the granary. Royal workshops, especially for the processing of wool into textiles, were part of the central economy. The products and raw materials could also be converted into silver, which could then be invested by advancing loans to citizens in need of cash for various commercial transactions. The maintenance of important public facilities was a shared responsibility of the local authority and the state, especially the dredging of waterways running through the city and the upkeep of the fortifications.

The local authority operated on a different level from the administrative offices that dealt with the central government and concerned itself with the affairs of the city itself. Sippar was divided into wards (*babtum*), the administration of which was mainly concerned with sanitation and policing. The ward could also be a judicial body. Each ward was represented by an official (*hazannu*), but there was also a city corporation, simply called 'the city', which functioned as a legal entity and landlord of intramural city property. The mayor (*rabianum*) was superior in rank to the *hazannu*. Mayors were appointed for a limited period, usually for one year. For some reason they often appeared as witnesses in property transactions.

The commercial sector of Sippar was represented by the port authority (*karum*), which seems to have been primarily a judicial body to settle disputes within the merchant community. By the time of Samsuiluna, it had become the principal administrative body, charged with tax collection and the supervision of the royal granaries. The 'Overseer of the Merchants' rose in status with the growing importance of the *karum*. This was an annually held office, with the exception of one individual who maintained the position for a record twenty-two years. Overseers were apparently all wealthy citizens and there is no evidence that they were themselves merchants. There were, of course, many other administrative posts and offices in the city, from the army to the judiciary, quite apart from the 'civil service' of the local authority or the state.[23]

That the temple estates were important factors of the city's economy is demonstrated by the temple archives. They had large landholdings worked primarily by temple personnel, including slaves, as well as by people under obligations to perform corvée work. The yield was used to support the temple and its personnel and any surplus was stored. It could be given out in small quantities as loans to the needy or invested in business loans.

According to the available evidence, the Ebabbar was by far the richest temple in Sippar during the Old Babylonian period.[24] The importance of the sun-god at this time can also be gleaned from the large numbers of people who had names compounded with Shamash.[25] Other deities were represented at Sippar. There were smaller temples for the moon-god Sin and the weather-god Adad – of great importance to the inhabitants of northern Mesopotamia as the bringer of rains; for the newly introduced Babylonian god Marduk,[26] as well as for Enlil, Ea, Nergal and the Amorite god Amurru. Annunitu was the most important of the female deities in Sippar, whose cult grew in importance during the reign of Samsu-iluna. Aya, 'bride of Shamash', was housed in a chapel within the Ebabbar. Ishtar, as Inanna was now called, had her own temple, as did the healing goddess Gula. The archives from the Ebabbar and other legal and administrative texts contain the names and titles of many officials, priests and workers employed by the sanctuaries, from the highest ranking *sanga*, the head of the entire personnel, to the managers, cult personnel, scribes, dream interpreters and diviners, down to the temple slaves.[27]

THE *NADITU* WOMEN OF SHAMASH AT SIPPAR

We will now take a closer look at the *gagum* and its inhabitants, the *naditu* women.[28] Other cities had similar institutions, notably Babylon, Nippur and Kish, but these enclosures were peculiar to the Old Babylonian period, and, perhaps because of their close connection to the Babylonian kings, did not survive the demise of the dynasty. The earliest record dates from the reign of Immerum (1880–1845), who ruled at Sippar before the kings of Babylon assumed power in the late nineteenth century.[29]

The *gagum* should not be confused with the *giparu*, encountered at Ur,[30] which was the household and cult place for a single priestess, the *entu*, and her staff. The *gagum* was inhabited by many women, usually from the wealthiest families of the city, including at least one princess. These women, known as *naditu* women, had to support themselves from the proceeds of their private estates. They actively participated in the economy of the city, investing in large and small business ventures. The word *naditum* means 'fallow' or 'taboo' and thus designates their special gender identity. Such women were regarded as set apart from the customary female roles, but how this distinctiveness manifested itself seems to have varied in place and time. In Sippar the *naditu*s could not marry, while those dedicated to Marduk at Babylon could.[31] Those of Ninurta at Nippur were also celibate, but were apparently not living in a *gagum*.[32] One important characteristic was the injunction that the *naditu*, like other women connected with the cult, should not bear children. To what extent this also entailed virginity and lifelong chastity is another question. The threat of a death penalty in the Code of Hammurabi against a *naditu* frequenting taverns, the customary place for casual sexual encounters, has been taken as an indication of their tabooed sexuality.

Although there are isolated cases of a *naditu* seeking a wet-nurse, it is clear that the women in the enclosure did not have children. This greatly enhanced their chances of survival, since they were spared the risks of pregnancy and the debilitating effects of having to give birth during their fertile years, as did most other women at the time. As a result of this sterility and their social segregation within the *gagum*, which protected them from the various epidemics not uncommon in Mesopotamian cities, a *naditu* could reach a relatively advanced age; some are known to have lived in the *gagum* for forty years and more.[33]

The other significant gender deviation from the norm was the control a *naditu* had over her share of the paternal estate. While other women of the day passed their inheritance on to their husbands at marriage, the *naditu* could administer hers at her will. She was supposed to pass it back (with any accrued dividends) to her paternal family, but the documents make it clear that such conventions could be subverted by adopting a young girl to succeed her as a *naditu* and take care of her in old age. *Naditu* all came from wealthy families, some being the daughters of kings and local rulers, and they did not have to be natives of Sippar. It seems it was seen as highly prestigious to have a daughter serving the gods in a *gagum* and families often decided that a girl should be dedicated in this way at birth.[34] They lived in an age when the female legal status had changed in favour of male control over women. Daughters therefore had little choice in the matter of marriage or whether they should become servants of gods.[35]

One *naditu*, reproaching her stepmother for not looking after her needs, states this very clearly:

> I am a king's daughter! You are a king's wife! Even disregarding the tablets with which your husband and you made me enter the *gagum* – they treat well soldiers taken as booty! You then, treat me well![36]

A *naditu* probably joined the *gagum* at puberty. The initiation ceremony included offerings to Shamash and Aya, a memorial banquet for deceased *naditu*s and the formal presentation of the neophyte to the deities.[37] For very high-ranking women, an omen was performed to confirm the god's approval. The administration of the *gagum* paid for a 'betrothal gift' which in fact covered the expenses of the initiation. Her family was obliged to draw up an agreement as to how the new *naditu* was to be supported. Hammurabi's code distinguishes three possibilities. Her share of the inheritance could be administered by her brothers for a guaranteed life-long supply of clothing and subsistence, or, if they failed to do so, by appointing another person of her choice. Alternatively she could decide to manage and leave her share to anyone she decided, if her father consented to it in writing. Should she receive no share, she was to inherit on equal terms with her brothers.[38] The legal tablets show that such arrangements were not always carried out as anticipated and the courts sometimes had to rule on the validity of claims made by *naditu*s or their families.

The *gagum* at Sippar lay within the Ebabbar precinct, but it was surrounded by walls and had its own gate. The houses of the *naditu*s and their officials within the compound numbered several hundred. They also had their own granary, an administrative building and perhaps workshops, as well as a small arable plot of land. As the institution became popular and attracted new incumbents, and because the women had quite a long life expectancy, the *gagum* became rather overcrowded by the time of Hammurabi.[39] The office of overseer of the *naditu*s was originally held by a *naditu*. Later, in keeping with the state's efforts to secularize religious establishments, a man, probably appointed by the king, was put in this influential position, which carried a very high rank, second only to the *sanga* of the Ebabbar. Several *naditu* women were literate and functioned as scribes.[40] A certain Amat-Mamu, for instance, served in this capacity for some forty years.

In some cases, families were keen to perpetuate a tradition of sending girls to the Sippar enclosure. It is interesting to see how some of the *naditu* managed to increase their original share through various business enterprises. There was one who traded in tin through an intermediary. They would make loans of barley or silver or other commodities, or own a business, such as a tavern – too risqué to be entered, but acceptable as an investment. They also cooperated with each other in joint ventures and by buying adjacent plots of land or sharing a field.[41] The princess Iltani, daughter of Sin-muballit and Hammurabi's sister, was by far the richest of the *naditu*s. Not only did she possess vast tracts of arable land, she also invested in livestock and once hired six herders to look after the 1,085 head of cattle she owned.[42]

The active engagement of Iltani and other *naditu*s in the economic affairs of the city is well documented. It gives the impression that the *naditu*s were shrewd businesswomen, forever battling with male family members over their inheritances and making lucrative deals. The letters of Ereshti-Aya, the princess from Mari, remind us, however, that this is to give a very one-sided impression.[43] Although she complains a lot about her family's negligence in keeping her supplied with provisions, she makes it very clear that her main function was a religious one. She repeatedly tells her father that she performs a vital service by praying for him continuously before Shamash and Aya. In return she expects to be properly provisioned:

Now the daughters of your house ... are receiving their rations of grain, clothing and good beer. But even though I alone am the woman who prays for you, I am not provisioned!

Again and again she mentions that she is the 'emblem' (*surinnum*):

Am I not your praying emblem who constantly prays for your life?

Am I not your praying emblem who gives you a favourable report in the Ebabbar?

She compares herself to the famous emblem of the sun-god, which was thought to represent the deity in various contexts, such as the administration of oaths or the action of perpetual prayer (*karibtum*). She sees herself as an animate votive statue donated to the temple to be in the presence of the deity 'for ever', a substitute for the donor. She defines her main duty as being to pray for her father's life. It is not clear to what extent other *naditu*s were equally engaged in such a duty to their parents. They all had to make offerings twice daily in the temple as well as a special offering for every twentieth day of the month, known as *piqittum*,[44] which consisted of meat, bread and beer. In cases when they did not administer their own property, their families or executors were obliged to supply the offering. It seems that the *naditu*s were also expected to attend religious feasts, perhaps taking part in processions,[45] and to fulfil certain obligations towards the gods.

The institution of the *gagum* was seen to have a primary religious purpose, though it was clearly distinguished from other female cultic offices. Although the *naditu*s were not part of the temple personnel, they came under the authority of the temple chief official. Their lawsuits were conducted in the temple courts and witnessed by temple officials. There is no evidence that they performed any rituals in the temples and their contributions to the daily offerings were additional to those provided by the temple. As with the *piqittum*, these were probably consumed by the *naditu*s and other officials.[46]

A *naditu*'s relationship to Shamash was expressed as that of *kallatum*, a term with a range of meanings connected to the status of 'betrothed'.[47] The reference to brides does not necessarily entail either the presence or absence of sexual activity. It can also be seen as marking a marginal and transitional female status between childhood and adulthood, between the paternal patrilineal family and integration into the husband's family. The *naditu*s were to spend their whole life in this social limbo, grown up yet childless, dissociated from the paternal family yet only loosely integrated into the household of the god. It therefore categorizes the gender status of the *naditu* without having theological implications.

Ereshti-Aya's emphasis on her duties as *karibtum*, translated as 'perpetual prayer', reveals the religious purpose of the institution. The economic contribution of the *naditu* has received far more attention only because of the large amount of documentary material. It has been suggested that the dedication of a daughter to the *gagum* served to preserve the integrity of estates and to prevent the diffusion of property.[48] However, since many *naditu*s did not pass their share of the inherited estate back to their families, but preferred to bequeath it to persons who would more reliably provide for them in old age, this cannot have been a major consideration.

That their diverse engagements in the local economy, primarily through land agricultural holdings but also as creditors, gave a significant boost to the city economy is beyond doubt. To have one or even several female members in the enclosure enhanced the social prestige of a family, not least because the *gagum* harboured women from the very top of the social hierarchy. Rulers aspiring to legitimize their power found it politically useful to dedicate their daughters and establish an indirect though long-lasting connection to important gods and their sanctuaries.[49] Again, Ereshti-Aya's metaphor of the living votive statue seems more than apt.

There is a passage in the story of Atra-hasis, the Old Babylonian flood epic,[50] which points to the ecological purpose of women such as the *naditu*s. When the god Ea repopulates the earth anew, he makes some adjustments so as to lessen the excessive noise and bustle of humankind that had caused Enlil to send the flood. Ea decrees that there should be women 'who give birth yet not give birth successfully' and that there be demons 'to snatch the baby from the mother's lap', and he declares that some women 'shall be taboo and thus control childbirth'.[51] Although the text does not specifically mention the *naditu*s, they were obviously in the same category, 'fallow' women who did not contribute to population growth, which was clearly already seen as problematic.

The archives of the *naditu* women of Sippar allow us not only to perceive some of the prevailing institutions and attitudes, they are also unique in representing a female perspective at this period. This is no doubt an anomalous and very privileged group of women, but evidence of the contributions women could make to the urban society of their time is nevertheless abundant.

OTHER PEOPLE AT OLD
BABYLONIAN SIPPAR

The administrative and legal texts recovered from the *gagum* contain the names of some 18,000 people. Many were labourers, hired hands and slaves, others appear to have been professionals.[52] The tablets thus reveal something of the social complexity of the city. There were millers working for the royal households or the garrison, leather-workers, fullers, an important occupation in a town with a thriving textile economy – they were organized into some sort of professional association. Weavers were mainly employed by the large organizations belonging to the state or the temples and, unlike in the Ur III period, both men and women were engaged in all aspects of textile manufacture.

Other craft activities could be conducted on an independent basis; such as goldsmiths, who may have had their shops in the main streets to attract rural customers. Bakers either worked privately, under a licence, or were employed by the cloister or temple. Tavern keepers, some of whom made their own beer, seem to have had to pay a special tax or licence. Apparently it was a lucrative business, and one that the wealthy *naditu* women liked to invest in. There were also many scribes, though during the period covered by the archives at least there is no indication of learned institutions or families of scholars such as are known from Nippur.[53] Their main duties were to serve the adminis-tration and the judiciary, and to record economic transactions. Sippar is not known for having an interest in literature or the sciences. The fact that quite a few scribes had Sumerian names nevertheless shows a certain pride in the intellectual tradition of their profession.[54]

FOREIGN TRADE

Of great importance to the prosperity of Sippar and the Old Babylonian kingdom generally was foreign trade.[55] We lack any coherent tablet collection from the Harbour, but because some of the *naditu* women were engaged in trade, there are references in the texts from the enclosure that allow an insight into the city's export and import business. Sippar was particularly well suited geographically for trading with the north and the east, along the Euphrates and the Tigris. The trade commodities listed in the *naditu* tablets were luxury items, such as juniper oil, myrtle oil and perfumes ('Look out for good quality and take it!')[56] to be sold in eastern regions for silver, and 'splendid Gutian slaves' (also from east of the Tigris) to be traded for oil or silver in Mesopotamia. The tree oils and essences were in turn imported, probably from the mountainous regions of Lebanon.

Sippar also shipped textiles to Ashur, where they were traded against silver, gold and copper from Anatolia.[57] The presence of Assyrian merchants in Sippar itself may be seen from tablets written in Assyrian, as well as from the personal names of those who were given loans in silver.[58] Wine was sent from Carchemish in northern Syria along the Euphrates by boat, as were timber and wooden furniture. This town was also a trading centre for horses, also mentioned in the texts, though it is unclear whether they were used for transport or sold.

Other important trading posts were Haleb (modern Aleppo) and Emar on the Euphrates. The river traffic was subject to government control and ships were stopped at customs posts to pay any dues and show a royal permit of passage.[59] Merchants also used donkeys to transport their wares, particularly for journeys further east. In prosperous and politically stable times, as during most of the Old Babylonian period, demand for luxury items was high and investment in trade therefore made sound business sense, as the *naditu* ladies realized. In periods of general instability, when the safety of the caravans or boats could no longer be guaranteed by governmental control of agreements, trading ventures became too fraught with risk to remain profitable.

SIPPAR'S SOCIAL SYSTEM

The social structure of the city was a complex and interconnected system based on the obligations and duties individuals owed towards the various institutions in return for contributions towards subsistence, military protection and other services, including the judicial and ritual.

The Code of Hammurabi makes a legal distinction between people on the basis of their status as free, unfree (slave) or semi-free. Punishments for offences against an *awilum* (literally 'man', the person in possession of full rights) are higher than those against a *muškenum* (who had lesser rights), while the slave (*wardum*) was not considered a legal person and compensation for any injury was to be paid to his (or her) owner. The meaning of the word *muškenum* is still unclear. It appears primarily in legal compilations such as the Code of Hammurabi.[60] In the Sippar texts, the term occurs very rarely and may have a topographical connotation, referring to people living at a particular place.[61]

Early attempts to characterize Old Babylonian society as having a three-tier class structure composed of nobles (*awilum*), burghers (*muškenum*) and slaves have never been substantiated, while the validity of the so-called law codes as an accurate reflection of social reality has likewise been questioned. Generally the categories of 'free' and 'unfree' were not fixed since an individual could pass from one state to the other in a lifetime. Debt slavery could either be incurred voluntarily by adults for a fixed term in lieu of payments, or, more frequently, through the sale of legal dependants, children and women.

Any change of status was signalled by a characteristic hairdo. A lock of hair was removed on manumission when a former slave reassumed the status of *awilum*. Prisoners of war and foreign-born slaves were less likely to change status. With the expansion of centralized economic enterprise by the crown and the temples, more foreign slaves, especially from Subartu (later Assyria), were 'imported' to man the textile workshops and other enterprises. A general change occurs between the early periods covered by the texts and later part of the eighteenth century. At the outset slaves are not a significant factor in the economy, but are mainly found as domestic workers from private households, and marriages between former slaves and free citizens are not uncommon. The paternalistic framework that characterizes relationships between masters and slaves is also shown by the personal names of the slaves, which use kinship terminology to express the relationship.[62] With a growing centralization of the economy, slaves then began to fill gaps in the labour markets. Kings would donate slaves captured in raids and wars to the temple estates, which could then be more intensively worked to produce greater surpluses, some of which had to be paid in taxes to the crown. The demand for increased productivity affected not only temple estates but all landholdings, and the number of slaves owned by private households and crown estates rose accordingly. As a result social stratification also increased and the gulf between free and unfree citizens widened.

The network of obligations also became more tightly controlled by the centralized regime of the Old Babylonian state. Free citizens too were required to provide services for the king, especially military duties and corvée work on public projects, such as the dredging of canals or the maintenance of public buildings, quite apart from the taxation of landholdings or licences for professional activities.

Many relied for a livelihood on their services for the large estates, whether temple owned or private. They worked parcels of land in return for a share of the crop, or worked in other capacities in return for rations. Not even such economically self-sufficient persons as merchants or craftsmen like the Sipparean goldsmiths were exempt from obligations to the city authority or the crown in terms of labour and taxes. If obligations could not be met, perhaps because of illness, crop failure or some other misfortune, people would take out a loan (the temples seem to have given loans without interest to poor clients) at a rate imposed by the lender. In some cases indebtedness could become unmanageable and debt slavery be the only way out of the dilemma.

The various political problems of the state, especially the loss of control over southern Mesopotamia and such tribal population movements in the north as the immigration of Kassite groups, had repercussions in all the remaining corners of the kingdom. Correspondence between the king and the city officials of Sippar from the time of Abi-esuh (1711–1684) onwards reveals their preoccupation with military defences.[63] Economic difficulties that could be linked with population increase and intensified exploitation of the land may also have contributed to social unrest. The penultimate king of the First Babylonian Dynasty, Ammi-saduqa (1646–1626), issued a decree that attempted to alleviate some of the symptoms. He sanctioned the release of private debts in barley and silver, wrote off outstanding tax payments due to the crown and various other crippling debts owed by whole districts. At the same time, he reduced the payments on tenancies and leased land, and released people from debt slavery.[64]

Sippar is not explicitly mentioned as being affected by this edict. It is not clear whether conditions in the city were better than those experienced in other parts of the realm or whether the king sought to consolidate his authority elsewhere. During the reign of his successor, Samsu-ditana (1625–1595), Sippar was probably destroyed, since it is then that written records cease abruptly.

NEO-BABYLONIAN SIPPAR

The second group of texts from Sippar date from more than a thousand years later than those of the Old Babylonian *gagum*. Most of these texts were acquired by various museums from S. Rassam in the early part of the twentieth century. They come from Abu Habbah, and constitute the archives of the Neo-Babylonian temple of Shamash. The shrines of Sippar had been substantially renewed by the last king of Babylon, Nabonidus (555–539), who, having some difficulties with the Marduk priesthood in the capital, concentrated his efforts on restoring old cults in some of the provincial centres of the kingdom. He was keen as well to revive former institutions, as the example of the *entu* office at Ur showed.[65] He also made attempts to revitalize the *naditu* office, which had disappeared after the end of the First Dynasty of Babylon. As work at the ancient sanctuaries progressed, workmen came across the old foundation documents his royal predecessors had deposited beneath the brick walls. The very same tablet that Rassam first uncovered had also been handled by the last king of Babylon, who, in accordance with Mesopotamian custom, restored the tablet to its place.

The temple and the city revived, as the tablets clearly show. They concern primarily the estate of the Ebabbar, where, as in previous ages, the fields were sown with barley and wheat, though date-palm groves were also planted, as well as orchards with pomegranate and fig trees, and even some vines.[66] The town may have had a much smaller population than earlier, and the temple estates had to lease or subcontract two thirds of their lands to institutions of private land-owners. This is in marked contrast to the Old Babylonian period, when 67 per cent of the agricultural land owned by the temple was worked by temple dependants.[67] The new farming entrepreneurs not only had to furnish the labour but also needed to invest their own money in the means of production, to acquire seed, sort out traction and irrigation, and so on. Methods of farming had not changed. Independent smallholders could also lease temple property and furnished teams of three or four ploughmen to work on fields together.

The archive gives some indication of the temple administration and of a close interconnection between the citizens and the temple through hundreds of posts, offices and duties. But because the late Sippar tablets have been published only relatively recently and are still being examined, the contemporary and far more voluminous temple archives from Uruk have been a better source for investigations of this kind.[68] That scribal arts were also being practised again at Sippar is proved by the numerous exercise tablets with excerpts from lexical lists and various literary texts. A library excavated in 1986 contained several well-preserved examples.

SHAMASH, GOD OF SIPPAR

The personality of the Babylonian sun-god Shamash resembles in many ways that of the Sumerian solar deity Utu. Their temples were often called Ebabbar, which means the 'shining (white) house'. Utu's was located at the southern city of Larsa. In the Sumerian pantheon, the sun-god is the son of the moon-god, and in some compositions he is described as the brother of Inanna.[69] One curious text explains that Utu had a connection with beer brewing, and he accompanies the goddess Inanna to the Mountain of the Cedars, where aromatic resins, silver, salt and lapis lazuli are to be found. She wants to go to this place because 'what concerns women, (namely) men, I do not know, what concerns women, (namely) love-making, I do not know, what concerns women, (namely) kissing, I do not know'.[70] To gain that experience she has to eat 'what is there in the mountain' – perhaps from a tree? It is interesting to find references to tree oils in this text, written in Sumerian during the Old Babylonian period, since we know that the trade in aromatics was important in Sippar. Perfumes and unguents were used within the cult, but also played a role in women's preparations for love-making, which could explain the aetiological connection with Inanna's journey.

Shamash is also the deity who protects the hero Gilgamesh. With his help Gilgamesh and his friend Enkidu overcome the demonic guardian of the Forest of Cedars, the monstrous Huwawa, whom Enlil appointed to stop anyone from entering the forest. Throughout Gilgamesh's subsequent wanderings he is under the divine protection of Shamash and eventually returns safely to Uruk.

One of the most beautiful of Mesopotamian hymns is the one dedicated to the sun-god.[71] It is exactly 200 lines long, with 100 couplets, and probably dates from the Neo-Babylonian period but incorporating older material. Most extant copies are Neo-Assyrian, but one piece does come from Sippar. It is most likely that this composition was recited in the temple since it constitutes the most comprehensive summary of Mesopotamian solar theology. Shamash is praised primarily as the giver of light throughout the universe who bestows his splendour on all creatures alike. To his all-seeing eyes secrets are revealed, and he can communicate the hidden in dream oracles. Since the sun was seen as being constantly on the move, Shamash became the patron of travellers and merchants and the protector of all those journeying on dangerous roads and across treacherous waters.[72]

> Illuminator, dispeller of darkness of the *vault* of the heavens,
> Who sets aglow the *beard* of light, the cornfield, the life of the land.
> Your splendour covers the vast mountains surveying the earth, you
>   suspend from the heavens the circle of the lands.
>
> (. . .)
>
> Whatever has breath you shepherd without exception,
> You are their keeper in the upper and lower regions.
> Regularly and without cease you traverse the heavens,
> Every day you pass over the broad earth.
>
> (. . .)
>
> In the underworld you care for the counsellors of Kusu, the Anunnaki,
> Above, you direct all the affairs of men.
> Shepherd of that beneath, keeper of that above,
> You Shamash, direct, you are the light of everything.
>
> (. . .)

The whole of mankind bows to you
Shamash, the universe longs for your light.
You enlighten the dream priests and interpret dreams.
(. . .)
You dismiss (to the underworld) the rogue who is surrounded . . .
You bring up from the underworld river him entangled in a lawsuit.
What you say is a just verdict, Shamash . . .
Your manifest utterance may not be changed, and is not . . .
You stand by the traveller whose road is difficult,
To the seafarers in dread of the waves you give . . .
(. . .)
You save from the storm the merchant carrying his capital,
The . . . who goes down to the ocean you equip with wings.
You point out settling places to refugees and fugitives,
To the captive you point out routes that (only) Shamash knows.

The sun-god is also the ultimate judge and the hymn lists a number
of offences against Shamash, especially malpractices in justice and
business.

You give the unscrupulous judge experience of fetters,
Him who accepts a present and yet lets justice miscarry, you make bear
    his punishment.
As for him who declines a present, but nevertheless takes the part of the
    weak,
It is pleasing to Shamash, and he will prolong his life.
A circumspect judge who pronounces just verdicts
Controls the palace and lives among the princes.
(. . .)
The merchant who [practises] trickery as he holds the scales,
Who uses two sets of weights, thus lowering the . . .
He is disappointed in the matter of profit and loses [his capital].
The honest merchant who holds the scales [and gives] good weight –
Everything is presented to him in good measure . . .

Shamash protects those who are away from the comforts of civilization,
people like huntsmen, travellers, even highwaymen:

He whose family is remote, whose city is distant,
The shepherd [amid] the terror of the steppe confronts you,
The herdsman in warfare, the keeper of sheep among the enemies.
(. . .)
The prowling thief, the enemy of Shamash,
The marauder along the tracks of the steppe confronts you.
The roving dead, the vagrant soul,
They confront you, Shamash, and you hear all.
You do not obstruct those that confront you.
For my sake, Shamash, do not curse them.

The hymn then describes the festival of the twentieth day – twenty was
the number sacred to the sun – when he was offered beer and granted
the wishes of the worshippers.[73]

On the twentieth day you exult with mirth and joy,
You eat, you drink their pure ale, the barman's beer from the market,
They pour the barman's beer for you, and you accept.
You deliver people surrounded by mighty waves, in return you receive
    their pure, clear libations,
You drink their mild beer and ale,
Then you fulfil the desires they conceive.

The rest of the hymn repeats a number of earlier topics, Shamash also
being praised, for instance, as the one who regulates the climate and
the seasons of the year. The hymn ends with a note of domestic
comfort: 'May [Aya your spouse] say to you in the bedchamber: ["Be
appeased"]' a passage which the translator did not find a 'worthy
conclusion to the elevated thought of the whole'.[74]

This composition reveals that Shamash, more than any other Mesopotamian god, stood for the values of social justice, the protection of
the weak and principles of fairness in business. Evidence from the
economic tablets tempts us to portray the people of Sippar as hard-
headed businessmen and businesswomen, for whom profit was a
primary motive. We also tend to view the temples as mainly centres of
production, our perspective coming from the overwhelming number
of administrative documents concerned with labourers, harvest calculations and teams of oxen. The hymn of Shamash provides a corrective

balance, reminding us that the rituals in the temples also served to inculcate moral values and ethical standards.

As an epilogue I would like to quote a legal ruling concerning a divorce case heard in Old Babylonian Sippar. It is about an ordinary woman and offers a glimpse of the perennial problems of marital relations. It also shows a compassionate jury at work, who protect the wife from a wilful rejection by her husband and ensure she will at least be no worse off than when she first married:

In the presence of these witnesses they questioned Aham-nirshu: 'Is this woman your wife?'

He declared: 'You can hang me on a peg, yea dismember me (but) I will not stay married to her (any longer)!' thus he said.

Then they questioned his wife and she answered: 'I still love my husband.' He, however, refused. He knotted up her hem and cut it off.[75]

The gentlemen questioned him (again): 'A woman who has come to live with your family and whose status as a married wife is known in (all) your ward, is she to depart simply like that? (You must) fit her out exactly as (she was when) she moved in with you.'[76]

8 ASHUR

The next two cities, Ashur in this chapter and Nineveh in Chapter 9, were Assyrian, located on the limestone plateau of northern Mesopotamia. Both the geography and to some extent the social system of this region differ from the cities of the southern plain,[1] yet the urban culture of the north still owed much to southern developments. This is particularly evident from the written records discovered at Assyrian sites. Ashur and Nineveh both had unusually long histories of occupation, whereas most other capitals, such as Nimrud or Calah, which furnished some of the best-known examples of Assyrian sculpture, were inhabited by the king for only brief periods of less than a century.

Ashur and Nineveh were more than short-lived capitals built on a whim by powerful kings; both were sacred sites – the former the seat of the eponymous god Ashur, the latter dedicated to the goddess of love and war, Ishtar. The role of these cities before and after Assyria asserted its might, and how they fared within the context of the Assyrian state, is worth particular attention. The archaeological evidence has revealed the complexities of architectural sequences, while the tablet collections from both cities tell about early trading ventures, the careers of kings, their care for the cities and something about the religious practices and rituals of the ancient temples.

ASHUR AND ITS EXCAVATIONS[2]

The city of Ashur was built on a rocky limestone cliff that forced the fast-flowing Tigris into a sharp curve. The main stream was also joined by a side-arm in antiquity, so that an oval-shaped island was created with a shoreline of 1.80 kilometres. Rocky outcrops rose some 25 metres above the valley floor, with steep sides. This naturally sheltered position had strategic importance as it made the site comparatively easy to defend, besides forming a landmark with a wide view over the valley. To the west lay the steppeland of the Jezirah, while to the east and north the valley was fertile and suitable for ploughing. The city was between the two Zab rivers, closer to the Lesser than to the Greater Zab, and there was an important pass across the Zagros on to the Iranian plateau.

In the nineteenth century, the mound of Ashur, known as Qalat Sherqat, was, as well as the other Assyrian sites, one of the remotest and least developed corners of the Ottoman Empire. Although its dramatic cliff-top setting aroused the curiosity of a British consul-general in Baghdad, Claudius James Rich, who discovered it in 1821 and published an account of his findings,[3] it was not considered a major site. Austen Layard and Hormuzd Rassam went to it in 1840, and returned there briefly in 1847.[4] They were rewarded by the discovery of the first Assyrian statue ever found, a life-size effigy of Shalmaneser III, seated on a throne completely covered with cuneiform writing. The inscription later turned out to contain a detailed description of the walls of Ashur. Two years later, the clay prism of Tiglath-Pileser I turned up, unearthed by workmen employed by Rassam, who passed on their finds to Mosul. This text was used to verify the decipherment of the Assyrian script, based on Henry Rawlinson's pioneering efforts in reading cuneiform.

The British-backed investigators did not embark on any serious excavations at Qalat Sherqat; they returned now and again, picked up some tablets (Rassam in 1853 and George Smith in 1873, when he discovered the foundation document of Adad-nirari I which describes his temple-building activities). In general they concentrated their efforts on the more promising Assyrian sites near Mosul. The German Oriental Society, which began excavating Babylon in 1899, decided to target another mound which would yield material older than Babylon for one of their scientific and systematic explorations. The neglect of Qalat Sherqat by the French and the British, together with the evidence indicating its potential riches, made it an attractive proposition to the Germans. Furthermore, the Ottoman sultan, Abdul Hamid II, was keen to be of service to the German Kaiser and presented him with the ruin site, which happened to belong to his private estate. This initiated the German excavation, which lasted from 1903 till 1913.

Robert Koldewey came from Babylon to set everything up before passing overall responsibility for the site to Walter Andrae, who had worked with him at Babylon from the beginning. As at Warka, the excavators were all trained architects and, having developed a method for tracing mudbrick walls, they concentrated their efforts on the buildings. They removed layer after layer to establish the sequence of walls and plans, but paid little attention to the contents of the rubble, pottery, tablets, bones or other detritus. Nor did they show much interest in tablets and epigraphy. Even the immensely useful evidence of the Shalmaneser throne inscription continued to be ignored for years. Epigraphists far away in Berlin were given the task of dealing with the tablets as if they had little connection with the site where they were found. The publications of Andrae and his colleagues instead dealt primarily and thoroughly with the architectural structures and demonstrated the stratified sequence of buildings one above the other.

The number of important monuments at Ashur justified their procedure to some extent. Andrae also made sensitive and evocative drawings and reconstructions of the city as he imagined it must have looked, and he wrote a popular monograph[5] in which he attempted to animate the dry archaeological material. He describes how a Greek 'with clear eyes and keen senses' would have experienced Ashur in 688 BC and, by identifying closely with the 'European' sensibilities of the 'Ionian', he evaluates the culture and technologies of the Assyrians in a way that is embarrassingly, though by the standards of his time only mildly, anti-Semitic. His scientific excavation reports, despite their emphasis on architecture, are exemplary and exhaustive.[6]

Although Andrae had hoped to reach well beyond the first millennium structures, the Neo-Assyrian monumental buildings covered such a large proportion of the inner city that systematic attempts to uncover coherent layers of the second millennium and third millennium were impracticable. Therefore it was the major religious buildings of Ashur – the Anu-Adad temple, the Ashur temple, the temple of Sin and Shamash – as well as the palace of Adad-nirari I, with the royal tomb vaults, and the city walls that received most of the attention. Deep soundings were taken only in the area of the Ishtar temple, where Early Dynastic and Ur III levels were uncovered.

Although Ashur had played an important role in the early second millennium, hardly any of the city's remains from the Old Assyrian period were excavated. The fifteenth- and thirteenth-century buildings became better known and later reconstructions of the same buildings simply followed the old plans. There was important inscribed material, especially several rows of stelae,[7] from the Middle Assyrian period, but the best-documented parts of the city date from the ninth and eighth centuries, though even these substantial buildings were much denuded. The city had been attacked and destroyed by the Medes in 614 and the ruins left to the elements for nearly five hundred years till the Parthians established themselves in the area. They then built above the levelled remains of the old Assyrian capital a new city with a typical Hellenistic layout, though the temples on the 'acropolis' still housed some sanctuaries dedicated to Assyrian gods. The largest building was the huge Parthian palace. The Parthians stayed at 'Assor', as it was then called, for three hundred years. Thereafter the road along the Tigris ceased to be maintained until the Sassanian or early Islamic period (seventh or eighth century AD), when a caravanserai was built near the old ruins. The area was to remain a provincial backwater throughout the early Islamic and especially the Ottoman periods.

The third millennium remains

The earliest levels of Qalat Sherqat are those associated with the 'archaic Ishtar-temple', which dates from the Early Dynastic III period (c.2600–2350).[8] The timber and mud roof had fallen in when the temple was destroyed, thus preserving many of the furnishings of the cult room. Precious items, except for minor pieces, had been looted, but small-scale gypsum and alabaster statuettes of female worshippers, clothed in fringed skirts typical of the period, had been left behind, as had large pottery stands, some of them shaped like miniature buildings, found lying on the floor. One small painted gypsum piece shows an elaborately tattooed naked female lying on a bed. A beautifully carved small female head of alabaster may represent a priestess, indicated by its headband that seems to be characteristic for the en. Large pottery vessels and smaller votive gifts, jewellery and ivory figurines were also recovered. Only sections of the temple were excavated, consisting of a narrow court leading to courtyards surrounded by oblong rooms, one of which was identified as the main cult area from its contents and a central offering stand.

The foundation of this sanctuary dates from the early third millennium, at the beginning of the Early Dynastic period, maybe by the Hurrians, who were then beginning to settle in the East Tigris area.[9] Perhaps the site was then a small hill sanctuary[10] dedicated to a female deity. The objects found within the cult room resemble those of other north Mesopotamian sites of the period, such as Mari, Khafadji and Eshnunna, and show that the temple was patronized by the local élite. It seems to have flourished throughout the Early Dynastic and Akkadian periods and perhaps its destruction had something to do with the invasion by the Gutians, who were thought to have originated from the Zagros mountains.[11] The site was called Ashur during the Akkadian period (c.2350–2150), but probably not before.[12] During the time of the Third Dynasty of Ur (c.2150–2000) the temple was rebuilt on the same spot and with the same type of layout, only with thicker walls and slightly larger proportions, by one of the governors of Amar-Sin of Ur, and identified as the sanctuary of Ishtar. The well-appointed graves and several large domestic buildings suggest that Qalat Sherqat had a wealthy population with access to prestige goods (lapis-lazuli seals, copper tools and weapons, pearl necklaces), but there is no indication of the size of the settlement at this period.

ASHUR IN THE OLD ASSYRIAN PERIOD (C.1990–1400)

The archaeological evidence for this period is very patchy. Apart from some building inscriptions, we know only about the early levels of the Ashur temple, those of the old palace and parts of the city walls. Most of these projects date from the time of Shamshi-Addu I (1813–1781), a contemporary of Hammurabi of Babylon, but hardly any of the residential parts of the city have been excavated. The few building inscriptions and a few tablets comprise all the historical evidence from Ashur. However, this is one of the instances where written evidence discovered at a completely different location more than fills the gap. Some 16,000 cuneiform tablets found at the Turkish village of Kültepe, near Kayseri in Cappadocia, turned out to have been part of the economic records of Assyrian businessmen and traders who had established themselves in a commercial enclave a few minutes' journey from the local city of Kanesh. The headquarters of these Assyrian firms, operating in Anatolia, were situated in Ashur. The tablets, which are still not completely published, form the main source of information about the city before Shamshi-Addu. For about a hundred years (*c*.1900–1800), caravans went back and forth between Ashur and central Anatolia. Although the records concern only particular trading connections, namely, the exchange of tin and textiles against silver, gold and copper, they reveal much about the extent of a particular component of the 'international' commercial activities of the time, and especially how it was organized, financed and carried out.[13]

Just how and when Ashur became a rich trading city is still unclear. The majority of the Cappadocian tablets date from *c*.1900 to 1830 BCE. Some business archives were found more or less intact, others had to be pieced together from scattered tablets.[14] They are written in cuneiform in the language known as Old Assyrian, in an anachronistically archaic manner when compared with contemporaneous texts from Babylonia. Since they are tersely written business documents, concerned with shipment of goods, receipts, instructions on purchase policy, taxes paid and reports of transactions, they contain hardly any references to the political situation in the home country. Evidence of the historical background to the Ashur trading ventures therefore had to be pieced together from other, not very reliable sources. For example, the Assyrian King-list (composed *c*.609) contains the names of all the rulers from the beginning of the second millennium down to Ashur-uballit II (611–610).[15] It says that the first 'seventeen kings lived in tents', a reference to the tribal origin of Assyrian royalty. The names of these kings also appear in Hammurabi's list of ancestors and may have been honorary rather than actual antecedents.

In the building inscriptions found at Ashur, which preserve the names of some of the rulers, they called themselves simply 'governor of the god Ashur'. It appears that the cult of this deity became established in the twentieth century BC and that the god may have been named after the city, as 'the one of Ashur', in a shift from the earlier titular female deity.[16] The oldest extant royal inscription is by Ilushuma I (c.1960–1939):

Ilushuma, governor of Ashur, beloved of the god Ashur and the goddess Ishtar, son of Shallim-ahhe, governor of Ashur, son of Puzur-Ashur, governor of Ashur:

(. . .)

The god Ashur opened for me two springs in Mount Ebih and I made bricks for the wall by the two springs.

(. . .)

The 'freedom' of the Akkadians and their children I established. I purified their copper. I established their freedom from the border of the marshes, Ur and Nippur, Awal and Kismar, Der of the god Ishtaran, as far as the city [i.e. Ashur].[17]

Walter Andrae, the German excavator, did indeed find 'water channels and other hydraulic installations, carefully waterproofed with bitumen and wells constructed with trapezoid bricks'.[18] Ilushuma's reference to the 'freedom of the Akkadians', combined with the mention of the purified copper, is now taken to reflect attempts by Ashur's ruler to establish a sort of free-trade zone, enticing traders to do business with Ashur by granting them special privileges.[19]

It is possible that the city had already managed to control the import of tin, a metal vital for the manufacture of bronze, widely used for weapons and other implements. The tin was brought to Ashur by way of a long chain of traders from somewhere in the east, probably Afghanistan. By giving the south Mesopotamian merchants an incentive to buy their tin at Ashur and to sell their wares, particularly fine textiles as well as perhaps copper imported from the Gulf via Ur, Ilushuma made Ashur the hub of commercial connections. His successor, Erishum, claims to have made 'silver, gold, copper, tin, barley and wool exempt from taxes',[20] thereby extending the favourable conditions for trade even further.

The copper and cloth that the Akkadians brought to Ashur were sold for silver and tin, but business with the tin merchants was not conducted in writing. The eastern traders probably conveyed their wares in person. Hence we know little about this exchange. It is likely that they took silver and cloth with them, and the Assyrians themselves set up their own trade representations in Anatolia, then a provincial country divided into many small principalities, rich in minerals and metals, and eager to acquire the latest fashion garments and cloth from Mesopotamia. Tin and Babylonian textiles, in several qualities, were transported from Ashur to central Anatolia, where the trading post (Assyrian *karum*) near Kanesh served as the main entrepôt. Although the government for Ashur seems to have levied some taxes, this was not a state but a private enterprise.

The merchants were entrepreneurs 'driven by the desire to make profit'.[21] Merchants worked in teams, usually composed of family members. The tin and cloth were transported to Kanesh by donkey caravan. They could either be sold there for silver and gold, which were sent back to Ashur, sealed, and with a letter advising the recipient of the exact sum to expect, or else converted into other commodities, such as wool and copper, which were then taken to other Anatolian towns, as far afield as the Black Sea, and exchanged there for silver and gold. The selling price for both tin and textiles was double the purchase price.[22] Although various expenses for transportation, costs for lodgings and taxes had to be deducted from this gain, the merchants were left with enough profit to make it all worth while. Textiles were more bulky to transport and only half as valuable as tin, but since they were much in demand as a foreign luxury, they were also imported.

A typical caravan from Ashur to the Kanesh *karum* would consist of a team of five or six donkeys, in which each beast could carry a weight of 60 to 90 kilograms (2 to 3 talents). They were loaded with textiles and tin, as well as fodder for at least the first stages of the journey, which took between five and six weeks. The donkeys also formed part of the capital, as they could be sold on arrival. Silver, gold and other precious metals (iron) and stones were lighter and much less bulky than tin or cloth. For journeys within Anatolia, especially on level ground, wagons could be bought or hired, drawn by donkeys or oxen.[23] The routes taken by the caravans and the time they took to travel between Ashur and central Anatolia have not been clearly established and probably varied. It seems the actual transport was handed over to specialist haulers who acted as representatives of the company.

Security does not seem to have been a great problem since the local princes benefited from the passing trade through being able to levy various duties. Merchants across the Near East at that time had diplomatic immunity.[24] The ruler of Kanesh also had a right of pre-emption and all caravans were obliged to 'go up to the palace first'. As the texts show, the merchants were well aware that ethical practice was essential to inspire confidence and secure repeat business. Weight stones were carefully checked and precise accounts were demanded by the partners of the company.

Many merchants are well known from their tablets. Some came to live in Anatolia in their youth and stayed for many years. A merchant could marry a local wife in addition to any wife he may have had in Ashur, so long as both were equally provided for. The correspondence between merchants in Anatolia and their wives in Ashur shows how women acted as their husbands' representatives in all kinds of commercial and legal situations.[25] They were also the producers of a great variety of textiles, assisted by other females in the household. They were expected to respond quickly to changes in taste and fashion, as some of the letters show. While sheet-like cloth seems to have been the main bulk item of the textile trade, elaborately finished embroidered garments fetched a high price and were eagerly bought by the Anatolian élite.[26] For their labours women were given some of the profit and they seem to have had considerable control over financial matters.[27]

Not all business conducted in the *karum* of Kanesh was between Ashur and the colony. Some firms seem to have specialized in the Inner Anatolian trade, especially in copper, which was rarely exported to Assyria.[28] There were also entrepreneurs in Ashur who did not engage directly in trading but specialized in providing capital for trade ventures.[29] This was often a form of long-term investment over several years with the profit allocation between trader and creditor being agreed in advance.[30] As we have also seen, Assyrians had resident representatives in other Babylonian cities, such as Sippar, Mari and Nippur. This network of merchants was able, for some hundred years, to create a circuit of trading operations that brought great wealth and experience to Ashur. Nevertheless, just because Ashur and its Anatolian market are particularly well documented, it does not mean that Ashur had a monopoly on trade or somehow controlled all the commercial activity throughout upper Mesopotamia. On the contrary, it is rapidly becoming clear, as more archives are discovered, that Ashur constituted just one among several trade circuits. Emar and Mari on the Euphrates, Carchemish in northern Syria and Sippar and Babylon, of course, also operated networks of exchange in other areas.[31]

The tablets from Cappadocia also contain information about the governing institution at Ashur, which is always referred to simply as 'the city'.[32] This was probably a board composed of the leaders of the great merchant houses, who seem to have met in a building called the 'city house' (*bit alim*). The committee made decisions on commercial policy, fixed the rates of export tax and sealed the bales of caravans leaving the city. It also acted as a diplomatic body (a bit like the British East India Company) and controlled relations with Anatolian rulers on whose cooperation and protection the caravans and resident merchants relied.

Powerful businessmen were also holders of another office, that of the *limmu*, translated as 'eponym', since the years were not retrospectively named after important events as in southern Mesopotamia, but after the *limmu* himself. The official was chosen by lot and officiated for one year. It is likely that the chairman of the city board was the current eponym and the office rotated among a small group of influential citizens. The ruler, who in the inscriptions always calls himself 'governor (*iššiakum*) of the god Ashur', seems to have had a complementary rather than a superior role.[33] He was responsible for public works, for overseeing the judiciary, and took a leading part in the city's religious and ceremonial rites.[34] The title *ruba'um* marks him as the head of the aristocratic lineage, with the highest status in Ashur's society.[35]

The merchant accounts have nothing to say about relations between the city and the local population, or about the role of the temples. This produces an impression that Ashur in the twentieth century BC was primarily a capitalist trading state whose wealth depended exclusively on mercantile enterprise, rather like the Abbasid Baghdad of *The*

Thousand and One Nights. Any intensive commercial activity is likely to stimulate a local economy, but we know little about the organization of Ashur's local textile production, for instance, or how the farmers and pastoralists were affected. However, the prosperity of the city must have produced benefits in the form of the improvements to local amenities, such as Ilushuma's wells, the city walls and the temple buildings, as the rulers claim in their inscriptions.

Ashur under Shamshi-Addu I

At the time when Shamshi-Addu I seized control of Ashur, the Anatolian trade had just collapsed and the *karum* in Kanesh been hastily abandoned. As a result the 'city' lost its main source of revenue, which may have precipitated a crisis that could be exploited by a powerful outsider. Information about Shamshi-Addu's rule comes from the archives of Mari, at the time another thriving trading city on the Euphrates, and from the numerous inscriptions left by the king himself and the Assyrian King-list.

Shamshi-Addu was the son of an Amorite chief, Ilu(a)-Kabkabi, who operated from a base at Terqa on the Euphrates and fought with other local leaders, such as the one of Mari, Yaggid-Lim, who claimed to have driven him out of Terqa.[36] Shamshi-Addu seems to have gone to Babylonia, as the Assyrian King-list notes, at a time when the struggle for political influence and territorial control was intense, especially in the Middle Euphrates region. It was vital for him to be informed of the key players and to keep abreast of any developments, alliances, quarrels and military actions, and the Mari tablets are certainly full of intelligence reports about the situation across a wide geographical area. In these circumstances, any quick-witted, well-informed and decisive person, able to exploit an opportunity to build influence, ruthless in the pursuit of power and calm enough to preserve it, could be a man to make history. Shamshi-Addu was just such a man, who rose from obscurity to be 'king of the world'.

The exact sequence of events cannot be reconstructed and only the highlights of his ascent have been transmitted. He seized Ekallate, a town on the Tigris not far north of Ashur, and ousted the local ruler Erishum I,[37] but there is no evidence to show he operated out of Ashur, let alone made it the capital of an Old Assyrian 'empire', which certainly did not exist at that time.[38] Any impression that this was the case rests entirely with the Assyrian King-list, which integrated Shamshi-Addu, the usurper, into a coherent dynastic line. During his thirty-two-year reign, Shamshi-Addu gradually extended his territory by a mixture of diplomacy cemented by dynastic marriages and military force. He conquered Mari and installed his younger son as regent. From Ekallate he eventually controlled the whole of the Jezirah, the Middle Euphrates region, with Terqa and Karana, up to the Habur valley, where Shubat-Enlil (modern Tell Leilan) became a thriving provincial capital. His power extended further east into the Zagros mountains, thereby securing access to the Iranian plateau along the pass of Shamshara. He adopted the old Mesopotamian royal title *šar kiššati*, 'king of the universe', a pun that plays both on the old epithet 'king of Kish' (which Shamshi-Addu did not control!) and the notion of 'totality'.[39] He seems to have regarded Ashur as city of special status that conducted its own affairs. At one point Ashur was even involved in arbitrating a dispute between Ekallate and another city.[40]

Shamshi-Addu, perhaps following the example of Babylonian rulers, manifested his authority by engaging in building operations and having written inscriptions composed for him. He seems to have employed Babylonian scribes for this task, since all were written in standard Babylonian and not in the Old Assyrian dialect. The German architectural excavators were delighted by the high quality of his building works, from the purity and solidity of the clay used for bricks to the coherent and lucid layout of the buildings.[41] Shamshi-Addu's main work was what later became the Ashur temple, which he, according to his numerous foundation documents, dedicated to the Babylonian god Enlil. This also demonstrated that his imperial ambitions were based on southern Mesopotamian patterns and that he was not, as has been claimed, forging the first 'Assyrian' empire. He was no Assyrian and made no efforts to conform to the city's particular attachment to its own god Ashur.

The temple occupied the highest part of the cliff in the north-east corner, where the rocky plateau formed an extended oval. The temple, rectangular in shape, 110 metres long and 60 metres wide, with two successive courts, connected by a ramp to overcome the 2-metre difference in gradient, fitted snugly into this position. Its courts were paved with burnt bricks and surrounded by a row of chambers, and the walls were carefully structured with recesses and niches. Brick-building skills were highly developed at this period in Upper Mesopotamia. The temple façade was artfully articulated by engaged round columns and pilasters built with specially manufactured bricks.[42] Shamshi-Addu may also have built the ziggurat connected to this temple,[43] and a palace perhaps on the remains of an older structure from the Akkadian period. The palace was a compact, well-laid-out building, almost square in shape, with a central square courtyard around which reception rooms were grouped and several subsidiary courtyards in the lateral sectors. This building was also to persist relatively unchanged into the first millennium, becoming the burial place for many Assyrian monarchs.[44]

The political unification of Upper Mesopotamia did not last beyond the death of Shamshi-Addu. Although he may have had 'a brilliant foresight'[45] of the possibility of controlling the whole of the north-east, it was premature. He in fact divided the territories between his two sons, Ishme-Dagan and Yasmah-Addu. The archive of Mari has preserved some of Shamshi-Addu's letters to Yasmah-Addu, after he installed him there as governor, in which he frequently criticized his son for being an ineffective administrator, spending too much time with women and driving around in fast chariots.[46] In due course Yasmah-Addu was ousted by Zimri-Lim, when he returned from exile in Aleppo to claim his ancestral throne. Neither did the older son, Ishme-Dagan, always held up in his father's letters as an example of tough manliness, last long in Ekallate and the east Tigris area after he took it over.

At Ashur the old 'city' administration asserted itself once again,[47] but little is known about what happened between Ishme-Dagan and Ashur-uballit I in the fourteenth century, a period therefore considered a 'dark age' in Assyrian history. But the fact that the regime of Shamshi-Addu was considered illegitimate in the generation after Ishme-Dagan is borne out by an inscription on an alabaster slab by Puzur-Ashur, who does not feature in the Assyrian King-list:

When (I), Puzur-Ashur, vice-regent of the god Ashur, son of Ashur-bel-shame, defeated . . . son of Asinum, [descendant] of Shamshi-Addu, whose dress [was improper] for . . . who did wrong [against] Ashur-bel-shame.

(. . .)

Further, I destroyed that palace of Shamshi-Addu, his grandfather, a man of foreign extraction, not of Assyrian blood, who had destroyed the shrines of the city [Ashur] and built that palace.[48]

ASHUR AS THE CAPITAL
OF THE ASSYRIAN EMPIRE

During the mid second millennium, the political scene in the Ancient Near East was dominated by aristocratic élites of 'foreign' origin who ruled over the indigenous populations. The longest lasting of these dynasties was that of the Kassites in Babylonia, who ruled from c.1600 to 1155. In Anatolia an Indo-European aristocratic group formed the Hittite empire (1420–1200), and in Great Mesopotamia another Indo-European leadership ruled a kingdom known as Mitanni (c.1500–1370). All the rulers of these kingdoms engaged in a more or less intense form of diplomatic exchange, which involved the pharaohs of Eighteenth Dynasty Egypt, who had dominion over much of the coastal area of Syria.

The language used for correspondence between the various courts was Babylonian, and some of the letters sent to Egypt from the Babylonian, Hittite, Mitanni and Syrian courts were found in the archives of Akhenaton's city at modern Tell al-Amarna. Influence over Syria and Upper Mesopotamia was much contested between Egypt, the Hittites and Mitanni, and led to various military campaigns. The tension between Hittites and Egyptians ended with a draw after the battle of Qadesh in c.1275, but Mitanni had lost its independence to the Hittites back in the mid fourteenth century. The resulting disintegration of the Mitanni state into a Hittite province paved the way for a new north Mesopotamian power and the kings of Ashur took control, with the reign of Ashur-uballit I (c.1365–1330) marking the beginning of the Assyrian state. He sent an exploratory letter to Egypt, together with gifts, to test out how these overtures would be received. Evidently he continued to enlarge his territories and influence to an extent where, in his next missive to Amenophis IV, he felt able to adopt a high-handed tone and insist on equality of status, addressing the pharaoh as brother and demanding substantial amounts of gold:

May it be well with you, your family, and your land. When I saw your messengers I was extremely glad. Your messengers are entertained with all due honour in my court. I have dispatched to you as a peace offering a beautiful royal chariot (from among those) that I myself drive and two white horses that I likewise drive (myself); one chariot without a team of horse; and one seal of beautiful lapis lazuli. Are the offerings of great kings like this? Gold is like dust in your land. One simply gathers it up. Why does it appear so valuable to you? I am in the process of building my new palace. Send me enough gold to decorate it properly. When Ashur-nadin-ahhe, my ancestor, wrote to Egypt, he was sent twenty talents of gold. When the king of Hanigalbat wrote to Egypt to your father, he sent him twenty talents of gold. {now} I {am the equal} of the king of Hanigalbat[49] but to me you have sent [a mere . . . talents] of gold. It is not enough to pay my messengers for their trips to and fro! If you are seriously disposed towards friendship, send me much more gold! It is all in the family! Write to me what you (yourself) need and it will be supplied. We are distant lands. Should one messenger keep running to and fro like this?[50]

Although there had been tensions between Babylonia and Assyria, Ashur-uballit seems to have improved relations and even married his daughter, Muballit-sherua, to Karaindash, son of the Kassite king Burnaburiash. When the son born of the union was killed in a palace revolt, Ashur-uballit interfered. He killed the usurper who had assumed kingship and installed a relative of the previous king on the Babylonian throne. Sources for these events are contradictory, however, and it is not clear whether the new incumbent was an infant, the child of Muballit-sherua, or a grown-up other son of Burnaburiash II.[51] During his thirty-five-year reign Ashur-uballit consolidated the claims of Assyria to be a power to rank equal with Babylonia, the Hittites and Egypt.

Ashur-uballit's two immediate successors had some trouble securing the borders in the northern and eastern mountains and subduing the tribal populations there. The next stage in the expansion of Assyria came with the reign of Adad-nirari I (1307–1275), who gained territories in the south at the expense of Babylonia, pushing back the frontiers to the Diyala area. He also capitalized on the difficulties the Hittite king had to face in Anatolia and conquered the Hittite vassal state Mitanni, which gave him control over the middle Euphrates regions as far as Carchemish. His successor, Shalmaneser I (1274–1245), consolidated the Assyrian domination of this area by building a number of new fortifications and restructuring the administration. The Mitanni vassal ruler was replaced by an Assyrian palace official and Assyrian colonists were settled to develop the agricultural potential of the region.[52] His royal inscriptions now additionally contain accounts of military campaigns and no longer report only building works, as had been the custom. He refers to himself by a number of epithets stressing his warlike character as a 'valiant hero, capable of battle with his enemies, whose aggressive battle flashes like a flame and whose weapons attack like a merciless death-trap'.[53] This was henceforth to set the tone for all Assyrian royal inscriptions.

The reign of Shalmaneser I's son, Tukulti-Ninurta I (1244–1208), marks the high point of the first Assyrian empire. His reign is also remarkably well documented, thanks to the discovery of numerous archives.[54] He turned Assyria into the most formidable military and economic power of his day, and the way he attained his goals is described in the royal inscriptions. The following excerpt demonstrates how an initial show of strength would be followed by a formal treaty for tribute obligation and a declaration of loyalty to Assyrian rule:

At that time they banded together against my army in rugged (and) very mountainous terrain. They fiercely took up position for armed conflict. Trusting in Ashur and the great gods, my lord, I struck (and) brought about their defeat. I filled the caves and ravines of the mountains with their corpses. I made heaps of their corpses (like grain piles) beside their gates. Their cities I ravaged, (and) turned into ruin hills ... Thus I became lord of the extensive land of the Qutu.

(...)

The hordes of princes of Abulli ... (king of the land) of Uqumenu I captured (and) brought them bound to my city Ashur. I made them swear by the great gods of heaven (and) underworld, I imposed upon them the (exacting) yoke of my lordship, (and then) released them to return to their lands ... fortified cities I subdued at my feet and imposed (upon them) corvée. Annually I receive with ceremony their valuable tribute in my city Ashur.[55]

Despite such repeated shows of strength, Assyrian control over the far-flung corners of the empire and the ever-expanding borders of the state was continuously subverted by the local population. Pastoralist tribes in particular evaded direct confrontations but continued to raid the border country. Tukulti-Ninurta seems to have been successful in subduing the north but to have had more problems in the south. His most controversial victory was over Babylonia. He defeated Kastiliash V, a Kassite ruler, taking him and members of the court captive to Assyria. He then simply annexed Babylonia and assumed the traditional Babylonian royal titles. The first period of Assyrian rule over their southern neighbour was to last thirty-two years and resulted in a strong and lasting Babylonian influence on the élite of Ashur. In terms of the international balance of power, on the other hand, the occupation of Babylonia and the loss of west–east trade strengthened the territorial claims of Elam, a state in western Iran that was to grow to be a major adversary to Assyria in the years to come.[56]

By the thirteenth century the city of Ashur had grown into a populous city, the capital of the world power. The old part of town was still the centre of religious, ceremonial and administrative functions, but a new, primarily residential part, known as the 'New Town' (*alu eššu*), had grown up in the southern side. The layout of the centre of the inner city was an irregular large square, surrounded by four monumental buildings: the palace and the three temples. To the south was the double sanctuary of the moon and the sun (Shamash and Sin), built by Ashur-nirari I *c.*1500, a completely symmetrical building linked by a central square courtyard with cult rooms off to either side.

Tukulti-Ninurta I also rebuilt the temple of Ishtar. He began to raze the old walls but then changed his mind. He left the old temple as it was and built a new one on a much larger scale alongside it. The new cult room was dedicated to the local manifestation of Ishtar, *aššuritu*, 'the Assyrian one'.[57] It measured 32.5 by 8.7 metres. The façade was dominated by projecting square gate towers. A transverse courtyard led directly into the vast, oblong cella, where the image of the goddess stood on a pedestal along the narrow side, under a baldachin and on a higher level that was accessed by a flight of steps. No less than nine foundation documents by Tukulti-Ninurta have been discovered in this temple, inscribed with the standard text, as well as an extra one that explained the change of plan. He chose different materials, from large limestone slabs to alabaster, lead and gold,[58] and deposited them on cushions of pearls and shells, stone chips and leaves drenched in honey and oil.

Tukulti-Ninurta was an energetic builder. Other than the reconstruction of the Ishtar temple, he strengthened and substantially rebuilt the city walls, excavated a moat nearly twenty metres wide and began work on a large palace for which enormous amounts of earth were moved to provide a platform. Little is known about the building because of later structures having been built in subsequent higher layers. But his most ambitious project was to build a new town three kilometres north of Ashur, called Kar-Tukulti-Ninurta, which became, for a short while, his main residence. The motivation for such an undertaking, which was to be repeated by several later Assyrian kings, was probably partly megalomania – to demonstrate the absolute power of the king by huge construction programmes – and partly paranoia. In his new palace the king hoped to gain greater control over Ashur while distancing himself from the old city, which he may have seen as being rife with intrigue.

The sack of Babylon and the abduction of the gods had been far more difficult to legitimize than the brutal suppressions of barbarian peoples at the fringes of the empire. Babylonia was acknowledged as having an older cultural tradition than Ashur and Babylon was a sacred city. The king's actions may therefore have provoked negative reactions among educated senior officials in Ashur. At Kar-Tukulti-Ninurta he was to put royal power on a more secure footing, quite literally on virgin soil. The new city was meant to house a people loyal to the king and he spared no expense in making it beautiful. The palaces and temples were decorated with brilliantly coloured glazed tiles and wall paintings. It was watered by its own canal and he planted gardens. He financed the new city by tribute and booty, using people deported from other parts of the empire to supply labour. It would be to no avail. Perhaps it was his very success at demonstrating power that provoked a reaction. According to an Assyrian chronicle, there was a palace rebellion when he was locked into a room and assassinated by one of his sons.[59] Intense struggles for the succession followed and the vast empire of Tukulti-Ninurta I, which had stretched from north-east Syria to southern Mesopotamia, gradually shrank back within its north Mesopotamian limits.

In the twelfth century the thirty-eight-year reign of the energetic Tiglath-Pileser I (1114–1076) represented another period of Assyrian expansion that could only be achieved and maintained by continuous military campaigns coupled with large-scale deportations. Especially troublesome were the incursions of Aramaean tribes, who also raided and threatened the Babylonian north. It was a sign of this king's considerable strength and energy that he also found time for pursuits other than warfare. His lengthy royal annals describe his expeditions to the Mediterranean, where he went to sea and killed 'a sea-horse' (probably a dolphin), as well as other hunting expeditions. He also collected exotic plants and trees and created a kind of game reserve, stocked with animals which had either been given to him as presents (a monkey and a crocodile from the king of Egypt) or else he had captured himself (four live elephants from the Habur region).

He also put up temples and monuments in many cities. In Ashur he built a very individual structure, the huge double temple dedicated to the sky-god Anu and the weather-god Adad. Its walled forecourt, accessed by a central gate flanked by projecting buttresses, led to the twin sanctuaries, each of which abutted against a ziggurat (36.6 by 35.1 metres), probably reached from the roof of the double cellas between them. This, in its simple monumentality, must have been a very impressive sight.

Tiglath-Pileser's son, Ashur-bel-kala (1073–1056), also had continuous problems with the Aramaean tribes, who had, by then, penetrated into all areas of Great Mesopotamia. He seems to have managed to retain Assyrian supremacy and to have made a treaty with the Babylonians, but after his death the Assyrian empire disintegrated and, as in Babylonia, another 'dark age' set in, for which written sources were few and scattered. Assyria then revived again in the beginning of the first millennium, to become more powerful than ever before, but this expansion of the empire was primarily westwards and northwards. As a result, Ashur came to occupy a marginal position.[60] It was also relatively close to the vulnerable border with Babylonia, and these facts may have contributed to Ashurnasirpal II's decision to move the court to Calah, further to the north, in 879 BC. Ashur ceased to be a capital city and became a sacred city, the burial place of Assyrian monarchs who were laid to rest in huge marble sarcophagi in vaults beneath the Old Palace. It also preserved the historical records of Assyrian kings and high officials in the form of stone stelae placed in an open square along the south side of the inner city wall.

From the fourteenth century *limmu* officials and other dignitaries had put up such stones recording their names and title of office. Since Adad-nirari I, kings had also erected stelae, placed opposite those of the officials. The exact function of these monuments is still debated, but it seems no accident that the stelae of officials faced those of kings. This underlined the strength of the aristocratic élite at Ashur at the same time as suggesting that the continuity of Assyrian culture was safeguarded by an office demonstrably older than kingship.

The presence of many temples in the city (some thirty-four in all), but especially the towering sanctuary of Ashur on the northern promontory, made Ashur the main official religious centre, the most important place for all the crucial rituals of kingship, such as coronations and the celebrations of seasonal festivals.

THE ASHUR TABLET COLLECTIONS

As in Babylonia, the temples were not just places of worship but also centres of learning. When Tukulti-Ninurta I brought Babylonian officials to his capital, he also enlarged his tablet collections immensely. The strong Babylonian influence of the fourteenth century was to have a lasting impact on the development of Assyrian literature and many archive collections were discovered at Ashur.[61] Most of the texts from the Middle Assyrian period (the time of Tukulti-Ninurta I and Tiglath-Pileser I) were found in the south-east corner of the Ashur temple. They contained the standard reference works (sign lists, lexical lists, vocabularies), omen lists, hymns, prayers, rituals and also more specialized texts, such as perfume recipes (written to the instruction of female perfume makers), a horse training manual, lists of pharmaceutical plants and literary compositions, some in Sumerian ('The Return of Ninurta'),[62] some bilingual (creation myths), and a catalogue of song titles. The availability of such works made a great impact on the scribes and inspired them to compose a 700-line epic in praise of Tukulti-Ninurta abounding in learned references and literary artifice.[63]

Most of the archives from the first millennium come from the private houses in the new city that belonged to grandees of Ashur society. Some were families of scribes and the tablets reflect their interests and professional orientation. In the house of the chief singer Ashur-shuma-ishbu, for instance, many hymns, including several royal hymns, were found,[64] as well as literary texts such as the Anzu myth, the story of Etana and the highly erotic 'divine love-lyrics' which concern the affair between Marduk and Ishtar and the jealous ravings of Marduk's wife Zarpanitum.[65]

A family of exorcists had a very large private library comprising exorcists' manuals, oracles, prayers, diagnostic texts and many prescriptions for spells and rituals to counteract any number of complaints and evils. Many little figurines, destined to be used in their apotropaic rituals, were also discovered. The learned priests also had a collection of literary texts and a very interesting topography of the city of Ashur, describing the temples, ziggurats, bastions and gates.[66]

In total, some 4,300 tablets were found in these archives, which gives us some idea of the intensity of literary activity in the city and the wide range of sources available. Ashur's reputation as a centre of learning was acknowledged by the title *al nemeqi*, 'city of wisdom'.[67]

RELIGION AND RITUAL

The Babylonian influence on Ashur goes back to the end of the third millennium, when the city was part of the Ur III state. Shamshi-Addu I had also stressed his connection to the south and may have favoured the cult of Enlil over that of Ashur. Such exposure to southern Mesopotamian ideas and practices, especially with regard to religion and ideology, must have left some mark, though the scarcity of theological texts from the early period makes it impossible to substantiate any direct importation of Babylonian thought.[68] But certainly by the time of Tukulti-Ninurta I, and during the reigns of Sennacherib's successors, which brought an influx both of Babylonian professionals and their archives, scholars were repositioning the local god Ashur as occupying the same if not a superior status to that of Marduk in the south. This led to an Assyrian version of the creation epic that features Ashur in the role of Marduk and other similar compositions. To what extent these were intellectual exercises which did little to change the older cult traditions is another matter since we know so little about such traditions in the first place.[69]

Peculiar to the Assyrian ritual is the close involvement of the king and the royal family. The gods even came to visit the palace. Adad-nirari I talks of a room inside his palace, 'within which the dais of the god Ashur, my lord, was built and annually the god Ashur, my lord, proceeds to that dais to take up residence'.[70] Tukulti-Ninurta curses any future ruler who 'prevents [the gods who dwell in] the city [Ashur] from [entering] my palace [during festivals]',[71] and Tiglath-Pileser I reports that the gods are being offered sheep when they visit the palace. More regular were the rituals in which the king had to perform for Ashur, although only fragments of texts describing such ceremonies survive:

... the king has made ... rise ... to the temple of Anu he brought (statues of the goddesses) Sherua, Kippat-mati ...

(. . .)

to the temple of Anu they have gone. He has made Ashur sit in his seat, a ... and torch he has lit, and sacrificial sheep he has slaughtered, a pot with food he has put down, *hammurtu* beer he has offered, he has taken up his position, the king has left, salt on the pickled mutton that was in the *qersu* sanctuary he has strewn, *bušu* containers they have rubbed, the king goes straight to the palace. On the sixth day the king has left the palace ...

(. . .)

the queen has risen, she collected (everything needed?), '(the statue of the goddess) Sherua has started out' she has said three times.[72]

The royal inscriptions endlessly reiterate the old notion that the king is the vice-regent of Ashur as well as his chief priest, and that his authority rests on the command of his lord Ashur and the other great gods. This is a continuation of the very ancient Mesopotamian tradition of regarding the ruler as the mediator between mankind and the gods.

The gods also visited each other's shrines; one fragment describes Ashur's stay in the chapel of the weather-god Dagan. Another special occasion was the Akitu festival, which could be performed at various times during the year and was not exclusively a New Year celebration.[73] The most important feature of this feast was also an outing for the gods, who went to some open space, like a garden, generally within the city. When Sennacherib built a new, special Akitu house, he did so in imitation of a Babylonian custom which located the festival house outside the city walls. Sennacherib located his in a level part of town, north of the Tabira Gate. He incorporated a pleasure garden into the design and must have made it a pretty sight, with regular rows of bushes and trees within a central courtyard. He had to construct special installations for the water supply; Andrae found traces of a well and water channels that had been carved out of the rocky surface.[74] The statues of the gods were transported along the specially paved streets on wagons pulled along bronze rails. Each had his or her own niche in the main cult room. At the end of the ceremonies the gods returned to the city by boat, taking advantage of the current.

The god Ashur

After the destruction of Ashur when the city revived again in the Parthian period, so did the cult of Ashur. Very little is known about this god's personality. There are no myths or stories about Ashur, and not even his symbol has been clearly identified. On some Assyrian reliefs there appears a winged sun-disc with a bearded male wielding bow and arrows; that has been interpreted as a representation of Ashur, but this has never been confirmed by written identification. It could as easily refer to some other deity. Ashur's origins are obscure. He may have been a West Semitic deity, or a Hurrian one. He was probably one of the many manifestations of a weather-god, especially on Mount Ebih, since he is listed as 'lord of Ebih' in texts from the Ur III period. In the course of time, many other powers were ascribed to him. Inspired perhaps by the example of the Sumerian Enlil, he became a supreme ruler of the pantheon. But in comparison with the Babylonian deities, whose cosmic powers were part of a coherent theological system and whose family relationships also stemmed from a complex pantheon, Ashur was undefined.

Only in the aftermath of Sennacherib's anti-Babylonian policy, which culminated in the destruction of Babylon and the abduction of Marduk and other Mesopotamian deities, did Ashur's divine persona become more complex, if clearly patterned on the example of Marduk. The creation epic was rewritten to feature Ashur instead of Marduk and, as we have seen, Sennacherib built a festival house in order to celebrate a Babylonian style New Year festival.[75]

Sennacherib's efforts to make Marduk redundant were not followed through by his successors. Esarhaddon returned the statue of Marduk to Babylon and rebuilt the temple his father had destroyed. Ashur once again became what he always had been, the local deity, not just of the city of Ashur but of the whole empire. His most important function was to be a focus of Assyrian identity. This is borne out not only by the official inscriptions which stress the close connection between king, state and god, but also by the frequent use of Ashur in personal names. The epicentre and the origin of this cult was the city of Ashur. Ashur may have been the 'national' deity in the times of great empires, when his name struck fear into the populations of distant lands, as the inscriptions tell us, but ultimately Ashur is the god of the city of Ashur. He was there at the beginning of history and was still there long after the demise of the powerful Mesopotamian states. Even today the few remaining Nestorian Christians, who live in northern Syria and northern Iraq, as well as in exile abroad, call themselves 'Assyrians' and their official symbol is the god within the sun-disc whom they believe to be Ashur, not as a deity but as a guardian of their assumed identity.

The ancient mound of Nineveh is nowadays almost engulfed by the urban sprawl of the city of Mosul. Dual carriageways pass just outside the old ramparts and modern houses cover a large area of the old city. The offices of the university, where some Iraqi Assyriologists may be found at work, oversee the partially restored walls and gates of the Assyrian capital. But Nineveh's proximity to a living city means it is implicated in the political affairs of our time. The looting of antiquities has become more common as clandestine markets have generated some form of undeclared income in an economy crippled by the UN sanctions against Iraq. A lack of finance and materials for the maintenance of the ruin sites has accelerated the deterioration of the monuments, creating a 'world heritage disaster' according to one American archaeologist who formerly worked at the site.[1]

The explorations of the past and the efforts of historians and epigraphists have allowed us a glimpse at Nineveh. We therefore know its history relatively well for the short span of time when it was the capital of a world empire; that is, for less than a hundred years, from 705 until its destruction in 612. Even so there are many questions that remain unanswered. The architectural evidence is very scanty because the mid-nineteenth-century excavation methods were crude and records often inexact.

In the mid nineteenth century the dimensions of Nineveh could still be clearly seen: a not quite rectangular site enclosed by a massive wall some twelve kilometres in length. The largest mound lay along the west side of the city walls and was known by its Turkish name of Kuyunjik. A smaller mound was occupied by a mosque built within the remains of an earlier Christian monastery, which was known as

Tell Nebi Yunus, the Mound of the Prophet Jonah, who was believed to have been buried there. This smaller mound was also inhabited by some villagers and is still so occupied to this day. Only a few soundings and limited excavations have therefore ever been possible on this mound. Most attention was thus concentrated on Kuyunjik, which was more than a mile long and a quarter of a mile in width, with enough accumulated debris to raise the surface of the mound ninety feet above the surrounding plain.[2]

The proximity of the ruins to the district capital of Mosul made them conspicuous to early explorers. Various items, such as inscribed tablets, had been finding their way into the hands of visiting dignitaries since the late eighteenth century. The first person to take a serious interest in the site was the French consul at Mosul, Émile Botta.[3] He started digging on Kuyunjik in 1842, but found little except accumulated mudbrick. He diverted his attention to another mound in the vicinity, known as Khorsabad, where he discovered the first of the Assyrian sculpted reliefs. While thus busily engaged at finding ever more splendid monuments, he did not give up hope on Kuyunjik. A younger man, the Englishman Austen Layard, had meanwhile arrived, eager for adventure and determined to secure the rights to other promising mounds. He was given permission to explore the southern side of Kuyunjik and began work there in 1845. Although the new French supervisor, Rouet, who replaced Botta on the site, felt the French had prior rights, Layard persisted with his trial shafts and in 1847 found a palace:

I opened not less than seventy-one halls, chambers, passages, whose walls, almost without exception, had been panelled with slabs of sculptured alabaster, recording the triumph and the great deeds of the Assyrian kings. By a rough calculation about 9,880 feet, or nearly two miles, of bas reliefs, with twenty-seven portals formed by colossal winged bulls, lion sphinxes, were uncovered in that part alone during my researches.[4]

The slabs of 'sculptured alabaster' made the tracing of walls relatively easy. They had been set in a groove below floor level against a mudbrick wall. With the removal of the slabs the walls soon disintegrated and since we only have Layard's hasty sketches, the architectural layout of the palaces is known only very partially. Despite his success at uncovering some of the finest Assyrian antiquities, Layard tired of this occupation and left the Middle East in 1851 to pursue a career in politics. His successor at Nineveh on behalf of the British Museum was Hormuzd Rassam, the brother of the British vice-consul at Mosul, Christian Rassam.[5] The brothers were natives of the city, from a Christian family and great anglophiles. Hormuzd was particularly keen to serve the British cause and determined to gain any advantage he could over the French, who still considered they had a prior claim on the site.

Rassam made his workmen sink some exploratory trenches in the French part of the mound under cover of darkness, and, when they duly found more sculptured slabs, declared that under new rules of his own devising the discovered palace was his to explore. Even though the French conceded defeat, the money for Rassam's excavations was running out. In great haste he tore the reliefs from the walls and shipped them to London, where scenes of hunting that showed king Ashurbanipal killing lions, onagers and gazelles have continued to be much admired for their naturalism and sense of pathos. He also came across a large collection of cuneiform tablets, subsequently considered to be from the library of the royal palace.

In 1854 Colonel H. C. Rawlinson, the distinguished scholar and celebrated decipherer of cuneiform, arrived in Mosul for a year, having enlisted the support of the Assyrian Excavation Fund. He continued Rassam's work at the palace of Ashurbanipal. In 1873 another scholar, George Smith, came to the site, sent by a mission organized by the *Daily Telegraph* in order to locate a missing portion of the Assyrian flood story that had been written on one of the 'library tablets' from Kuyunjik. Smith found the fragment without much trouble but died from dysentery near Aleppo in 1876. From then on the aim of all the subsequent British Museum excavations was to find more tablets. Rassam, followed by Budge and King, both British Museum curators, were at Nineveh from 1876 until 1903.

The arrival of Campbell Thompson in 1904 signalled a change of direction, since he was keen to establish scientific excavation and to pay more attention to architecture. He discovered the Nabu temple, but the project was discontinued for lack of funds and only resumed more than twenty years later in 1927 when Campbell Thompson, assisted by the young Max Mallowan, soon to be married to the crime writer Agatha Christie, returned to Nineveh and embarked on a gigantic deep sounding of the site of the Ishtar temple to determine the archaeological sequence of habitation.[6] The earliest levels before virgin soil was struck dated to the sixth millennium, as the pottery sequence showed. A few building levels of the temple were partially revealed, but there was no provision for any large-scale exploration of layers earlier than the first millennium.

In the 1960s the Iraqi Directorate of Antiquities resumed work at Nineveh, alarmed by the speed at which the modern city was beginning to engulf the site. The objective was to make the antiquity of the site a visible reminder of the past and turn it into a museum. To preserve the integrity of the perimeter of the inner city, the Iraqi team restored parts of the old city wall and some of the gates. Between 1987 and 1990 American archaeologists from Berkeley joined the Iraqi team and worked on some of the city residential quarters and the so-called Halzi Gate, where gruesome evidence of a last desperate struggle against the Median and Babylonian enemy was discovered.

This summary of events clearly shows how little of the long history of Nineveh has so far come to light. The artistic treasures of the great Assyrian palaces have been shipped to London, together with large numbers of cuneiform tablets. For earlier historical periods we so far have only the evidence from texts found elsewhere, as well as some samples of pottery and a few other artefacts from the temples. Nineveh was found too early, before archaeology had been invented. The story of its discovery reflects Victorians' preoccupation with origins and the political mastery of the Orient, even as its neglect after the First World War and the ransacking of the ruins during the time of the UN sanctions reflect the post-colonial situation of the twentieth century. In the biblical accounts, for centuries the main source for stories about the city, Nineveh was doomed to be punished, a city the Hebrew God wanted to see brought low, to have even the memory of it erased in retaliation for what the Assyrians had done to the Jews. It would be a cruel irony if the last remains of Nineveh were to disappear as the result of the vengeful spirit of a Western superpower.

HISTORY OF SETTLEMENT

Nineveh lies well within the Assyrian heartland, in a well-watered and fertile country situated on the best or most frequented of the Tigris crossings and the focus of greater routes serving all the settled regions of the Near East.[7] There are no surface survey data from Nineveh and the archaeological sequence derives solely from Campbell Thompson's work on the lower levels of the Ishtar temple[8] and Mallowan's subsequent deep sounding at the same place,[9] when it became clear that the temple foundations had been cut into prehistorical layers from the late fourth millennium. The accumulated debris making up these early layers was surprisingly thick (20 metres), which accounts for the differential in the levels of central Kuyunjik and the surrounding city area. The sequence makes it clear that Nineveh was continuously occupied from the fifth to the third millennium. The earliest levels are represented by Chalcolithic painted pottery,[10] followed by Uruk layers, replete with cylinder seals and masses of 'bevel-rimmed bowls' and other Late Uruk artefacts.

This was obviously an important place during the second half of the fourth millennium, even though the excavators failed to locate any architectural structures through their lack of time and experience in tracing mudbrick. The latest levels of the prehistoric city date from c.3000–2800, a period known as Nineveh v in Campbell Thompson's sequence, characterized by a particular type of pottery common in the north but not found in the southern regions of Mesopotamia. The Kuyunjik sequence breaks off at this level and it is possible that the main area of settlement shifted to the Nebi Yunus site, which has never been explored because of the presence of the Muslim shrine and cemetery at its summit.[11] The earliest phases of the Ishtar temple were assigned by the excavators to the Akkad period. Shamshi-Addu I, king of Ashur, records that Manishtusu, the grandson of Sargon, was its founder.[12]

The status and extent of Nineveh during the Akkad and then the Ur III periods are unclear. Later Assyrian sources all claim Shamshi-Addu I to be the founder of the Ishtar temple and it may have been in his time that the city came under direct control from Ashur. The temple foundations, built in rough limestone, were *c.*26 by 9 metres. The cult of the Ninevite goddess prospered in the second millennium and the Mitanni king Tushratta (mid fourteenth century) offered to send to the ailing Egyptian pharaoh the image of Ishtar, which was believed to have curative powers. Ashur-uballit I (1365–1330), the great Middle Assyrian king, rebuilt the temple, though none of his building inscriptions survive. The city lies on a geological fault and experienced several serious earthquakes, one of which is mentioned by Shalmaneser I (*c.*1280) in connection with his repair of the temple. He also built himself a palace. Some of the large burnt bricks that he used for foundations were discovered by George Smith. Tiglath-Pileser I also repaired the Ishtar temple, and so did Ashur-dan after yet another earthquake in *c.*1187.[13]

The very beautiful life-size limestone statue of a naked female torso (now in the British Museum) was dedicated by Ashur-bel-kala 'for the delight of the populace' (*c.*1080). He also claimed to have had a palace at Nineveh, as did Shamshi-Addu IV (*c.*1000). It appears that from this time onwards the kings of Assyria maintained at least a summer palace at Nineveh.[14] In the first millennium, when Assyria became a great political power, the kings began to endow Nineveh with temples, starting with Ashurnasirpal II (883–859), who substantially enlarged the Ishtar temple. His edifice was to last for the next two hundred years, standing on a solid brick platform 2 metres thick and some 100 by 50 metres in area. The devastating destruction suffered during the sack of Nineveh in 612 means that very little else remains of this temple.

Sargon II (721–705) built a temple dedicated to the Babylonian god Nabu, the son of Marduk, who was particularly venerated in Assyria as a god of victory. Sennacherib made Nineveh into the last official capital of the empire and built a huge palace. It was also inhabited by his successor Esarhaddon, though he may have resided in the so-called Arsenal, the *ekal mašarti* on Nebi Yunus, which served as the headquarters of the Assyrian army.[15] Ashurbanipal (668–627) built the last Assyrian palace in the northern part of Nebi Yunus, but then moved his court to Harran in Syria. Nineveh never regained the status of a city after the catastrophe of 612, but the site was occupied by the Hellenistic and the Parthian periods, as pottery finds demonstrate.

NINEVEH FROM SENNACHERIB
TO ASHURBANIPAL (705–612)

The story of Nineveh during the height of the Neo-Assyrian empire is closely tied to the fate of the Assyrian kings. The proliferation of sources from this period – annals, chronicles, letters, astrological reports, quite apart from biblical accounts – means there is a lot of historical information. We even gain a picture of the personalities of the Assyrian kings, and their attitude to cities, both abroad and at home, explains the development of the royal cities, especially Nineveh. The restless campaigning, the constant movement of troops and peoples, made this a time of rapid change. The capitals became not only places for the central government and administration but also the symbolic hubs of a multinational empire. At the same time, they were still Assyrian cities, with old sanctuaries and a conservative aristocratic élite.

The investment in the old cities, and the construction of brand-new royal cities, reflects an inherent tension between autocratic rule and traditional privileges. Nineveh was at the time both a very ancient city and, intermittently, a capital. The following historical sketch should help to describe how the status of the city oscillated between being a centre of power and a centre of resistance.

Sennacherib (705–681)

Sennacherib was the son of Sargon II, who was probably not a direct descendant of the royal line and who had to suppress a number of revolts against his rule.[16] Sargon was a tireless campaigner, constantly on the march against some rebellious ruler or another. Sargon's predecessors had ruled from Calah (Nimrud), a city founded in the thirteenth century and much enlarged during the reign of Ashurnasirpal II (883–859). Sargon probably never trusted the court at Calah, and he moved his entourage to a new city called Sargon's Fort (Dur-Sharrukin), where he constructed a huge palace, which Botta excavated. Sargon died a soldier's death fighting in Anatolia, and not even his body could be recovered for burial. Despite the recognition that war was a royal duty, death in battle was not considered to be honourable but a sign of divine punishment for some act of hubris. It was to cloud the memory of this king for all the subsequent generation of Assyrian rulers.

Sennacherib was not the eldest son of Sargon II, as his name, 'Sin (the moon-god) has replaced the brothers', clearly indicates. His brothers probably died in infancy, for Sennacherib's position as crown prince was never contested. At his father's succession he was already a young man and entrusted with important affairs of state, representing Sargon at the capital during the latter's prolonged absence on campaigns. He communicated with his father by letters, several of which are preserved.[17] He reported on intelligence missions in the north, the distribution of tribute and internal issues, and there are texts that reveal his interest in trees and orchards.[18] At this time he probably lived in the northern palace at Nineveh, the traditional residence of a crown prince.

After Sargon's sudden death in 705, Sennacherib took over the throne of Assyria. He was no longer young – most likely in his early forties – but he was an experienced politician.[19] The letters between him and his father had shown mutual respect, but after Sargon's ignominious death in enemy territory the son was eager to distance himself from his parent, whom he never once mentioned by name in any of his inscriptions and whose great project at Dur-Sharrukin he left abandoned and unfinished.[20] Sargon's death was also a signal for Marduk-apla-iddina, an old enemy of Assyria, to return from exile and assert his hold over Babylonia. This was the beginning of a protracted and ultimately ruinous engagement in southern Mesopotamia, which was to overshadow the whole of Sennacherib's reign. Sennacherib had set out resolutely to deal with the situation and marched southwards, but Marduk-apla-iddina evaded direct confrontation and took refuge in the marshes close to his home province of Bit-Yakin. He was very good at guerrilla tactics, and epitomized the opportunist schemer and tribal leader who manages to activate resistance against the most powerful state in the world of the day.

The Assyrian kings hated Marduk-apla-iddina with undying enmity because he made them look powerless, even ridiculous at times, but the southern rebel leader was a useful if unpredictable ally for the Babylonians, who were never comfortable under Assyrian dominion. After the situation reached a stalemate, Sennacherib vented his anger on Babylon, plundering the royal treasury and marching with his army to ransack the rebellious southern cities. He also appointed a new king over Babylonia, a native nobleman who had been educated in Assyria – a compromise meant to render Assyrian sovereignty more acceptable. Although the exact sequence of events is not completely clear, Sennacherib finally considered the situation in the south to be secure enough for him to tackle problems in other regions of the empire, in the Zagros mountains and in the west, where various Syrian cities had refused to pay tribute. The Bible reports his unsuccessful attempt to take Jerusalem whereas the Assyrian palace reliefs and annals concentrate on the sack of the fortresses of Lachish and Azekah. These campaigns were on the whole a success as the region once again recognized an Assyrian domination that was to last until the demise of the empire.

Meanwhile the situation worsened in Babylonia, where Marduk-apla-iddina and another Chaldean, Mushezib-Marduk, were back and actively fomenting rebellion while successfully evading capture. Sennacherib decided the time had come for direct control. He deposed the puppet ruler and appointed his crown prince Ashur-nadin-shumi as king of Babylon.[21] Before Sennacherib launched his punitive raid against the Bit-Yakin in their Elamite refuge, he made his son come to Babylon and installed him on the Babylonian throne (700). This seems to have consolidated the situation for the time being. For the next six years, Sennacherib was able to concentrate on building and irrigation projects at Nineveh. He had no interest in continuing his father's unfinished capital of Dur-Sharrukin, nor did he decide to reactivate Ashurnasirpal's capital, Calah. He preferred to move the court to the old religious centre of Nineveh, at this time a relatively small and rather run-down city, though he may have recognized its potential as a military base and administrative centre much earlier.[22] It certainly had a symbolic connection with the armed forces. Ashurnasirpal II had started his military campaigns from Nineveh and it was the city to which tribute was delivered.

When Sennacherib moved the whole of his administrative apparatus to Nineveh, he was also planning to exert much more direct control over the city. The new palace, called 'palace without rival', was conceived not only as a royal residence but also as the headquarters of his government. The size of this building, twice as large as Sargon's palace, reflects this purpose. All Sennacherib's undertakings show considerable pragmatism combined with an acute sense of his representative duties and the symbolic dimension of kingship. His ambition, to create a truly magnificent capital and create a sustainable environment for a large population, reveals considerable understanding of urban planning and a keen interest in the agro-technical aspects of development in an almost modern manner. For the rest of his reign, he concentrated on this enormous project, using displaced persons from peripheral regions as a source of labour, and war booty and tribute for finance. Of particular interest were his hydraulic engineering works, which considerably extended the arable land around the city as well as supplying water to the numerous parks and orchards that were Sennacherib's particular delight. Some of these well-constructed tunnels, dams and aqueducts are still in use today.[23] It is possible that he used the expertise of Urartian technicians whom his father had resettled from western Anatolia after his victory over the Urartian army in 714. The Urartians were well known for their skill in hydraulic installations.

Sennacherib was well aware of his pioneering efforts for Nineveh, as his 'standard inscription' shows:

In those days (this is what happened): Nineveh, the lofty city, beloved by Ishtar, which contains all the rites of gods and goddesses, the ever-lasting and ancient foundation, whose plan has been determined since the days of old in accordance with the heavens' signs, whose structure is plain to see, the artfully fashioned place, the secret place, wherein all manner of artifice, all rites and hidden depths of the Lalgar are assembled; (in this place) earlier kings, my ancestors, had exercised their kingship over Assyria, ruled the subjects of Enlil, and received year after year the tribute of the whole world. (However) not one among them had given his thoughtful attention to, nor carefully considered, the palace therein, the sacred and royal dwelling, which had become too small, (nor) had he turned his mind to lay out the streets in the city, to widen the squares, to dig a canal, and plan orchards. Then I Sennacherib, king of Assyria, conceived of the plan in accordance to divine inspiration and occupied my mind. I deported Chaldeans, Arameans, people from the lands of Mannaya, Que, Cilicia, Philistia and Tyre, who had not bowed to my yoke, and I imposed corvée work on them and they made bricks. I cut reeds that grew in Chaldea and had the mighty plants transported by the prisoners I made, to accomplish the plan.

(. . .)

A park, the image of Mount Amanus, in which all kinds of spices, fruit trees and timber trees, the sustenance of the mountains and Chaldea, I had collected and I planted them next (to my palace).

In order to plant orchards I gave to the inhabitants of Nineveh 2 *panu* of land and let them have it. In order to make the fields flourish, I tore open mountain and valley with iron picks to dig a canal. From the Hosr I caused a ceaseless stream of water to flow for 1½ double hour.

I enlarged Nineveh, my capital, I widened its squares and made streets and avenues as light as day. In front of the gate to the Inner City I had a bridge built of burnt brick and white limestone.

(. . .)[24]

He was particularly keen to extend the area under cultivation and to indulge in his passion for botanical gardens and orchards. For this purpose he diverted smaller streams in the vicinity, constructed new canals and personally inspected mountain springs for their suitability as water sources. The palace, situated on the south-west side of the city mound, was of enormous proportions and abundantly lined with reliefs. The purpose of the pictorial scenes, which document in a very realistic way the workings of the Assyrian war machinery engaged in specific campaigns, was to impress any visitor with the might of the Assyrian army and to create a visual everlasting record of the king's achievements.[25] Foreign rulers who came to present tribute or swear allegiance to the king, would have had time to contemplate these scenes as they waited in the corridors and antechambers. They provided a graphic reminder of the dire consequences of insurrection and rebellion. But they also commemorated Sennacherib's civil engineering works. Thus we find depictions of the transport of the colossal portal bulls, which protected the entrances to the city and the palace; or we see the king supervising the quarrying of stone, while in his inscriptions he talks about inventing a new mechanism for casting bronze columns.

Sennacherib also restored the temples of Nineveh and built the famous city walls, pierced by eighteen monumental gates. The citadel and the palace were made secure by their own system of fortifications.

To the inhabitants of the city, swollen by deportees from all over the empire, he allotted newly irrigated land and encouraged the cultivation of non-native fruit trees and crops, including vines. It was now that Nineveh began to acquire its reputation as a great royal city, with straight streets, large residential quarters, splendid palaces[26] and temples, surrounded by green fields, orchards and parks. Inspired by the landscape of southern Babylonia, the king even ordered a reed marsh to be created, which he stocked with wild boar, deer, birds and fish, 'Which brought forth young in abundance.'[27] The marsh, besides being a nature reserve, also fulfilled the practical purpose of absorbing the surplus water his canals generated after the winter months and furnished valuable building material for the royal palace. He also experimented with cotton and made reports on the 'wool-bearing trees'.

Continuing rebellions in the north necessitated his absence for a while, though he did delegate command over the armed forces to high officials who subdued outlying provinces in Anatolia. It is not clear what prompted his next move against southern Babylonia, but he prepared for a completely new form of Assyrian attack – by sea. He ordered ships to be built and had them transported overland and down the Tigris to the Persian Gulf to launch a surprise assault on his old south Babylonian enemies, primarily the Chaldeans,[28] who had established themselves on the Elamite (Iranian) side. Sennacherib then waited for the safe return of his 'navy', which seems to have succeeded in destroying some cities and taking many prisoners. This unique event was duly immortalized on the palace walls at Nineveh, but the diverting escapade had serious consequences in so far as the king of Elam, Hallushu-Inshushinak, set out to avenge the Assyrian trespass of his territory. Even as Sennacherib was celebrating victory at the mouth of the Ulay river (also depicted on the reliefs), Hallushu-Inshushinak launched an attack against northern Babylonia and captured Sippar. He entered Babylon, took hold of Ashur-nadin-shumi, Sennacherib's son and the ruling king, and led him to Elam, where he probably killed him. He then appointed a new ruler from a local family to be king of Babylon.

The Assyrian reaction was swift and the army regained control over southern Babylonia, conquered Uruk and removed the statues of the city's gods. In a battle fought near Nippur, the Assyrians won and captured the Babylonian king, who was executed, but Mushezib-Marduk, a Chaldean, assumed the kingship in Babylon and sent a delegation, laden with treasure, to Elam with a request for military assistance against Assyria. The plan was to unite all opposition against Assyria and confront Sennacherib's army.

The culminating battle was fought at Halule, and although the Assyrians claimed complete victory, they were not immediately able to capitalize on their gains. Sennacherib therefore decided to deal with the problems in the south-west and he organized a campaign against the Arabs, who were under the leadership of a queen. He captured thousands of camels and made the Arabian queen prisoner, and with this front pacified and the Elamite king out of action following a stroke, he began his siege of Babylon, which lasted for fifteen months until 689.

The destruction of Babylon was as systematic as the planning of Nineveh had been.[29] He gave explicit orders to his soldiers to kill, loot and burn, and to destroy the divine statues. And as ingeniously as he had manipulated waterways to make his city in Assyria bloom, he diverted a branch of the Euphrates to flood the ruined Babylon. To complete the annihilation he took away to Assyria the statues of Bel (Marduk) and other deities, as well as colossal amounts of treasure from the Babylonian temples. The policy had the desired effect of pacification. For the last seven years of his reign Sennacherib encountered little opposition. But the destruction of the sacred city of Babylon demanded from him some gesture to restore the balance. In his last years he therefore concentrated on temple-building projects and on religious reforms at Ashur rather than Nineveh, with the aim of making Ashur the new Babylon. As we saw earlier, he even built the 'festival house' in conscious imitation of Babylonian rituals to celebrate the New Year.[30]

The death of Ashur-nadin-shumi, his murdered son whom he had appointed king of Babylon, was to have further repercussions. For some reason Sennacherib decided to appoint Esarhaddon, the son of his main wife and queen Naqi'a-Zakutu, as the crown prince. This caused considerable resentment among his other sons, who thought they had stronger claims to the succession, especially one who had been the designated crown prince since infancy. Sennacherib thought it prudent to remove Esarhaddon from Nineveh, without, however, revoking his decision. This prompted a palace conspiracy and on the twentieth day of the tenth month 681 Sennacherib was killed in his 'palace without rival'. As the chronicles report, the act took place 'between two bull colossi', the ponderous, curly-bearded bull-guardian spirits of gateways who were meant to keep evil at bay.

Sennacherib's restless experimentation, his interest in innovative technical solutions and his flexible strategies make him an unusual Assyrian ruler. In the monuments he created for his own memorial, especially the palace reliefs and the royal inscriptions, the creation of parks and irrigation projects is shown to be as important as warfare. While his inscriptions dwell on the punishment and torture meted out to rebels or those who dare to challenge Assyrian rule, he also displays a lively interest in the topography and ecology of 'the enemy lands'. He liked to show that his campaigns and projects took place in a real world, not some abstracted space. His father, Sargon, had initiated the custom of including topographical details in scenes of military campaigns. This was developed further under Sennacherib, with closely observed almost ethnographic details showing the inhabitants of the marshes hiding in the reeds; the dress, hairstyle and house types of the regions conquered by his soldiers. Even the bull colossi now only sported four legs rather than the five shown previously.[31]

He also allowed wives and sons considerably more influence than had other kings before him.[32] The queen Naqi'a-Zakutu especially enjoyed many privileges and had enormous wealth. She built a palace for her son, Esarhaddon, at Nineveh, had her own 'royal inscriptions' written and requested various divination reports not just for private use but also for state and military occasions.[33] Sennacherib is the only Assyrian king to have immortalized his affection for a woman. His last wife, Tashmetum-sharrat, who must have been a young woman when he married her, was his favourite during his last years. He built a special residence for her and called it 'the palace of love, happiness and joy', an extension to the south-west palace reached through a portal guarded by two stone lions whose bodies were, like most other gate sculptures, covered with an inscription. This praises the beauty of Tashmetum-sharrat, whom 'the goddess Belet-ili had endowed with grace not given to any other woman', and it ends in a prayer that she and her monarch may both 'live long and happily in these palaces and be sated with well-being'.[34]

Sennacherib may have removed populations from their homelands, but he also made sure they were settled in regions suitable for cultivation. The heterogeneous people of Nineveh in particular were to benefit from the parks, plantations and irrigated fields. He delighted in making wildlife flourish, another unusual trait for an Assyrian monarch. Even his death was extraordinary. We do not know what prompted Sennacherib to prefer Esarhaddon's succession over that of his other sons. His death between the bulls meant to ward off all evil from the palace was a counterpoint to the death of his father on campaign. But while the latter was considered an *Unheilsherrscher*, an ill-fated ruler, Sennacherib, though a victim of parricide, was never denied by his descendants.

Esarhaddon (681–669)

When news of Sennacherib's death reached the exiled crown prince Esarhaddon, he knew he would have to fight for his accession. He also counted on the support of the Assyrian nobility, who had been made to swear an oath of loyalty to the chosen successor. The following passage in his annals records the events:

My brothers went mad and did all that is abhorrent to the gods, at Nineveh they formed evil plans, resorted to the use of arms, fighting for sovereignty and butting each other like billy goats.

I marched rapidly along the road to Nineveh despite difficulties, but in the land of Hanigalbat (Upper Mesopotamia) all their experienced troops barred my way, sharpening their weapons.

But fear of the great gods cast them down; when they saw my tremendous attack they lost their senses. Ishtar, the lady of battle and war, who loves my priesthood, moved to my side, broke their bows, and dissolved their battle order. Then there sounded in the army the cry, 'This is our king!'

At their (the gods') lofty command they all came over to my side and stood behind me, crowding around like lambs and imploring my lordship. The Assyrians, who had sworn loyalty to me by the great gods, approached me and kissed my feet.[35]

This account conflates several events, but it shows that the acceptance of Esarhaddon followed his victory over his enemies. The identity of his father's assassin is never mentioned in his inscriptions, and scholars often suspected that Esarhaddon himself was behind the plot. The royal 'murder mystery' was finally ingeniously solved by the Finnish scholar Simo Parpola. There is a report in the Bible that a certain Adrammelech (later also transmitted as Adramelos) was the killer. A Babylonian letter was then found to contain further clues. It told the story of how some loyal subject hoped to warn Sennacherib of an assassination plot and requested an audience to reveal the identity of the conspirator. He was admitted to the palace and faced the king, who had his face veiled, as was the custom, and revealed his secret unaware that he was in the presence not of the king but of the murderous prince himself, whom the letter names as Arda-Ninlil. Since Ninlil became Mulissu in Assyrian, the prince's name, Arda-mulissu, could easily have been transmitted as Adramelos or Adrammelech in the Hebrew sources, especially since the Hebrew letters 'k' and 's' look closely alike in inscriptions of the time.[36]

The historical sources for Esarhaddon's reign are unusually varied. Besides the official display inscriptions, which combine accounts of military campaigns, building projects and religious activities (though not unfortunately in chronological order), there are letters, administrative records and a great number of oracular reports. The Babylonian Chronicle also fills in events omitted from the official Assyrian historiography.

Esarhaddon's main military achievement was the invasion of Egypt.[37] The primary reason for the attack was the fact that, under the Kushite Dynasty, Egypt once again made claims on the Syrian coastal region, that came under Assyrian control. The war against Egypt lasted several years and was not without its setbacks. In 671, after careful preparations, the Assyrians made a concerted effort. A large force crossed the Sinai desert, escorted by Arab camel riders who had been forced to provision the army and its horses with water. After three battles, Memphis was captured and the pharaoh Taharka fled. Esarhaddon then appointed men of his choosing as governors and administrators and returned home carrying substantial booty from the Egyptian capital.

The situation in the northern and north-eastern provinces, important as a source of metals and horses, had become increasingly difficult as the result of massive movements of new peoples, many of whom spoke Indo-European languages, including the Cimmerians, the Manneans, the Medes and the Scythians. They threatened and attacked the Assyrian vassal states and provinces, which then appealed to Assyria for help. The newcomers were also quick to exploit any possibility of allying themselves with the Assyrian power should the opportunity arise, though both parties were equally aware that such arrangements were likely to be short lived and unreliable.

Esarhaddon's treatment of Babylonia was in marked contrast to that of his father, though he was not prepared to give up Assyria's domination of the southern kingdom. Instead he concentrated on improving the efficiency of its administration and restoring some confidence in Assyria's goodwill. He appointed his elder son, Shamash-shumu-ukin, to officiate as the designated future king of Babylon and entrusted him with supervising the Assyrian administration. To demonstrate his policy of appeasement further, Esarhaddon invested heavily in the restoration of cities in Babylonia, and especially in the rebuilding of the capital, which his father had sacked. He rebuilt the Esagila temple and its ziggurat, the Processional Way and the city walls. In his building inscriptions he was very careful to lay the blame for the destruction of the holy city not on the anger of Sennacherib but on 'evil people' in Babylonia who had plundered the temple treasure in order to bribe the Elamites to attack Assyria. This, he argues, made Marduk so angry that he punished his faithless city by decreeing seventy years of misfortune. Only through favourable omens did he change his mind towards Babylon, shortening the seventy years to eleven.[38]

Esarhaddon also re-established the city's special status that exempted it from various taxes and conscription, and he was careful not to place the Assyrian gods above those of Babylon. The decision to return the abducted statues of Babylonian gods was of the utmost importance. It was a tricky matter since endless oracular decisions were necessary to determine exactly the right time and procedure.[39] These efforts to combine tight control and show signs of respect for the sanctity of the city and its inhabitants (he also allowed deported

Babylonians to return to their homeland and restored their property), seem to have been effective, since no major disturbances disrupted the country during the rest of his reign.

Since the reconstruction of Babylon was seen as a priority, Esarhaddon's building projects in Assyria were modest in comparison with those of his predecessors. He found it judicious not to antagonize the priesthood of Assyria's holy city of Ashur and embarked on substantial building works on the Ashur temple. In Nineveh he enlarged the arsenal, because 'the (arsenal) which my royal ancestors had built to keep the military equipment, to stable horses, mules and to store chariots, equipment, arms and booty of the enemy, to gallop horses and to drive chariots, had become too small'.[40]

Despite the success of his policy in Babylonia, his victory in Egypt and the relative stability of his frontiers, Esarhaddon was troubled by a deep sense of insecurity and unease. It comes across in his official inscriptions, and even more so in his letters to his advisers, physicians and diviners. More than any other known Mesopotamian ruler, he was aware of the precarious nature of the royal position as ultimate mediator between humanity and the gods and the need to know the gods' will. As early as the third millennium various forms of divination, such as the casting of lots, were used to obtain affirmative or negative answers to specific questions. Such 'randomizing of decision making', as anthropologists characterize divination, was used for the appointment of important officials, especially when there were several candidates who had the right credentials. As governments became more autocratic, so were greater efforts needed to substantiate claims to legitimate power. Divination became a very important medium to demonstrate that all major public ordinances were done with divine approval through the systematic use of omens and oracular pronouncements. The procedures to determine divine intentions had become a veritable science by the time of Esarhaddon.

The epistemological basis for divination was the idea that the gods communicate their intentions and preferences by leaving all kinds of hidden clues that can be read and understood by specialists.[41] The whole universe, from the planets to the 'creeping things on earth', could be seen as encoded with messages about the future. This meant that any observation of something unusual was portentous and had to be noted. Over many centuries, huge amounts of data were collected and eventually systematically organized to provide a paradigm of interpretation assembled on cuneiform tablets and categorized into series according to the sources of an observation: *šumma izbu* deals with physical deformities, for instance, and *šumma alu* with unusual forms of human and animal behaviour. The gods could also be formally requested to communicate through a specific medium in a particular setting. The patterns made by oil on water or the smoke of incense could then be scrutinized for answers. However, the preferred method in Mesopotamia was the observation of the viscera of animals, especially the liver of lambs selected for the purpose. The gods would be invited to inscribe their message within the body of a sacrificial animal that would after slaughter be scrutinized by experts who had spent many years learning how to decipher the divine writing.

Since this was more oblique than the older binary code of 'yes and no' decisions, the interpretations could be as cryptic as the original 'message'. An uncertain answer to a specific question could then be challenged on the grounds that the extispicy had been performed in a less than professional manner or that some blemish adhered to either animal or diviner and thus invalidated the result. Needless to say, other diviners were keen to cast doubts on the procedures of colleagues and it could take a long time to arrive at a satisfactory conclusion, by which time the problem may well have been solved by other means. In contrast to this arcane and 'scientific' way of communicating with mankind, the gods could also speak directly to a person in a state of receptivity, who was either asleep or in a trance. Gudea of Lagash, in the late third millennium, described how he sought in this way his city god's approval for the rebuilding of a temple.

In north Mesopotamia, perhaps under the influence of more western countries, the custom of prophecy was established at least as early as the beginning of the second millennium, as the Mari letters demonstrate. Here persons without rank or training, often women, could become the mouthpiece of a god. Their utterances in a state of trance were often addressed to the king and formed an effective check to any abuse of power. During the Neo-Assyrian period, at the time of Esarhaddon, all these forms of divination and prophecy, as well as astrology, a relatively recent discipline, were taken into account. With the acute concentration of power centred on the personality of the king, he became the primary subject of inquiries, as to a lesser extent were members of his family. A strong, self-confident king could manipulate the soothsayers and astrologers to achieve his own will, but Esarhaddon, though by no means a weakling, was either too conscientious or too anxious to act independently.[42] Here is what he has to say about his kingship:

Sin and Shamash, the twin gods, pursued their courses month after month, on the 13th (?) and 14th day they regularly appeared together. Venus the most brilliant of the stars appeared in the west on the path of Ea's stars, to strengthen the land and appease the gods; she reached the Hypsoma and disappeared. Mars, who decides the fate of the Amurru, shone brilliantly on the path of Ea's stars, she showed the rule which gave strength to the kings and his country as his sign. Messages of ecstatics were constantly sent to me. The favourable forces appeared which announced the foundation of my priestly throne for ever. They communicated to me again and again in dreams and blessings. They announced the foundation of my throne (?) and government to old age. When I saw these favourable omens my heart grew confident and my mind happy.[43]

However, his mind was rarely at rest for long and he constantly sought reassurance. Here is a message from a prophet serving Ishtar of Arbela, at the time a cult centre specializing in inspired prophecy. Unlike the prophets of the Mari period, these men and women were highly educated and well versed in Babylonian literature, as their carefully composed messages show:

I am the Lady of Arbela: To Esarhaddon, whose bosom [Ishtar] of Arbela has filled with favour. Could you not rely on the previous utterances which I spoke to you? Now you can rely on this later one too.
Praise me! When daylight declines, let them hold torches. Praise me before them!
I will banish trembling from my palace. You shall eat safe food and drink safe water and you shall be safe in your palace. Your son and grandson shall rule as kings in the lap of Ninurta.
By the mouth of La-dagi-ili of Arbela.[44]

Any illness in the royal family was cause for great concern. Not only were physicians consulted but diviners had to establish whether or not the intended cure was going to be efficacious. The following is an excerpt from an oracle request:

[Should Ashurbanipal, the crown prince of the] Succession Palace,
[drink this drug which] is placed [before] your great [div]inity, [and in drinking this drug will he] be rescued and spared?
[Will he live and get well? Will he . . . be s]aved and escape? [Will the illness] of his [body] be released? Will it leave (him)? Does your great divinity know it?

(. . .)

I ask you Shamash, great lord, whether this drug which is now placed before your great divinity, and which Ashurbanipal, crown prince of the Succession House (is to) drink – (whether by drinking this drug he will) be saved, (and escape). Be present in this ram, place (in it) a firm positive answer . . .[45]

Another manifestation of Esarhaddon's sense of vulnerability was the revitalization of an ancient custom of appointing a 'substitute king' (šar puḫri) to occupy the throne during inauspicious times. During the latter part of his reign, this happened on several occasions.[46] Eclipses of stars and the moon were seen to be particularly dangerous as they could result in the king's death, but it was possible that fate could be tricked into claiming the wrong king. A surviving fragment indicates that the hapless substitute was to die at the end of his mock reign.[47] During these periods (which could last up to several months) the real king was addressed as a 'peasant' and no state affairs could be discussed. Obviously this allowed his ministers and generals to assume control meanwhile, and they may well have played on the anxious disposition of Esarhaddon in such a way as to periodically exclude him from power.

Ashurbanipal and the fall of Nineveh

Esarhaddon was, however, shrewd enough to resist excessive interference and was determined to regulate his succession in such a way as to eliminate the sort of violent struggle that had cost his father's life. In 672 he assembled representatives from all parts of the empire and made them swear oaths to the great gods and the gods of their countries to respect his wishes and be loyal to his successors.[48] Ashurbanipal, the grandson of the formidable queen Naqi'a, had been nominated as crown prince of Assyria and taken up residence in the House of Succession (*bit reduti*) at Tarbisu. His elder brother, Shamash-shumu-ukin, also a son of Esarhaddon's Babylonian wife, Esharra-hammat, was to be king of Babylon.

In 669 the situation in Egypt had deteriorated to such an extent as to make a further military offensive inevitable. Esarhaddon set out on what would be his last campaign since he died on the way. Naqi'a immediately summoned the vassals who had sworn allegiance to her son and made them confirm their vows, and Ashurbanipal was duly crowned king of Assyria in 668. His first priority was to restore Assyrian control in Egypt, first by sending troops to quell insurrections against the Assyrian garrisons and later by a full-scale invasion culminating in the fall of Thebes in 663. This brought a huge amount of booty, signalled the end of the Kushite Dynasty, and ensured there would be no further Egyptian interference in Syro-Palestine.

Difficulties with the Cimmerians, Manneans and Medes continued as they had during his father's reign, and these Ashurbanipal counteracted with a mixture of diplomacy and aggression to protect his northern and north-eastern borders. The most problematic conflict he faced, however, was a war against Babylon[49] after various factors contributed to a growing alienation between him and his half-brother. No doubt Shamash-shumu-ukin, originally appointed to be his father's successor to the imperial throne, had felt resentment when his younger sibling was preferred. Furthermore, a lack of commitment towards Babylon by Ashurbanipal was taken as a slight. He had been slow to respond to appeals for help when Elamites and various tribes invaded Babylonian territory, and the restoration of gods and cult furniture initiated by Esarhaddon was allowed to lapse for years. Shamash-shumu-ukin came to identify himself with the cause of Babylonian independence and enlisted the support of various other political groups in an Anti-Assyrian coalition that included Elam, the Chaldean 'sea-land', as well as Aramean and Arab tribes. After initial Babylonian successes, they began to suffer setbacks and the alliance broke apart. Babylon itself came under siege to the great hardship and suffering of the population. After two years the city fell in 648. Nothing more was recorded of Shamash-shumu-ukin, who probably died in his city.

Ashurbanipal's next target was Elam, the other old enemy of Assyria. Having led the Assyrian war machine to Elam, he took the old capital Susa and reduced it to a ruin heap. Then, before moving on to take revenge on Babylonia's other allies, the Arabs, he ordered that salt be strewn over the devastated fields to ensure the site would remain uninhabitable for ever. It was the end of Elam as a political entity, but it did not result in peace for Assyria since into the vacuum created by its destruction came the Medes. Pressure continued to mount on all sides, but a lack of written sources for the last years of Ashurbanipal's reign means we have no knowledge of whether he moved his residence to Harran, aware of the dangers facing the Assyrian heartland, or whether he remained in Nineveh until his death.

Here he also left his mark by building the last of the great Assyrian palaces in the grounds of the *bit reduti* where he had spent his youth, called the North Palace by the nineteenth-century explorers. Its walls were lined with reliefs and he put up many statues; he planted gardens with exotic trees. One famous relief shows him relaxing in a grape arbour in the company of a wife who may be Ashur-sharrat, well known from an inscribed stele she set up in Ashur. The artistic style of Ashurbanipal's period displays a formidable sense for the dramatic spacing of figures, and animals and plants especially are rendered vividly and realistically, in contrast to the more static and stereotypical manner of representing human beings. The lion-hunting scenes in particular have received much comment. The practice of royal hunting, particularly the killing of lions, should not be seen as merely an aristocratic pastime. It was a public performance of the ancient duties of the king, to protect his subjects from evil. The symbolic connection was underlined by the fact that the hunt took place at the time of the New Year festival, when the king was acting out a number of roles. As the reliefs show clearly, eighteen lions were released into a staked-off arena on the plain before the city, clearly corresponding to the eighteen gates. The killing of eighteen lions thus 'symbolically secured each exit from the capital, every gate and road leading out of it'.[50]

The most enduring legacy of Ashurbanipal's reign was his tablet collection, or 'library', discovered by Rassam. It has been suggested that since Ashurbanipal was not originally destined for kingship he had an education more suitable for high official or priest which entailed literacy:

I am versed in the craft of the sage Adapa; I studied the secret lore of the entire scribal craft, I know the celestial and terrestrial portents. I discussed with competence in the circle of the masters, I argue about (the work) 'If the Liver is a Correspondence of the Sky' with expert diviners. I can solve the most complicated divisions and multiplications which do not have a solution. I have read intricate tablets inscribed with obscure Sumerian and Akkadian, difficult to unravel, and examined sealed, obscure and confused inscriptions on stone from before the flood.[51]

Ashurbanipal certainly took a close interest in all branches of Mesopotamian learning and gave orders to requisition tablets from the various Babylonian scribal centres and thus accumulated the largest and most comprehensive cuneiform library. The reference works contained in the Ninevite library greatly facilitated the work of Western scholars 2,500 years later in their attempts to decipher 'obscure Sumerian and Akkadian'.

Like his father, Ashurbanipal was keen on divination, ecstatic prophecies and dream oracles. The latter seem to have caught his particular interest. But although the messages of the soothsayers and prophets were full of reassurances ('Fear not Ashurbanipal'), the downfall of the great empire would follow within a few years of his death. There is still considerable confusion as to the sequence of events and who ruled Assyria at the time, but it is known that in Babylonia a ruler of the Sealand called Nabopolassar, who had begun his career as an official in Assyrian service, asserted independence and evicted the last Assyrian governor. He defeated the Manneans, who were allied with Assyria at the time, and in 614 concluded a treaty with Cyaxares, king of the Medes. Together they marched into Assyria and launched serious attacks on the major cities. Nineveh and Calah held out, but Ashur was destroyed. The counter-offensive of the Assyrian king, Sin-sharishkun, supported by Scythian allies, only provoked another punitive expedition by the joint Babylonian–Median forces. In 612, their host, augmented by various tribal contingents, launched an unexpected attack against Nineveh. The siege lasted a mere three months and, as the excavations of the Berkeley team have shown, the defenders desperately tried to narrow the gates.[52] Skeletons of guards, complete with arrows lodged in the bones, were found in a heap within the gate chambers. The sheer size of the city militated against any effective defence and there were too many gates, which may not all have been in the best condition. The large numbers of besiegers and concerted assaults at several points then sealed the fate of Nineveh.

According to the Babylonian Chronicle, Nabopolassar set up court in the royal palace for some months, probably to oversee the transport of valuables to his own capital before giving the signal for the city's destruction. He returned to Babylon with the ashes of Nineveh. The city was set on fire, its temples and statues smashed, before, in a final act of revenge, Nabopolassar flooded it in a gesture of ritual annihilation. That the Babylonians may have used Sennacherib's carefully constructed waterways to reverse the treatment he had meted out to Babylon gave the story a final ironic twist.

This was the end of the metropolitan history of Nineveh: a huge ruin field which in later centuries was partially inhabited. In the biblical account of Jonah, Nineveh was described as a city 'of three days' journey', but it was not just its size or even its splendidly appointed public buildings or the luxurious gardens which made Nineveh and the other Assyrian capital cities so special. They had large and cosmopolitan populations; some 120,000 people have been estimated in the case of Nineveh.[53] Once the Assyrians had decided to create a capital, they had had to achieve in a few years what had taken millennia in other places. They had enormous resources at their disposal, including raw materials and costly furnishings, but their most important resource was the ability to mobilize an incredible labour force that, at the same time, provided inhabitants and instant citizens for the newly created metropolis.

'To the great city of Nineveh deportees were brought from Hilakku (Cilicia), Manna, Philistia, Babylonia, Arabia, Egypt, Shubria and other places,'[54] as Sennacherib recorded. They were forcibly removed from many different parts of the empire, usually trouble spots where tension could be lessened by a large removal of population, but the Assyrians did not split up existing communities. Instead they settled them in clusters and according to existing kinship structures.[55] Despite the ethnic and cultural pluralism of the new population, in Nineveh as much as in the other royal cities, efforts were made to integrate it into forming a community. As Sargon says, he tried to make the people of

Dur-Sharrukin into 'one mouth' with the help of Assyrian scribes.[56] Naturally, the élite remained Assyrian, though the rise of Arameans to the highest positions in the administration showed there were no intrinsic barriers to minorities achieving high status. It was official policy to make deportees be 'counted as Assyrians', liable to taxation but also with the rights of citizens. As Grayson points out, 'the Assyrians could afford to be tolerant of foreigners, since they ruled most of those they knew'.[57]

Nineveh was as much a social experiment as Uruk had been in the fourth millennium, a collective engagement in the physical creation of the city being common to both. The monumental building projects symbolized the current ideology, and it is worth remembering that Nineveh had already been a city once before in the Uruk period. In the biblical accounts, Nineveh became a symbol for the transience of human ambition. From the perspective of a subject people, as the Hebrews were at the time, the fall of the mighty was experienced as delivery.

In the long story of Nineveh, which is far from finished, a curious ambiguity emerges, and a desire to overcome existing dichotomies. The goddess of Nineveh, Ishtar, was worshipped here 'wearing a beard like Ashur', but otherwise in a female form. In the eighth and seventh centuries it was both a holy city and the headquarters of the army; it was the capital of Assyria yet largely inhabited by foreigners; it was a northern Mesopotamian town with marshland as in the Persian Gulf and forests as in Anatolia. Its intellectual traditions originated in Babylonia and its scholars discussed variant translations of ancient Sumerian; while the language spoken in the streets was Aramaic.

Even the memory of Nineveh came to be distorted during the Greek and Hellenistic period. Many of the special features attributed to Babylon were actually Ninevite: Semiramis was Shammu-ramat, the wife of Shalmaneser V, who, according to a stele, accompanied her husband on military campaigns.[58] The 'Hanging Gardens of Babylon' are much more likely to refer to Sennacherib's complex artificial plant-ations and waterworks in Nineveh.[59] In a famous painting showing the king Ashurbanipal lounging at ease in his garden, listening to his female musicians and being fanned by his wife, the severed head of his arch-enemy is seen hanging from a tree. In present-day Nineveh, engulfed by the city of Mosul with its Kurdish minorities, the scanty remains of Sennacherib's palace are stripped to defy international sanctions that are meant to humiliate a modern dictator who feels an inherent kinship with Assyrian rulers and who likes to be portrayed in the pose and dress of Nineveh's ancient rulers. Such incongruities and reversals, half comic, half tragic, might have amused the bearded Lady of Nineveh.

10 BABYLON

The Bible and some classical writers left descriptions of Babylon that were the main sources of any knowledge of the city for hundreds of years. The biblical accounts of Mesopotamia clearly reflect the memory of a people oppressed by Assyrian or Babylonian imperialism. The Babel of the Bible is therefore synonymous with decadence, political ruthlessness and the excesses of urban life in general. The years of captivity were remembered with bitterness and there was no enthusiasm for any of the architectural wonders of the ancient city. On the contrary, the great ziggurat – the prototype for the Tower of Babel – became a powerful symbol for human foolishness and arrogance.

The Greek writers, on the other hand, notably Herodotus, took a very different attitude to the Oriental civilizations. Their descriptions of buildings and customs reveal an almost ethnographic interest totally absent in the biblical writings. They also collected narratives and traditions, such as the stories of Semiramis and Ninus, and classified the 'Hanging Gardens of Babylon', which none of them had actually seen, as one of the Seven Wonders of the World.

One of the earliest European accounts of the ruins of Babylon, which had kept the name Babil, dates from the twelfth century AD. Rabbi Benjamin of Tudela had travelled to Mesopotamia to visit the Jewish communities there and reported on the sights. Later, the Englishman John Eldred in 1583 and the Italian Pietro della Valle and the Frenchman J. Beauchamp in the late eighteenth century also left descriptive accounts.[1] All these travellers had obviously hoped to see the remains of the fabled Tower of Babel and the natives inevitably obliged them by taking them to the mound at Birs Nimrud, which, though close to the site of Babylon, is in fact the remains of another ziggurat.

Claudius James Rich was the first to make tentative excavations, between 1811 and 1817.[2] Austen Layard and Hormuzd Rassam also made some surface explorations but were put off the site by the vast accumulations of debris they found. It was in 1897 that Robert Koldewey and E. Sachau toured the Middle East with a view to locating a site suitable for large-scale excavations for Germany. They visited a number of sites, but their decision to choose the mound of Babil was taken only after a second visit. Koldewey had picked up some colourful glazed tiles, and it was the 'singular beauty and the art historical value' of these which persuaded the director of the Royal Museum in Berlin to recommend the excavation of the Babylonian capital.[3] The German Oriental Society (Deutsche Orientgesellschaft) was formed in 1898 and raised 500,000 Marks for the project.

Excavations began under Koldewey's command in March 1899, at the actual site (called 'Kasr' by the locals) where he had found the coloured tiles. His very first trench revealed the structure of the city gate and the Processional Way, with many of the glazed tiles still *in situ*. Pavement slabs with stamped inscriptions made it clear that this was indeed the Processional Way of Marduk, built by Nebuchadrezzar II (605–562), king of Babylon. By 1900 Koldewey had cleared this street as far as the north-east corner of the North Citadel (the Kasr) and also surveyed the whole of the extensive site with all its constituent mounds (Babil, Kasr, Merkez, Amran and Homera), an area of some 18 square kilometres. The Kasr, location of Nebuchadrezzar's palace, and the outer fortifications of the city were the main target of the excavations. The museum directors in Berlin were most anxious for tablets, and in 1900 Koldewey began work on Amran ibn Ali, the highest part of the site, where the debris was up to 24 metres thick. He ordered a railway and an engine from Germany and engaged a large workforce of 200 to 250 men to tackle the mound. They found the remains of the temple precinct, with Marduk's main sanctuary, Esagila, but no tablets. A second mission, however, in nearby Borsippa, then yielded the highly desired written artefacts in great quantities.

With tireless energy, supported by a number of other German architects, such as J. Jordan, A. Unger and H. Noeldecke, Koldewey was determined to investigate systematically. The scale of the work was unprecedented, not only because of the outspread nature of the big city but as a result of the huge deposits covering the first millennium strata. His method was to define major tasks for each season, combining work on some of the large, complex mounds like the Kasr with further exploration at other places. In this way he gained information about all the major parts of the city and the archaeological sequence, from the highest Parthian layers, followed by Hellenistic and Neo-Babylonian levels, down to the late second millennium. Koldewey had also hoped to reach the lower levels of the city to reveal the Old Babylonian Babylon, the capital of Hammurabi, but this proved to be inaccessible on account of the high water table.

Koldewey devoted his life to the excavation of Babylon and worked there for fourteen years, winter and summer, day after day, with few interruptions. He carried on digging even after war had broken out in 1914, and was briefly commissioned to non-military duties in Syria. He returned as soon as the British had sufficiently withdrawn, and stayed until 1917.[4] His health was ruined by the exertions and the punishments he inflicted on himself in a misguided attempt to prove the mind's mastery over the body. For instance, he would wear thick clothes during the summer heat and only the lightest covering in winter; and when he became seriously ill refused medical attention up to the last moment.[5] In 1924, the year before he died, having supervised the publication of the excavation reports, he was able to conclude with some satisfaction that 'the most important points of the great, illustrious city had been dealt with'.[6]

The most fitting memorial to Koldewey's efforts is without doubt the reconstructed Ishtar Gate and the Babylonian throne-room façade. This is where it had all begun. Between 1899 and 1900 he had established the position of the Processional Way and the Ishtar Gate, both covered in glazed tiles above street level, with a relief-decorated but unglazed sub-structure. He also recovered the façade of the throne room of the main citadel. The tiles were collected, numbered and packed into crates, which were transported entirely by water, first down the Euphrates to Basra, and from there to Hamburg, down the Elbe and Spree, right to the gates of the Pergamon Museum. The cleaning, restoration and final reassembly took many years of painstaking labour. Sadly Koldewey never lived to see the grand opening of the reconstructed Ishtar Gate in 1930.

Though the southern citadel and Processional Way were the high-lights of his excavations, he also uncovered the north citadel, the Greek theatre, the Parthian palace, various temples, apart from Esagila, the ziggurat mound, the residential quarters in Merkez and especially the fortifications of the city. After Koldewey's departure and the removal of portable artefacts to Berlin, the ruins of Babylon were for decades once again left to the elements. The Germans returned in 1970 to begin further investigations on the site of the ziggurat and north of the Kasr where the Festival House was thought to have been. The State Organization for Antiquities and Heritage of Iraq then began work in 1978, which continued until 1989. Their brief was the excavation and restoration of specific monuments, such as the Greek theatre, the Processional Way, the Southern Palace and the area south of the Ishtar temple. Here a new temple, dedicated to the god Nabu, and remnants of the temple archive were discovered.[7] Private houses and many graves were also found, from the Old Babylonian period onwards, and excavations of the Ishtar temple revealed three successive phases of building during Neo-Babylonian times. The Iraqi team reconstructed the lateral walls of the Processional Way, the theatre and parts of the palace of Nebuchadrezzar.

In recent years, the site of Babylon has become a popular destination for Iraqis from nearby towns. The ambitious reconstruction work of the old city, as at Nineveh, was part of a government plan to make the population of Iraq aware of their heritage and to link the name of their present ruler to the kings of antiquity. To this end, Saddam Hussein ordered that the reconstruction be carried out regardless of archaeological accuracy, often using thermalite blocks so as to create a theme-park Babylon for the urban masses of the twentieth century AD. He even had inserted into the new walls special bricks that bear stamped inscriptions saying, 'Rebuilt in the era of the leader Saddam Hussein.'[8]

THE HISTORY OF BABYLON

Babylon is not one of the oldest cities of Mesopotamia. In the fourth millennium the Euphrates ran further to the east and it only gradually shifted westwards. Because of the high water table at the site, hardly any archaeological data are known from periods earlier than the first millennium. There is little evidence that Babylon was anything other than a small town before the Old Babylonian period (1800–1600). Much later texts, such as the Babylonian Chronicle or some of the historical omens, relate that Sargon of Akkad had destroyed Babylon and used its earth to build his own city. These narratives are anachronistic and were invented to give Babylon a greater historical depth to correspond with that of other ancient cities.[9]

It was probably only in the nineteenth century, after the collapse of the Ur III empire, that Babylon became a city. From year names preserved in the records of other sites, including nearby Sippar, we hear that an Amorite chief called Sumu-abum (c.1894–1881) built the city walls and fortifications and made Babylon the centre of his operations. Sumu-abum founded a dynasty which was to rule Babylon for 300 years. At the beginning, the aim was to carve out a new sphere of influence and gradually gain control over the established and flourishing cities in the immediate neighbourhood, Sippar, Dilbat, Kish and Borsippa. After four generations things began to gain momentum under the rule of Sin-muballit (1812–1793) and that of his son, Hammurabi (c.1792–1750). The latter, after thirty years of patient manoeuvring, managed to break the hegemony of Larsa, ruled by the powerful king Rim-Sin, and thereby gained control over all of southern Mesopotamia. He conquered Eshnunna, which gave him access to the eastern trade routes. He defeated his Amorite rival, Shamshi-Addu I of Ashur, which extended his territory northwards to include the Assyrian heartland.[10] He also destroyed Mari, despite the fact that the city had been a Babylonian ally for generations, and secured thereby the western regions of the middle Euphrates. He ended up with an empire almost as large as that of the Ur III kings.

The inscriptions of Hammurabi record building activities in many Mesopotamian cities and especially at Babylon. Some parts of the residential quarters from this period have been recovered in the Merkez mound. However, the Babylonian hegemony proved to be short-lived. By the end of the reign of Hammurabi's successor, control over the south had been lost and Babylon was reduced to roughly the same area as it had been at the start of the dynasty. Recent studies, which take astronomical and archaeological data into account, have revised the date of Babylon's fall to 1499,[11] when a raid by the Hittite king Murshili I resulted in the destruction of the city and signalled the end of the First Dynasty of Babylon. This also reduced the long break previously assumed between the end of this dynasty and the next. It appears that, in the immediate aftermath of Babylon's fall, the Kassites, a people who spoke a Caucasian language and probably originated from the Caucasus region, consolidated control over Babylon under their leader Agum-kakrime (II), who called himself king of Babylon, a title all Kassite rulers retained. Later tradition says that he managed to retrieve for Babylon the statues of the tutelary god Marduk and his spouse Zarpanitum. The Kassite kings, having established themselves in Babylon, then expanded their dominion over an area that included southern and central Mesopotamia, from the Persian Gulf to the Lower Zab.[12]

At the beginning of the fourteenth century, Babylon counted as one of the world powers, on a par with the Mitanni kingdom, the Hittites and Egypt. Like Ashur-uballit I, the ruler of the emergent Assyrian state, the king of Babylon (by now called by its Kassite name Karduniash) was writing to the pharaoh requesting gold in return for his presents.[13] It was the beginning of an age when distances between territorial states began to shrink. The use of horses for transport had made communications faster and horse-drawn chariots allowed armed forces to penetrate more quickly into enemy territory. International competition over areas deemed to be peripheral to the centres of power became fierce and the net of colonial dominion meshed more closely. Kassite Babylonia did not participate directly in this expansion of territorial claims, opting rather for internal stability in so far as the meagre records preserved from the first half of the long-lasting Kassite dynasty reveal. In the thirteenth century Babylonia itself became the target of Assyrian as well as Elamite efforts to extend their control ever further.

This political passivity of Babylonia is well reflected by the fate of the tutelary divine couple, Marduk and Zarpanitum, whose statues, as we have already heard, Agum-kakrime restored during his reign. It is unlikely, however, that the Hittites had taken them, as he claimed. He may simply have restored the statues a previous Kassite ruler had removed to another Babylonian town. Since the deities represented the city, their abduction spelled the loss of political independence. The Assyrian king Tukulti-Ninurta I took them away in 1250 after he had annexed Babylonia and declared himself king of Babylon, removing them to Ashur, where they received offerings.[14] It was the removal of Marduk rather than the invasion of Babylonia that was considered to be a risky if not a sacrilegious strategy by some Assyrian circles, and after sixty-six years the statues were returned. However, they had been reinstalled in Esagila, the main temple of Babylon, for scarcely eight years before the Elamite king Kutir-nahhunte took them off to Susa (1176), having descended on the country 'like a flood' and turned Babylon and other cities into a 'ruin heap', as his own inscriptions record. He not only took the statues of Marduk and other gods with him to Elam, but also Enlil-nadin-ahhe, the thirty-sixth and last of the Kassite rulers.

The vacuum left by the demise of the Kassite kings was soon filled by a ruler of the Second Dynasty of Isin, which had established itself in south Mesopotamia in the twelfth century. The first act of Nebuchadrezzar I (1126–1105) after seizing the Babylonian throne was to embark on a military campaign against Elam that enabled him to recover the stolen statues. This did much to improve morale in Babylonia, as well as to legitimize his own rule. It may be that he capitalized on his success by declaring Marduk to be not only the tutelary god of the city of Babylon but the supreme god of the Babylonian pantheon; previously Marduk was just the son of Ea, who had a comparatively minor role in the general hierarchy of Mesopotamian deities; Enlil of Nippur continuing to be the chief deity during the Kassite period.[15] With the rise of Babylon's fortunes, Marduk's eminence rose accordingly. His emblem was the *mušhuššu*, a hybrid creature with a lion's body and a snake's head and tail.

Nebuchadrezzar seems to have been extremely adept at manipulating public opinion and, to secure himself a place in Mesopotamian history, he commissioned a large number of literary works, most of which either glorify his success against Elam or demonstrate the greatness of Marduk.[16] He was keen to be seen as acting strictly in accordance with tradition, and adopted the old royal titles (such as 'king of Sumer and Akkad') and appointed his daughter to the position of *entu*, priestess of the moon-god at Ur.[17]

Thus the city of Babylon once more became a capital, for the Kassite kings from the time of Kurigalzu early in the fourteenth century had ruled from a new foundation, Dur-Kurigalzu, further north, within the main areas of Kassite settlements and near modern Baghdad. It is not clear whether the poetic Babylonian creation myth (the *Enuma eliš*) was also composed at this time, but the central position Marduk and the city of Babylon have in the text suggests that it was at least adapted for a period when Babylon became not only the political but also the religious and ceremonial centre of Babylonia. In the creation myth Marduk is given the decisive role in the process of creation, embodying, as he does, the active principle of order which overcomes the archaic, inert, creative potential of the old forces of nature, personified by Tiamat, Mummu and Apsu.[18] Having fashioned a rationally ordered universe out of the slain body of Tiamat, he creates man from a mixture of clay and the blood of a guilty god. This is a traditional theme of Mesopotamian cosmogony, except that in the older myths either a mother goddess or Ea was the maker of mankind. The assembled Anunnaki gods, grateful to Marduk for having been released from corvée duties, then ask:

'What shall be the sign of our gratitude before you?
Come, let us make (something) whose name shall be called "Sanctuary".'
(. . .)
When Marduk heard this, his face shone exceedingly, like the day, (and he said:)
'So shall Babylon be, whose construction you have desired,
Let its brickwork be fashioned, and call (it) a sanctuary.'
The Anunnaki wielded the hoe.
One year they made bricks for it,
When the second year arrived,
They raised the head of Esagila on high, level with the Apsu.
After they had built the lofty stage tower of the Apsu,
They established an abode therein(?) for Marduk, Enlil, (and) Ea.
He sat down before them in majesty.
(. . .)
After they had completed the construction of Esagila the Anunnaki built themselves shrines.
. . . of them were gathered.
They sat in the elevated shrine which they had built as his dwelling.

> He had the gods his fathers sit down to a banquet.
> 'Here is Babylon, your favourite dwelling place.
> Make music in [its] place (and) be seated on its square(?).'[19]

The temple precinct of Esagila was certainly an old foundation, going back to at least the First Dynasty of Babylon. The *Enuma eliš* was recited annually on the occasion of the New Year festival, which in Babylon took place in the month of Nisan (April). The king's participation was of vital importance in this ritual, since he had to grasp the hands of the Marduk statue in a symbolic transfer of legitimate power. The ceremony also underlined the prime importance of Babylon as the ritual centre; hence all the other major city gods and goddesses had to be transported to Babylon for the duration of the festival. The festival could not be celebrated in the absence of these gods or without the statue of Marduk. When the Aramaean raids became more widespread in the tenth century, there was a period of nine years when it became too risky for the gods to be taken to Babylon.

Towards the end of Nebuchadrezzar's reign the economic and political situation had deteriorated badly. There was widespread civil disorder and famine as a result of the destruction of crops and irrigation works. The situation is described in the long literary text known as the Erra Epic,[20] extant copies of which date from the first millennium and come mainly from the collections of Ashur and Nineveh. A colophon states that the whole composition was revealed to its author, one Kabti-ili-Marduk, in a dream, but it should be seen not as a contemporary record of the bad years or the 'dark age' of Babylonia but as a learned and not unhumorous mythical answer to the question as to why such things happen at all. There is no narrative as such; events are conveyed entirely through direct and reported speech. The main dialogue involves the irascible plague god Erra, his calm and rational 'captain' Ishum, the rabble-rousing and dangerous 'Seven' and the god Marduk.

The Seven taunt Erra that he lives too comfortably with his wife in retirement and evoke the former joys of warfare; even his weapons have become rusty. If he does nothing about this state of affairs, everyone will laugh at him. Erra is sufficiently roused by this speech to get up and go to find Marduk at Esagila, where he is shocked to discover how lacklustre the statue of the great god has become. Marduk answers that he is well aware of this, but he cannot possibly leave his temple and city to procure the necessary precious stones and metals because every time he does so something terrible happens. Erra now offers to look after things in Marduk's absence, a proposal to which Marduk, surprisingly, consents. The text is broken at this point, but it seems that Erra tries to subvert or delay Marduk's efforts to collect the materials he needs. Evil portents begin to appear in the sky; in particular Erra's star (the Dog Star) waxes brightly. The goddess Ishtar tried to placate the god, who has talked himself into a state of terrible anger. He launches into a long speech that reads like an incantation (and similar passages do indeed occur in Babylonian magic spells):

> I shall cover the face of the moon in the middle of the night (. . .)
> I shall finish off the land and count it as ruins (. . .)
> I shall destroy mountains and fell cattle (. . .) I shall fell people and leave no life (. . .)
> I shall let a [barbarian] enter a god's shrine where evil men should not go (. . .) I shall devastate the city (etc.).[21]

Ishum tries, in his compassion for the sufferings of mankind, to deter Erra from further violence, but Erra retorts that it was after all inevitable, since Marduk 'the king of the gods has risen from his dwelling so how can all the lands stay firm?' – to which Ishum answers that, in Marduk's absence, he controls the whole earth and rules the land, asking, 'Does conflict ever happen without you, or warfare take place in your absence?' He then launches into a graphic description of the evils unleashed by Erra and the distress he caused to the city gods, in a manner very like that of the 'Lamentations',[22] which also describe a complete inversion of the customary norms in times of peace and prosperity. Even Marduk himself is affected, causing him to curse his own city:

> Woe to Babylon which I made as lofty as a date-palm's crown, but the wind shrivelled it.
> Woe to Babylon, which I filled with seeds like a pine-cone, but whose abundance I did not bring to fruition.
> Woe to Babylon, which I planted like a luxuriant orchard, but which never tasted its fruit. (. . .)[23]

Erra defensively retorts that he can no more change his nature than a shepherd can stop letting sheep out from their pen – 'like one who does not plant the orchard I am not slow to cut it down' – and Ishum finally manages to placate him by flattery, suggesting a rest now 'that we all know that nobody can stand up to you'. At this Erra's features brighten and he launches into a comprehensive blessing, decreeing that 'the temples which were allowed to become damaged, lift their heads (up) as high as the rising sun' and the provisions be once again delivered to Esagila and Babylon.

This text is an interesting counterpart to the creation story annually recited precisely to banish all evil from the city and the whole country. Here a more realistic picture emerges that acknowledges the fundamental inscrutability of divine providence. Marduk, well aware that his absence always leads to chaos, is here seen not only to be forced to make his own statue but to entrust the running of the world to the most unsuitable candidate. The author seems to suggest that the theological explanations for political disasters can be manipulated, and that the resolution of conflict is as much a whim of some god as its cause. Here Erra responds to flattery; it does not need the return of Marduk for peace to be re-established. This text, which is neither an 'epic' nor a myth, stands in the same intellectual tradition as certain other deeply sceptical works which also probe the limitations of official religious beliefs for the solution to moral and ontological problems and the Job theme of justice and the purpose of suffering.[24]

The fundamental uncertainty of the age which the Erra Epic so eloquently describes is echoed by the changing fortunes of the reign of Nebuchadrezzar I. His efforts to expand Babylonian territory were thwarted by Assyrian reprisals, which led to the destruction of a number of Mesopotamian cities, including Sippar and Babylon. Relations with Assyria remained strained, despite periods of cooperation (as under Ashur-bel-kala). With the expansion of the northern state in the ninth century, Babylonia lost its independence to its more powerful neighbour, who was swift to check any signs of resistance and rebellion. The most drastic retaliation for a bid for independence was Sennacherib's campaign against Marduk-apla-iddina II, which culminated in the sack of Babylon in 689. The incursions of western Semitic tribes, like the Aramaeans in the north and the Chaldeans in the south, also made an impact.

At first, as on previous occasions when nomadic peoples had begun to infiltrate the Mesopotamian regions, the effect was primarily disruptive, since the mobile and socially distinct newcomers fought for land and pasture at the expense of the settled population, leading to the abandonment of rural settlements. Gradually, the newcomers learnt to adapt and some sort of equilibrium evolved. In the north, where the climate and geographical situation was more suitable for pastoralist pursuits, the Aramaeans remained more aloof from contact and assimilation; in Assyria, their acculturation proceeded more swiftly. The Chaldeans, who occupied the regions along the southern Euphrates, around Ur and the marshland of the Persian Gulf, adopted a sedentary lifestyle more quickly, since the options of continued pastoralist subsistence were less favourable here. These tribes acknowledged a common ancestor and were led by sheikhs. Some of these sheikhs, especially the Chaldeans, became very powerful and played a decisive role in the Babylonian struggle for independence.[25] The most famous of them was the chief of the Bit-Yakin, known by his Babylonian name as Marduk-apla-iddina II, who became the arch-enemy of Sargon and Sennacherib.

The dominant form of settlement, despite a trend towards village and small (unfortified) town settlements, remained the city, which had at this time a cosmopolitan and socially heterogeneous population. The new tribal people, while retaining the option of mobility, also established ties with existing urban centres through individual families taking up residence there or helping to build their own.[26] The cities, with their formidable fortifications and massed populations, were the main foci of civil, economic and religious life. The traditional prestige of the old cultural centres allowed them to exert considerable influence and to retain their customary privileges, especially Nippur, Sippar and Babylon.

Although the Assyrians were politically dominant for most of the period between 900 and 612, they were generally reluctant to treat Babylonia as if it were just another vassal state or dependent province. There were few garrisons stationed in the country and to maintain control the Assyrians relied on intelligence reports and loyalty oaths.

Another tactic was to curry favour with the residents of the old cities. Assyrian kings invested in the restoration of temple buildings, sent handsome offerings to the great deities and extended the privileges that only some cities had traditionally enjoyed to others, such as Ur, Uruk and Eridu. The idea was to foster solidarity of the urban élites with the Assyrian cause against the troublesome tribal groups in the rural areas and the southern marshland.[27]

Yet, for all these efforts, the Babylonians never came to accept Assyrian hegemony. The experience of strong outside control overrode internal divisions based on social systems, subsistence and ethnic origin. Assyrian attempts to exploit rivalries between cities, between tribal peoples and urban centres, and to pit clan against clan within tribes, were not without success, but eventually a common purpose emerged that in turn contributed to the creation of a new Babylonian identity. Various forms of resistance were employed, from riots and civil protests against taxation to guerrilla warfare which made full use of environmental features. The marshes, with their extensive reed thickets, were ideal for retreats and sudden sorties and unsuitable for conventional fighting, and the watercourses, canals and rivers could also be manipulated for strategic ends. The most successful tactic of resistance, however, was to broaden the base of operations by enlisting allies in the anti-Assyrian cause. With the support of the east, first of Elam and then of the Medes, and the west, of the Arab tribes of the desert, the rebel forces drew the Assyrians into ever more strenuous and draining counter-campaigns. The Elamites were the most consistently supportive of the Babylonian struggle, though dynastic instabilities (for instance, the quick succession of rulers) and internal dissent sometimes neutralized the effectiveness of their role.

Despite persistent acts of subversion and occasional outbreaks of violent insurrection, which the Assyrians repressed with greater or lesser degrees of swiftness and brutality, the Assyrian domination continued for some two hundred years. The last effort to break free from the 'yoke of Ashur' was the Great Rebellion of 652–648, which was, ironically, led by Shamash-shumu-ukin, the elder half-brother of the Assyrian king Ashurbanipal.[28] It epitomized the ambiguity of Assyria's relationship to Babylonia that an official Assyrian monarch should come close to breaking the supremacy of Assyria. In the end,

Ashurbanipal prevailed, the uprising was suppressed and a new king, Kandalanu, was appointed, who ruled until 627, the year of Ashurbanipal's death. This marked the fading of Assyrian rule.[29]

Like any other province of the Assyrian empire, Babylonia had been made to pay tribute. Rebellion was punished by the destruction of cities and the countryside, the plundering of treasures and the removal of large sections of the population, especially from among the tribal peoples. However, there were also benefits that materialized particularly in the later period, when local rulership stabilized. The incorporation of the country into a world empire stimulated the economy, creating a much wider market for Babylonian goods[30] and securing access to international trade routes. The mainstay of the Babylonian economy was still agriculture (barley and dates) and animal husbandry. High-quality textiles made of wool and linen were as highly prized as before, as were other craft and luxury articles, for which there was a flourishing market in the royal capitals and provincial centres. New crops were introduced, such as cotton, and even certain kinds of timber and vine began to be grown on a commercially viable scale. Being part of greater Assyria also made the import of new materials and technology possible: in the seventh century Babylon became part of the iron age.

The deportation policies of the Assyrians, which brought so many foreign groups into the country, also broadened the cultural and ethnic composition of the population. Together with the contacts forged by international trade, this widened cultural horizons. Another advantageous factor was the unifying force of the Aramaean language, which was by then spoken throughout the Near East. Although written communication for archival and literary purposes still made use of cuneiform, the Aramaic alphabet made literacy a far less privileged and complicated procedure. This fact is often overlooked because there are so few written sources in Aramaic as a result of the impermanent nature of the writing material. The Aramaization of the Near East was no doubt facilitated by the Assyrian imperial structure and its administrative needs. An easily acquired written language was a much more useful tool in a multicultural and multilingual world than the cumbersome cuneiform system. Many people, of course, used spoken Aramaic as a lingua franca for commerce and in daily life. In fact, by the time of the empire's demise, the commonly spoken language throughout Syria and Mesopotamia was not Assyrian but Aramaic.

In contrast to this social levelling effect, the much debated influence of Babylonian culture on Assyria was limited to an educated élite. Assyrian kings prided themselves on their familiarity with Babylonian learning and tried to stock their libraries with complete editions of cuneiform literature and science. They also made efforts to follow the examples of Babylonian public ritual and cult, especially during periods when the Babylonian deities were 'hostages' in Assyria. But it is doubtful whether these cultural borrowings penetrated more deeply than this into Assyrian society. An exception is the great popularity of the god Nabu, a patron god of scribes and of comparatively minor importance in Babylonia, who acquired a more martial aspect in Assyria that assured his widespread veneration.

THE NEO-BABYLONIAN
EMPIRE (626-539)

With the death of Kandalanu, the last king appointed by Assyria, Babylonia did not automatically gain independence and unity. The Assyrians still exerted their influence, and the successors of Ashurbanipal ruled at least nominally as kings of Babylonia, though the Babylonian Chronicle asserts that no king was recognized at the time. It was a period of confusion, and the struggle for political control over the country, fought bitterly and persistently not just by Assyria but by various factions within the country, lasted some six to eight years. The first Neo-Babylonian ruler, Nabopolassar, who officially acceded to the Babylonian throne as early as 626, had called himself 'son of a nobody', and although later sources refer to him as a Chaldean, it is not at all certain that he actually belonged to the Chaldean tribe. His background remains obscure, but it is certain that he founded the last dynasty to rule over an independent Babylonia. By 616 he had consolidated his position in southern Mesopotamia and entered into a fateful alliance with the Medes, who had established themselves on the previously Elamite territories.[31]

The Medes had built up a capable and well-equipped army, and with their support Nabopolassar was able to launch his attacks against Assyria, where he destroyed the nerve centres of the government: the ceremonial capital Ashur, the administrative and residential capital Nineveh, as well as Tarbisu, Calah and the last capital of the empire Harran. Babylonia had by then triumphed over Assyria and become the new main power in the Near East. The defeat of Assyria had mobilized Egypt, first to bring them to the defence of their former enemy Assyria, then to contend against Babylonian control over Syro-Palestine.

Nabopolassar's son and crown prince, Nebuchadrezzar, secured a decisive victory over the Egyptians in 605 at Carchemish and again at Hamath.[32] After his father's death in the same year, Nebuchadrezzar II acceded to the throne without opposition. Aware of the need to maintain a strong military presence in the area of northern Syria, he returned there soon afterwards. The consolidation of Babylonian control in the face of persistent Egyptian resistance remained his most important task during the following years. The struggle against Egypt was fanned and exploited by various smaller states and tribal confederacies, including Judah and the Transjordanian kingdoms. By 601 Nebuchadrezzar had won the upper hand, and Egypt chose not to interfere, as the hapless Judaean king Johoiakin was to learn when he initiated a revolt against Babylon, vainly counting on Egyptian support. His insurrection was punished by exile, and when the newly appointed governor Zedekiah also rebelled, Nebuchadrezzar responded in the 'Assyrian' manner and destroyed Jerusalem (587). The port cities of Tyre and Sidon also fought to retain their independence and were conquered after protracted sieges.[33]

Nebuchadrezzar's eastern campaigns not only brought vast amounts of tribute and booty to Babylonia, but also secured undisputed possession of the major trade routes to the Mediterranean and beyond. The control over the equally important southern Anatolian provinces, providers of iron and other metals, was achieved less arduously since Cilicia, Pirindu and Lydia could be persuaded by diplomatic means to accept Babylonian overlordship. By decades of concerted efforts Nebuchadrezzar had built an empire larger than the one lost by Ashurbanipal. A capable and shrewd ruler, he was able to balance diplomacy with ruthlessness to keep his dominions in order. At home, he was scrupulous in basing his kingship on popular support, carefully orchestrated through public ceremonial and religious ritual. Again in the imperial modes of the Assyrians, he invested much of the accumulated booty and tribute in urban development throughout the country, but especially in the capital Babylon which was to eclipse the fame of Nineveh to such an extent that later historians conflated the reputation of both capitals.

Nebuchadrezzar's Babylon

The inner layout of Babylon, the main quarters and streets, had been established long before the Neo-Babylonian empire.[34] In the residential area on the Merkez mound, where earlier levels have been accessible, the street pattern had changed little over the centuries since the Kassite occupation. The Assyrian kings, especially Esarhaddon, had contributed to the beautification of the city – especially the main sanctuary of Marduk, Esagila – plastered some streets and repaired the defences. The project to make Babylon into a metropolis grand enough to represent the aspirations of an empire, however, was initiated by his father, Nabopolassar. He began work on the Southern Palace, his residence, built a temple to Ninurta, constructed the quay walls of the Arahtu (as the Euphrates was then named) and began the most ambitious architectural undertaking of all, the reconstruction of Etemenanki, 'Foundation of Heaven and Earth', as the 'Tower of Babel' or ziggurat was called.

This vast undertaking, which was to take forty-three years to complete, became the symbol of the new Babylon. While the Assyrians had built vast palaces to accommodate the royal residence and the civil service, their ziggurats were modest box-like structures, accessible from the roofs of abutting temple buildings. The free-standing ziggurat, like the one built by Urnammu at Ur, was a type commonly found in the south. In Babylon, though the palaces were also very large, the biggest building was entirely for ceremonial and religious purposes, standing alone in a vast terraced precinct, in the very centre of the city. It characterized the southern Mesopotamian attitude to monumental architecture that we already observed in the fourth millennium. The vast dimension of the ziggurat ensured that this building was indeed the largest ziggurat to be built in Mesopotamia and manifested the triumph of Babylonia over its enemies.

The foundation document of Nabopolassar describes how, after his victory over Assyria, he had received a summons from the gods to restore the sacred structure which had suffered long neglect. The dimensions were calculated in accordance with divine revelation: 'I gathered the oracles of Shamash, Adad and Marduk and in my heart I kept the measurements which the great gods had decided upon in the oracle.' It had to be built on safe foundations, 'on the heart of the Apsu', with its summit equal to heaven; in other words, the height should equal the base. The building therefore anchored the whole city within cosmic parameters.

New soundings by the German Archaeological Institute at the ziggurat core, combined with a careful evaluation of cuneiform material, have led to new insights into the original appearance of the ziggurat.[35] Of crucial importance was a cuneiform tablet that George Smith had already published in paraphrase in 1876. It dates from the Seleucid era and is a copy of an earlier version, written by Anu-bel-shunu. It may have served as the blueprint for the construction of Etemenanki. The tablet gives the dimensions for the base in three different systems of measurements, but the most important factor is that the dimensions of the side-walls of the base were to be equal to the total height of the building[36] (approximately 92 × 92 × 92 metres). Another tablet, from the British Museum, shows the elevation and the access ramp, also with proportions indicated.[37] The elevation and the size of the structure were to some extent dictated by the remains of the old mudbrick ziggurat, which may well date back to the time of Hammurabi and no doubt had been intermittently repaired. Sennacherib destroyed what was left of this in 689, and his successors, Esarhaddon and Ashurbanipal, had tried to restore it by adding a new mudbrick facing tied to the core with wooden brackets. However, this outer skin had come loose and the whole structure was in a sorry state.

Nabopolassar's architects came up with a new scheme to incorporate the remains of the old ziggurat and, at the same time, to dignify it. Nabopolassar first cleared the ground for the new temenos to make it safe from flooding. He then rebuilt the river wall and constructed a large platform 3.5 metres above water level, well above the lower courses of the old ziggurat. At the ceremonial commencement of the building operations, the king himself, his sons and selected officials carried the first baskets of clay, mixed with wine and honey. It took two and a half years to build the mantle around the existing mudbrick core of the old structure. The new facing was to be made of baked bricks, laid in bitumen mortar. The original height of the old ziggurat was to be represented visually by the first two stages, which rose in sheer, monumental masses from the ground. A centrally placed stepped ramp at the south façade was to lead straight to the top of the second stage, which was, in fact, the emplacement of the old high temple. Two lateral flights of stairs then led to the first stage, indicating the old level of the first high terrace. Above the second stage, with its wide platform, rose the subsequent stages, a ziggurat above a ziggurat. This consisted of four regularly stepped terraces with an internal staircase. The high temple on the topmost platform was organized as a sequence of rooms around an open courtyard. Here were the chapels of the great gods and the monumental bed of Marduk, and on the opposite side his throne.

Such was the plan devised during Nabopolassar's reign. The basic proportions and dimensions had been established with due divine guidance and a long period of construction was envisaged. Nebuchadrezzar duly continued his father's work and saw it to completion after some forty-three years. It has been calculated that at least 17 million bricks had to be made and fired. The sight of the building, even before completion, made such an impression on the exiled Jews that the story of the Tower of Babel was never to be forgotten.

But this was not the only project Nebuchadrezzar supervised. He reigned for forty-three years and had command over limitless resources of wealth and materials, of skilled as well as unskilled manpower recruited from resettled populations. During his reign Babylon became the new metropolis of the world. It is clear from an early first millennium topographical text that Babylon was already by that stage a large city with numerous sacred buildings. This text, preserved on five tablets, lists the many names and epithets of Babylon in a litany-like enumeration:

> Babylon the creation of Enlil,
> Babylon that secures the life of the land,
> Babylon, city of abundance,
> Babylon, city whose citizens are overwhelmed by wealth,
> Babylon, city of festivities, joy, and dancing,
> Babylon, the city whose citizens celebrate ceaselessly,
> Babylon, privileged city which frees the captive,
> Babylon, the pure city.[38]

The next three tablets list all the major and minor shrines of the city, according to districts. This has made it possible to identify some of the excavated temples.[39] The last tablet contains information about the city gates, walls, waterways, canals, streets and city quarters. The old inner city of Babylon had covered about a square mile. In the twelfth century, the walls were extended so that the area measured more than three square miles. The fortifications were particularly impressive, as Herodotus noted. They consisted of a double line of walls, the inner one being 6.5 metres thick and probably higher than the outer one, which measured just 3.7 metres thick. Both were built of mudbrick and had regularly spaced projecting towers. The space between was wide enough to take an elevated military roadway.[40]

At the point where the Euphrates enters the city in the north, Nebuchadrezzar added a particularly strong wall, built in baked brick set in bitumen, and there sited the Northern Fortress. A moat, also strengthened with baked brick, added another line of defence. Since the Euphrates was also the most important medium for traffic, all major streets led to the river, and Nebuchadrezzar built a new wall on the eastern bank with a broad quay for ships to anchor. The Euphrates,[41] flowing from north to south, could be crossed at several bridges, including one made of stone.

The centre of the city was the religious precinct, the vast courtyard of Etemenanki, the ziggurat, with Esagila, the temple of Marduk, to the south of it. The temple Esagila had its own enclosure, courtyard and cellae. The statue of Marduk had traditionally been kept in Esagila, and the temple functioned like a royal palace, as a residence and reception area for visiting deities, surrounded by all the practical

amenities: places for slaughter and sacrifice, for storage and administration. The high temple on top of Etemenanki was by contrast a
purely symbolic space, reserved for the display of divine images and
the performance of special rituals. The inner staircase connecting the
second stage with the high temple allowed for unobserved access by
the gods' servants. The ziggurat temenos was the ritual epicentre of
the city, and from there of the whole of the empire. Here, where heaven
and earth were connected, where gods hovered in elevated security
above the city, the hub of the state could be contemplated as a cosmic
pillar assuring continuity and renewal.

From the ziggurat temenos a beautifully paved street led directly
northwards, past the temples of Ishtar and Belet-ili to the east and the
temple of Nabu to the west, skirting the Southern Palace, to the Ishtar
Gate. This was the Processional Way which led to the Festival House
outside the walls. It had originally been paved with limestone slabs.
The plan and the side-walls of the northern end of the street and the
Ishtar Gate itself had a very deep substructure (15 metres), buried
when the level of the street was raised. This was all that was left of
the street and the gate when Koldewey dug there, but because the
foundations were so substantial, it allowed for the gate to be reconstructed with its tall square towers and high vaulted inner chambers.
At Babylon itself, the formerly buried building now stands exposed.
Even the famous relief decoration of the sculpted animals was found
preserved under a carefully applied plaster coating. The superstructure,
the part visible in the sixth century, was completely covered by colourful glazed tiles, with sacred animals on a deep blue background. The
whole building has been reconstructed with the original tiles that lay
scattered about the ground in thousands of pieces, and visitors to the
Berlin Museum today are able to admire the reconstituted bulls of
Adad and the dragons of Marduk. The Processional Way was used for
the ceremonial departure and return of the army under royal command, the Babylonian name of the street being *ai-ibur-šabu*, 'May the
proud not flourish'. It was the greatest boulevard of the city, with
the main palaces and temples built along it, and it terminated at the
temenos of Etemenanki. When the New Year was properly celebrated,
which could only happen when there was both a king and the Marduk
statue present at Babylon, the procession of the great gods passed

down it, out through the Ishtar Gate and into the Festival House outside the city walls. The lavish decoration of the walls lining the street and the gate itself were tributes to its sacred purpose.

Another major project of the Neo-Babylonian kings was the construction of a suitably grand royal residence and administrative centre, 'a palace as the seat of my royal authority, a building for the admiration of my people, a place of union for the land'. This summarizes the ideological as well as the representative function of the Mesopotamian palaces. In Assyria, the palaces also incorporated shrines and chapels to stress the link between king and gods. In the past, especially during the Assyrian hegemony, the kings of Babylon 'used to build palaces and establish residences wherever they pleased, and stored their possessions in them and piled up their belongings there and only in the New Year festival came to Babylon to please Marduk'.[42]

Nabopolassar had built his own residence just south-west of the Ishtar Gate, abutting to the north against the double city walls. Nebuchadrezzar realized that the Euphrates would always be problem for any large building in its proximity. To protect the temples in the centre and the planned palaces from erosion and flooding, he diverted the river further west by constructing a huge bulwark with walls up to 25 metres thick. The palaces were built on a vast platform made of burnt brick, and consisted of various compounds grouped around large courtyards and protected by massive walls. The Southern Citadel (Südburg), as Koldewey called it, had been begun by Nabopolassar. Nebuchadrezzar added more wings and later also built a second palace (Hauptburg) just beyond the double city wall. Both buildings abutted against the western side of the Processional Way and the Ishtar Gate. The walls of these palaces too had been completely denuded and Koldewey traced their foundations, which were built of large, square bricks.

There were vast storage rooms in subterranean vaulted chambers, which used to be interpreted as the substructure of the 'Hanging Gardens'.[43] The interior fittings of the palace were suitably luxurious, with rich wood panelling inlaid with ivory and lapis lazuli. The walls of the throne-room were glazed with the same blue tiles as the Ishtar Gate, with rampant lions and palm trees. But the Babylonian kings eschewed the Assyrian practice of depicting their deeds on the palace walls. Instead of the figurative scenes that lined the rooms and corridors of the Assyrian palaces, they relied on architectural means to demonstrate the power of their empire. The sheer size of their buildings, the often disproportionate thickness of the walls, the baked brick instead of the traditional mudbrick and the architectural decorations all not only suggested the state's command over unlimited manpower and wealth, but also introduced an unprecedented scale – everything was much bigger and higher than before.

This method can be observed quite clearly in the way the palatial doorways were constructed. There were intermediate passages, almost chambers, set within the depth of walls several metres thick. Walls and ceilings were panelled with precious wood and inlaid with silver and gold, ivory and lapis lazuli, while lintels and thresholds were cast in bronze. In these doorways of rooms within and between rooms, important affairs could be conducted and contacts made, but apart from such social uses, the emphasis on the doorways is also characteristic of the Babylonian preference for making indirect but effective statements about political power. It is a subtly conveyed message, since there was often a practical and rational reason for the use of thick walls, baked brick or the massive size of public monuments: defence, damp-proofing, the existence of earlier structures that were to be incorporated in the new. Close inspection reveals, however, that the solutions went way beyond necessity.[44] The kings also displayed antiquities and curiosities in the palace, including the Ur III period statues from Mari, which may have been part of the booty Hammurabi removed to Babylon in the early second millennium; an inscribed paving slab by Adad-nirari II; late north Syrian relief stone stelae and similar objects.[45] The display of such relics of the past enhanced the prestige of the present royal incumbents. They could be seen as heirs of a venerable local tradition and the conquerors of alien peoples.

The palaces and temples, defences and quays, the streets and gates, bridges and moats, were not only decorated with a stupendous magnificence, using the most costly materials – gold, silver, lapis lazuli and hardwood timber – they also showed a new interest in structural durability. Nebuchadrezzar wanted his buildings to survive in the form and state of his period for ever. Nobody had ever built so much in baked brick before, or used lime mortar and bitumen in such quantities.

Nor had anyone before him taken such wide-ranging measures to protect the buildings and the city from the vagaries of the Euphrates. The old Mesopotamian cities were always more or less in decay, since mudbrick, once the plaster covering and roof protection become neglected, begins to crumble quickly. But this continual process of disintegration had at the same time contributed to the very substance of the city's volume as buildings were erected on top of the levelled remains of obsolete structures. Decay and renewal were part of a process of growth and cyclical development.

Nebuchadrezzar's Babylon signalled, by contrast, a desire for everlasting monumentality, and this time he was not satisfied with a mere proclamation of that intention in foundation documents, as was the habit of older times. He had thousands of bricks stamped with his written identification and inserted hundreds of commemorative plaques into his walls, and he went even further in choosing an incorruptible material. Ultimately he succeeded in his quest. For millennia after his death the peasants of the area built their homesteads with his top-quality bricks, and today the Neo-Babylonian lime and bitumen mortar still bind the surviving masonry and brickwork with unyielding strength.

In Mesopotamia, the last indigenous dynasty managed to perpetuate its version of the city into the future. Nebuchadrezzar set out to build a city commensurate with Babylonia's status as a new international power, as victor over Assyria and Egypt, at the time the only metropolis in the world but also a city with a venerable and ancient cultural tradition, that had the most advanced science and the most sophisticated arts. No opportunity to flaunt its wealth was missed, with a conspicuous use of precious materials, but it was also done in a manner to emphasize the cultural rather than the martial superiority of Babylon, as heir to the oldest civilization in the world.

Yet this desire for physical permanence may betray doubts about the sustainability of it all, and a growing awareness of danger and inherent changes. The feverish building activities, the huge endowments to the temples, the lavishly staged public rituals and, most tellingly, the investment in massive defence structures such as the so-called Median wall between the Euphrates and Tigris in the Sippar region – all seek to stave off the fate that befell Assyria: the collapse of a mighty empire.

After the death of Nebuchadrezzar in 562, his son, Amel-Marduk, the Evil-Merodach of the Bible, reigned for barely a year before being deposed and perhaps murdered by the husband of his sister, Kashshiya, a certain Nergal-sharra-usur, or Neriglissar (559–556).[46] Neriglissar had been a high official and wealthy entrepreneur before becoming Nebuchadrezzar's son-in-law. Not much is known of his activities; he led a military campaign against an Anatolian province and died soon afterwards. His chosen heir was then eliminated to allow Nabonidus, who also had served as a senior official, to take over the kingship, a move which seems to have found general acceptance. The instability of the royal succession had meanwhile sparked off rebellions in the Syrian provinces and Nabonidus went with his army to re-establish Babylonian supremacy. He brought back large numbers of prisoners of war and much booty, most of which he spent on building projects in the major Babylonian cities. As was mentioned earlier he seems to have been something of an archaeology buff and to have liked discovering ancient documents and statues. He even made his daughter serve as *entu* priestess at Ur, after he found an old inscription about this practice, which had been defunct for centuries.

The Syrian and Levantine regions were not to be so easily subdued, however. He had to engage in further campaigns there and also came into contact with the Arab tribes in the western desert region. According to the Babylonian Chronicle, which is generally rather unkind about Nabonidus, he spent ten years away from Babylon, at the oasis city called Teima, leaving government affairs in the hands of his son, Bel-shar-usur (Belshazzar). This has been explained as the result of a rift between the priesthood of Bel (Marduk) and the king who was engaged in rebuilding the old city of Harran, the last official Assyrian capital. It is more likely that his motives were to try to find a safer base of operation further east, and to capitalize on the new international trade routes through the Arabian desert, which had, since the domestication of the camel (*c.*1000 BC), opened new lucrative markets in the spice and incense trade.

Nabonidus also renewed the moon temple at Harran, where his mother, Addu-Guppi, who was probably a descendant of the last Assyrian royal house, officiated as a high cult functionary.[47] When she died in 547, she was buried with great ceremony, and Nabonidus erected two stelae at Harran to commemorate her extraordinary life in an pseudo-autobiographical style:

Out of his love for me who worships him and have laid hold of the hem of his garment, Sin, the king of all gods, did what he had not done before, had not granted to anybody else, he gave me (a woman) an exalted position and a famous name in the country. He added (to my life) many days (and) years of happiness and kept me alive from the time of Ashurbanipal, king of Assyria, to the 9th year of Nabonidus, king of Babylon, the son whom I bore, (i.e.) one hundred and four happy years (spent) in that piety which Sin, the king of all gods, has planted in my heart. My eyesight was good (to the end of my life), my hearing excellent, my hands and feet were sound, my words well chosen, food and drink agreed with me, my health was fine and my mind happy. I saw my great-great grandchildren, up to the fourth generation, in good health and (thus) had my fill of old age.

(. . .)

I have obeyed with all my heart and have done my duty (as a subject) during the 21 years in which Nabopolassar, the king of Babylon, the 43 years in which Nebuchadrezzar, the son of Nabopolassar, the four years in which Neriglissar, the king of Babylon, exercised their kingship, (altogether) 68 years. I have made Nabonidus, the son whom I bore, serve Nebuchadrezzar, son of Nabopolassar, and Neriglissar, king of Babylon, and he performed his duty for them day and night by doing always what was their pleasure. He also made me a good name before them and they gave me an elevated position as if I were their real daughter.[48]

This account bore testimony not only to an unusually blessed life for a woman of her time, enjoying a healthy old age and great-grandchildren, but also to someone who was a direct and very important link between the Assyrian and the Babylonian empires. Having witnessed the decline and fall of the former, she saw the rise of the new state and the accession of her own son to supreme office. Since she must have been at Harran for most of her adult life, she chose Sin, the moon-god of Harran, the last seat of the Assyrian kings, to be the centre of her devotion, and at Harran she was buried. Addu-Guppi was one of the few royal women who could help to shape history rather than be only a pawn in the political game played by their fathers. Her diplomatic skills and persistence must have been highly developed to maintain her influence successfully through four successive regimes and see her son, whose claim to legitimacy was tenuous, find acceptance as king of Babylon. He rewarded her by the preservation of her memory.

The activities of Nabonidus in the west and his prolonged absence from Babylon caused unease, especially since it meant that the ideologically crucial New Year festival had to be cancelled for the duration of his stay in Arabia. Although he had made his son Bel-shar-usur co-regent, with full responsibility, the priesthood of Marduk would not countenance his participation in the rite. At long last Nabonidus seems to have heeded the advice of his diviners and returned to the capital in time to celebrate the festival (in 543 or 542). It was to be the last time an indigenous king clasped the hands of the Marduk statue. Nabonidus' concentration on Arabia had deflected him from the real problem: the new political power in the old Elamite territory, which was now ruled by the Persian dynasty called after their founder, Achaemenes. In 539 king Cyrus II marched down the Diyala valley and fought a victorious battle at Opis. Nearby Sippar surrendered. Nabonidus, who had commanded the Babylonian army, fled. Within days the Persians were in Babylon, which had offered no resistance. Nabonidus surrendered and survived, according to Berossus, in exile. His son, Bel-shar-usur, was probably killed.

This was the end of Babylonian independence, but the assumption of political control by the Achaemenids did not result in any radical change in the lives of the Babylonians. Throughout the sixth century Babylonia had experienced a steady rate of economic growth, built on a solid base of agricultural productivity, manufacturing and trade. This trend for sustained prosperity and productivity continued throughout the following centuries when Babylonia was ruled by foreign dynasties.[49] When Cyrus took Babylon, he interfered as little as possible with the *status quo* so as to minimize any disruption and loss of revenue. The Achaemenid king was also quick to exploit the resentment of the Babylonian élite against Nabonidus' neglect of the 'holy city' and styled himself as a traditional Babylonian ruler. He celebrated the New Year festival and thus confirmed the supremacy of Marduk. He also commissioned a royal inscription to be written in the style of Ashurbanipal, regarded by Babylonian historians of the time as an exemplary universal ruler.[50] He also followed the customs of the Mesopotamian kings by restoring temples and public buildings, and he returned displaced cult statues to their original temples.

Local Babylonian officials continued to occupy their posts as before. The city of Babylon enjoyed special status. According to classical sources, it was even considered as an imperial capital. It housed the royal treasury and archive. The wealth and economic activity of the city are reflected in the business archives of the period. Koldewey had failed to discover extensive tablet collections, not least because local people had been digging out tablets by the thousand between the 1870s and 1900. These were sold to dealers in Baghdad and dispersed throughout private and museum collections in Europe and the United States. As has become clear, most of these economic tablets belonged to the private sector, mainly to families of rich entrepreneurs who dealt in agricultural produce, livestock and banking.[51] However, Babylonia was also subjected to heavy taxation and exploitation of its resources, which caused economic stress and a rise in interest rates. By the second half of the fifth century rates of interest had increased to 50 per cent from the 10 per cent charged during Nebuchadrezzar's time.[52]

Under Darius I (522–486), the expansionist phase of the Persian empire came to an end and he invested in the ideological underpinning of the imperial power by building ceremonial Persian centres, most famously Persepolis, and by stressing Iranian cultural and political dominance, a policy further pursued by his successors. The territorial integrity of the old Babylonian empire was divided into smaller units, and the Mesopotamian part became an integral component of the empire, rather than a tribute-paying associate state under Persian general command. The Babylonian ruling élite was gradually replaced by Persian nobles and the temple estates were obliged to hand over part of their produce and revenue and have their records subjected to state control.

When Darius had acceded to the throne, there had been an uprising in Babylon, led by a man who claimed to be a son of Nabonidus who adopted the name Nebuchadrezzar III. He was recognized as legitimate ruler in Babylonia, but half a year later was defeated in battle and killed by Darius.[53] Similarly, Darius' son Xerxes, after he succeeded in 486, had to put down two revolts in Babylon. According to classical sources, he destroyed temples and temporarily removed the Marduk statue, but there is little evidence that the sanctuaries suffered a decline.[54] He did, on the other hand, abolish the title 'king of Babylon'.

The layout of the city hardly changed during the Achaemenid period, and the temples and palaces continued in use; only Darius added a relatively small Persian-style palace on the Kasr, west of the South Citadel. The city during the fifth century was described most memorably by Herodotus. The people of Babylon, he reported, smelled good because they liked to apply fragrant unguents to their bodies. They kept their hair long, covered with high caps, and wore several layers of clothes made from linen and wool, with a short cape around the shoulder. This description fits well with the representation of Babylonians on the Apadana frieze in Persepolis. The nobles liked to sport a walking stick and everyone had their own cylinder seal.[55]

Herodotus remarks upon the fact that the city was full of houses with three or more storeys, and that the streets were straight, aligned either parallel with or at right angles to the river. The population was very heterogeneous. Jews and Syrians, Persians and Egyptians, as well as Greeks lived in the city. The language of communication throughout the empire was still Aramaic, as it had been during the first half of the millennium. The old Mesopotamian literary tradition continued to flourish in the great scribal centre, which carried on perfecting the sciences of divination, astronomy and astrology, as well as the study of the literary compositions and religious texts.

The same state of affairs continued after Alexander the Great defeated Darius III (331) and thus inherited the Persian empire. Having destroyed and burnt Persepolis, he wanted Babylon to become the capital of his new empire and planned the reconstruction of Etemenanki, the ziggurat, which had fallen into disrepair. But he died before he could realize any of his projects for Babylon. In the ensuing division of his territorial conquests, Babylonia came to be governed by one of Alexander's Macedonian generals, Seleucus I (305–272), and his descendants. There is little evidence of any radical change or Hellenization of the city during the Seleucid era.[56] Despite later foundations of other cities, most notably Seleucia on the Tigris, Babylon remained the administrative, ceremonial, religious and economic centre of the region.

There was a Greek-Macedonian presence in Babylon. Koldewey excavated the small and relatively well preserved theatre in the area known as Homera,[57] as well as a gymnasium and an agora, as mentioned by Diodorus. This community, referred to from outside as 'Babylonian', represented an enclave in a multinational but predominantly Babylonian city. Nothing supports the assumption that Babylon became a Greek *polis* in organization or urban redevelopment, or that there was a widespread Hellenization of the local population. The texts testify to the continuing vitality of Babylonian society and culture. The traditional cuneiform learning was still practised and the Greeks adopted the use of clay tablets as a medium for public documents written in Greek.[58] On the other hand, Babylonian scribes made transliterations of Akkadian and Aramaic texts in the Greek alphabet, and there are a few tablets which have a cuneiform version of one side and a Greek one on the other. The astronomical diaries, which record the daily market price of standard commodities such as oil and barley, the water levels of the Euphrates and planetary positions, continued to be recorded until *c.*AD 75.[59]

The ritual for that most characteristic of Babylonian ceremonies, the New Year festival, was also recorded during the Seleucid period. During the second and first centuries, however, as the long struggle continued against the Parthians, the new Persian power that had taken over Iran, records from Babylonia became very sparse. The situation was particularly dire in the years between 141 and 126, when central Babylonia was first occupied by Mithridates I. It suffered repeated devastations as the fight raged for the possession of the city and region. In the ensuing struggle between Rome and the Parthian kingdom, Babylon was only very indirectly involved, being at a safe distance from the border, which ran just south of Dura-Europos on the middle Euphrates. It also meant that the river trade lost its importance, and that Babylon became a provincial town with a dwindling population and deserted and derelict city quarters.

The process of shrinkage accelerated under the Sassanian occupation (AD 226–636), until only small parts of the former settlement were occupied and the temples became abandoned. At the time when the real Babylon disappeared under drifts of sand, the Hebrew holy writings, which had been codified, were translated into Latin and Greek. The memory of the old Mesopotamian cities was thus bequeathed to a new age and a new civilization.

Glossary

(* An asterisk indicates a cross-reference within the glossary)

Achaemenids: Persian dynasty named after the founder Achaemenes. Having defeated the Medes* in Iran (middle of the sixth century BC), they built an empire that comprised the Iranian heartland to the borders of India, all Mesopotamia and most of Anatolia, Syro-Palestine and Egypt. The last king, Darius III, was defeated by Alexander the Great in 333.

agriculture: the production of food as opposed to procurement from the wild (hunting and gathering). Agriculture is also distinguished from horticulture (the cultivation of small, garden-like plots) as being more labour-intensive and associated with technologically sophisticated and socially complex societies. Some of the Neolithic cultures in the ancient Near East are strictly speaking horticultural, or extensively agricultural, as distinct from the later intensification of production.

Akkadian: linguistic term for various Semitic dialects spoken in Mesopotamia over a period of 2,000 years (such as Old Akkadian, Babylonian*, Assyrian*). The name derives from the region and city called Akkad.

Amorites: term for Semitic-speaking tribes, called in Akkadian *amurru*. Towards the end of the third millennium they settled in increasing numbers in northern and middle Babylonia. The influx of Amorite tribes contributed to the downfall of the Ur III* dynasty.

annals: yearly reports, primarily concerning military expeditions and building works, composed on behalf of Assyrian kings. They were apparently introduced by Adad-nirari I in the beginning of the thirteenth century BC.

Aramaeans, Aramaic: a group of peoples speaking a western Semitic language (Aramaic), originally tribal pastoralists. In the middle of the second millennium BC they formed small states in Syria and northern Mesopotamia. In the first millennium BC Aramaic became the most widely spoken and understood language in western Asia. Written Aramaic, using different types of alphabetic scripts, first appeared c.800 BC.

Assyrian: east Semitic dialect of Akkadian* spoken in Assyria. In accordance with the different historical periods, one distinguishes between Old, Middle and Neo-Assyrian.

Babylonian: dialect of Akkadian* spoken in Mesopotamia since the beginning of the second millennium BC. There are certain differences between Old, Middle and Neo-Babylonian.

Babylonian Chronicle: there were several chronicles written in Babylon from the middle of the second millennium BC onwards. Chronicle P records the dealings of the Kassite dynasty with their Assyrian and Elamite neighbours; another deals with the period 744–688 and dates from c.500/499. They depict events from a Babylonian point of view and thus often contradict and/or supplement other sources, like the Assyrian annals and royal inscriptions.

building inscriptions: the building of civic structures such as canals, city walls and quays, as well as palaces and temples, was the responsibility of kings and governors. In third millennium Mesopotamia, tablets or cone-shaped objects listed the name of the person responsible for the construction or restoration, its purpose, and usually a date.

Calah (modern Nimrud): Assyrian city on the Tigris, founded by Shalmaneser I in the thirteenth century, much enlarged in the ninth century by Ashurnasirpal II, who made it his capital. The Medes* and Babylonians destroyed the city in 612 BC.

Chalcolithic: the so-called 'copper age' which followed the Neolithic period, marked by the ability to smelt and work copper. In Mesopotamia this period is divided into several sub-periods, not all of which are attested for the whole of the country. The term is therefore rarely used in the archaeological context of Mesopotamia.

Chaldeans: Semitic tribal peoples in southern Mesopotamia. They formed a dynasty that ruled Babylonia from 625 to 539. The term Chaldean was from that time also used to denote Babylonia until well into the Roman period.

chiefdoms: a form of social organization in which chiefs govern at the head of a social hierarchy, determined by birth and closeness of relationship to the chief. Chiefdoms usually practise redistribution, encouraging craft specialization. Large-scale public works, such as architectural or irrigation projects, can be organized by the central authority. Chiefs may be elected or inherit their office. There are 'simple' and 'complex' chiefdoms, the latter being similar to states. One of the salient differences between them is that simple chiefdoms do not exercise a monopoly of force.

Cimmerians: group of nomadic tribal peoples who invaded Anatolia in the first quarter of the first millennium BC. They were feared for their intrepid mounted warriors, who raided the country.

cuneiform: a system of writing in which a cut-reed stylus is pressed into soft clay to leave a wedge-like imprint (Latin *cuneius*), invented in Mesopotamia *c.*3000. Different versions of cuneiform writing were used to write various Near Eastern languages: Sumerian, Akkadian, Eblaite, Elamite, Ugaritic, Hittite and Hurrian. It was superseded by alphabetic scripts after the mid first millennium.

Early Dynastic period: a period of time in the third millennium in southern Mesopotamia (between the Jemdet Nasr period and the beginning of the Akkadian dynasty: *c.*3000–2350). There are three subdivisions, ED I, II and III. The age is associated with the development of independent city states and increasing urbanism. Historical records are mainly from ED III A (mid third millennium), which in this context is also known as the Fara time.

Ebla (modern Tell Mardikh): city in the Orontes valley in Syria. In the mid third millennium it was the capital of a wealthy kingdom well known for its textile production. The archives found at Ebla give details of the wide trade connections and the rich agricultural potential of the area. The city was destroyed *c.*2250, but repopulated in the Old Babylonian period, until finally destroyed *c.*1600. The texts were written in a Semitic language, now simply called Eblaite.

Elam: region east of southern Mesopotamia, in south-west Iran, which had strong cultural links with Mesopotamia from prehistoric times. The inhabitants spoke a language (Elamite) not connected with any other known language, which they wrote in cuneiform. During the last quarter of the second millennium BC Elam became a powerful state. It was closely involved in the history of Babylonia and Assyria until the sixth century.

en: Sumerian official title. The precise meaning is difficult to establish, and no doubt it shifted from place to place and time to time, but in some cases at least it seems to imply a high position in the temple hierarchy.

ensi: Sumerian title that means something like 'governor' of a city. It could be used to describe the appointment issued by an overall ruler, as for instance in Elam during the Akkadian domination, or else to refer to an independent ruler.

entum: Babylonian term derived from the Sumerian word **en**. It denotes a high priestly office held by a woman, often a member of the ruling dynasty. This tradition was established from at least the Akkad period. **Entus** certainly lived in the Gipar, within the temenos of the temple, in the Ur III period, and in the sixth century when the custom was revived by Nabonidus, king of Babylon.

eponym (Assyrian *limmu*): Assyrian high official selected each year to give his name ('eponym') to the current year. This constituted a dating system in use from the Middle Assyrian period*.

Eshnunna (modern Tell Asmar): Mesopotamian city in the east Tigris area. Before and during the Old Babylonian period* it was the capital of an independent kingdom until its conquest by Hammurabi.

Fara time: *see* Early Dynastic period.

Gutians: a people who lived in the Zagros mountains, east of southern Mesopotamia. From a small power base in the Diyala region, they invaded the kingdom of Akkad early in the twenty-second century and established their own dynasty.

Halaf: an archaeological period of the Chalcolithic age of northern Mesopotamia, named after the north Syrian town Tell Halaf (fifth millennium). Characteristic of it was fine pottery with elaborate designs in glossy paint. The age is associated with permanent settlements and farming.

Harran: city in northern Upper Mesopotamia, conquered by the Assyrians in the eighth century BC. It was to be the last royal residence of Assyrian kings. Thereafter it came under Babylonian control. It was an important cult centre of the moon-god Sin.

Hassuna: a mound near Mosul that gave its name to a culture sequence which spans the transition from the Neolithic to the end of the Chalcolithic age in northern Mesopotamia. Excavations have shown a sequence of six settlement layers from nomadic camps to farming villages (sixth to mid fifth millennium).

Hittites: an Indo-European people who settled in Anatolia in the eighteenth century BC. They took the name of the indigenous population, the Hatti, whose territory, along the bend of the river Halys (Kizilirmak), they conquered. By the mid second millennium they had become a major military power, on a par with Egypt, Assyria and Mitanni*. The Hittite empire disintegrated in the thirteenth century BC.

Hurrians: a group of peoples speaking a Caucasian language, who inhabited the north-eastern borders of Mesopotamia from the last quarter of the third millennium. To judge from their personal names, Hurrians were present in all parts of the Near East for most of the second millennium, but especially in south-east Anatolia, northern Mesopotamia and eastern Iran. They achieved the height of their political importance between 1500 and 1200, within the framework of the kingdom called Mitanni*. The Hurrians wrote their language in cuneiform*.

Isin: city of central Lower Mesopotamia. After the collapse of the Ur III state, Ishbi-Erra founded the First Dynasty of Isin (c.2017–1794). It was conquered by Rim-Sin of Larsa.

Jemdet-Nasr: a period of time named after the archaeological site. It marks the transition from the late Uruk period to the Early Dynastic age in southern Mesopotamia (c.3200–3000).

Kanesh (modern Kültepe): city in Cappadocia. In the beginning of the second millennium it was inhabited by the local, Hattian population. The site is well known because of the extensive Old Assyrian* texts that have been found in excavations of the Assyrian trade colony (*karum* Kanesh) near by, which deal in the import/export of metals and textiles.

Kassites: a people speaking a little-known language, who migrated into Mesopotamia from the Caucasus region at the beginning of the second millennium BC. After the Old Babylonian dynasty, kings with predominantly Kassite names ruled Babylonia (from the sixteenth to the twelfth century), an epoch known as the Kassite period.

Kish (modern Tell el-Ohemir): Mesopotamian city near Babylon. It was an important town, the seat of several dynasties, during the third millennium.

Lagash (modern Telloh): Sumerian city state, including Girsu. It had considerable importance in the Early Dynastic period* and the second half of the third millennium.

Larsa (modern Senkereh): city in southern Mesopotamia. In the first quarter of the second millennium the seat of an Amorite* dynasty conquered by Hammurabi of Babylon.

Manneans: a people inhabiting the mountainous regions of the Zagros in the first millennium referred to as Mannaea by the Assyrians. They came under the domination of the Assyrians under Tiglath-Pileser III.

Mari (modern Tell Hariri): Mesopotamian city in the middle Euphrates region. It was an independent city state in the Early Dynastic period, and also flourished in the first quarter of the second millennium, when it was capital of an Amorite* kingdom. It was destroyed by Hammurabi of Babylon c. 1759. The extensive archive dates mainly from the eighteenth-century period.

Medes: an Iranian people, closely related to the Persians*, who inhabited the area of Hamadan in the first half of the first millennium. They probably did not form a coherent state, but some of their rulers, such as Cyaxares, extended their power into eastern Anatolia. They also contributed to the final defeat of the Assyrians as allies of the Babylonians. In the sixth century they were defeated by the Persians under Cyrus II.

Middle Assyrian period: the time, c. 1400–1050, when Assyria re-emerged as an important political power after a long decline. Some of the most important rulers of this period were Ashur-uballit I and Tiglath-Pileser I.

Mitanni: kingdom in northern Mesopotamia and Syria. From the sixteenth to the fourteenth century it was one of the most influential powers in the Near

East. It then came into conflict with the Hittites*, who reduced it to a vassal state. The Hurrian* element was strong in the Mitanni kingdom, while the ruling élite had mainly Indo-European names.

naditum: Akkadian* term for women who fulfilled some form of ritual or priestly role during the Old Babylonian period*. They were mainly dedicated to the sun-god, lived in seclusion and were not allowed to have children. Some were from wealthy or even royal families. Because of their childlessness, they tended to reach a greater age than was usual for women at the time.

Neo-Assyrian period: the time, *c.*934–610, when Assyria expanded rapidly to dominate the whole of the Near East, from Iran to Egypt, until its collapse and final defeat by the Babylonians and Medes*.

Neo-Babylonian period: the time, *c.*900–539, when Babylonia, freed from the domination of the Assyrians, became a powerful state in western Asia under such kings as Nabopolassar and Nebuchadrezzar II.

Old Assyrian: like 'Old Babylonian'*, this term has philological connotations as the language used in the written sources of the period, particularly those found in Cappadocia referring to the trading activities of the city of Ashur (*c.*2000–1800).

Old Babylonian period: time from the end of Ur III to the end of the First Dynasty of Babylon (*c.*2000–1600), whose best-known king was Hammurabi. It is also used as a linguistic term, referring to the Akkadian* dialect used in the documents of the time.

omens: there was a great variety of divinatory techniques in the ancient Near East, and the collection of omens and their interpretation were the responsibility of highly trained scribes in Mesopotamia.

pastoralists: people whose main form of subsistence is the herding and raising of sheep and goats who lead a nomadic or semi-nomadic way of life. Pastoralists have existed in the Near East for millennia since the area allows them to utilize land that is too marginal for the growing of crops. Pastoralists are usually tribally organized with a strong kin loyalty and are often good fighters.

Parthians: Iranian people from the area around the Caspian Sea. They rebelled against the Seleucids* and formed an empire which lasted from 140 BC to AD 224 and eventually included Mesopotamia.

Persians: Iranian people who formed two empires in the ancient Near East. The first was the Achaemenid empire, founded *c.* 550 by Cyrus II and conquered by Alexander the Great between 334 and 323. The second was the Parthian empire (140 BC–AD 224).

reciprocity: a form of exchange in which goods are transferred between individuals or groups in the context of social obligations without any central authority being involved. Balanced reciprocity involves exchanges of equal value (usually within the family or community).

redistribution: a form of exchange of goods and commodities within and between groups that is organized by a central authority. This can include collection and pooling of locally produced goods and subsequent reallocation, which involves storage facilities and some system of bookkeeping. It can stimulate the development of craft specialization, since the central authority can take on subsistence needs and the procurement of raw materials. Exchange is also possible with outside communities, sometimes at considerable distances. Such externally procured items are usually treated as prestige objects and reserved for people with high social status. Redistribution is often associated with relatively complex societies, with differences in social rank and a central authority, often chiefdoms.

Sealand: translation of an Akkadian* term for the marshes of southern Babylonia. In the mid second millennium there was a Dynasty of the Sealand, mentioned in the King-lists, which profited from the Gulf trade. There was a Second Dynasty of the Sealand in the eleventh century BC. In the Neo-Babylonian period*, it was mainly occupied by Chaldean* tribes who fought against the Assyrians, often in alliance with Elamites.

Second Dynasty of Isin: a Babylonian dynasty based on Isin* (1158–1027). Nebuchadrezzar I was its most prominent and successful ruler.

Seleucids: Hellenistic dynasty (305–64 BC), founded by Seleucus I Nicator (a general of Alexander the Great), who exercised control over Mesopotamia until the Parthian* conquest.

status: the position of an individual in society in relation to other members. This can be seen as referring either to a role or a position, the fulfilment of a function within the social organization. More commonly, status is defined in terms of stratification (along with wealth and power). High status does not therefore necessarily imply political power or wealth.

Sumer: name for southern Mesopotamia from the third to the mid second millennium. It did not form a political unit in itself, but was divided into several city-state-like entities.

Sumerians: inhabitants of southern Mesopotamia in the third millennium who spoke Sumerian, a language that has no connections with any other known linguistic group. Sumerian was written in cuneiform* and, like Latin in Europe in the Middle Ages, remained in use for some text genres long after it ceased to be a spoken language.

Ubaid period: prehistoric period in southern Mesopotamia named after the site Tell al-Ubaid, near Ur, which precedes the Uruk period. Early Ubaid levels begin in the sixth millennium. The duration of Ubaid sequences varies from site to site (between 4000 and 3500 BC). Like the contemporary northern levels of (late) Halaf* and Hassuna*, the Ubaid culture has characteristic painted pottery and is associated with settled farming communities and the beginnings of social stratification.

Umma: Sumerian city in southern Mesopotamia, mainly known from tablets, discovered at Girsu, which describe its long-standing war with Lagash* in the Early Dynastic period*.

Ur III (Third Dynasty of Ur): a dynasty founded by Ur-Nammu, which ruled over most of Mesopotamia and parts of Elam*, c.2112–2004. It relied on a centralized and highly differentiated bureaucracy that used Sumerian as the main means of written communication.

Uruk period: time-span in Mesopotamia, c.4000–3200 BC, based on evidence found in the prehistoric archaeological sequence discovered at the site of Warka (ancient Uruk). Characteristic artefacts, such as pottery and later cylinder seals, and architectural features have been found widely distributed throughout the Near East, from northern Syria and southern Anatolia to western Iran. The period is associated with bureaucratic administration, inter-regional exchange of commodities and the beginnings of urbanism.

ziggurat: Babylonian word which describes a type of religious building consisting of several superimposed platforms, accessible by one or more ramps. Several examples have been excavated (the ziggurat of Ur, for instance), and there are descriptions and architectural sketches on cuneiform* tablets. At least some ziggurats, like the famous Etemenanki at Babylon, had a shrine on the uppermost platform.

Notes and References

1 ERIDU

1. Heidel (1951), p. 62.
2. For descriptions, see Thesiger (1964); Salim (1962); Maxwell (1957).
3. Green (1975), p. 4.
4. See Chapter 7, page 168.
5. Mythological accounts were frequently added to magic texts to make them more efficacious. The cosmogonic account had much older prototypes.
6. Written during the Isin-Larsa period (beginning of the second millennium), but utilizing earlier records. See Michalowski (1983).
7. Quoted from Kramer (1963), p. 328.
8. See Chapter 8, page 196; Chapter 9, page 219.
9. Mustafa in Safar, Mustafa and Lloyd (1981).
10. See ibid.
11. ibid., pp. 36–7.
12. See Chapter 5, page 126.
13. See Huot (1989).
14. See Woolley (1929), p. 21.
15. Opinion of Charvát (1993), p. 70.
16. See Oates (1960), p. 45.
17. See Earle (1991). For the ancient Near East, see Charvát (1993), p. 105; Berman (1994).
18. See Chapter 2, p. 34.
19. See Safar, Mustafa and Lloyd (1981), p. 160, fig. 74, and p. 171, fig. 81.
20. Hole (1983).
21. C. S. Coon, University Museum, University of Pennsylvania, quoted in Safar, Mustafa and Lloyd (1981), p. 308.
22. See Charvát (1993), p. 71.
23. See Vértesalji (1989).

24. Infants under the age of two are rarely found at Eridu. Perhaps there was an infant cemetery at some other location, as at Tell as-Sawwan. No intramural burials were found in the small sample of houses excavated at Eridu. See Safar, Mustafa and Lloyd (1981), p. 125.

25. See Charvát (1993), pp. 105ff.

26. ibid.

27. See Pollock (1999), p. 5.

28. See ibid., pp. 81–2.

29. According to Charvát (1993), p. 177.

30. See Chapter 2, p. 54.

31. Safar, Mustafa and Lloyd (1981), p. 46.

32. Unger (1933), *Reallexikon der Assyriologie und Archaeologie* 2, p. 464.

33. See Chapter 2, pp. 54–5, for similar instances from Uruk.

34. See Chapter 5, p. 118.

35. Klein (1981).

36. cf. Sallaberger (1993).

37. Charpin (1986), pp. 343–86.

38. Benito (1969); Alster (1987); Farber-Flügger (1973); Reiner (1961).

39. Green (1975), pp. 154–85.

40. See Leick (1994), ch. 1, pp. 12ff.

41. Or another pair, Lahmu and Lahamu, in another version.

42. Her name was actually written with the sign **engur**, which was also used for Apsu.

43. See Steinkeller (1999).

44. Benito (1969).

45. Galter (1981).

46. Galter (1981), pp. 98–9.

47. For example, the myth of Inanna's descent into the underworld, when Enki creates sexless beings who are able to penetrate the underworld and claim the body of the dead goddess by feigning sympathy for the sad Stygian queen.

48. For more about Inanna, see Chapter 2, pp. 57–60.

49. Farber-Flügger (1973).

50. This runs parallel with the situation of Eridu as being primarily a place of symbolic importance but not as somewhere wonderful to live in.

51. See Jacobsen (1987), pp. 181–204.

52. For editions of the text, see Picchioni (1981). See also Dalley (1989), pp. 182–8.

53. See ibid., p. 292.

54. Even earlier versions are known from Abu Salabikh, dating from the Early

Dynastic III period. Although it appears in this ancient context, the hymn to E-unir, as the Enki temple was called, was still not the earliest.

55. Sjöberg and Bergmann (1969), No. 1.

56. ki is a derminative that follows place-names and makes them identifiable as such to the reader. The etymology of the place-name Eridu is unknown as it is not a Sumerian word. It may preserve a much older 'proto-Euphratian' word belonging to an earlier language. In Sumerian it was written with the sign NUN, which represents a kind of tree, or even a reed. Whether this was the original meaning of the ancient word is uncertain.

57. Safar, Mustafa and Lloyd (1981), p. 36.

58. See Chapter 5, p. 109.

59. According to Steinkeller (1999).

2 URUK

1. Quoted in Loftus (1857), p. 159. The currently used name 'Uruk' is the Babylonian version of the Sumerian **Unug**. The etymology and origin of the toponym are not known.

2. There were three international conferences in 1998 alone, and a growing number of publications are devoted to exploring the Uruk phenomenon.

3. Loftus (1857), p. 124.

4. Finkbeiner (1991).

5. Adams (1981); Adams and Nissen (1972).

6. This means that archaeologists now work only in those areas previously regarded as 'peripheral to the centre', which was located in southern Iraq. This enforced dislocation has resulted in an interesting shift of perspective so that it has become fashionable for archaeologists to minimize or even deny the significance of what was formerly seen as the centre.

7. See Finkbeiner (1991).

8. Level XVIII was carbon dated to 5300–4574.

9. See Charvát (1993), ch. 5; Pollock (1999).

10. There was quite a different situation in the Early Dynastic period, when the planoconvex bricks were invented to speed up construction and economize on labour.

11. Charvát (1993).

12. Nissen, Damerow and Englund (1993).

13. See Charvát (1997).

14. Nissen (1988).

15. Wittvogel (1977).

16. This is especially well documented, but Habuba-Kabira is now submerged beneath the waters of the Assad dam. See Strommenger (1980).

17. Tell Brak on the Habur, a tributary of the Euphrates; Habuba-Kabira and Samsat and Carchemish on the Euphrates; Nineveh on the Tigris.

18. Algaze (1993), drawing inspiration from the 'world system' theories first formulated by Wallerstein (1974).

19. See Kuhrt (1995), p. 26.

20. Charvát (1993).

21. Charvát (1998).

22. He interprets the bevil-rimmed bowls found in huge numbers in all the Uruk culture sites, not as containers for measured grain, as have most archaeologists, but as moulds for a bread or sweetmeat eaten by everyone and at every location. The symbolic social value of people eating the same food is well known in anthropology, especially as this applies to types of bread and 'breakfast habits', which help to define national or regional identity.

23. See Wright (1994); Stein and Rothman (1994), pp. 67–84.

24. Pollock (1999), pp. 93ff.

25. Adams and Nissen (1972).

26. Nissen (1988), p. 71.

27. In later tradition there were two deities worshipped in Uruk, the goddess Inanna (later called Ishtar), who resided at Eanna, and the sky-god An, associated with Kullab.

28. This contradictory treatment of wall surfaces is also characteristic for other incipient architectural styles, such as the imitation of reed walls in the Saqqara complex of Egypt's Old Dynasty, the dense vegetative ornamentation of early Ummayid palaces and mosques (eighth century AD) or the tapestry-like decorated doorways of Seljuk monumental buildings.

29. Charvát (1993), p. 126.

30. For comparisons between social structures and patterns of decoration (weaving, pottery, facial painting), see, for instance, Lévi-Strauss (1966, 1995).

31. See Lenzen (1949).

32. Boehmer (1991), p. 468.

33. See Pollock (1999), p. 194.

34. For the ritualization of exchange as 'offerings', see pp. 52–3 below on the iconography of the Warka Vase.

35. The custom of open access might also explain the many acts of sealing: containers and storage rooms were perpetually being officially sealed and unsealed.

36. Charvát (1993) believes that the monuments served as repositories for prestige goods dedicated to specific purposes but apparently belonging to a collective entity and not an élite person or group. They could have had a function like treasure-houses, perhaps safeguarding precious articles for future needs, as did the treasure-houses in the early mosques. But the fact that they mixed the valuables with 'rubbish' speaks against this hypothesis.

37. The missing figure in a skirt appears in other images, where he is engaged in such acts as feeding sheep, shooting predators or overseeing the executions of prisoners.

38. See also the article by Selz (1998), p. 292, where he expresses reservations about the absolute rule of the **en** and suggests that Uruk may have been governed by an 'oligarchic autocracy' with the **en** having primary responsibility for the administration and distribution of foodstuffs.

39. This process may be observed in many subsequent historical contexts: the Greek *polis*, the Roman *urbs*, the English colonial centre. All were architecturally idiosyncratic lessons in brick and stone as to what it meant to be a part of Greek, Roman or Western European 'civilization'.

40. For the Gilgamesh Epic tablets I and XI, see Dalley (1989), pp. 15 and 120.

41. See Nissen (1972).

42. Dalley (1989), tablet I, p. 50.

43. See Chapter 5, p. 131.

44. See Chapter 1, p. 22.

45. Dalley (1989), p. 158.

46. ibid., p. 305.

47. See Frymer-Kensky (1992); Leick (1994); Lambert (1992); and, most recently, Asante (1998).

48. ibid., p. 43.

3 SHURUPPAK

1. Martin (1988).

2. See Chapter 5, p. 136.

3. Nissen (1988), pp. 129ff.

4. Martin (1988), p. 125.

5. See Nissen, Damerow and Englund (1993).

6. See, most recently, Römer (1999), p. 3, where he dates the Sumerian 'immigration' to around 3000 or the late Uruk period. He declares,

furthermore, that writing 'dient mit Sicherheit zur Wiedergrabe des Sumerischen' ('certainly served to render Sumerian').

7. See 'The Poor Man of Nippur' tale in Chapter 6, pp. 164–5.

8. Not least because there is still no generally accepted grammar and only the first few volumes of the Sumerian Dictionary have as yet been published. Sumerian is therefore still learned 'at the feet of a master' and its acquisition has greater kudos than Akkadian.

9. See Walker (1987); Nissen, Damerow and Englund (1993).

10. The convention is to pronounce it in English as the 'a' in 'glass'.

11. Hieroglyphic Egyptian uses the same principle.

12. When this change came about is uncertain, but it was probably towards the end of the Early Dynastic period.

13. Pettinato (1980).

14. Biggs (1974), p. 8.

15. Bottéro quoted in Michalowski (1990), p. 51.

16. Alster (1974), pp. 11–18.

17. Krebernik (1984).

18. Pomponio and Visicato (1994), p. 9.

19. Biggs and Postgate (1978).

20. See Leick (1983).

21. See Green (1984).

22. Krebernik (1986).

23. See, for instance, Lévi-Strauss (1966), pp. 35ff.

24. This was also the case in Ebla and Abu Salabikh.

25. Pomponio and Visicato (1994), pp. 8–9.

26. Martin (1988), p. 128, surmises that the huge grain silos discovered by Schmidt may have been designated for feeding the **guruš**.

27. Jacobsen (1957), pp. 121–2.

28. See Chapter 5, p. 112.

29. Charvát (1993).

30. Pomponio and Visicato (1994).

31. Martin (1988), p. 107.

32. Charvát (1986), p. 47.

33. See Matthews (1991), p. 13.

34. See Pollock (1999), p. 117.

35. Gelb (1979), p. 11.

36. Charvát (1993), pp. 279–81.

37. Katz (1993).

38. Gibson (1976).

39. Pomponio and Visicato (1994), p. 16.

40. See Chapter 4, p. 90.
41. Martin (1988), p. 126.

4 AKKAD

1. Also written as 'Agade' or 'Akkade'.
2. See Horowitz (1998), pp. 67–95.
3. Michalowski (1993), p. 89.
4. See Chapter 6, p. 143.
5. Frayne (1993), p. 2.
6. Hallo (1998), p. 119: '. . . they even displayed a kind of scholarly interest in the original'.
7. Sollberger and Kupper (1971), text number 1A2a.
8. ibid., text number 1B5c.
9. Franke (1995).
10. Charvát (1971), p. 69.
11. Sollberger and Kupper (1971), text number 1H2b.
12. Charvát (1997), p. 69.
13. See Heimpel (1992), pp. 13–14.
14. See also Chapter 5, p. 114.
15. See Chapter 3, p. 71.
16. Heimpel (1992), p. 12.
17. ibid., p. 18.
18. Postgate (1992), p. 31.
19. See also Chapter 7, p. 167.
20. In Mann (1986), p. 133.
21. Perhaps to be compared with the borderland between Wales and England, which in the Middle Ages was also known as a 'march'.
22. Frayne (1993), p. 6.
23. Eannatum of Lagash, for instance, called himself 'king of Kish' – Nissen (1988), p. 145.
24. See Liverani (1993).
25. All dates for the third millennium are provisional. An alternative shorter chronology by Glassner proposes 2296–2240 for Sargon's reign.
26. See below, p. 101.
27. Kramer (1963), p. 330.
28. Nissen (1988), p. 166.
29. cf. such other names as 'Sharru-dan'; see Frayne (1993), p. 7.

30. Cooper and Heimpel (1983).

31. Westenholz (1997), pp. 36–7.

32. Which were well known for their abortifacient properties – no doubt a punning reference in the context, as Joan Westenholz remarks; ibid., p. 39, n. 4.

33. McEwan (1980); Wall-Romema (1990).

34. ibid., p. 208.

35. Horowitz (1998), pp. 67–95.

36. Westenholz (1997), pp. 102ff.

37. See Chapter 8, p. 204.

38. Liverani (1993), pp. 54–5; see also Chapter 8, p. 206.

39. Wall-Romema (1990).

40. Nissen (1988), p. 161.

41. We speak today of the east Semitic language described in these texts as 'Old Akkadian', while the generic term 'Akkadian' is used for all the different Semitic dialects (Assyrian, Babylonian) rendered in cuneiform.

42. 'The royal title at once symbolized the transfer of power to a central authority in a specific area, as well as the aspirations of Sargon and his descendants to universal dominion' – Michalowski (1993), p. 88.

43. See Chapter 6, p. 145.

44. 'One can safely guess that Sumer and Akkad, as well as areas to the north, east and west, were inundated with public monuments, both with and without writing' – Michalowski (1993), p. 97.

45. Amiet (1976).

46. See, for instance, Lloyd (1985), p. 143.

47. See Chapter 5, p. 114.

48. Postgate (1992), pp. 41, 94–5.

49. Foster (1982), pp. 31–2.

50. ibid., p. 116.

51. Liverani (1993), pp. 59ff.; text in Westenholz (1997), pp. 221ff.

52. Quoted in Kuhrt (1995), p. 51.

53. Liverani (1993), pp. 62ff.; Westenholz (1997), pp. 263ff.

54. Foster (1982), p. 111.

55. See Michalowski (1993).

56. ibid., pp. 73–4.

57. al-Khalifa and Rice (1986).

58. Cooper and Heimpel (1983); Cooper (1993), pp. 16–17.

59. See Chapter 5, pp. 102–3.

60. See Chapter 6, pp. 147ff.

61. Cooper and Heimpel (1983), pp. 52–3, ll. 13–54.

62. Jacobsen (1987), pp. 386–444; Edzard (1997).
63. See Chapter 10.

5 UR

1. See Chapter 10.
2. Woolley (1925, 1929, 1930, 1931, 1932, 1933, 1934, 1955).
3. Woolley (1952), p. 25.
4. For other flood stories and their interpretation, see the discussion in Chapter 3, pp. 82–4.
5. Charvát (1993), pp. 228ff.
6. See Pollock (1985), pp. 129–59. Her scheme of dating, based on an analysis of pottery and seals, has the Royal Cemetery (RC) strata I and II correlating with Early Dynasty (ED) IIIa; RCIII with EDIIIb; RCIV with Early Akkadian; RCV with Mature to Late Akkadian; and RCVI with Post-Akkadian times. As this shows, the cemetery was in use for some 600 years up to a time shortly before the Third Dynasty of Ur.
7. Pollock (1991).
8. The name used to be read as 'Shub-ad'.
9. The current museum exhibit shows no facial features.
10. Woolley (1952), p. 46.
11. ibid., p. 47.
12. ibid., p. 50.
13. See Charvát (1993), pp. 306–7.
14. ibid., p. 30.
15. Pollock (1991).
16. See Charvát (1998), pp. 87–9.
17. Charvát (1993), p. 309.
18. See Alster (1980).
19. Moorey (1984).
20. Nissen (1988), pp. 92–3.
21. For Abu Salabikh, see Matthews and Postgate (1987), pp. 107ff.
22. See the discussion on the guruš in Chapter 3, pp. 77–8.
23. Pollock (1999), p. 180.
24. Paynter (1989), p. 384.
25. At Khafaje the houses between and around the temple show differentiations in size and in the wealth of the occupants; see Delougaz, Hill and Lloyd (1967).

26. See Jagersma (1990).

27. Pollock points out that the presence of the First Dynasty sealings above the 'Royal Tombs' could have been the result of disturbances of the strata as successive graves were dug in the same area. It is therefore possible that Meskalamdug and Mesannepada fit into periods I–II of the sequence.

28. See Sollberger and Kupper (1971), text number B6a.

29. Zgoll (1997).

30. See Chapter 1, p. 26.

31. See Durand (1987).

32. The title is taken from the initial line, which in Kramer's translation (1969) means: 'queen of all the *me*, radiant light'.

33. Zgoll (1997). For the earlier translations, see Hallo and van Dijk (1966); Kramer in Pritchard (1969), pp. 579–82.

34. It is by no means certain that she was his biological daughter. The title could be used to encompass a younger family member or even a symbolic affiliation.

35. See Chapter 4, p. 99.

36. See Mooret (1984).

37. For Utu-hegal's triumphal inscription, see Sollberger and Kupper (1971), text number IIK3a.

38. Wilcke in Garelli (1974), p. 180, n. 67.

39. Mesannepada, it will be recalled (p. 119), did use the title 'king of Kish', but there is little evidence that he exercised control over 'the land' for more than a brief period.

40. See Jones (1975).

41. See Wright (1996), pp. 79–110.

42. See Steinkeller (1987).

43. Woolley (1952), p. 96.

44. ibid., p. 92.

45. ibid., p. 97. A ladder features in the stele of Ur-Nammu, a ten-foot-high arch-shaped slab stone (now in the Pennsylvania University Museum). It is divided into five horizontal registers and shows Ur-Nammu receiving the divine consent to his building operation. First he lays a petition before the god, who is shown seated on a throne. Then he is presented with the measuring line and rod by Nannar and Ningal. Another image shows the king shoulder-ing the tools of a builder, assisted by a priest. The rest has been broken away, save for a propped-up ladder and a pair of feet next to it. This fragmentary monument sets the building activity of the king within a theological frame-work: it is being undertaken and brought to fruition through divine command and assistance. See Frankfort (1970), pp. 109–11, figs. 110–11.

46. The pyramids of Egypt, though based on a different conceptualization, have similar connotations.

47. See Weadcock (1975).

48. ibid., p. 166.

49. ibid., p. 104.

50. ibid., p. 112.

51. See, most recently, Steinkeller (1991), pp. 106ff., esp. pp. 126ff.

52. See Kuhrt (1995), pp. 68–9.

53. Michalowski (1987).

54. See Hallo (1975), pp. 181–204, 205–316.

55. From 'Three Shulgi Hymns' in Klein (1981), pp. 74–5.

56. A rendering in English from the German translation in Wilcke (1975), pp. 241–2.

57. From 'Two Šulgi Hymns' in Castellino (1972), pp. 196ff.

58. For the practice of liver reading, see Chapter 9, p. 236.

59. See Leick (1994), pp. 111–29.

60. See Chapter 2, p. 57, and Chapter 4, p. 103.

61. See Leick (1994), ch. 7.

62. Klein (1981), pp. 135–66.

63. See Leick (1994), ch. 9.

64. See Chapter 2, p. 58.

65. Berlin (1979), ll. 62–3, 87–90.

66. See Steinkeller (1987), pp. 20–21.

67. Maekawa (1999), p. 93.

68. Klein (1981), pp. 135–66.

69. Michalowski (1989).

70. ibid., pp. 6ff.

71. cf. Gurney (1983).

6 NIPPUR

1. See Postgate (1992), p. 15.

2. McGuire Gibson suggests that the Shatt el-Nil trough was probably the oldest Euphrates bed – Gibson (1992), p. 37.

3. See Geere (1904), p. 170.

4. See Kuklick (1996).

5. The decision was taken in 1884: 'England and France have done noble work of exploration in Assyria and Babylonia. It is time for America to do

her part. Let us send out an American expedition.' See Zettler (1992), p. 327.

6. Geere (1904), p. 173; see also Lloyd (1980), p. 165.

7. For a curiously hagiographic account of the Shakespearean heroism displayed by the excavator Haynes, see Westenholz (1992), pp. 291–6.

8. Kuklick (1996), p. 88. The director of the 1970s campaign, McGuire Gibson, found the excavation diaries of Peters, Meyer and Fisher useful and reliable for the location of find-spots, though he was far less impressed by Hilprecht in this regard; cf. Gibson (1992), p. 37.

9. Jastrow, quoted by Kuklick (1996), p. 135.

10. Hilprecht (1906, 1910).

11. For the first three seasons. The last two were undertaken jointly between the Chicago Oriental Institute and the Baghdad School of Oriental Research.

12. The first ten seasons ran in consecutive years from 1948; thereafter they were 1973–6, 1981–2, 1985, 1987, 1988–9, 1990.

13. Stone (1987).

14. See McCown and Haines (1967); Zettler (1992).

15. Gibson (1980).

16. Gibson (1975), p. 7.

17. Gibson (1992), p. 39.

18. Pollock (1999), p. 65.

19. Zettler (1992).

20. Gibson (1992), n. 41.

21. Stone (1987).

22. Gibson (1992), p. 44.

23. Gibson (1978), pp. 118–19.

24. See Chapter 9, p. 234.

25. Gibson (1992), p. 48.

26. Oded (1979).

27. Zadog (1978a, 1978b).

28. Wiseman (1985). This was no new tradition: by the Middle Babylonian period (late second millennium) prisoners of war had already been settled there. See Walker (1980).

29. Stolper (1985).

30. For the Nippur Lamentation, see Tinney (1996).

31. cf. Eridu, Chapter 1, p. 1

32. See Chapter 1, p. 20.

33. See Chapter 5, p. 133.

34. See Chapter 4, p. 103; Cooper (1983).

35. The emphasis on acceptance and submission to an imponderable divine will is also a characteristic of Islam.

36. See especially the elaborate introduction to Enannatum's victory stele, where Ningirsu, the god of Lagash, appears to Enannatum in a dream and exhorts him not to put up any longer with the pillages of Umma, the city that had been embroiled in a quarrel with Lagash over a disputed territory. See Cooper (1986), p. 34; and the legend written next to the relief figure of Enannatum, which reads: 'Enannatum who subjugates foreign lands for Ningirsu' – ibid., p. 370.

37. The *topos* appears for the first time in the royal inscriptions of Lugal-kigine-dudu, a king of Uruk, to legitimize his exercise of lordship over Uruk and kingship over Ur. It is interesting to note that Enlil appears as a variant to the more logical choice of Inanna, goddess of Uruk; see Sollberger and Kupper (1971), p. 85, text number 1E1c and d. In connection with a supremacy over the whole land, Lugalzagesi of Umma appears as the instigator of Enlil's primary role.

38. Jacobsen (1957) reprinted in Moran (1970).

39. ibid., p. 105.

40. 'Kengi' is the Sumerian term for 'Sumer'.

41. Sigrist (1984), p. 14.

42. See Michalowski (1983).

43. See Sollberger (1962).

44. This was especially important for dynasties that had a more dubious claim over Mesopotamian rulership, particularly such foreign dynasties as the Kassites, who invested heavily in rebuilding traditional sacred places. The Assyrian interest in Nippur during the reign of Ashurbanipal may have been motivated by similar concerns.

45. See Sigrist (1984), p. 16, for examples.

46. See Selz (1992), pp. 190–92; Charvát (1993), p. 283; Lieberman (1992).

47. For god-lists see Selz (1992), pp. 196–200; see also Chapter 3, p. 73.

48. In the so-called 'stele of vultures' commemorating his victory over Umma. See Cooper (1986), pp. 34–7.

49. cf. Lugal-kigine-dudu of Uruk, though he opportunistically had a duplicate made of his main inscription that credits Inanna with the bestowal of his leadership! See ibid., p. 101, Uk. 1.1.

50. See Sigrist (1984), p. 13; cf. the Gudea cylinder.

51. Selz (1992), p. 203.

52. His 'reform' inscriptions had survived; cf. Cooper (1986), pp. 70–83.

53. See Cooper (1986), p. 94, Um 7.1.

54. See Chapter 4, p. 88.

55. Frayne (1993).

56. Lieberman (1992), p. 133.

57. This is fully documented by Sigrist (1984), pp. 24–40.

58. See Lambert (1992), pp. 119–26.

59. See Michalowski (1998), p. 242.

60. ibid., where he cites the older spelling of the name as still incorporating the sign of NUN, traditionally associated with Enki.

61. See Leick (1999), p. 164.

62. See Dalley (1989), Atra-hasis, Gilgamesh tablet XI.

63. See Leick (1999) p. 80; see also Michalowski (1998), p. 243.

64. Behrens (1978).

65. Michalowski (1998); see also Civil (1983).

66. Michalowski (1998), p. 244.

67. See Chapter 5, p. 133.

68. Römer (1989).

69. Sjöberg (1976), pp. 411–26.

70. Cooper (1978).

71. van Dijk (1983).

72. See Behrens (1989).

73. Römer (1969).

74. Ferrara (1973).

75. See Zettler (1992b) and Steinkeller (1999).

76. Bernhardt and Kramer (1975).

77. See Chapter 4, p. 103.

78. See Sigrist (1984), p. 19.

79. See Goodnick-Westenholz (1992).

80. Stone and Owen (1991).

81. Sigrist (1984); Robertson (1992).

82. Stone (1987).

83. ibid., p. 127.

84. See Sjöberg (1975).

85. ibid., p. 161.

86. These are texts in Sumerian, mainly in dialogue form, which are set in the é-dub-ba milieu. See Kramer (1963b), pp. 229–48, for examples.

87. It was mainly boys who were educated, though female scribes also existed, usually being employed in such specialist institutions as the Gipar. See Waetzoldt (1988).

88. See Çig and Kizilyay (1959).

89. Sjöberg (1975), p. 163.

90. See also Chapter 3, p. 73.

91. See Landsberger (1937).

92. In the context of a largely unlettered population, Mesopotamian letters always began with the formula: 'To so-and-so to say the following'.

93. Sjöberg (1975), p. 167.

94. Such as the establishment of Igmil-Sin at Ur. Nearly 2,000 tablets were in his house at 'Number 1 Broad Street', according to Woolley (1931), p. 365.

95. Sjöberg (1975), p. 176.

96. See Foster (1993), p. 23, IV.

97. Foster (1995), pp. 363ff.

98. Joannès (1992).

99. See Beaulieu and Rochberg (1996).

7 SIPPAR

1. See de Meyer, Gasche and Paepe (1971), pp. 25–6.

2. Rassam (1897), p. 402.

3. It is also interesting to note that the Hebrew name is in the dual form indicating two of a kind.

4. Rassam (1897), p. 407.

5. For a summary, see Walker, C. B. and Collon, D. in de Meyer (1980), pp. 93–111.

6. Budge (1920).

7. Scheil (1902).

8. Andrae and Jordan (1934).

9. Baqir and Mustafa (1945).

10. See de Meyer (1978, 1980).

11. According to Harris (1975), p. 14.

12. See Charpin (1988).

13. ibid., p. 26.

14. See below, p. 175.

15. For this and the following account of the Old Babylonian history of Sippur, see Harris (1975), pp. 5–9.

16. For the prologue to his stele inscribed with the laws, see Driver and Miles (1955), p. 32, col. II.

17. Kuhrt (1995), p. 379. This terrible time of unrest and lawlessness was remembered in a literary composition known as the Erra Epic. See Chapter 10, p. 253.

18. Andrae and Jordan (1934), p. 53. The precinct measured 320 × 240 metres.

19. MacGinnis (1995); Bongenaar (1997); Jursa (1995).

20. Harris (1975).

21. See Gallery (1978), who scathingly criticizes the work as 'thinly disguised file-cards'; and Jeyes (1983), p. 261.

22. See below, p. 184.

23. See Harris (1975), pp. 77–142.

24. The E-ulmash, Annunitu's temple, was perhaps not much smaller, but because far fewer texts have been recovered from the period at ed-Der, information is much more limited. See ibid., pp. 178ff.

25. Such as 'Shamash gave an heir' or 'Light-of-Shamash'.

26. See Chapter 10, p. 246.

27. See Harris (1975), pp. 158–88.

28. See Harris (1962, 1964) and (1975), pp. 188–98, 303–5; Jeyes (1983). cf. also Stone (1982).

29. See Jeyes (1983), p. 262.

30. See Chapter 5, p. 128.

31. The code of Hammurabi contains passages that deal with the implications of this: the married *naditu* was barred from having children, but could choose a secondary wife for her husband and make her her heir.

32. See Postgate (1992), p. 131.

33. Harris (1962).

34. They were given names composed either with the element Aya, the wife of the sun-god, or Shamash. There are some typical *naditu* names that no other woman should be given. Harris suggests that they came to the enclosure with such names, a sign of their early dedication – Harris (1964), p. 114.

35. Some of the daughters of Zimri-Lim, king of Mari, complained bitterly when they found themselves sent away to a potentially hostile territory as wives to locale potentates. One Mariote princess, Ereshti-Aya, had been sent to the *gagum* at Sippar, where she railed against her family's neglect of her. See Batto (1974), pp. 93–102.

36. ibid., p. 99.

37. See Jeyes (1983), pp. 263–4.

38. Driver and Miles (1952), paras. 178–80.

39. Jeyes (1983), p. 263.

40. Harris (1962), pp. 2, 3.

41. Harris (1975), p. 214.

42. ibid., p. 6.

43. Batto (1974); see also n. 35 above.

44. Harris (1964), pp. 121, 128–30.

45. Harris (1975), pp. 199–200.

46. ibid., p. 306.

47. Therefore under an obligation to remain chaste. See Finkelstein (1970), pp. 264ff.

48. Harris (1975), p. 307.

49. For an oracle sent to Zimri-Lim in which the sun-god was reputed to have requested of him not just a throne but also 'your daughter which I already requested from you', see Batto (1974), p. 95.

50. See Chapter 3, p. 82.

51. See Dalley (1989), p. 36.

52. See Harris (1975), pp. 270–302.

53. See Chapter 7, p. 000.

54. Harris (1975), pp. 289–302.

55. Leemans (1960).

56. ibid., pp. 93–4, no. 8.

57. See Chapter 8, p. 200.

58. Walker (1980).

59. Leemans (1960), pp. 108–9.

60. Postgate (1992), p. 239.

61. Harris (1975), p. 334.

62. Harris (1976), p. 145.

63. Harris (1975), pp. 8–9.

64. Kraus (1958); see also Postgate (1992), pp. 196–8.

65. See Chapter 5, p. 130.

66. Jursa (1995), pp. 191–2.

67. ibid., p. 196.

68. See also Kuhrt (1995), pp. 618–21.

69. Leick (1994), pp. 80–89.

70. Kramer (1985).

71. Lambert (1960), pp. 121–38.

72. Lambert surmised that the passages about the merchants either reused or incorporated an Old Babylonian text since the vocabulary here is anachronistic in comparison with the main text – ibid., p. 122.

73. It was also the day on which the *naditu* women brought their *piqittu* offerings!

74. Lambert (1960), p. 121.

75. Thus symbolically cutting the bond of marriage.

76. Veenhof (1976).

8 ASHUR

1. See preface, p. ix.
2. See Unger (1928), pp. 170-95; Lloyd (1978), pp. 10, 108, 179.
3. Rich (1831).
4. Rassam (1897).
5. Andrae (1977).
6. Andrae (1909, 1913a, 1913b, 1922, 1931); Andrae and Lenzen (1933).
7. See p. 199.
8. Andrae (1922).
9. Hrouda, in Andrae (1977), pp. 303-4, n. 63.
10. Oppenheim (1964), p. 131.
11. Andrae (1977), p. 112.
12. Kuhrt (1995), p. 82.
13. See Larsen (1967, 1976, 1987); Veenhof (1972); Dercksen (1996).
14. See Ichisar (1981); Larsen (1982); Michel (1991).
15. Larsen (1976), pp. 34-40.
16. See p. 216 below.
17. Grayson (1987), number AO 32.2.
18. Andrae (1977), p. 121.
19. Larsen (1976).
20. Kuhrt (1995), p. 87.
21. Dercksen (1996), p. 2.
22. Larsen (1967), p. 4; cf. also ibid., p. 168 for an example.
23. Dercksen (1996), p. 64.
24. Charpin (1997), p. 377.
25. Veenhof (1972), p. 123.
26. ibid., pp. 104-5, where one robe fetches half a mina of silver.
27. ibid., p. 119.
28. Dercksen (1996).
29. Rosen (1977).
30. Veenhof (1987).
31. Charpin (1997), p. 377.
32. Larsen (1976).
33. Larsen (1974), p. 288.
34. Larsen (1976).
35. Larsen (1974), p. 293.
36. Birot (1985), p. 223. The origins of Ila-Kabkabu remain obscure.
37. For Ashur during this period, see Charpin (1997).

38. Larsen (1974), p. 288; Charpin (1997).

39. Grayson (1972), p. 19, n. 58.

40. Charpin (1997), p. 373.

41. Andrae (1977), p. 122.

42. For a contemporary example, see the temple at Tell al-Rimah: see Dalley (1984).

43. Haller (1955).

44. Preusser (1955).

45. Charpin (1997), p. 382.

46. Dossin (1950, 1952).

47. Charpin (1997), p. 373.

48. Grayson (1972), pp. 29–30.

49. i.e. Mitanni.

50. Grayson (1972), pp. 48–9.

51. Kuhrt (1995), p. 352.

52. ibid., p. 354.

53. Grayson (1972), pp. 80–81.

54. Pedersen (1985), vol. I, pp. 34ff.

55. Grayson (1972), pp. 123–4.

56. Kuhrt (1995), p. 356.

57. The older sanctuary was originally meant to be dedicated to the Akkadian Ishtar, but the text was later changed to 'Dinitu'. See Grayson (1972), p. 113.

58. See Andrae (1977), pp. 160–61.

59. Grayson (1972), p. 134.

60. See Reade (1981), p. 144.

61. Pedersen (1985).

62. See Chapter 6, pp. 155–6.

63. Lambert (1957–8).

64. Pedersen (1985), p. 34.

65. See Leick (1994), pp. 234–46.

66. George (1989), pp. 92–3.

67. Thureau-Dangin (1912), pp. 113, 201.

68. It has been suggested that the story about Sargon's expedition to Anatolia may have been composed at the behest of Shamshi-Addu in an attempt to revitalize the lapsed trading ventures with Cappadocia. See Liverani (1993), p. 55.

69. van Driel (1969).

70. Grayson (1972), pp. 69–70.

71. ibid., p. 105.

72. van Driel (1969), pp. 130–31.

73. van Driel (1969), p. 162.
74. Andrae (1977), p. 219.
75. Frahm (1997), pp. 282–8.

9 NINEVEH

1. Russell (1998).
2. See Campbell Thompson (1934), p. 10.
3. See also Curtis and Reade (1995), pp. 10ff.; Larsen (1994), pp. 202ff., 228–35.
4. Layard (1853), p. 589.
5. See also Chapter 6, p. 241.
6. Her crime novel, *Murder in Mesopotamia*, draws on her experiences as an archaeologist's wife.
7. Oates (1968), p. 21.
8. Campbell Thompson and Hamilton (1932).
9. Mallowan (1933). For a re-evaluation of the pottery sequence, see Gut (1995).
10. A much better picture of this period was provided by Mallowan's excavations at a site close to Nineveh, Tell Arpachiyah. See Mallowan and Rose (1932).
11. See Oates (1968), p. 30.
12. Grayson (1972); see also Chapter 4, pp. 98–9.
13. Campbell Thompson (1934), p. 99.
14. ibid., p. 100.
15. Turner (1970).
16. Frahm (1997), p. 1.
17. Parpola (1987); Lanfranchi and Parpola (1990).
18. Frahm (1997), p. 3.
19. ibid., p. 8.
20. A later literary text describes how Sennacherib was anxious to find out through divination what his father's sin could have been, suspecting it was the fact that he had 'esteemed the gods of Assyria too much, placing them above the gods of Babylon' – an explanation Sennacherib would not have found acceptable! See Livingstone (1989), p. 77.
21. For a Babylonian perspective on these events, see Brinkman (1984), pp. 39–65.
22. See Reade (1981), p. 145.

23. Jacobsen and Lloyd (1935).

24. From Sennacherib's standard inscription, after Frahm (1997), pp. 59–61.

25. 'Into flat slabs of brecchia and alabaster and into large limestone slabs I carved the homeland of my enemies which I captured with my own hands, and I placed them along the walls of (my palace) to make into a spectacle' – ibid., p. 82.

26. Sennacherib also built the *Ekal mašarti* on Nebi-Yunus and a third palace in the east of the city.

27. Jacobsen and Lloyd (1935), p. 35.

28. The Chaldeans were Semitic tribal people who settled in southern Mesopotamia between 1000 and 900 BC.

29. Brinkman (1984), pp. 67ff.

30. See Pongratz-Leisten (1997).

31. This was done to reconcile the front and side views of the beast, which had to look complete from any angle, hence the two front legs and the four legs seen from the side.

32. Reade (1987).

33. Grayson (1991), Cambridge Ancient History III/2 (CAH), p. 138.

34. Frahm (1997), p. 121.

35. Borger (1956), p. 42.

36. Parpola (1980).

37. Grayson (1991), CAH III/2, pp. 123–5.

38. In cuneiform signs this is easily done. See ibid., CAH III/2, p. 134.

39. In fact the most important statue, that of Marduk, was returned only after Esarhaddon's death, the delay apparently having been the result of unfavourable omens. See Lambert (1988).

40. Borger (1965), p. 65.

41. For a good overview of this topic, see Oppenheim (1964), pp. 206–27.

42. See also Parpola (1970), p. 112.

43. Borger (1956), p. 31.

44. Parpola (1997), p. 9.

45. Starr (1990), no. 187.

46. Grayson (1991), CAH III/2, p. 137.

47. Lambert (1957–8, 1959–60).

48. Wiseman (1958).

49. See Grayson (1991), CAH III/2, pp. 147–51; Brinkman (1984), pp. 93–104; Grayson (1991), CAH III/2, pp. 47–57.

50. Weissert (1997), p. 355.

51. Streck (1916), vol. II, pp. 252–3.

52. Stronach (1997), pp. 307–24.
53. See Grayson (1991), CAH III/2, p. 209.
54. Luckerbill (1924), pp. 60, 73.
55. Oded (1979), pp. 22ff.
56. ibid., p. 31.
57. ibid.
58. Schramm (1972).
59. Dalley (1997).

10 BABYLON

1. Unger (1928).
2. Rich (1839).
3. Koldewey (1990), p. 7.
4. See Andrae (1952).
5. See ibid., p. 219.
6. Koldewey (1990), p. 11.
7. Hrouda in Koldewey (1990), p. 303.
8. al-Khalil (1991), p. 71.
9. See Cooper (1980).
10. See Chapter 8, p. 204.
11. Gasche, Armstrong and Cole (1998).
12. ibid., p. 88.
13. See Chapter 8, p. 208.
14. See Chapter 8, pp. 209ff.
15. Lambert (1971).
16. See Kuhrt (1995), pp. 378–9.
17. According to the report by Nabonidus concerning the enthronement of his own daughter, where he reported that he found an inscription of Nebuchadrezzar I about the ritual. See Kuhrt (1995), p. 381.
18. See Chapter 1, p. 20.
19. Heidel (1951), pp. 148–9.
20. Cagni (1977); Dalley (1989), pp. 282–316.
21. ibid., p. 297.
22. See Chapter 5, p. 137.
23. Dalley (1989), p. 304.
24. See especially, 'The Poem of the Righteous Sufferer' and 'A Babylonian Theodicy' in Lambert (1960), pp. 21–91.

25. Brinkman (1984), pp. 12–15.

26. ibid., p. 18.

27. ibid., pp. 21–3.

28. See Chapter 9, p. 239.

29. Brinkman (1984), pp. 105–11.

30. ibid., p. 35.

31. Zawadzki (1988).

32. Oates (1991), ch. 25.

33. Wiseman (1985), pp. 26–9.

34. Koldewey (1990), p. 300.

35. Schmid (1995).

36. Powell (1982).

37. See Wiseman (1985), fig. 12.

38. George (1992).

39. 'Altogether: 43 temples of the great gods, 55 sanctuaries of Marduk, 300 pedestals of the Igigi, 600 of the Anunnaki, 180 chapels of Ishtar, 180 pedestals of Lugalgirra and Meslamtaea, 12 pedestals of the Seven, 4 pedestals of the rainbow, 2 pedestals of the Evil God, 2 pedestals of the city guardian.'

40. Though probably not for two chariots, as Herodotus and Curtius Rufus report; cf. Wetzel (1930).

41. Opinion is still divided as to whether it was the main arm of the Euphrates that flowed through Babylon at the time or still only the Arahtu arm. Both terms appear in the inscriptions of the period.

42. Wiseman (1985), p. 55.

43. See Chapter 9, p. 243.

44. See the discussion on measurement by Heinrich and Seidl, 1968.

45. Koldewey (1990), pp. 163–70.

46. Sack (1994).

47. Mayer (1998).

48. Oppenheim, A. L., in Pritchard (1969), pp. 560–62.

49. Stolper (1985), p. 2.

50. Kuhrt (1983). The cylinder with its cuneiform inscription was discovered by Rassam in 1879.

51. van Driel (1985–6); Wunsch (1993).

52. Haerinck in Koldewey (1990), p. 373.

53. Cuyler-Young (1988), p. 58.

54. Kuhrt and Sherwin-White (1987).

55. Haerinck in Koldewey (1990), p. 381.

56. Sherwin-White and Kuhrt (1993), pp. 149–61. See also van der Speck (1987) and Sherwin-White (1987).

57. It was built of bricks, many of which came from some of the Neo-Babylonian structures that had by that time fallen into disrepair. See Koldewey (1990), pp. 290–99.

58. ibid., p. 160.

59. Sachs and Hunger (1988, 1989).

Bibliographies

1 ERIDU

Adams, R. McC. (1970), 'The Study of Ancient Mesopotamian Settlement Patterns and the Problem of Urban Origins', *Sumer* 25, pp. 111–23.
—— (1981), *Heartland of Cities*, Chicago.
Alster, B. (1987), 'Enki and Ninhursag', *Ugarit Forschungen* 10, pp. 15–27.
Benito, C. A. (1969), 'Enki and Ninmah' and 'Enki and the World Order' (dissertation, University of Pennsylvania), Ann Arbor, Mich.
Berman, J. (1994), 'The Ceramic Evidence for Sociopolitical Organization in Ubaid Southwestern Iran' in G. Stein and M. Rothmann (eds.), *Chiefdoms and Early States in the Near East: The Organizational Dynamics of Complexity*, Madison, Wis., pp. 23–33.
Bernbeck, R. (1995), 'Die Obed-Zeit: religiöse Gerontokratien oder Häuptlingstümer?' in K. Bartl, R. Bernbeck and M. Heinz (eds.), *Zwischen Euphrat und Indus: aktuelle Forschungsprobleme in der vorderasiatischen Archäologie*, Hildesheim, pp. 44–56.
Charles, M. (1988), 'Irrigation in Lowland Mesopotamia' in *Irrigation and Cultivation in Mesopotamia, Part 1, Bulletin on Sumerian Agriculture*, 4, pp. 1–39.
Charpin, D. (1986), *Le Clergé d'Ur au siècle d'Hammurabi (XIXᵉ–XVIII siècles av. J.C.)*, Geneva.
Charvát, P. (1993), *Ancient Mesopotamia: Humankind's Long Journey into Civilization*, Prague.
Dalley, S. (1989), *Myths from Mesopotamia*, Oxford, New York.
Earle, T. (ed.) (1991), *Chiefdoms: Power, Economy, and Ideology*, Cambridge.
Farber-Flügge, G. (1973), *Der Mythos 'Enanna und Enki' in der Berücksichtigung der Liste der me*, Rome.
Forest, J. D. (1983), *Les pratiques funéraires en Mésopotamie du cinquième millénaire au début du troisième: étude de cas*, Paris.

Galter, H. D. (1981), *Der Gott En/Enki in der akkadischen Überlieferung*, Graz.

Garfinkel, Y. (1994), 'Ritual Burial of Cultic Objects: The Earliest Evidence', *Cambridge Archaeological Journal* 4, pp. 159–88.

Green, M. (1975), *Eridu in Sumerian Literature*, Chicago.

Hallo, W. W. (1970), 'Antediluvian Cities', *Journal of Cuneiform Studies* 23, pp. 57–67.

Heidel, A. (1951), *A Babylonian Genesis*, Chicago.

Hendrickson, E. and I. Thuessen (eds.) (1989), *Upon this Foundation: The Ubaid Reconsidered*, Carsten Niebuhr Institute Publications 10, Copenhagen.

Hole, F. (1983), 'Symbols of Religion and Social Organisation at Susa' in T. C. Young, P. E. L. Smith and P. Mortensen (eds.) (1983), *The Hilly Flanks and Beyond: Essays on the Prehistory of Southwestern Asia Presented to Robert J. Braidwood, November 15, 1982* (Studies in Ancient Oriental Civilization 36), Chicago.

Huot, J. (1989), 'Ubaidian Villages of lower Mesopotamia: permanence and evolution from "Ubaid O" to "Ubaid 4" as seen from Tell el 'Oueili' in E. Hendrickson and I. Thuessen (eds.) (1989), *Upon this Foundation: The Ubaid Reconsidered*, Copenhagen, pp. 19–42.

Jacobsen, Th. (1987), *The Harps That Once . . . Sumerian Poetry in Translation*, New Haven and London.

Klein, J. (1981), *The Royal Hymns of Shulgi, King of Ur*, Ramat-Gan.

Kramer, S. N. (1963), 'The Sumerian Sacred Marriage Texts', *Proceedings of the Society of Biblical Archaeology* 107, pp. 485–525.

Kushner, D. (1977), *The Rise of Turkish Nationalism 1876–1908*, Guildford, London and Worcester.

Leick, G. (1994), *Sex and Eroticism in Mesopotamian Literature*, London, New York.

Maxwell, G. (1957), *People of the Reeds*, New York.

Michalowski, P. (1983), 'History as charter: some observations on the Sumerian king list', *Journal of the American Oriental Society* 103, pp. 237–48.

Nissen, H. (1988), *The Early History of the Ancient Near East, 9000–2000 B.C.*, Chicago, London.

Oates, J. (1960), 'Ur and Eridu, the prehistory' in M. E. L. Mallowan and D. J. Wiseman (eds.), *Ur in Retrospect, Iraq* 22, pp. 32–50.

Pariselle, C. (1985), Le cimetière d'Eridu: essai d'interprétation', *Akkadica* 44, pp. 1–13.

Picchioni, S. A. (1981), *Il poemetto di Adapa*, Budapest.

Pollock, S. (1999), *Ancient Mesopotamia: The Eden that Never Was*, Cambridge.

Postgate, J. N. (1992), *Early Mesopotamia: Society and Economy at the Dawn of History*, London.

Reiner, E. (1961), 'The Etiological Myth of the "Seven Sages"', *Orientalia* N. S. 30.

Safar, F., M. A. Mustafa and S. Lloyd (1981), *Eridu*, Baghdad.

Salim, S. M. (1962), *Marsh Dwellers of the Euphrates Delta*, London.

Sallaberger, W. (1993), *Der kultische Kalendar der Ur III Zeit*, Berlin, New York.

Sjöberg, A. W. and S. J. Bergmann (1969), *The Collection of Sumerian Temple Hymns*, Locust Valley, NY.

Stein, G. and M. Rothmann (eds.) (1994), *Chiefdoms and Early States in the Near East: The Organizational Dynamics of Complexity*, Madison, Wis.

Steinkeller, P. (1999), 'On Rulers, Priests and Sacred Marriage: Tracing the Evolution of Early Sumerian Kingships' in K. Watanabe (ed.), *Priests and Officials in the Ancient Near East*, Heidelberg, pp. 103–38.

Thesiger, W. (1964), *The Marsh Arabs*, London.

Vértesalji, P. P. (1989), 'Were there supralocal cemeteries in southern Mesopotamia of late Chalcolithic times?' in E. Hendrikson and I. Thuessen (eds.), *Upon this Foundation: The Ubaid Reconsidered*, Copenhagen, pp. 181–98.

Woolley, Sir L. (1929), *Ur of the Chaldees*, London.

2 URUK

Adams, R. McC. (1965), *Land Behind Baghdad*, Chicago.

—— (1966), *The Evolution of Urban Society*, Chicago.

—— (1981), *Heartland of Cities*, Chicago.

Adams, R. McC. and H. Nissen (1972), *The Uruk Countryside*, Chicago.

Algaze, G. (1993), *The Uruk World System: The Dynamics of Expansion of Early Mesopotamian Civilization*, Chicago.

Asante, J. (1998), 'The kar.kid (*harimtu*): Prostitute or Single Woman?' *Ugarit Forschungen* 30, pp. 5–97.

Boehmer, R. M. (1991), 'Lugalzagesi, der Bauherr des Stampflehmgebäudes in Uruk', *Baghdader Mitteilungen* 22, pp. 165–74.

Charvát, P. (1993), *Ancient Mesopotamia: Humankind's Long Journey into Civilization*, Prague.

—— (1998), *On Peoples, Signs and States: Spotlights on Sumerian Society c. 3500–2500 B.C.*, Prague.

Dalley, S. (1989), *Myths from Mesopotamia*, Oxford, New York.

Finkbeiner, U. (1991), *Uruk Kampagne 35–37 1982–84: die archäologische Oberflächenuntersuchung (Survey)*, Ausgrabungen in Uruk-Warka Endberichte 4, Mainz.

Frymer-Kensy, T. (1992), *In the Wake of the Goddesses: Women, Culture and the Biblical Transformation of Pagan Myth*, New York, Oxford.

Johnson, G. (1975), 'Locational Analysis and the Investigation of Uruk Local Exchange Systems' in J. Sabloff and C. C. Lamberg-Karlovsky (eds.), *Ancient Civilization and Trade*, Albuquerque, pp. 285–339.

Kuhrt, A. (1995), *The Ancient Near East c. 3000–330 B.C.* (2 vols.), London.

Lambert, W. G. (1992), 'Prostitution' in V. Haas (ed.), *Aussenseiter und Randgruppe: Beiträge zu einer Sozialgeschichte des Alten Orients*, Konstanz, pp. 127–57.

Leick, G. (1994), *Sex and Eroticism in Mesopotamian Literature*, London, New York.

Lenzen, H. J. (1974), 'Die Architektur in Eanna in der Uruk IV Period', *Iraq* 36, pp. 111ff.

Lévi-Strauss, C. (1966), *The Savage Mind*, London.

—— (1995), *Tristes tropiques*, Paris.

Loftus, W. K. (1857), *Travels and Researches in Chaldea and the Susiana, with an account of excavations at Warka, the 'Erech' of Nimrud, and Shush, 'Shusha', the Palace of Esther*, London.

Millard, A. (1988), 'The Bevelled Rim Bowls: Their Purpose and Significance' *Iraq* 50, pp. 49–57.

Nissen, H. (1972), 'The City Wall of Uruk' in P. J. Ucko, R. Tringham and G. Dimbleby (eds.) *Man, Settlement and Urbanism*, London.

—— (1986), 'The Archaic Texts from Uruk', *World Archaeology* 17, pp. 317–34.

—— (1988), *The Early History of the Ancient Near East, 9000–2000 B.C.*, Chicago, London.

Nissen, H., P. Damerow and R. Englund (1993), *Archaic Bookkeeping: Early Writing and Techniques of Economic Administration in the Ancient Near East* (translated by P. Larsen), Chicago.

Pollock, S. (1999), *Ancient Mesopotamia: The Eden that Never Was*, Cambridge.

Postgate, J. N. (1992), *Early Mesopotamia: Society and Economy at the Dawn of History*, London.

Powell, M. (1994), 'Elusive Eden: Private Property at the Dawn of History', *Journal of Cuneiform Studies* 46, pp. 99–104.

Schmandt-Besserat, D. (1992), *Before Writing: from Counting to Cuneiform* (2 vols.), Austin.

Selz, G. J. (1998), 'Über mesopotamische Herrschaftskonzepte' in M. Dietrich and O. Loretz, *Dubsar anta-men. Festschrift für Willem H. Ph. Römer zur Vollendung seines 70. Lebensjahres*, Münster, pp. 189–226.

Strommenger, E. (1980), *Habuba-Kabira: eine Stadt vor 5000 Jahren*, Mainz.

Wallerstein, I. (1974), *The Modern World System*, vol. I, New York.

Wittvogel, A. (1977), *Die altorientalische Despotie, eine vergleichende Untersuchung totaler Macht*, Berlin.

Wright, H. T. (1994), 'Prestate Political Formulations' in G. Stein and M. Rothmann, *Chiefdoms and Early States in the Near East: The Organization of Complexity*, Madison, Wis.

Wright, H. T. and S. Pollock (1987), 'Regional Socio-Economic organization in Southern Mesopotamia: the Middle and Later 4th Millennium B.C.' in J. L. Huot (ed.), *Préhistoire de la Mésopotamie*, Paris.

3 SHURUPPAK

Alster, B. (1974), *The Inscriptions of Šuruppak*, Copenhagen.

—— (1997), *Proverbs of Ancient Sumer* (2 vols.), Bethesda, Md.

Biggs, R. D. (1974), *Inscriptions from Tell Abu Salabikh*, Chicago, London.

Biggs, R. D. and J. N. Postgate (1978), 'Inscriptions from Abu Salabikh', *Iraq* 42/1.

Charvát, P. (1986), 'The Name Anzu ^{d}Sud in the Texts from Fara' in K. Hecker and W. Sommerfeld (eds.), *Keilschriftliche Literatur en.Ausgewählte Vorträge der 32 Rencontre Assyriologique Internationale*, Berlin, pp. 45–53.

—— (1993), *Ancient Mesopotamia: Human Kind's Long Journey into Civilisation*, Prague.

Edzard, D. O. (1979), 'Die Archive von Šuruppak (Fara): Umfang und Grenzen der Aufwertbarkeit' in E. Lipínski (ed.), *State and Temple Economy in the Ancient Near East*, Leuven.

Frayne, D. R. (1989), 'The Early Dynastic List of Geographical Names', *Journal of the American Oriental Society* 74.

Gelb, I. J. (1979), 'Household and Family in Early Mesopotamia' in E. Lipínski (ed.), *State and Temple Economy in the Ancient Near East*, Leuven, pp. 1–99.

Gibson, McG. (1976), 'By state and cycle to Sumer' in D. Schmandt-Besserat (ed.), *The Legacy of Sumer*, Malibu, Ca.

Green, M. H. W. (1984), 'Early Sumerian Tax Collectors', *Journal of Cuneiform Studies* 36, pp. 93–5.

Heimpel, W. (1992), 'Herrentum und Königtum im vor- und frühgeschichtlichen Alten Orient', *Zeitschrift für Assyriologie* 82, pp. 4–21.

Jacobsen, Th. (1957), 'Early Political Development in Mesopotamia', *Zeitschrift für Assyriologie* 52, pp. 91–140.

Katz, D. (1993), *Gilgamesh and Akkad*, Groningen.

Krebernik, M. (1984), *Die Beschwörungen aus Fara und Ebla: Untersuchungen zur ältesten Beschwörungsliteratur*, Hildesheim, Zurich, New York.

—— (1986), 'Die Götterlisten aus Fara', *Zeitschrift für Assyriologie* 76, pp. 161–204.

Leick, G. (1983), 'Über Tradition und Bedeutung thematischer Listenwerke' in I. Seybold (ed.), *Meqor Hajjim: Festschrift für Georg Molin zu seinem 75. Geburtstag*, Graz, pp. 221–40.

Lévi-Strauss, C. (1966), *The Savage Mind*, London.

Martin, H. P. (1988), *Fara: A Reconstruction of the Ancient Mesopotamian City of Shuruppak*, Birmingham.

Matthews, R. J. (1991), 'Fragments of Officialdom from Fara', *Iraq* 53, pp. 1–15.

Michalowski, P. (1990), 'Early Mesopotamian Communicative Systems: Art, Literature and Writing' in A. C. Gunter (ed.), *Investigating Artistic Environments in the Ancient Near East*, Washington.

Nissen, H. (1988), *The Early History of the Ancient Near East 9000–2000 B.C.*, Chicago, London.

Nissen, H., P. Damerow and R. Englund (1993), *Archaic Bookkeeping: Early Writing and Techniques of Economic Administration in the Ancient Near East* (translated by Paul Larsen), Chicago.

Pettinato, G. (1980), *The Archives of Ebla*, New York.

Pollock, S. (1999), *Ancient Mesopotamia: The Eden that Never Was*, Cambridge.

Pomponio, F. and G. Visicato (1994), 'Early Dynastic Administrative Tablets of Suruppak', *Istituto Universitario Orientale di Napoli, Dipartimento di Studi Asiatici, Series maior* VI.

Römer, W. H. Ph. (1999), *Die Sumerologie: Einführung in die Forschung und Bibliographie in Auswahl* (2nd enlarged edition), Münster.

Selz, G. J. (1998), 'Über mesopotamische Herrschaftskonzepte' in M. Dietrich and O. Loretz, *Dubsar anta-men. Festschrift fur Willem H. Ph. Römer zur Vollendung seines 70. Lebensjahres*, Münster, pp. 189–226.

Steible, H. and F. Yildiz (1993), 'Kiengi aus der Sicht von Šuruppak', *Istanbuler Mitteilungen* 43, pp. 17–26.

Visicato, G. (1995), 'The Beaurocracy of Šuruppak', *Abhandlungen zur Literatur Alt-Syriens-Palästinas und Mesopotamiens* 10, Münster.

Walker, C. B. F. (1987), *Reading the Past: Cuneiform*, London.

4 AKKAD

Al-Khalifa, Sh. H. A. and M. Rice (eds.) (1986), *Bahrein Through the Ages: The Archaeology*, London.

Amiet, P. (1976), *Art d'Agadé du Musée du Louvre*, Paris.

Charvát, P. (1997), *On People, Signs and States: Spotlights on Sumerian Society c. 3500–2500 B.C.*, Prague.

Cooper, J. S. (1983), *The Curse of Agade*, Baltimore.

—— (1986), *Presargonic Inscriptions*, New Haven.

—— (1993), 'Paradigm and Propaganda. The Dynasty of Akkade in the 21st Century' in M. Liverani (ed.), *Akkad: The First World Empire. Structure, Ideology, Traditions*, Padova, pp. 11–23.

Cooper, J. S. and W. Heimpel (1983), 'The Sumerian Sargon Legend', *Journal of the American Oriental Society* 103, pp. 67–82.

Edzard, D. O. (1997), *Gudea and his Dynasty*, Toronto.

Foster, B. R. (1982), *Administration and Use of Institutional Land in Sargonic Sumer*, Copenhagen.

Franke, S. (1995), *Königsinschriften und Königsideologie. Der Könige von Akkade zwischen Tradition und Erneuerung*, Münster.

Frayne, D. (1993), *Sargonic and Gutian Periods (2334–2113 B.C.)*, Toronto.

Glassner, J. J. (1986), *La chute d'Akkade: l'évenement et sa mémoire*, Berlin.

Hallo, W. W. (1998), 'New directions in historiography' in M. Dietrich and O. Loretz (eds.), *Dubsar anta-men. Festschrift für Wilhelm H. Ph. Römer zur Vollendung seines 70. Lebensjahres*, Münster, pp. 122ff.

Heimpel, W. (1992), 'Herrentum und Königtum im vor- und frühgeschichtlichen Alten Orient', *Zietschrift für Assyriologie* 82, pp. 4–21.

Horowitz, W. (1998), *Mesopotamian Cosmic Geography*, Winona Lake, Ind.

Kramer, S. N. (1963), *The Sumerians: Their History, Culture, and Character*, Chicago.

Kuhrt, A. (1995), *The Ancient Near East, c. 3000–330 B.C.* (2 vols.), London.

Jacobsen, Th. (1987), *The Harps That Once . . . Sumerian Poetry in Translation*, New Haven and London.

Liverani, M. (ed.) (1993), *Akkad: The First World Empire: Structure, Ideology, Traditions*, Padova.

Lloyd, S. (1985), *The Archaeology of Mesopotamia: From the Old Stone Age to the Persian Conquest*, rev. edn, London.

Mann, M. (1986), *The Sources of Social Power: A History of Power from the Beginning to A.D. 1760* (vol. 1), Cambridge.

McEwan, J. G. P. (1980), 'Agade after the Gutian Destruction: The Afterlife of a Mesopotamian City', *Archiv für Orientforschung* 19, pp. 8–15.

Michalowski, P. (1993), 'Memory and Deed: The Historiography of the Political Expansion of the Akkad State' in M. Liverani (ed.), *Akkad: The First World Empire: Structure, Ideology, Traditions*, Padova, pp. 69–90.

Nissen, H. (1988), *The Early History of the Ancient Near East, 9000–2000 B.C.*, Chicago, London.

Pettinato, G. (1978), *The Early Dynastic List of Geographical Names*, American Oriental Series 74.

Pollock, S. (1999), *Ancient Mesopotamia: The Eden that Never Was*, Cambridge.

Postgate, J. N. (1992), *Early Mesopotamia: Society and Economy at the Dawn of History*, London.

Sollberger, E. and J. R. Kupper (1971), *Inscriptions royales sumeriennes et akkadiennes*, Paris.

Wall-Romema, C. (1990), 'An Areal Location of Agade', *Journal of Near Eastern Studies* 49, pp. 205–45.

Westenholz, J. G. (1997), *Legends of the Kings of Akkade: The Texts*, Winona Lake, Ind.

5 UR

Alster, B. (1980), *Death in Mesopotamia*, 26e Rencontre Assyriologique Internationale (Copenhagen, 1979), Copenhagen.

Berlin, A. (1979), *Enmerkar and Enšuhkešdanna*, Philadelphia.

Castellino, G. R. (1972), *Two Šulgi Hymns*, Rome.

Charvát, P. (1993), *Ancient Mesopotamia: Humankind's Long Journey into Civilization*.

—— (1998), *On People, Signs and States: Spotlights on Sumerian Society c. 3500–2000 B.C.*, Prague.

Cooper, J. (1993), 'Sacred Marriage and Popular Cult in Early Mesopotamia' in E. Matsushima (ed.), *Official Cult and Popular Religion in the Ancient Near East*, Heidelberg.

Delougaz, P., H. Hill and S. Lloyd (1967), *Private Houses and Graves in the Diyala Region*, Chicago.

Durand, J. M. (ed.) (1987), *La femme dans le proche-Orient antique*, 33e Rencontre Assyriologique Internationale (Paris, 1980), Paris.

Dyson, R. H. (1960), 'A Note on Queen Shub-Ad's "Onagers"', *Iraq* 22, pp. 102–4.

Frankfort, H. (1970), *The Art and Architecture of the Ancient Near East* (4th edn), Harmondsworth.

Garelli, P. (ed.) (1974), *Le palais et la royauté*, Paris.

Gibson, McG., H. Nissen, et al. (eds.) (1980) *L'archéologie de l'Iraq du début de l'époque néolithique à 332 avant notre ère*, Colloques internationaux du Centre National de la Recherche Scientifique, Paris.

Gurney, O. (1983), *The Middle Babylonian Legal and Economic Texts from Ur*, Oxford.

Hallo, W. W. (1975), 'Toward a History of Sumerian Literature' in S. J. Lieberman, *Sumerological Studies in Honor of Thorkild Jacobsen on his Seventieth Birthday, June 7 1974*, Chicago, London.

Hallo, W. W. and J. J. van Dijk (1966), *The Exaltation of Inanna*, New Haven, London.

Jagersma, B. (1990), review article of A. Albert and F. Pomponio, *Pre-Sargonic and Sargonic Texts from Ur Edited in UET (2)*, *Bibliotheca Orientalis* 47, no. 5/6, pp. 671–4.

Jones, T. B. (1975), 'Sumerian Administrative Documents: An Essay' in S. J. Lieberman (ed.), *Sumerological Studies in Honor of Thorkild Jacobsen on his Seventieth Birthday, June 7, 1974*, Chicago, London.

Klein, J. (1981), *Three Shulgi Hymns*, Ramat-Gan.

Kuhrt, A. (1995), *The Ancient Near East c. 3000–333 B.C.* (2 vols.), London.

Leick, G. (1994), *Sex and Eroticism in Mesopotamian Literature*, London.

Matthews, R. and J. N. Postgate (1987), 'Excavations at Abu Salabik', *Iraq* 49, pp. 91–119.

Michalowski, P. (1987), 'Charisma and Control: On Continuity and Change in Early Mesopotamian Bureaucratic Systems' in McG. Gibson and R. D. Biggs (eds.), *The Organization of Power: Aspects of Bureaucracy in the Ancient Near East*, Chicago.

—— (1989), *The Lamentation over the Destruction of Sumer and Ur*, Winona Lake, Ind.

Moorey, P. R. S. (1984), 'Where Did They Bury the Kings of the Third Dynasty of Ur?' *Iraq* 46, pp. 1ff.

Nissen, H. (1988), *The Early History of the Ancient Near East, 9000–2000 B.C.*, Chicago, London.

Paynter, R. (1989), 'The Archaeology of Equality and Inequality', *Annual Review of Anthropology* 18, pp. 369–99.

Pollock, S. (1985), 'Chronology of the Royal Cemetery of Ur', *Iraq* 47, pp. 129–59.

—— (1991), 'Women in a Man's World: Images of Sumerian Women' in J. Gero and M. Conkey (eds.), *Engendering Archaeology – Women and Prehistory*, Oxford, pp. 366–87.

—— (1999), *Ancient Mesopotamia: The Eden that Never Was*, Cambridge.

Pritchard, J. B. (ed.) (1969), *The Ancient Near East: Supplementary Texts and Pictures Relating to the Old Testament*, Princeton.

Römer, W. H. Ph. (1965), *Sumerische Königshymnen der Isin Zeit*, Leiden.

Sollberger, E. and J. R. Kupper (1971), *Inscriptions royales sumeriennes et akkadiennes*, Paris.

Steinkeller, P. (1987), 'The Administrative and Economic Organization of the Ur III State: The Core and the Periphery' in McG. Gibson and R. D. Biggs (eds.), *The Organization of Power: Aspects of Bureaucracy in the Ancient Near East*, Chicago.

—— (1999), 'On Rulers, Priests and Sacred Marriage: Tracing the Evolution of Early Sumerian Kingship' in K. Watanabe (ed.), *Priests and Officials in the Ancient Near East*, Heidelberg, pp. 124–7.

Weadcock, P. N. (1975), 'The Giparu at Ur', *Iraq* 37, p. 103.

Wilcke, C. (1975), 'Formale Gesichtspunkte in der sumerischen Literatur' in S. J. Lieberman (1975), *Sumerological Studies in Honor of Thorkild Jacobsen on his Seventieth Birthday, June 7 1974*, Chicago, London.

Woolley, Sir L. (1925), *The Antiquaries Journal* 5.

—— (1929), *The Antiquaries Journal* 9.

—— (1930), *The Antiquaries Journal* 10.

—— (1931), *The Antiquaries Journal* 11.

—— (1932), *The Antiquaries Journal* 12.

—— (1933), *The Antiquaries Journal* 13.

—— (1934), *The Antiquaries Journal* 14.

—— (1934), *Ur Excavations II: The Royal Cemetery*, London.

—— (1952), *Ur of the Chaldees*, Harmondsworth.

—— (1955), *Ur Excavations IV: The Early Periods*, Philadelphia.

Wright, R. P. (1996), 'Technology, Gender, and Class: Worlds of Difference in Ur III Mesopotamia' in R. P. Wright (ed.), *Gender and Archaeology*, Philadelphia, pp. 79–110.

Zgoll, A. (1997), *Der Rechtsfall der En-hedu-Ana im Lied nin-me-šara*, Münster.

6 NIPPUR

Beaulieu, P. A. and F. Rochberg (1996), 'The Horoscope of Bel-šunu', *Journal of Cuneiform Studies* 48, pp. 89–96.

Behrens, H. (1978), *Enlil and Ninlil*, Rome.

—— (1989), *Die Ninegalla Hymne: die Wohnungsnahme Inanna's in Nippur in altbabylonischer Zeit*, Stuttgart.

Bernhardt, I. and S. N. Kramer (1975), 'Die Tempel und Götterschreine von Nippur', *Orientalia* 44, pp. 96–102.

Charvát, P. (1993), *Ancient Mesopotamia: Humankind's Long Journey into Civilization*, Prague.

Çig, M. and H. Kizilyay (1959), *Zwei altbabylonische Schulbücher aus Nippur*, Ankara.

Civil, M. (1983), 'The Marriage of Sud', *Journal of the American Oriental Society* 103, pp. 64–6.

Cooper, J. S. (1978), *The Return of Ninurta to Nippur*, Rome.

—— (1983), *The Curse of Agade*, Baltimore.

—— (1986), *Sumerian and Akkadian Royal Inscriptions, vol. 1: Pre-Sargonic Inscriptions*, Winona Lake, Ind.

Dalley, S. (1989), *Myths from Mesopotamia*, Oxford, New York.

Ferrara, A. J. (1973), *Nanna-Suen's Journey to Nippur*, Rome.

Foster, B. R. (1993), *Before the Muses*, Bethesda, Md.

—— (1995), *From Distant Days: Myths, Tales and Poetry of Ancient Mesopotamia*, Bethesda, Md.

Frayne, D. R. (1993), *Sargonic and Gutian Periods (2334–2113 B.C.)*, Toronto.

Geere, H. V. (1904), *By Nile and Euphrates: A Record of Discovery and Adventure*, Edinburgh.

Gibson, McG. (1975), 'Excavations at Nippur: Eleventh Season', *Oriental Institute Communications* 22, Chicago.

—— (1978), 'Nippur 1975', *Sumer* 34, pp. 114–21.

—— (1980), 'Current Research at Nippur: Ecological, Anthropological, and Documentary Interplay' in *L'Archéologie de l'Iraq*, Paris, pp. 193–205.

—— (1992), 'Patterns of Occupation at Nippur' in M. deJong Ellis (ed.), *Nippur at the Centennial*, papers read at the 35e Rencontre Assyriologique Internationale (Philadelphia, 1988), Philadelphia, pp. 38–54.

Goetze, A. (1970), 'Early Dynastic Dedication Inscriptions from Nippur', *Journal of Cuneiform Studies* 23, pp. 39–56.

Goodnick-Westenholz, J. (1992), 'The Clergy of Nippur' in M. deJong Ellis (ed.), *Nippur at the Centennial*, papers read at the 35e Rencontre Assyriologique Internationale (Philadelphia, 1988), Philadelphia, pp. 297–310.

Hansen, D. P. and G. F. Dales (1962), 'The Temple of Inanna, Queen of Heaven', *Archaeology* 15, pp. 75–84.

Hilprecht, H. V. (1903), *Exploration in Bible Lands during the Nineteenth Century*, Philadelphia.

—— (1906), *Mathematical, Meteorological, and Chronological Texts from the Temple Library of Nippur*, Philadelphia.

—— (1910), *The Earliest Version of the Babylonian Deluge Story and the Temple Library of Nippur*, Philadelphia.

Jacobsen, Th. (1957), 'Early Political Development in Mesopotamia', *Zeitschrift für Assyriologie* 18, pp. 91–140.

Joannès, F. (1992), 'Les archives de Ninurta-ahhe-bullit' in M. deJong Ellis (ed.), *Nippur at the Centennial*, papers read at the 35e Rencontre Assyriologique Internationale (Philadelphia, 1988), Philadelphia, pp. 87–100.

Kramer, S. N. (1963a), 'The Sumerian Marriage Texts', *Proceedings of the Society of Biblical Archaeology* 107, pp. 485–525.

—— (1963b), *The Sumerians: Their History, Culture and Character*, Chicago.

Kuklick, B. (1996), *Puritans in Babylon: The Ancient Near East and American Intellectual Life 1880–1930*, Princeton.

Lambert, W. G. (1992), 'Nippur in Ancient Ideology' in M. deJong Ellis (ed.), *Nippur at the Centennial*, papers read at the 35e Rencontre Assyriologique Internationale (Philadelphia, 1988), Philadelphia, pp. 119–260.

Landsberger, B. (1937), *Materialien zum sumerischen Lexikon* (vol. 1), Rome.

Leick, G. (1996), *A Dictionary of Ancient Near Eastern Mythology* (2nd edn), London.

—— (1999), 'The Erotication of Landscape in Mesopotamian Literature' in L. Milano, S. Martino, F. M. Fales and G. B. Lanfranchi (eds.), *Landscapes: Territories, Frontiers and Horizons in the Ancient Near East*, papers presented to the 44e Rencontre Assyriologique Internationale (Venice, 1997), Padova, pp. 79–82.

Lieberman, S. J. (1992), 'Nippur: City of Decisions' in M. deJong Ellis (ed.), *Nippur at the Centennial*, papers read at the 35e Rencontre Assyriologique Internationale (Philadelphia, 1988), Philadelphia, pp. 127–36.

Lloyd, S. (1980), *Foundations in the Dust: A Story of Mesopotamian Exploration* (rev. edn), London.

McCown, D. E. and R. C. Haines (1967), *Nippur I: Temple of Enlil, Scribal Quarter, and Soundings*, Chicago.

McCown, D. E., R. C. Haines and R. D. Biggs (1978), *Nippur II: The North Temple and Soundings*, Chicago.

Michalowski, P. (1983), 'History as Charter: Some Observations on the Sumerian King List', *Journal of the American Oriental Society* 103, pp. 237–48.

—— (1998), 'The Unbearable Lightness of Enlil' in J. Prosecky, *Intellectual Life of the Ancient Near East*, papers presented at the 43e Rencontre Assyriologique Internationale (Prague, 1996), Prague, pp. 237–48.

Moran, W. L. (ed.) (1970), *Towards the Image of Tammuz and Other Essays on Mesopotamian History and Culture*, Cambridge, Mass.

Oded, B. (1979), *Mass Deportations and Deportees in the Neo-Assyrian Empire*, Wiesbaden.

—— (1984), 'Ninurta's Pride and Punishment', *Orientalia* 54, pp. 231–7.

Pollock, S. (1999), *Ancient Mesopotamia: The Eden that Never Was*, Cambridge.

Postgate, J. N. (1992), *Early Mesopotamia: Society and Economy at the Dawn of History*, London.

Robertson, J. F. (1992), 'The Temple Economy of Old Babylonian Nippur: The Evidence for Centralized Management' in M. deJong Ellis (ed.), *Nippur at the Centennial*, papers read at the 35e Rencontre Assyriologique Internationale (Philadelphia, 1988), Philadelphia, pp. 177–89.

Römer, W. H. Ph. (1969), 'Eine Hymne mit Selbstlob Inannas', *Orientalia* 38, pp. 161–253.

—— (1989), 'Die Heirat des Gottes Mardu', *Ugarit Forschungen* 21.

Selz, G. J. (1992), 'Enlil und Nippur nach präsargonischen Quellen' in M. deJong Ellis (ed.), *Nippur at the Centennial*, papers read at the 35e Rencontre Assyriologique Internationale (Philadelphia, 1988), Philadelphia, pp. 189–226.

Sigrist, M. (1984), *Les Sattuku dans l'Ešumesa durant la periode d'Isin et Larsa*, Malibu, Ca.

Sjöberg, A. W. (1975), 'The Old Babylonian Eduba' in S. T. Lieberman (ed.), *Sumerological Studies in Honor of Thorkild Jacobsen on his Seventieth Birthday, June 7, 1974*, Chicago, pp. 159–80.

—— (1976), 'Hymns to Ninurta with Prayers for Susin and Bursin of Isin', *Kramer Anniversary Volume*, Neukirchen-Vluyn, pp. 411–26.

Sollberger, E. (1962), 'The Tummal Inscription', *Journal of Cuneiform Studies* 16, pp. 4–47.

Sollberger, E. and J. R. Kuppur (1971), *Inscriptions royales sumeriennes et akkadiennes*, Paris.

Steinkeller, P. (1999), 'On Rulers, Priests and Sacred Marriage: Tracing the Evolution of Early Sumerian Kingship' in K. Watanabe, *Priests and Officials in the Ancient Near East*, Heidelberg, pp. 124–7.

Stolper, M. W. (1985), *Entrepreneurs and Empire: The Murašu Archive, the Murašu Firm and Persian Rule in Babylonia*, Istanbul.

Stone, E. C. (1987), *Nippur Neighborhood*, Chicago.

Stone, E. and D. I. Owen (1991), *Adoption in Old Babylonian Nippur and the Archive of Mannum-mešu-lissir*, Winona Lake, Ind.

Tinney, S. (1996), *The Nippur Lament: Royal Rhethoric and Divine Legitimation in the Reign of Išme-Dagan of Isin (1953–1935 B.C.)*, Philadelphia.

van Dijk, J. (1983), *Lugal ud me-lám-bi Nir-gál: Le récit épique et didactique des Travaux de Ninurta, du Déluge et de la Nouvelle Création*, Leiden.

Waetzoldt, H. (1988), 'Die Situation der Frauen und Kinder anhand ihrer Einkommensverhältnisse zur Zeit der III. Dynastie von Ur', *Archiv für Orientforschung* 15, pp. 30–44.

Walker, C. B. F. (1980), 'Some Assyrians at Sippar in the Old Babylonian Period', *Anatolian Studies* 30, pp. 15–22.

Westenholz, A. (1992), 'The Early Excavators of Nippur' in M. deJong Ellis (ed.), *Nippur at the Centennial*, papers read at the 35e Rencontre Assyriologique Internationale (Philadelphia, 1988), Philadelphia, pp. 291–6.

Wiseman, D. J. (1985), *Nebuchadrezzar and Babylon: The Schweich Lectures of the British Academy*, Oxford.

Woolley, L. (1931), *Antiquaries Journal* 11, p. 365.

Zadog, R. (1978), 'The Nippur Region during the Late Assyrian, Chaldean and Achaemenid Periods Chiefly from Written Sources', *Israel Oriental Studies* 8, pp. 266–332.

—— (1978) 'Phoenicians, Philistines and Mobabites in Mesopotamia', *Bulletin of the American Society of Oriental Research* 230, pp. 57–65.

Zettler, R. L. (1992), 'Excavations at Nippur, the University of Pennsylvania, and the University's Museum' in M. deJong Ellis (ed.), *Nippur at the Centennial*, papers read at the 35e Rencontre Assyriologique Internationale (Philadelphia, 1988), Philadelphia, pp. 325–35.

—— (1992), *The Ur III: Inanna Temple at Nippur*, Berlin.

7 SIPPAR

Andrae, W. and J. Jordan (1934), 'Abu Habbah-Sippar', *Iraq* 1, p. 59.

Baqir, T. and M. Ali Mustafa (1945), 'Iraq Government Soundings at Der', *Sumer* 1, pp. 37–45.

Batto, B. F. (1974), *Studies on Women at Mari*, Baltimore, Md.

Bongenaar, A. C. (1997), *The Neo-Babylonian Ebabbar Temple at Sippar: Its Administration and Its Prosopography*, Istanbul.

Budge, W. (1920), *By Nile and Tigris*, London.

Charpin, D. (1988), 'Sippar: deux villes jumelles', *Révue d'Assyriologie 82*, pp. 13–32.

Dalley, S. (1989), *Myths from Mesopotamia*, Oxford.

de Meyer, L. (ed.) (1978), *Tell ed-Der: Progress Reports (First Series)*, Leuven.

de Meyer, L., H. Gasche and R. Paepe (1971), *Tell ed-Der I. Rapport préliminaire sur la première compagne, février 1970*, Leuven.

—— (ed.) (1980), *Tell ed-Der: Sounding at Abu Habbah (Sippar)*, Leuven.

Driver, G. R. and J. C. Miles (1955), *The Babylonian Laws* (vol. 2), Oxford.

Finkelstein, J. J. (1970), 'On Recent Studies in Cuneiform Law: A Review Article', *Journal of the American Oriental Society 90/2*, pp. 243–56.

Frayne, D. R. (1997), *Ur III Period (2212–2004 B.C.)*, Toronto.

Fuller, C. J. (1984), *Servants of the Goddess*, Cambridge.

Gallery, M. (1975), review of Harris in *Journal of the American Oriental Society 99*, pp. 73–80.

Harris, R. (1962), 'Biographical Notes on the *Naditu* Women of Sippar', *Journal of Cuneiform Studies 16*, pp. 117–20.

—— (1964), 'The Naditu Women' in E. Reiner (ed.), *Studies Presented to Leo A. Oppenheim*, Chicago, pp. 106–35.

—— (1967), 'The Journey of the Divine Weapon' in H. G. Güterbock and Th. Jacobsen (eds.), *Studies in Honor of Benno Landsberger*, Chicago.

—— (1975), *Ancient Sippar: A Demographic Study of an Old Babylonian City (1994–1595)*, Istanbul.

—— (1976), 'On Foreigners in Old Babylonian Sippar', *Révue d'Assyriologie 70*, pp. 145–52.

Jeyes, U. (1983), 'The *Naditu* Women of Sippar' in A. Cameron and A. Kuhrt (eds.), *Images of Women in Antiquity*, London, pp. 260–72.

Jursa, M. (1995), *Die Landwirtschaft in Sippar in Neubabylonischer Zeit*, Vienna.

Kramer, S. N. (1985), 'Bread for Enlil, Sex for Inanna', *Orientalia 54*, pp. 117–32.

Kraus, F. R. (1958), *Ein Edikt des Königs Ammi-Saduqa von Babylon*, Leiden.

Kuhrt, A. (1995), *The Ancient Near East c. 3000–330 B.C.* (2 vols.), London.

Lambert, W. G. (1960), *Babylonian Wisdom Literature*, Oxford.

Leemans, W. F. (1960), *Foreign Trade in the Old Babylonian Period*, Leiden.

Leick, G. (1994), *Sex and Eroticism in Mesopotamian Literature*, London, New York.

MacGinnis, J. (1995), *Letter Orders from Sippar and the Administration of the Ebabbara in the Late-Babylonian Period*, Poznán.

Postgate, J. N. (1992), *Early Mesopotamia: Society and Economy at the Dawn of History*, London.

Rassam, H. (1897), *Asshur and the Land of Nimrod*, New York.

Scheil, V. (1902), 'Une saison de fouilles à Sippar', *Mémoirs publiées par les membres de l'Académie Française d'Archéologie Orientale du Caire* (vol. 1), Paris.

Stone, E. C. (1981), 'Texts, Architecture and Ethnographic Analogy: Patterns of Residence in Old Babylonian Nippur', *Iraq* 43, pp. 19–33.

—— (1982), 'The social role of the *Naditu* women in Old Babylonian Nippur', *Journal of the Economic and Social History of the Orient* 25/1, pp. 50–70.

Veenhof, K. R. (1976), 'The Dissolution of an Old Babylonian Marriage According to CT 45–86', *Révue d'Assyriologie* 70, pp. 153–64.

Walker, C. B. F. (1980), 'Some Assyrians at Sippar in the Old Babylonian Period', *Anatolian Studies* 30, pp. 15–22.

8 ASHUR

Andrae, W. (1909), *Der Anu-Adad Tempel*, Berlin.

—— (1913), *Die Festungswerke von Assur*, Berlin.

—— (1913), *Die Stelenreihe von Assur*, Berlin.

—— (1922), *Die Archaischen Ischtartempel in Assur*, Berlin.

—— (1923), *Farbige Keramik aus Assur*, Berlin (translated: *Coloured Ceramics from Ashur* (1925), London).

—— (1931), *Kultrelief aus dem Brunnen des Assur-Tempels zu Assur*, Berlin.

—— (1935), *Die jüngeren Ischtar Tempel*, Berlin.

—— (1938), *Das wiedererstandene Assur*, Munich (2nd rev. edn by B. Hrouda (1977), Munich).

Andrae, W. and H. Lenzen (1933), *Die Partherstadt Assur*, Berlin.

Birot, M. (1985), 'Les chroniques "Assyriennes de Mari"' in *Mari: Annales de Recherches Interdisciplinaires* 4, pp. 219–43.

Braidwood, R. J. (1974), 'The Iraq Jarmo Project' in G. R. Willey (ed.), *Archaeological Researches in Retrospect*, Cambridge, Mass.

Charpin, D. (1997), 'Assur avant l'Assyrie' in *Mari: Annales de Recherches Interdisciplinaires* 8, pp. 307–91.

Dalley, S. (1984), *Mari and Karana: Two Old Babylonian Cities*, London.

Dercksen, J. G. (1996), *The Old Assyrian Copper Trade in Anatolia*, Istanbul.

Dossin, G. (1950), *Archives royales de Mari I: Correspondance de Šamši-Addu et des ses fils, transcrite et traduite*, Paris.

—— (1952), *Archives royales de Mari V: Correspondance de Iasmah-Addu, transcrite et traduite*, Paris.

Earle, T. (1991), 'The Evolution of Chiefdoms' in T. Earle (ed.), *Chiefdoms: Power, Economy, and Ideology*, Cambridge, pp. 1–15.

Frahm, E. (1997), *Einleitung in die Sanherib-Inschriften*, Vienna.

George, A. (1985), review of B. Menzel, *Assyrische Tempel Band I* in *Archiv für Orientforschung* 32, pp. 89–93.

Grayson, A. K. (1972/1976), *Assyrian Royal Inscriptions* (2 vols.), Weisbaden.

—— (1987), *Assyrian Rulers of the Third and Second Millennia*, Toronto.

Haller, A. (1955), *Die Heiligtümer des Gottes Aššur und der Sin-Šamaš-Temple in Assur*, Berlin.

Ichisar, M. (1981), *Les Archives cappadociennes du marchand Indilum*, Paris.

Kuhrt, A. (1995), *The Ancient Near East c. 3000–330 B.C.* (2 vols.), London.

Lambert, W. G. (1957–8), 'A Part of the Ritual for the Substitute King', pt 1, *Archiv für Orientforschung* 18, pp. 109–12.

Larsen, M. T. (1967), *Old Assyrian Caravan Procedures*, Istanbul.

—— (1974), 'The City and the King: On the Old Assyrian Notion of Kingship' in P. Garelli (ed.), *Le palais et la royauté*, 19e Rencontre Assyriologique Internationale (Paris, 1971), Paris, pp. 285–300.

—— (1976), *The Old Assyrian City-state and its Colonies*, Copenhagen.

—— (1982), 'Your Money or Your Life! A Portrait of an Assyrian Businessman' in J. N. Postgate (ed.), *Societies and Languages of the Ancient Near East: Studies in Honour of I. M. Diakonoff*, Warminster, pp. 214–45.

—— (1987), 'Commercial networks in the Ancient Near East' in M. Rowlands, M. Larsen and K. Kristiansen (eds.), *Centre and Periphery in the Ancient World*, pp. 47–56.

Leick, G. (1994), *Sex and Eroticism in Mesopotamian Literature*, London, New York.

Liverani, M. (1993), 'Model and Actualization: The Kings of Akkad in the Historical Tradition' in M. Liverani (ed.), *Akkad: The First World Empire: Structure, Ideology, Traditions*, Padova, pp. 41–67.

Lloyd, S. (1978), *The Archaeology of Mesopotamia from the Old Stone Age to the Persian Conquest*, London.

Michel, C. (1991), *Innaya dans les tablettes paléo-assyriennes*, Paris.

Oppenheim, A. L. (1964), *Ancient Mesopotamia: Portrait of a Dead Civilization*, Chicago, London.

Pedersén, O. (1985), *Archives and Libraries in the City of Assur: A Survey of the Material from the German Excavations*, Uppsala.

Preusser, C. (1955), *Die Paläste von Assur*, Berlin.

Rassam, H. (1897), *Asshur and the Land of Nimrod*, New York.

Reade, J. (1981), 'Neo-Assyrian Monuments in Their Historical Context' in F. M. Fales (ed.), *Assyrian Royal Inscriptions: New Horizons in Literary, Ideological, and Historical Analysis*, Rome, pp. 144–67.

Rich, C. J. (1831), *Narratives of a Residence in Koordistan and on the Site of Ancient Nineveh*, London.

Rosen, B. L. (1977), *Studies in Old Assyrian Loan Contracts*, Ann Arbor, Mich.

Scott, J. (1985), *Weapons of the Weak*, New Haven, Conn.

Stein, G. and M. Rothmann (1994), *Chiefdoms and early states in the Near East: The Organizational Dynamics of Complexity*, Madison, Wis.

Thureau-Dangin, F. (1912), *Une relation de la huitième campagne de Sargon*, Paris.

Unger, H. (1928), 'Assur' in *Reallaxikon der Assyriologie und Archäologie* 1, pp. 170–95.

van Driel, G. (1969), *The Cult of Assur*, Leiden.

Veenhof, K. R. (1972), *Aspects of Old Assyrian Trade and its Terminology*, Leiden.

—— (1987), ' "Dying Tablets" and "Hungry Silver": Elements of Figurative Language in Akkadian Commercial Terminology' in M. Mindlin, M. J. Geller and J. E. Wansbrough (eds.), *Figurative Language in the Ancient Near East*, London, pp. 41–75.

9 NINEVEH

Borger, R. (1956), *Die Inschriften Asahrhaddons, Königs von Assyrien*, Graz.

Brinkman, J. A. (1984), *Prelude to Empire: Babylonian Society and Politics, 747–626 B.C.*, Philadelphia.

Campbell Thompson, R. (1934), 'The Buildings on Quyunjik, the Larger Mound of Nineveh', *Iraq* 1, pp. 95–104.

Campbell Thompson, R. and R. W. Hamilton (1932), 'The Temple of Ishtar at Nineveh 1930–31', *Annals of Archaeology and Anthropology* 19, pp. 55ff.

Curtis, J. E. and J. E. Reade (1995), *Art and Empire: Treasures from Assyria in the British Museum*, London.

Dalley, S. (1997), 'The Hanging Gardens of Babylon at Nineveh' in H.

Waetzold and H. Hauptmann (eds.), *Assyrien im Wandel der Zeiten*, 39e Rencontre Assyriologique Internationale (Heidelberg, 1992), Heidelberg, pp. 19–24.

Frahm, E. (1997), *Einleitung in de Sanherib-Inschriften*, Vienna.

Grayson, A. K. (1972), *Assyrian Royal Inscriptions* (2 vols.), Wiesbaden.

—— (1991), *Assyrian Rulers of the Third and Second Millennia*, Toronto.

Gut, R. (1995), *Das prähistorische Ninive: zur relativen Chronologie der frühen Perioden Nordmesopotamiens*, Mainz.

Jacobsen, Th. and S. Lloyd (1935), *Sennacherib's Aqueduct at Jerwan*, Chicago.

Lambert, W. G. (1957–8), 'A Part of the Ritual for the Substitute King', pt 1, *Archiv für Orientforschung* 18, pp. 109–12.

—— (1959–60), 'A Part of the Ritual for the Substitute King', pt 2, *Archiv für Orientforschung* 19, pp. 119ff.

—— (1988), 'Esarhaddon's Attempts to return Marduk to Babylon' in G. Mauer and V. Magen (eds.), *Ad bene et fideliter seminandum: Festgabe für Karlheins Deller zum 21 Februar 1987*, Neukirchen-Vluyn, pp. 158–74.

Lanfranchi, G. B. and S. Parpola (1990), *The Correspondence of Sargon Part II: Letters from the Northern and North-Eastern Provinces*, Helsinki.

Larsen, M. T. (1994), *The Conquest of Assyria: Excavations in an Antique Land 1840–1860*, London, New York.

Layard, A. (1853), *Discoveries in the Ruins of Nineveh and Babylon, with Travels in Armenia, Kurdistan and the Desert*, London.

Livingstone, A. (1989), *Court Poetry and Literary Miscellanea*, Helsinki.

Luckenbill, D. D. (1924), *The Annals of Sennacherib*, Chicago.

Mallowan, M. E. L. (1933), 'The Prehistoric Soundage of Nineveh', *Annals of Archaeology and Anthropology* 20, pp. 127ff.

Mallowan, M. E. L. and J. C. Rose (1935), 'The Excavations of Tell Arpachi-yah', *Iraq* 2.

Oates, D. (1968), *Studies in the Ancient History of Northern Iraq*, London.

Oded, B. (1979), *Mass Deportations and Deportees in the Neo-Assyrian Empire*, Wiesbaden.

Oppenheim, A. L. (1964), *Ancient Mesopotamia: Portrait of a Dead Civilization*, Chicago, London.

Parpola, S. (1970), *Letters from Assyrian Scholars to the Kings Esarhaddon and Ashurbanipal*, vol. 1, Neukirchen-Vluyn.

—— (1972), 'A Letter from Šamaš-šumu-ukin to Esarhaddon', *Iraq* 34, pp. 21–34.

—— (1980), 'The Murder of Sennacherib' in B. Alster (ed.), *Death in Mesopotamia*, 26e Rencontre Assyriologique Internationale (Copenhagen, 1979), Copenhagen, pp. 171–82.

—— (1987), *The Correspondence of Sargon II, Part 1: Letters from Assyria and the West*, Helsinki.

—— (1997), *Assyrian Prophecies*, Helsinki.

Pongratz-Leister, B. (1997), 'The Interplay of Military Strategy and Cultic Practice' in S. Parpola and E. M. Whiting (eds.), *Assyria 1995: Proceedings of the 10th Anniversary Symposium of the Neo-Assyrian Text Corpus Project, Helsinki, September 7–11, 1995*, Helsinki, pp. 245–52.

Reade, J. (1981), 'Neo-Assyrian monuments in Their Historical Context' in F. M. Fales (ed.), *Assyrian Royal Inscriptions: New Horizons in Literary, Ideological, and Historical Analysis*, Rome, pp. 144–67.

—— (1987), 'Was Sennacherib a feminist?' in J. M. Durand, *La femme dans le proche-Orient antique*, 33ᵉ Rencontre Assyriologique Internationale (Paris, 1986), Paris, pp. 139–46.

Russell, J. M. (1998), *The Final Sack of Nineveh: The Discovery, Documentation, and Destruction of King Sennacherib's Throne Room at Nineveh, Baghdad* (New Haven, Conn. and London).

Schramm, P. (1972), 'War Semiramis assyrische Regentin?', *Historia* 21, pp. 513–21.

Starr, I. (1990), *Queries to the Sungod: Divination and Politics in Sargonid Assyria*, Helsinki.

Streck, M. (1916), *Assurbanipal*, I and II, Leipzig.

Stronach, D. (1997), 'Notes on the Fall of Nineveh' in S. Parpola and R. M. Whiting (eds.), *Assyria 1995: Proceedings of the 10th Anniversary Symposium of the Neo-Assyrian Text Corpus Project, Helsinki, September 7–11, 1995*, Helsinki, pp. 307–24.

Turner, G. (1970), 'Tell Nebi Yunus: The *Ekal mašarti* of Nineveh', *Iraq* 32, pp. 68–85.

Weissert, E. (1997), 'Royal Hunt and Royal Triumph in a Prism Fragment of Ashurbanipal (82-5-22,2)' in S. Parpola and R. M. Whiting (eds.), *Assyria 1995: Proceedings of the 10th Anniversary Symposium of the Neo-Assyrian Text Corpus Project, Helsinki, September 7–11, 1995*, Helsinki, pp. 339–58.

Wiseman, D. J. (1958), *The Vassal Treaties of Esarhaddon*, London.

10 BABYLON

al-Khalil, S. (1991), *The Monument: Art, Vulgarity and Responsibility in Iraq*, London.

Ali, S. M. (1979), 'The Southern Palace', *Sumer* 35, pp. 92–3.

Andrae, W. (1952), *Die versunkene Weltstadt und ihr Ausgräber Robert Koldewey*, Berlin.

Brinkman, J. A. (1984), *Prelude to Empire: Babylonian Society and Politics, 747–626 B.C.*, Philadelphia.

Cagni, L. (1977), *The Poem of Erra*, Malibu, Ca.

Cooper, J. (1980), 'Apodictic Death and the Historicity of "Historical" Omens' in B. Alster (ed.), *Death in Mesopotamia*, 26ᵉ Recontre Assyriologique Internationale (Copenhagen, 1979), Copenhagen, pp. 99–105.

Cuyler Young, T. (1988), in *Cambridge Ancient History*, vol. IV.

Dalley, S. (1989), *Myths from Mesopotamia*, Oxford, New York.

Gasche, H., J. A. Armstrong and S. W. Cole (1998), *The Fall of Babylon*, Ghent.

George, A. (1992), *Babylonian Topographical Texts*, Leuven.

Heinrich, E. and U. Seidle (1968), 'Mass und Übermass in der Dimensionierung von Bauwerken im alten Zweistromland' in *Mitteilungen der Deutschen Orientgesellschaft in Berlin* 99, pp. 5–54.

Koldewey, R. (1990), *Das wiedererstehende Babylon* (5th rev. edn), Munich.

Kuhrt, A. (1983), 'The Cyrus Cylinder and Achaemenid Imperial Policy', *Journal for the Study of the Old Testament* 25, pp. 83–97.

—— (1995), *The Ancient Near East c. 3000–330 B.C.* (2 vols.), London.

Kuhrt, A. and Sherwin-White, S. (1987), '"Xerxes" Destruction of Babylonian Temples' in H. Sancisi-Weerdenburg and A. Kuhrt (eds.), *Achaemenid History 2: The Greek Sources*, Leiden, pp. 69–78.

Lambert, W. G. (1960), *Babylonian Wisdom Literature*, London.

—— (1971), 'The Reign of Nebuchadnezzar I: A Turning Point in the History of Mesopotamian History' in W. S. McCullogh (ed.), *The Seed of Wisdom*, Toronto, pp. 3–13.

Mayer, W. R. (1998), 'Nabonids Herkunft' in M. Dietrich and O. Loretz (eds.), *Dubsar anta-men. Festschrift für Willem H. Ph. Römer*, Münster, pp. 245–62.

Oates, D. (1991), in *Cambridge Ancient History*, vol. II, pt. 2.

Powell, M. A. (1982), 'Metrological Notes on the Esagila Tablet and Related Matters', *Zeitschrift füt Assyriologie* 73, pp. 92ff.

Pritchard, J. B. (1969), *The Ancient Near East: Supplementary Texts and Pictures Relating to the Old Testament*, Princeton.

Rich, C. (1839), *Narrative of a Journey to the Site of Babylon in 1811*, London.

Sachs, A. J. and H. Hunger (1988), *Astronomical Diaries and Related Texts from Babylonia: vol. 1, Diaries from 652 B.C. to 262 B.C.*, Vienna.

—— (1989), *Astronomical Diaries and Related Texts from Babylonia: vol. 2, Diaries from 261 B.C. to 165 B.C.*, Vienna.

Sack, R. H. (1994), *Neriglissar – King of Babylon*, Neukirchen-Vluyn.

Schmid, H. (1995), *Der Tempelturm Etemenanki in Babylon*, Berlin.

Sherwin-White, S. (1987), 'Seleucid Babylonia' in S. Sherwin-White and A. Kuhrt (eds.), *Hellenism in the East: The Interaction of Greek and non-Greek Civilizations from Syria to Central Asia after Alexander*, London, pp. 1–32.

Stolper, M. W. (1985), *Entrepreneurs and Empire: The Murašu Archive, The Murašu Firm, and Persian Rule in Babylonia*, Istanbul.

Unger, E. (1928), 'Babylon', *Reallexikon der Assyriologie and Archäologie* 1, pp. 330–69.

van der Speck (1987), 'The Babylonian City' in S. Sherwin-White and A. Kuhrt (eds.), *Hellenism in the East: The Interaction of Greek and non-Greek Civilizations from Syria to Central Asia after Alexander*, London, pp. 57–75.

van Driel, J. (1985–6), 'The rise of the House of Egibi: Nabu-nadin-ahhe' in *Jaarsbericht van het Vooraziatisch-Egyptisch Genootschap 'ex Oriente Lux'* 29, pp. 50–67.

Wetzel, F. (1930), *Die Stadtmauern von Babylon*, Berlin.

Wiseman, D. J. (1985), *Nebukhadrezzar and Babylon: The Schweich Lectures of the British Academy*, Oxford.

Wunsch, C. (1993), *Die Urkunden des babylonischen Geschäftsmannes Iddin-Marduk. Zum Handel mit Naturalien im 6. Jahrhundert v.Chr.*, Groningen.

Zawadzki, S. (1988), *The Fall of Assyria and Median–Babylonian relations in the light of the Nabopolassar Chronicle*, Poznán.

Index